Kendall

of the Picayune

KENDALL

of

𝔗𝔥𝔢 𝔓𝔦𝔠𝔞𝔶𝔲𝔫𝔢

BEING HIS ADVENTURES
IN NEW ORLEANS, ON THE TEXAN SANTA FE
EXPEDITION, IN THE MEXICAN WAR,
AND IN THE COLONIZATION OF
THE TEXAS FRONTIER

by

FAYETTE COPELAND

NORMAN
UNIVERSITY OF OKLAHOMA PRESS

International Standard Book Number: 0–8061–0851–7

Copyright 1943 by the University of Oklahoma Press, Publishing Division of the University. Manufactured in the U.S.A. First edition, April, 1943. Second printing, March, 1970.

To Mrs. Georgina Kendall Fellowes

who is, after all, the
real biographer of her father
George Wilkins Kendall

Preface

When the rising tide of empire was gathering force to push the United States boundaries to the Pacific Ocean, a tremendous urge for westward expansion rose along the Gulf coast and particularly in New Orleans.

From this romantic old city, George Wilkins Kendall wrote, and rode out to fight, for the acquisition of the Republic of Texas. In 1837 he established the New Orleans *Picayune,* the first representative in the South of the vigorous, rollicking "penny press," and helped make New Orleans journalism unsurpassed in America in the 1850's. He accompanied the Republic of Texas expedition to Santa Fe and became famous as the historian of that tragic enterprise. During the Mexican War, which grew out of westward expansion, an eager nation, including President Polk and his cabinet, awaited the pony express from the New Orleans *Picayune* with Kendall's dramatic front-line stories.

From the battlefields of Mexico he hurried to cover the revolutions which were shaking the thrones of Europe to their foundations. Then, back in his beloved Texas, he settled down to help build the state into the empire of his dreams, paying in sacrifice and toil and disappointment the toll which nature always exacts of the pioneer. A restless, impatient adventurer in a fabulous generation, he left his mark on the exciting and sometimes forgotten pages of history.

Even in Kendall's time there were conflicting reports of the expedition to Santa Fe. The purposes, events, and route of that journey as related in this book are taken from Kendall's own account, his *Narrative of the Texan Santa Fe Expedition,* which was published after his return.

It is hoped that this biography may be a part of the history which records the contributions of pioneer newspapermen in the building of the nation. The study grew out of a year spent in examining the old newspaper collections in Baton Rouge and New Orleans. Inspiration for the succeeding six years of study and research which were involved came from Professor Walter Prichard and other members of the history faculty, from Professor Marvin G. Osborn, director of the school of journalism, and from Mr. James McMillen, librarian, all of Louisiana State University. Exhaustive study of Kendall's early life and his career as a Texas rancher was made possible through the kindness of Mrs. Georgina Kendall Fellowes, his daughter, who made available the extensive Kendall family papers, with his letters and diaries, and who read the manuscript and gave valuable suggestions. Acknowledgment is gratefully extended to Miss Frances Hunt and to many other friends who helped me pore over the microscopic print of faded newspaper files, copy manuscripts, and pursue elusive clues; to John P. McClure of the New Orleans *Times-Picayune,* and to my own colleagues at the University of Oklahoma who bore with me through this undertaking.

FAYETTE COPELAND

Norman, Oklahoma

Table of Contents

List of Illustrations

Kendall
of the Picayune

1

Apprentice to adventure

"I WON'T GO BACK!"

"But George, you're out of pocket. You have nothing to live on."

The boy shook his head stubbornly, but his face lighted up with an engaging smile. Captain Thomas Wilkins looked anxiously toward the river mail packet where the last of the passengers for New York were loading. When he turned again to the sturdy seventeen-year-old youth, his own solemn features broke into an answering smile.

"Your grandfather sent me to bring you home. I can't leave you here without funds."

As George Wilkins Kendall stood on the wharf at Albany and waved to Captain Wilkins when the mail boat whistled and started slowly downstream, his other hand was thrust deep into his pocket, clutching the fifty dollars his uncle had given him.

The boat passed beyond the wharf, down the river. The boy picked up his little leather-bound trunk and set his feet again on the runaway road to adventure, his heritage from a long line of pioneers.

Two centuries earlier this pathway of adventure had lured his ancestors to the shores of America. Bray Wilkins, younger son of John Wilkins, Lord Bishop of Cheshire, shipped from Wales with Governor John Endicott and landed in Salem in 1628. He married Mary Rugg, daughter of a Scotch carpenter, whom he had met on the boat, and moved over to Middleton to

3

operate a mill and a ferry and establish the Wilkins line in New England.

The Kendall ancestor, Francis Kendall, came from England in 1640 and landed in Charlestown, across the bay from Boston. He was a kinsman of James Kendall, M.P., who was Lord High Admiral and for five years governor of the Barbados, and who was buried, with his wife, in Westminster Abbey. Francis soon settled in Woburn where in 1644 he was married to Mary Tidd. Succeeding generations of the Wilkins and Kendall families helped push back the frontier in slow moving eddies.

Among the townships set aside as land grants for the heroes of King Philip's War was that of Souhegan West, across the line in New Hampshire, which was organized and settled in 1740. Here a year later the Rev. Daniel Wilkins was called as the first minister to the new meetinghouse at Amherst, and he welcomed to his congregation the first of the Kendalls who moved to the settlement in 1754.

In the nearby village of Mont Vernon George Wilkins Kendall was born on August 22, 1809, the first of five children of Thaddeus Kendall and Abigail Wilkins.

Perhaps the most influential man in the region at that time was Deacon Samuel Wilkins, George's grandfather. He was chosen as selectman of Amherst in 1768 and held the office fifteen times during the next twenty-one years. When disputes arose in the church, growing out of the separation of Mont Vernon from Amherst, he was named moderator. Then he became deacon, a position he held for forty-two years.

He served a term in the New Hampshire house of representatives in 1780, and was elected ten times as town clerk. Four of his sons fought at Bunker Hill, and two of them lost their lives in later battles of the Revolutionary War.

Thaddeus Kendall, George's father, was a war baby of the Revolution. Born in 1772 in Amherst, he was steeped in its glories throughout his childhood. His oldest brother, Nathan, just under twenty, fought at Bunker Hill with the four Wilkins boys, and

4

another brother, Joshua, marched on Ticonderoga. Thaddeus joined the local militia as soon as he could, working meanwhile in the village store which Nathan operated in Amherst.

When he decided to set up a store of his own, the site he selected was the new settlement of Mont Vernon, three miles up the turnpike from Amherst on the way to Vermont. Its one hundred and twenty-seven voters included his younger brother and two other Kendalls, his cousins, and a half-dozen of the Wilkins clan.[1]

Before moving, Thaddeus married Catherine Fletcher, but she died six months after their marriage. Seven years later he married Abigail, second of Deacon Samuel Wilkins' eleven children.

At first the store prospered. Trade multiplied on the post road that wound through Mont Vernon, and the settlement's nine taverns and grog shops were thronged with teamsters who paused on the long hauls from Boston and Lowell, Massachusetts, and Nashua, New Hampshire, on up toward the Claremont bridge that crossed the Connecticut river and into Vermont.

Aside from his growing family, the interest closest to the heart of Thaddeus Kendall was his military career. On Saturday afternoons from behind his counter he watched his hardy neighbors stride down from the hills, attired in homespuns and coonskin caps, each with a long rifle supported in the crook of his arm. Then he put on his cocked hat and became Captain Kendall of the Mont Vernon Company of the old Fifth New Hampshire Regiment.[2] When he stepped out on the common, his neighbors stood at attention and began to drill.

Brigadier General Benjamin Pierce and his staff came down from Concord to Amherst to inspect the thirteen companies of

[1] For the part which the Wilkins and the Kendall families played in the settlement and development of Amherst and Mont Vernon, see D. F. Secomb, *History of the Town of Amherst, Hillsborough County, New Hampshire* (Concord, 1883); and Charles J. Smith, *History of the Town of Mont Vernon, New Hampshire* (Boston, 1907).

[2] The family at one time had his commission as captain, signed by George Washington.

the Regiment, and Captain Thaddeus Kendall's company of lanky boys from Mont Vernon proved to be one of the best.[3]

When President Jefferson began to cut off trade with Great Britain, the embargo laws struck home to the crossroads stores, and Thaddeus had little merchandise to sell. As the War of 1812 began in earnest and trade was shut off entirely, he found that little except debts and bad accounts remained of his once comfortable business. He had no farm to fall back on for subsistence,[4] so he took his family down to Nashua, and kept a store with John Endicott. But by this time three other children had been born to the Kendalls—William, Thaddeus Richmond, and Catherine and the partnership in the little store could not feed so many.

Then Thaddeus heard there was a chance for a fight up around Lake Champlain, where the British were menacing settlers while the mouth of the St. Lawrence was under blockade. He bundled up his family and started northwest. But the war was soon over and peace failed to end the Kendall misfortunes. Times were hard, and Thaddeus moved his family from one Vermont settlement to another. Eventually they went to Montreal, where their fifth child, the frail little Abbie, was born.

George was now seven years old, an alert, intelligent boy who gave promise of being a help to the struggling family. He had inherited his father's keen sense of humor which had made the little store at Mont Vernon such a popular gathering place.

George's education, however, was a problem for the family. It still was unsolved when, in the fall of 1816, a friend from Amherst came by during a business trip to Montreal. He brought a

[3]Benjamin Pierce, Revolutionary soldier, and his wife, Anna Kendrick, were the parents of Franklin Pierce, fourteenth President of the United States. Anna Kendrick's sister, Sarah, married Nathan Kendall, oldest brother of Thaddeus Kendall, father of George Wilkins Kendall.

[4] The will of Nathan Kendall, dated November 30, 1789, shows that the homestead had been willed to Timothy, next older brother of Thaddeus. Nathan III, the oldest of the brothers, got only twenty shillings, while Thaddeus was willed "nine pounds in lawful coined money." A copy of the will is included among the papers in the possession of Kendall's daughter, Mrs. Georgina Kendall Fellowes. The collection is referred to hereafter as "Kendall papers."

message that Deacon Samuel Wilkins wanted George to return with the friend to Amherst for a short visit. The boy remained under his grandfather's roof for ten years. He had traveled over half of the continent and had attained his majority before he again visited his parents in their home.

Many times Thaddeus and Abigail planned to send for him, but repeated tragedy interfered. Little Abbie died in her first year. The family moved to Philipsburgh, just across the Vermont line in Canada, hoping to get a new start. The homesick mother wrote that she hoped they could contrive in some way to get George home that summer. But Thaddeus added a postscript to the letter stating that they were leaving again for Montreal where he planned to make some ready money.

Despite his bright hopes for this second venture into Montreal, his misfortunes continued, and the family headed back again into Vermont. George might have rejoined them in 1820, but that year his brother, William, was ill and the trip was postponed. The next letter Abigail wrote told him that William had died and was buried at St. Armand, up on Lake Champlain.

At Amherst, George was enjoying the life on his grandfather's farm. He started to school when it became evident that his return might be delayed for some time, and during his first two years he made probably the best marks of his brief and rather haphazard educational career.[5]

As his stay lengthened, his grandfather became more and more reluctant to send him back to his parents. Even at seven, he must have shown the same dynamic quality that later held acquaintances under his spell of warm and genial friendship. Although there were Kendall uncles and cousins at almost every crossroads George passed in his wanderings around southern New Hampshire, it was in the Wilkins tradition and under the par-

[5] Kendall papers, Abigail and Thaddeus Kendall to Mrs. Solomon Wilkins, April 26, 1818. His mother wrote, "We rejoiced to hear of the proficiency he made in school last winter, and wish him to be kept in school if possible." Thaddeus added, "George—you make every improvement in learning possible to be some advantage to yourself and parents."

ticular guidance of old Deacon Samuel Wilkins that he spent the most impressionable years of his life. He always included his middle name "Wilkins" in his later famous signature.

But George did not conform to the Wilkins pattern. Although the Deacon liked a good joke, he must have been puzzled many times by the boy's quick sense of the ridiculous, and the unflagging spirit of wit and merriment that had burst upon the household. Cousins told and retold to their grandchildren anecdotes of the times when they were boys with him. He was the favorite, too, of his three young uncles still living at home. But neither they nor his indulgent grandfather could understand or stem the boy's impatience with the conventional pattern. Quick to learn, he displayed keen understanding when things interested him, but he avoided schoolroom drudgery and went about learning as he pleased.[6]

While the schooling of his boyhood was brief, he picked up somewhere the ability to devour books he liked or chose to read. Geography was his favorite subject, and he was impatient to see for himself the places his old dog-eared text described. But books never became as important to him as music, great paintings and statuary, or the theater. And none of these were as real as the world of action.

As he dipped casually into his texts during the brief school terms in the long winters, he lived the normal life of a New England farm boy. Frequently he tramped the hills with dog and gun, alone or with his uncles or cousins, and he spent many summer hours fishing in the Souhegan and its small tributaries. These years he spent in his grandfather's home also were filled with interest in local politics, church and military affairs. At muster time he went with the family to the commons to watch Captain Thomas Wilkins drill his company of Amherst infantry. Occasionally he

[6] In one of Kendall's last letters he remarked that he never had a year's schooling in his life. He must, however, have had in mind a comparison of his own early school terms and those of his great grandfather, the Rev. Daniel Wilkins, or of his uncle, John Hubbard Wilkins, both of whom were graduated from Harvard College with honors.

went to visit a relative on the Kendall side, Franklin Pierce, the sheriff's son, who later became a president of the United States.[7]

When George went to the Presbyterian church with members of the Wilkins clan, he sat in the family pew of the old building that Deacon Samuel had helped raise in 1771. It had no stoves, and when in the desperately cold winter of 1818 there was popular agitation for their purchase, the townspeople voted the proposal down. When they came in from their nearby farms, the men went to the taverns to keep warm until services started, while the women and children found shelter in homes close at hand.[8] These convivial gatherings[9] were broken up by the tolling of the bells. Those who owned footwarmers would hastily fill them with coals and trudge to the meetinghouse. The less fortunate bundled up and endured the cold as best they could.

By 1824 the stove faction mustered enough votes to win the election, and thereafter the building was heated during services.

[7] Sheriff Benjamin Pierce was the principal actor in an exciting event in Amherst, the town's most famous jail delivery. During the bitter winter of 1818, when the thermometer fell, one Friday, to a record low of thirty-two degrees below zero, Captain Moses Brown, Isaac Lawrence and George Lancy were arrested and jailed for debt. The sheriff sought legal means to release them, and finding none, took the responsibility, paid their debts and set them at liberty. He even made an appropriate address to them, which was printed and circulated widely. That hard winter of 1818 also marked the beginning of the infirmities of old Deacon Samuel Wilkins and the end of his half-century of public service in the affairs of Amherst.

Hard times stalked through the New Hampshire hills again in 1820. Horace Greeley related in his *Recollections of a Busy Life* (New York, 1868), 49, that the sheriff and creditors seized the farm of his father, Zaccheus Greeley, in the eastern part of Amherst township, together with equipment, livestock and most of the family's household goods, to satisfy accumulated debts of $1,000. The family fled to Vermont.

[8] The "town" of Amherst covered several square miles of sparsely settled land in addition to the small settlement near the church, stores and taverns.

[9] Kendall, in a reminiscent letter to the New Orleans *Picayune,* dated New Braunfels, September 25, 1860, wrote, "He was fond of a joke six days in the week, was my grandfather, albeit a pious and godly man, and on Sundays he was fond of a Santa Cruz rum sling or toddy, with a toasted cracker in it, and would regularly every Sabbath, between the morning and afternoon service, adjourn to a neighboring tavern, and in company with a brother deacon, partake of his favorite beverage. This was before the invention of temperance, abolition and many other new fangled societies. . . ."

9

But this victory revived the movement to separate the church from the town government and permit citizens to support whatever church they chose. A universalist movement, started some years earlier, now found two eager young champions in Thomas G. Wells and Nathan Kendall Seaton, George's first cousin. To support this movement they launched the Amherst *Herald* on January 1, 1825, and Kendall went to work in their shop as an apprentice.

After deliberate, farsighted planning, the boy had announced to the Wilkins family his decision to become a printer. Old Deacon Samuel protested from his sickbed, and wrote Abigail and Thaddeus for their advice. They did what they could to dissuade George, although they did not absolutely forbid his becoming an apprentice.[10]

But George had precedents, close at hand, for his decision. Four years earlier his youngest uncle, John Hubbard Wilkins, had become a junior partner in a publishing house in Boston. This uncle, the one who perhaps influenced him most and who had the last restraining hand of the Wilkins family on George's career, was the author of a work on astronomy which was the standard text in New England schools for many years. His publishers persuaded him to join their firm and he became one of Boston's most substantial business men. Amos Kendall, descendant of the first Francis Kendall, was becoming known as a journalist in Louisville and was confounding Henry Clay by swinging over to support Andrew Jackson. And up at East Poultney, Vermont, Horace Greeley, an Amherst boy two years younger than George, was serving an apprenticeship as a printer. At fourteen he was beginning to make a name for himself. Later he and Kendall were to become warm friends.

When the Amherst *Herald* stopped publication in December,

[10] This incident, and others concerning Kendall's early years, are related in a letter written by William Rix, Kendall's brother-in-law, to Mrs. G. W. Kendall, dated "Spring of 1868," which is in the Kendall papers. Abigail Wilkins Kendall wrote to her son, "I would not like to see you running from door to door with a bundle of papers under your arms, delivering them to subscribers."

1825, George's friends thought that would end the nonsense of his wanting to be a printer. But his interest had become an obsession. Before long he persuaded his Uncle John, then a partner in the firm of Hilliard, Gray, Little & Wilkins in Boston, to take him to the city.

Working as an apprentice on the Boston *Statesman,* Kendall had his first opportunity to attend the theater, and developed a passion for the stage which stayed with him all his life. At the old Federal Street Theatre he saw Kean, Conway, Cooper, Mrs. Duff and Mrs. Powell "at their zenith." In his later opinion, "Those were the palmy days of the drama."[11]

But in less than a year he sought new experience. He had come to the city to learn the trade, but it is probable that janitor work, cleaning presses and throwing used type back into the cases proved too important a part of his education as a printer. The delay irked him. New York, the siren that has beckoned to newspapermen for generations, called to him, and a mail packet sailed at dawn.

Fog blew cold from the Boston harbor and blurred the flickering light from the street lamps as young George stepped out on the cobbled street. He paused to shift the weight of the small trunk on his shoulder and glanced back at his uncle's house to see if anyone had been aroused when he lowered himself from the window. Then he turned toward the water front.

In New York he tramped from shop to shop on the lower end of Broadway, but there was no job for a boy of seventeen who had served scarcely two years as an apprentice. The fare on the mail schooner from Boston to New York had taken most of his slim savings. It was too late to turn back. He counted his money and took the boat up to Albany. It was there that his Uncle Thomas found him and begged him to return home, and in the end gave him the fifty dollars and sent him on the road to adventure.

11 *Picayune,* March 21, 1840. Horace Greeley in *Recollections,* 202–203, tells of seeing his first "genuine dramatic performance" in New York in the winter of 1831. Journeymen printers were admitted on orders from the editors on Saturday evenings, when audiences were thin.

2

A typo
settles down

GEORGE WILKINS KENDALL was an engaging storyteller. At his editorial desk, around the campfire in the evening after a hunt on the prairies, in a social gathering or on the deck of a river boat or a transatlantic liner, friends gathered around to catch a flash of his wit or to hear one of his amusing yarns. Out of his casual references, and from anecdotes, a slender thread of narrative appears, tracing his adventures after he refused to return to Amherst with Captain Wilkins.

He soon found that he had neither the age nor the expertness needed to be a printer, and hired himself to a farmer in western New York during haying and harvest.

A wandering theatrical troupe came through the village and George followed the wagons off down the country lane. For a time he appeared as an actor in the provincial towns of New York. But this adventure came to a disastrous close and the proprietors found themselves jailed for debt.

He tried, between other jobs, to get work in print shops, but with little success, for times were hard in this region.

The month of October, 1828, found Kendall at Sandusky City, Ohio, with less than five dollars in his pocket. During the summer he had traveled the whole length of the Erie Canal, "and had run the gantlet of chills, fevers, and all the ills with which western New York was then afflicted." He was on his way to Cincinnati, "short of money, yet full of hope." There was no regular stagecoach, and he tramped every step of the way.

He and a companion, L. D. Campbell, who was later United States minister to the Juarez government in Mexico, found brief employment in Cincinnati, but soon Kendall was on his way again. With another wanderer, he headed for Columbus. During that journey he thought often of a cartoon ridiculing the rush of pioneers to the Ohio country, which had amused Deacon Samuel Wilkins. It showed two horsemen, one well groomed and mounted on a prancing charger. He said "I'm going to Ohio." The other, headed in the opposite direction, was ragged and gaunt and his horse a bag of bones. He said "I've been." Kendall wrote, "at every turn the picture of the miserable wretch on a broken-down horse was brought forcibly to my recollection."

They passed through the little towns of Bucyrus, Tiffin and others just springing into existence. Everywhere there was sickness, wretchedness and want. Often whole families were ill, and "third-rate saddle bags doctors, with fourth-rate medicines, were riding about from place to place—young men learning their trade—killing more than they cured." It was a poor place for a wandering apprentice.

Kendall still was far from his goal of learning the printing trade—farther than he had been when the Amherst *Herald* folded up during his first year's apprenticeship, and much farther than when he caught the boat at Long Wharf in Boston harbor and headed for New York. He found little work in Ohio and wandered on.

In the year 1829 he was in parts of Indiana, which he found even worse than Ohio, "for there the dreaded milk sickness obtained to such an extent that one was just as much afraid of a bowl of milk as the bite of a rattlesnake—either would kill in twenty four hours."

Finally, in Detroit, he began in earnest to learn the printing trade, and not until he was an able craftsman did he permit

13

his gaze to wander again to distant horizons. Then, with a skill he could exchange for ready money, he did what journeyman artisans had done since the days of the ancient guilds—he hit the highroad.

In a day when railroads were such a novelty that newspapers triumphantly announced the construction even of three-mile lines, there was an amazing amount of travel. Stages, hacks, gigs, and wagons were filled with travelers, many of whom were headed for Texas where colonization was getting into full swing.[1] However, Kendall was content for the time being to wander within the confines of the United States.

He passed through Illinois, visiting the settlement of Chicago which he found to be only "an old block house and picket, with several straggling log houses." From Wisconsin territory he followed the summer southward through Ohio, Iowa, Missouri, and Tennessee. Natchez fascinated him and he paused there briefly, but before long he was in New Orleans. He might have remained in the South at that time, but the voice that called him to New York was still unanswered and he soon was on his way.

These years of experience in different sections of the country formed in Kendall's mind a dislike for politics and a distrust of politicians. The decade was one of partisan strife and political controversy. Nullifiers, supporters of the tariff and opponents of the tariff, the Masons and the anti-Masons, the Abolitionists and the slave owners were bitter in their denunciation of each other. Kendall heard all the arguments and put no faith in politics. While he could always turn aside a serious controversy with a joke, he often confided to his diary that the salvation of the country lay not in politics but in work.

His wanderings led him across to Mobile, Alabama, where he

[1] Beginning with Iturbide's grant to Stephen F. Austin in 1823, which was confirmed by the Congress of the Republic when Iturbide fell, the number of grants to foreigners steadily increased until by August 1, 1835, more than half of the territory of Texas had been given to the colonists. See Carlos E. Castenada (ed.), *The Mexican Side of the Texas Revolution,* by the chief Mexican participants (Dallas, 1928), 393.

worked for Thaddeus Sanford on the old *Register*, then up through Augusta, Georgia, and Charleston, South Carolina. One who knew him during those years wrote of him, "Sometimes he was flush, sometimes strapped and seedy—but always genial, witty, gentlemanly."[2]

Winter caught up with him in North Carolina and he found it more profitable to operate a stage line than to look for work in a print shop. This was excellent training for his establishment of pony express lines, years later, to carry the news.

In the spring he returned to New York, where his reception was far different from that of his first visit to the city. In almost every shop he visited there were friends he had met in his carefree vagabond years, and with whom he had worked at the case or swapped tall tales at convivial gatherings. He was master of a trade that was proud of its importance, and noted for its frequent and lavish entertainments.[3] He was of age now, a grown man. That year, 1832, he went home to visit his family for the first time since he left as a boy of seven.

His father, still a poor man, had settled in Burlington, Vermont, where the family kept student boarders near the University campus. Kendall spent several weeks there, often hunting ducks in the coves north of Burlington, or fishing for trout in the stream under the brow of Mt. Mansfield. There he met William Rix, a student, who later was to marry his sister, Catherine.

After he became famous, legends grew up about Kendall's early life, and a number of these concerned the period he spent in New York following the visit to his father's home. Joseph Elliott, a printer who later served for many years as superintendent

[2] Kendall papers, undated clipping from San Antonio *Express*.

[3] Two typographical societies in Cincinnati planned a dinner at two dollars a plate during 1832. When the United States celebrated the French Revolution in 1830, with general suspension of business, and the trades appearing with their banners, sashes and emblems, the printers took a most important part. In Washington a press at work on a stage formed a part of the procession. In New Orleans, the society held an annual dinner that was always elaborately reported in the press, with a full account of the many courses of food and wines.

of the mechanical and publishing department of the New York *Herald,* told of seeing Kendall hurrying down Broadway during the terrible cholera epidemic in 1832. He reported that Kendall told him, "I'm off for New Orleans. You'll die of the cholera if you remain here."

Two decades later Kendall wrote to his friend, William T. Porter, "It does not seem, friend Bill, as though twenty odd years had passed over our heads since we first tumbled over a ten pin or two at Holt's, next door to the Old Pork—in those days the last saloon in all New York. Why, so long ago as '32, the great cholera year, . . . we were men grown together in Gotham, and I believe that you then reckoned yourself one of the old and established citizens. . . ."

A newspaper friend dug up a story after Kendall's death. It runs thus:

Kendall was a "typo" in the printing office of the *New Yorker,* but after hours he patronized the Astor House, the popular stopping place for southerners visiting New York. One evening he was agreeably surprised to meet several gentleman from Natchez whom he had known on his wanderings. After a few social "smiles" a game of poker was proposed. Kendall had only fifteen dollars, which he had borrowed from his fellow workers. At seven the next morning he appeared in the office of the *New Yorker,* paid back the borrowed money, and told Horace Greeley, his employer, that he would give up his job, "as he now had $700 with which he proposed to start a paper in New Orleans."[4]

A shower of meteorites on the morning of November 14, 1833, fixed firmly in Kendall's mind the date of his departure[5] from New York for Washington, where he soon was at work for Duff

[4] Kendall papers, undated clipping from San Antonio *Express.* There may have been some basis for this story, but Kendall had left New York before Greeley started the *New Yorker* on March 22, 1834. At intervals during 1832 Greeley worked on the *Spirit of the Times,* the sporting journal which William T. Porter had launched. Porter formerly had been foreman of West's printing shop at 85 Chatham Street, and it was he who gave Greeley his first job in New York.

[5] Kendall recalled that the cabman, who called for him at four o'clock in the morning, was almost too frightened to load his trunk on the hack.

Green on the *United States Telegraph*.[6] Then a job opened on the famous *National Intelligencer* and Kendall took it. At the next case was a young man from North Carolina named F. A. Lumsden. The two met again in New Orleans in 1835 when they worked as foremen of rival newspapers, and later they formed a business partnership and an enduring friendship.

Meanwhile, William Rix, who had gone south from Vermont for his health, returned in the summer of 1834. He had arranged to go back to Alabama before January 1, 1835, to take charge of an academy, and Kendall planned to go south with him. But Rix was delayed, and Kendall, always impatient, took ship for New Orleans. Rix followed later by the Mississippi and found George just getting up from yellow fever. He had arrived too soon, but benefited in the long run by that severe ordeal of acclimation.

Through the winter Kendall worked on the *True American,* spent part of the next summer on the *Sentinel* in Greensboro, Alabama, and in the fall returned on horseback to New Orleans. Soon afterward Rix received the first number of the *Picayune*.

A spirit of "go ahead" pervaded New Orleans when Kendall settled there, and the population was riding on a wave of financial inflation which was to result in panic and disaster at the close of Andrew Jackson's administration. Eight new banks were chartered in the city in 1836, and they issued paper money far exceeding their reserves. But at the time everyone was hopeful. Companies were formed to dig canals and build railroads, the population doubled during the decade, and there was building everywhere.

More than five hundred artisans, mechanics and laborers poured into the city during November, 1836, and newspapers declared that still more were wanted. "Inferior carpenters" made four dollars a day, and first-rate bricklayers were paid five dol-

[6] Duff Green (1791–1875) edited the *Telegraph* from 1825 to 1835. He was a member of Jackson's "Kitchen Cabinet," but in the quarrel between Jackson and Calhoun he attacked the administration and the government printing was taken away from the *Telegraph* in 1831. Green then edited it in Calhoun's interest, supporting nullification.

lars. A visiting editor was "actually astonished to witness the great number of large and splendid edifices which were under way. . . . Eighteen months ago we thought the progress of improvement great, but it was nothing to compare to that which has taken place within the past six months."[7]

Gas extracted from Pittsburgh coal was introduced in 1834, although a theater had been lighted with it some years before, and the gas works were finshed in 1837 at a cost of one hundred and fifty thousand dollars. Kendall did not care for the improvement, and often complained that it hurt his eyes.

During the years he worked on the *True American* Kendall watched the construction of the new United States barracks, the United States mint, two fine markets, and the St. Charles Hotel where he was to stay so many times in the coming years. It cost six hundred thousand dollars to build and one hundred and fifty thousand dollars to furnish.

The St. Charles Theatre, where Kendall witnessed many enjoyable performances, was built in 1835. It held four thousand people, and was the fourth in size in the world, only St. Petersburg, Milan, and Naples having larger ones. Newspapers published widely the description of its chandelier, which was made in London at a cost of ten thousand dollars. It weighed two tons, had 23,000 pieces of cut glass, and was lighted by 176 gas burners, giving the effect of "soft moonlight." Its top border, emblematic of the United States, was decorated with twenty-six eagles and stars, surmounted by a gilded cornice of fleurs-de-lis. The rowdy cosmopolitan New Orleans audience was not impressed, and rioted when the Italian opera company omitted the last scene of Rossini's opera, "Semiramide." The spectators tore up chairs and threw canes at the splendid chandelier, "the pride of the St. Charles." But the city mourned when the theater burned in 1842.

[7] *Niles' Weekly Register,* November 5, 1836, p. 160. The *Picayune,* June 10, 1852, looking back on this pre-panic period, said that the city was "a sort of California of the times," though a saying was current that "it required three partners to establish a 'house'—one to die of yellow fever, one to get killed in a duel, and one to wind up the business and come home."

New Orleans in that day was an excitement-loving place, where tempers flared quickly and duels were not infrequent. Men enjoyed the lusty sports of a pioneer society, and there was cock fighting and prize fighting of a sort. When an Englishman and an Irishman fought three rounds at the forks of the Bayou Sara Road, a general scrimmage resulted. The rioters came to town and congregated opposite the American Theater, and it required the police and the Washington guards to disperse them.

Noisy rowdies pitched dollars in the streets, wrestling and "doing all manner of disorderly tricks;" draymen drove at a rate "to endanger the lives and limbs of its citizens," and the gatherings at the coffee houses made "more noise than the inmates of an Italian bedlam could possibly produce."

Negro traders paraded slaves for sale on the narrow *trottoir* in front of the City Hall on Common Street, in spite of a city ordinance. All too often it was necessary for the newspapers to call attention to piles of dead fish in the streets, or to mudholes where horses and drays and even firemen bogged down with their "engines" on the way to fires.

But the levee, Kendall found, was a pleasant place to walk in the evening, when the cathedral bells chimed calling the people to vespers, and the flags of every nation were run up to the masthead to salute the sunset. The shipping stretched away as far as the eye could reach, three tiers deep, curving in a beautiful crescent for two miles up and down the river.

In spite of its mud, its epidemics and its slow mail service, twenty-nine days away from New York, he was fascinated by the city he now called home.

3

The Picayune *starts*
its first hundred years

U P FROM THE OLD QUARTER of New Orleans, four young men stood around the imposing stone in a crowded little room, eagerly waiting while George Wilkins Kendall finished his work at the nearby case. Their "sanctum" faced the cobblestones of Gravier Street near Magazine, and its two front "door windows" looked across to Banks' Arcade, which, with Hewlett's, was the exchange of New Orleans until the St. Charles Hotel was completed.

The imposing stone stood in the center of the room, with a pair of chases and their furniture, eight or ten galleys, and a pair of bellows. Five pairs of type cases ranged around the walls. A new broom stood in the corner, and above it hung the wash basin. At one side there were two small tables; one was the editorial desk, the other held the books of the "business department" for the establishment which had just come into being.

On that Tuesday evening, January 24, 1837, George's fingers skipped from compartment to compartment in the case, and when the last line was set up he turned and transferred the type from the composing stick to the waiting form. He locked it up and planed it down by pounding with a wooden mallet on a wooden block which he moved rapidly over the face of the type. Meanwhile Francis Asbury Lumsden stood by, ready to take the proof. Then they spread out the damp sheets and looked over the first page-proofs of the New Orleans *Picayune*.

THE PICAYUNE

VOL. 1. **NEW ORLEANS, WEDNESDAY MORNING, JANUARY 25, 1837.** **NO. 1.**

THE PICAYUNE

IS PUBLISHED DAILY, BY

F. A. LUMSDEN AND G. W. KENDALL.

TERMS.

Subscriptions received for three months only, at $2 50; weekly subscriptions, 25 cents; single numbers, 6¼ cents. All subscriptions in advance.

Advertisements, not exceeding ten lines, inserted for $1, for the first, and 50 cents for every subsequent insertion. Those of greater length, charged in proportion.

OLD WINTER IS COMING.

Old winter is coming again—alack!
  How icy and cold is he!
He cares not a pin for a shivering back,
He's a saucy old chap to white and black,
He whistles his chills with a wonderful knack,
  For he comes from a cold country.

A witty old fellow this winter is;
  A mighty old fellow for glee!
He cracks his jokes on the pretty sweet Miss,
The wrinkled old maiden, unfit to kiss,
And freezes the flow of their lids—for this
  Is the way with such as he!

Old winter's a frolicksome blade I wot—
  He is wild in his humor and free!
He'll whistle along for the "want of his thought"
And set all the warmth of our furs at nought,
And ruffle the faces, by pretty girls brought,
  For a frolicksome old fellow is he!

Old Winter is blowing his gust along,
  And merrily shaking the tree!
From morning till night he will sing his song;
Now moaning and short—now howling and long;
His voice is loud for his lungs are strong;
  A merry old fellow is he!

Old Winter's a wicked old chap, I ween;
  As wicked as ever you'll see!
He withers the flowers, so fresh and green;
And bites the pert nose of the Miss of sixteen,
As she triumphantly walks in maidenly sheen,
  A wicked old fellow is he!

Old Winter's a tough old fellow for blows,
  As tough as ever you'll see!
He will trip up our trotters, and rend our clothes,
And stiffen our limbs, from fingers to toes;
He minds not the cries of his friends or his foes;
  A tough old fellow is he!

A cunning old fellow is Winter, they say,
  A cunning old fellow is he!
He peeps in the crevices day by day,
To see how we're passing our time away,
And marks all our doings, from grave to gay;
  I'm afraid he is peeping at me.

From the New-York Mirror.

SCENES FROM LIFE.

The young Lord D. yawned Why did the young lord yawn? He had recently come into ten thousand a year. His home was a palace. His sisters were angels. His cousin was—in love with him. He, himself, was an Apollo. His horses might have drawn the chariot of Phœbus, but in their journey around the globe, would never have crossed above grounds more Eden-like than his. Around him were streams, lawns, groves and fountains. He could hunt, fish, read, flirt, sleep, swim, drink, muse, write or lounge. All the appliances of affluence were at his command. The young Lord D. was the admiration and envy of all the country. The young Lord D.'s step sent a palpitating flutter through many a lovely bosom. His smile awakened many a dream of bliss and wealth. The Lady S.,—that queenly woman, with her majestic bearing, and her train of dying adorers, grew lovelier and livelier beneath the spell of his smile; and even Ellen B.,—the modest, beautiful creature, with her large, timid, tender blue eyes, and her pouting red lips—that rosebud—sighed audibly, only the day before, when he left the room—and yet—and yet—the young Lord D. yawned.

It was a rich still hour. The afternoon sunlight overspread all nature. Earth, sky, lake and air were full of its dying glory, as it streamed into the apartment where they were sitting, through the foliage of a magnificent oak, and the caressing tendrils of a profuse vine, that half buried the verandah beneath its heavy masses of foliage.

'I am tired to death,' said the sleepy lord.

His cousin Rosalie sighed.

'The package of papers from London is full of news, and ——,' murmured her sweet voice timidly.

'I hate news.'

'The poetry in the New Monthly is—

'You set my teeth on edge. I have had a surfeit of poetry.'

'Ellen B. is to spend the day with us, to-morrow.'

Rosalie lifted her hazel eyes full upon his face.

'Ellen B.?' drawled the youth, 'she is a child, a pretty child. I shall ride over to Lord A's.'

Rosalie's face betrayed that a mountain was off her heart.

'Lord A. starts for Italy in a few weeks,' said Rosalie.

'Happy dog!'

'He will be delighted with Rome and Naples.'

'Rome and Naples,' echoed D., in a musing voice.

'Italy is a delightful heavenly spot,' continued his cousin, anxious to lead him into conversation.

'So I'm told,' said Lord D abstractedly.

'It is the garden of the world,' rejoined Rosalie.

Lord D. opened his eyes. He evidently was just struck with an idea. Young lords with ten thousand a year, are not often troubled with ideas. He sprang from his seat. He paced the apartment twice. His countenance glowed. His eyes sparkled.

'Rose—'

'Cousin—'

What a beautiful break. Rose trembled to the heart. Could it be possible that he was ——

He took her hand. He kissed it. eagerly, earnestly, and enthusiastically.

She blushed and turned away her face in graceful confusion.

'Rose!'

'Dear, *dear* cousin!'—

'I have made up my mind.'

'Charles!'—

'To-morrow!'

'Heavens!'

'I will start for Italy.'

* * * * *

'Ocean! Superb—endless—sublime, rolling, tumbling, dashing, heaving, foaming—*cœlum undique et undique pontus.* Lord D. gazed around. The white cliffs of Dover were fading in the distance. Farewell, England. It is a sweet melancholy, this bidding adieu to a mass—a speck in the horizon—a mere cloud, yet, which contains in its airy and dim outline, all that you ever knew of existence.

'Noble England,' ejaculated Lord D., 'and dear mother—Ellen B.—pretty fawn—Rose too—sweet pretty dear Rose—what could mean those glittering drops that hung upon her lashes when I said adieu. Can it be that?—pshaw!—I am a coxcomb. What! Rose? the little sunshiny Rose—the cheerful philosopher—the logical—the studious—the—the—the—!'

Alas! alas! What are logic, study, cheerfulness, sunshine, to a warm hearted girl of twenty—in love?

Lord D. went below.

* * * * *

Italy *is* a Paradise. Surely Adam looked on such skies, such rivers, such woods, such mountains, such fields. How lavish, how bright, how rich is every thing around. Lord D. guided his horse up a mountain near Rome. The sun had just set; the warm heavens stretched above him perfectly unclouded; what a time to muse! what a place! The young nobleman fell into a reverie, which, the next moment, was broken by a shout of terror—the clashing of arms—a pistol-shot, and a groan. He flew to the spot. A youth of twenty lay at the root of a tall tree, weltering in his blood. The assassin terrified at the sight of a stranger, fled.

'I die,' murmured the youth, with ashy lips.

'Can I aid you?' asked Lord D., thrilling with horror and compassion.

'Take this box. It contains jewels, and a *secret* which I would not have revealed for the world. Carry it to England, to the Duke of R—. Open it not, no matter what happens. Swear never to reveal to any human being that you possess it—swear.'

Lord D. hesitated.

'My life blood ebbs away apace. Speak, oh speak, and bless a dying man—swear.'

'I swear.'

'Enough. I thank you—hide it in your bosom.—God bless you—my——England—never see—home—again—never, nev—.'

The full round moon beautifully bright, went solemnly up the azure track of the sky.

Lord D. dashed a tear from his eye, as he gazed on the pallid features of the youth, who stretched himself out in the last shuddering agony and convulsion of death. He placed his hand upon the stranger's bosom. The heart had ceased to beat. No longer the crimson gore flowed from the wound. The light foam stood on his pale lips.

'And he has a mother,' said the chilled nobleman—'and a once happy home. For their sake, as well as his, his wishes shall be obeyed.'

The tread of horses feet came to his ear, and shouts and confused voices.

Lord D. thought that the fugitive ruffian was returning with more of the gang.

'Shall I fly like a coward?' was his first thought, but again, he said, 'why should I waste my life upon a set of banditti?'

He sprang to his saddle, in his hurry, leaving behind him a kerchief—dashed the rowels into the flanks of the snorting steed, and was presently lost in the winding paths of the forest.

* * * * *

The midnight moon was shining silently into the apartment, as Lord D's eyes closed in sleep, after having laid for some time lost in thought upon his couch. His senses gradually melted into dreams.

'Ah, Rosalie. Dear Rosalie.'

The maiden suddenly grasped his throat with the ferocity of a fiend, when—hah! no Rosalie—but the iron gripe of a muscular arm dragged him from the bed, and shook his idle dreams to air.

'Bind the villain,' said a hoarse voice.

'Away, away to the duke's!'

Bewildered, indignant, alarmed, the astonished lord found himself bound, and borne to a carriage—the beautiful and soft fragments of Italian scenery flew by the coach windows.

* * * * *

If you would freeze the heart of an Englishman, and yet suffocate him with anger, thrust him into a dungeon. Lord D. never was so unceremoniously assisted to a change of location. A black-browed, dark-complexioned, mustachio-lipped soldier hurled him down a flight of broken steps, and threw after him his bundle of clothes.

'By St. George, my friend, if I had you on the side of a green English hill, I would make your brains and bones acquainted with an oaken cudgel. The uncivilized knave.'

He lay for hours on a little straw. By-and-by some one came in with a lamp.

'Pray, friend, where am I?'

The stranger loosened his cord, and motioned him to put on his clothes. He did so—unable to repress the occasional explosion of an honest, heartfelt execration. When his toilette was completed, his guide took him by the arm, and led him through a long corridor, till, lo! a blaze of sunshiny daylight dazzled his eyes.

* * * * *

'You are accused of murder,' said the duke, in French.

'Merciful Providence!' ejaculated D.

'Your victim was found weltering in his blood, at your feet. You left this kerchief on his body. It bears your name. By your hand he fell. You have been traced to your lodgings. You must die.'

* * * * *

A witness rushed forward to bear testimony in favor of the prisoner. Lord D. *could* not be the perpetrator of such a crime. He was a nobleman of honor and wealth.

'Where are his letters?'

He had brought none.

'What is the result of the search which I ordered to be made at his lodgings?'

'This box, my lord duke, and—'

The box was opened. It contained a set of superb jewels, the miniature of the murdered youth, and of a fair creature, probably his mistress.

Lord D. started.

'By heavens, it is Rosalie! I am thunderstruck.'

'Enough,' said the duke, 'guilt is written in every feature. Wretch, murderer! To the block with him. To-morrow, at daybreak, let his doom be executed.—Nay, sir, lower that high bearing, those fiery and flashing eyes, that haughty and commanding frown. Not thus should you meet your Creator.'

* * * * *

Night, deep night. How silent! How sublime!—The fated lord lay watching the sky through the iron grating of his cell.

'Ay, flash on, myriads of overhanging worlds—ye suns whose blaze is quenched by immeasurable distance. To-morrow just so with your calm, bright, everlasting faces, ye will look down upon my grave.—Jupiter, brilliant orb! How lustrous! How wonderful! Ha! the north star—ever constant! Axis on which revolves this stupendous, heavenly globe. How often *at home* I have watched thy beams with Rosalie on my arm. Rosalie, *dear* Rosalie—'

'I come to save you,' said a soft, sweet voice.

'What! Boy—who art thou? Why dost—'

The young stranger took off his cap.

'No—yes! That forehead—those eyes—enchanting girl—angel—'

'Hush!' said Rosalie, laying her finger upon her lip.

* * * * *

Ocean—again—the deep, magnificent ocean—and life and freedom.

'Blow, grateful breeze—on, on, over the washing billows, light-winged bark. Ha! land a-head? England! Rosalie, my girl, see—'

Again on her lashes tears stood glittering.

How different from those that—

* * * * *

Onward like the wind, revolve the rattling wheels. The setting sun reveals the tall groves, the great oak, lawns, the meadows, the fountains.

'My mother!'

'My son!'

'Friends!'

A package from the duke.

'The murderer of —— is discovered, and has paid the forfeit of his crimes. Will Lord D. again visit Italy?'

'Ay, with my *wife*—with Rosalie.'

'And with *letters* and a *good character*,' said Rosalie, archly.

PROSPECTUS
OF THE
Commercial News and Reading Room
OF
THE TRUE AMERICAN.

THE growing importance of this metropolis of the West, and the daily extension of its commerce, almost ensure the success of any undertaking which would tend to facilitate our merchants in those dealings which are the foundation of the greatness of our city. With the increase of its commerce, New Orleans itself increases; and in the ratio of this commerce we will see new improvements and ameliorations rise up in every quarter. The subscriber consequently runs but little risk in establishing a *New Reading Room*, and in calling upon the public to give it their patronage. He confidently expects that the liberal encouragement he has heretofore received from this community, will not in this instance be withheld.

The location of the Reading room proposed, will be at the corner of Magazine and Natchez sts. in Banks' Arcade buildings.

All the best Newspapers in the United States will be found at the room; and care will be taken that the *latest* papers be placed on the tables, immediately after the arrival of the mails.

A LIBRARY, composed of several hundred volumes of the best authors, will be attached to the room, for the use of subscribers who may wish to refer to it for information.

A complete set of *Niles' Register* will form a part of the Library.

The *Reviews*, and other literary periodicals of the U. States and Europe, will be laid on the table.

Holding out these inducements, the subscriber hopes that, in his expectation of public patronage, he will not be disappointed.

Conditions: Ten dollars per annum, payable semi-annually in advance.

jan 25 JOHN GIBSON.

REPUBLICTION of the London, Edinburgh, Foreign and Westminster Quarterly Reviews Published by Theodore Foster, corner of Broadway and Pine streets, New York, and by the different agents to Blackwood's Magazine.

TERMS.

The numbers of each work are published separately and from an exact reprint of the original copies. They are issued as soon after they are received from Europe as is consistent with their proper publication.

Price for the whole series, comprising the regular numbers of the London, Edinburg, Foreign and Westminster Reviews, $8 per annum, payable in advance; for three of them, $7 per annum; for two, $5; for one, $3. Any individual forwarding $30 free of charge shall have five copies of the entire series of this republication sent for one year.

jan 25 C. H. BANCROFT, agent, N. Orleans

REPUBLICATION OF BLACKWOOD'S AND THE METROPOLITAN MAGAZINES.—Published by Theodore Foster, 25 Pine st. New York, and also by the several agents to the republication of the London, Edinburgh, Foreign and Westminster Quarterly Reviews.

Blackwood's Magazine is republished in a most superior style of execution, fully equal to the original and is an exact copy of the same in every particular. The price is $5 per annum. The Metropolitan is republished all with the exception of the appendix. Its price is $4 per annum. When taken together the price of the two works will be but $8 per annum. Mail subscribers must in all cases pay in advance. The publisher and his agents reserve to themselves the right of collecting from all others at such times as they may think proper.

The importation price of these journals is about $20. They are here offered in a style equally neat and attractive, for less than half these sums. To those individuals who suppose that the price is still disproportionate to the price of the republication of the Reviews issued by the same publisher, it may be suggested that the Reviews are each of them Quarterly publications, and that these magazines are issued monthly and that a number of the magazines to an average contain three-fourths of the amount of matter that a number of the Reviews do. Consequently they are cheaper than the republication of Reviews, the publisher relying on the more extended sale, which they will probably obtain, for a proportionate profit.

jan 25 C. H. BANCROFT, agent, N. Orleans.

SATURDAY CHRONICLE.

$200 IN PREMIUMS.

THE Publishers of the Philadelphia Saturday Chronicle anxious to contribute their mite towards encouraging native talent, and desirous of showing their gratitude for the liberal patronage bestowed upon their publication, beg to offer to American writers the following premiums for approved original articles:

$100

For the best original tale—the subject left to the discretion of the writer.

$50

For the best original poem, not to exceed seventy lines.

$50

For the best original essay, either historical, moral, biographical or scientific.

The articles placed in competition for the prizes must be forwarded to the publishers, free of postage—(otherwise they will not be received)—on or before the 1st of February, 1837, when they will be placed in the hands of the following named literary gentlemen, who have kindly consented to act as the examining committee:

Joseph R. Chandler, Esq., editor of the United States Gazette.

Robert Morris, Esq. editor of the Pennsylvania Inquirer.

Willis Gaylord Clarke, Esq., editor of the Philadelphia Gazette.

David Paul Brown, Esq. author of "Sertorius," &c.

Dr. John A. Elkinton, author of "Last Moments of a Dying Man," "Lake George," &c.

The publication of the present articles will commence as soon as the decision of the committee is announced, and the premiums will be forwarded to the successful competitors, on the day the articles are published. All tales, essays, and poems, sent in competition, will be considered as the property of the publishers, but the author of each article accepted for publication will be entitled to the Saturday Chronicle, gratis, for one year.

Address, *post paid*,
MATTHIAS & TAYLOR,
No. 74 South Second street, Philadelphia.

jan 25

TERMS—Two dollars a year, payable in advance; $2 50 if not paid before the expiration of six months; and $3 00 if payment is delayed until the end of the year. For six months, $1 00—in advance.

☞ Advertisements neatly and conspicuously inserted, on reasonable terms.

☞ Postmasters and others remitting $10 00, will be furnished with six copies of the Chronicle for one year.

☞ Orders of postage addressed to the publishers, at No. 74 South Second street, Philadelphia, will meet prompt attention.

☞ Small notes on all solvent banks, received at par, in payment for subscription.

GREAT National Work.—AMERICAN MAGAZINE of useful and interesting knowledge to be illustrated by numerous engravings, by the Boston Bewick Company. The success which has attended the publication of the best magazine from the English press has led to preparations for issuing a periodical more adapted to the wants and tastes of the American public. While it will be the object of the proprietors to make the work strictly what its title indicates, it will nevertheless contain all articles of interest to its patrons which appear in foreign magazines.

Extensive preparations have been entered into with artists of the Union for drawings and illustrations of every subject of interest, which the publishers confidently believe will enable them to issue a work honorable to its title and acceptable to the American people.

Portraits and Biographical Sketches of distinguished Americans. Views of public buildings, monuments and improvements, landscape scenery, the boundless variety and beauty of which in this country, will form an unceasing source of instruction and gratification. Engravings and descriptions of the character, habits, &c. of beasts, birds, fishes, and insects, together with every subject connected with the geography, history, natural and artificial resources of the country illustrated in a familiar manner.

Boston, February 6th, 1836.

The American Magazine furnished to the subscribers at the low price of two dollars per annum. j 25

TO Printers.—E. WHITE & WM. HAGAR, respectfully inform the Printers of the United States, to whom they have been individually known as established Letter Founders, that they have now formed a copartnership in said business, and from their united skill and extensive experience, they hope to be able to give satisfaction to all who may favor them with their orders.

The introduction of machinery in place of the tedious and unhealthy process of casting type by hand, a desideratum by the European founders, was by American ingenuity and a heavy expenditure of time and money on the part of our senior partner, first successfully accomplished. Extensive use of the machine cast letter has fully tested and established its superiority in every particular over those cast by the old process.

The Letter Foundry business will hereafter be carried on by the parties before named, under the firm of White, Hagar & Co. Their specimen exhibits a complete series, from Diamond to sixty-four line pica. The book and news type being in the modern light and style.

White, Hagar & Co. are agents for the sale of the Smith and Rust Printing Presses, which they can furnish at manufacturers' prices. Chases, cases, composing sticks, ink, and every article used in the printing business, kept for sale and furnished on short notice. Old type taken in exchange for new, at nine cents per lb.

N. B. Newspaper proprietors who will give the above three insertions, will be entitled to five dollars in such articles as they may select from our specimens.

jan 25 E. WHITE & HAGAR.

SADDLERY and Harness Ware—The subscribers have received by the packet ships Kentucky, Louisville, and Orleans, and other late arrivals from New York, a large assortment of Saddlery and Harness Ware, which with their former stock, makes their supply very ample and complete, comprising every variety of article in their line of the best quality and style of workmanship, and which they offer for sale at wholesale and retail at the lowest prices and on liberal terms. They will also continue to receive through the season fresh supplies of goods by the packets from N York.

SMITH, HUBBARD & Co.
30 corner Customhouse and Chartres s.

j 25

Page One of the First Picayune

(about three-quarter size)

To Kendall and Lumsden this meant more than checking proofs for four pages of small type. It was the beginning of a newspaper publishing venture that had been more than three years in the planning, a venture which was to link their names with its growing stature throughout the remainder of their lives.

Through the late afternoon William H. Flood and W. H. Birckhead had worked, setting type for the four pages of the little paper and joking with H. C. Kelcey as he worked at his case supported on a stand improvised from drygoods boxes. When the young men had checked the last item on the proofs and corrected the pages, they carried the forms down to the job office of George Short at Camp and Common streets. There, in the hours before dawn, Lumsden ran off the first issue which was to greet the people of New Orleans on Wednesday morning.

Undoubtedly the partners debated over the number to be printed. Would three hundred be enough? Could they gamble on five hundred? Kendall had the final word, and they printed a thousand copies. By February 7 the *Picayune* was saying triumphantly, "On Sunday we printed and sold 1800 copies of our paper, and could have disposed of more had they been printed."

Kendall and Lumsden had precedent for their venture. Printers everywhere had watched the amazing success of the *Sun,* which Benjamin H. Day, a printer, had launched from his little shop in New York in 1833. It startled the world with its famous "moon hoax" stories, and laughed off its lies as a huge joke, safe in the assurance that it would be read by the man in the street. For the *Sun* had brought the newspaper within the reach of the masses for the first time, and the masses poured a rising tide of pennies into its circulation office. The *Sun,* early in 1837, boasted a larger circulation than any other newspaper in the world.

Other printers, amazed but somewhat assured by Day's success, began to imitate the *Sun.* There appeared the New York *Mirror,* the *Gazette,* the *True Sun,* and the *Ladies' Gazette,* and James Gordon Bennett's *Herald* which lived and became famous because its founder gave a new and gossipy twist to the day's news. Then Arunah S. Abell and a couple of his fellow typos from New York went down to Philadelphia and tried out the experiment of a small cheap paper. They called it the *Ledger,* and when it prospered Abell moved on to become a partner in establishing the Baltimore *Sun.*

Kendall and Lumsden started the first cheap paper in the South. While it did not sell for a penny a copy, like the *Sun* and the *Herald* in New York, it was a paper that the poor man could afford to buy. Establishing newspapers was a popular enterprise in the boom days of early 1837, for ten newspapers already flourished in the city of New Orleans, and eight more were started during the year.[1]

In a city of seventy thousand population, where the old Spanish and French setting provided an exotic backdrop for a panorama of queer and unusual scenes, the appearance of the *Picayune* caused a mild sensation. First, there was the name, derived from the old Spanish "picayon," the smallest coin in circulation at that time and valued at six and one-fourth cents. The new paper sold four issues for a quarter, while the other local papers sold for not less than ten cents. Then there was the size, four pages, eleven by fourteen inches and four columns to the page. All of the *Picayune's* contemporaries were large sheets, especially the *Commercial Bulletin,* which was printed "extra imperial," big enough to paper the wall or blot out the landscape. The *Picayune* taunted these larger papers, declaring that a man in New Orleans looked for three days for the advertisement he had inserted in the *Bulletin,* "and couldn't find it in the *horse blanket* he had spread out."

[1] *Le Vrai Republicain, Le Moquer, L'Ecureuil,* the *Daily Commercial and Ledger, Commercial Prices Current, The Magnolia,* the *Southerner,* and the *Picayune,* were established in 1837, while the *Commercial Bulletin,* the *Bee,* the *True American, The Echo,* the *Advertiser,* the *Merchant,* the *Courier,* the *Observer,* the *Herald,* and the *Rambler* already were in existence.

Since his days in Washington, Lumsden had been foreman of the shop of the New Orleans *Standard,* and Birckhead and Kelcey were on his staff. When fire swept through the buildings at 68 to 76 Camp Street opposite the American Theater, the *Standard* shop at No. 72 was destroyed, and its discouraged proprietors did not rebuild the plant. The New Orleans *Observer,* at No. 70, also was destroyed.

The *Bulletin* gave the *Picayune* a very friendly, very solemn announcement five days after its appearance, but the *True American* said, "The *Picayune* is a very nice little paper, but what we admire in it, is its excessive modesty. . . . We wish the little thing well; but have some fears that it will die of a surfeit of self praise."

There is small wonder that its contemporaries looked on it as an audacious little sheet. Its tone was determined, at least until it was firmly established, by the salutation in the first issue which Kendall set in type as he stood, laughing, at the case. Digging into his notebook full of jokes, and into the vast reservoir of his fun-loving past, he greeted New Orleans thus:

To the Public: In selecting our title, we intend the word to have a double application, as to its limited dimensions and demands.

> *Man wants but little here below,*
> *Nor wants that little long.*

Some may object to our Anglo-Spanish spelling of the title, and call for the derivation; but when we exchange *our Picayune* for *your* picayune, and we derive a profit, it will be time enough to *touch the Spanish.* . . .[2]

The puns came fast as the editors joked through a half-column of comic bows to prospective purchasers.

The *Sun* in 1833 and the *Herald* in 1835 had introduced in New York the English system of selling papers to newsboys who hawked them on the streets or delivered them to their own cus-

[2] Although Congress authorized the coinage of the copper cent in 1793, the half-dime in 1794, and the dime in 1796, metal for coins for domestic retail trade was so scarce that the act of 1793 also legalized the circulation of foreign coins. Popular among the Spanish-American coins was the old silver "medio real," valued at one-sixteenth of a dollar, known by various names in different parts of the United States. In Pennsylvania, Virginia, and nearby states it was called "fipenny bit," or "fip;" in New England, "fourpence ha'penny," or "fourpence;" in New York, "sixpence," and in Louisiana "picayon," or "picayune." In 1837 this was still the smallest coin in wide circulation in New Orleans, and thus the *Picayune's* competitors welcomed the new paper as "the penny press." Congress, in 1857, repealed the law which legalized the circulation of foreign money and these coins soon disappeared.

tomers. This "little merchant" plan apparently was put into effect with the first issue of the *Picayune*.

To begin with, the *Picayune* had little to recommend it to the public, aside from its catchy name, its small size, its cheap price and Kendall's jokes and puns. As a newspaper, it had few of the characteristics of the press of today.

It had no wire news. Samuel F. B. Morse, professor of art at Columbia University, had been experimenting for five years, trying to find out how electrical impulses could be transferred. Seven years were to pass before the first message was sent by wire from Washington to Baltimore, and ten years before the *Picayune* made use of the telegraph in gathering news. Even then it was to prove so costly and unsatisfactory that at first it was used only for market news and flash news of great importance.

The paper carried no illustrations except the small, quaint headings for want ads, depicting horses and ships. The first page of the initial issue showed liberal use of the scissors. Two of the four columns were devoted to a romantic "short short" story, headed "Scenes from Life," and honestly credited to the New York *Mirror*. Seven stanzas of jingling rhyme, lamenting the coming of winter, occupied a half-column under the masthead. The rest of the front page was filled with advertisements. These announced American magazines and reprints of British magazines, a printing wholesale house,[3] and the establishment of a reading room where for the price of twenty dollars per year a subscriber might read the latest papers and a few well selected books.

Even the local news on the inside pages could hardly be called a detailed picture of the times. The widespread practice of omitting names and of making only vague references to time and place gave early issues of the *Picayune* the appearance of being hastily and carelessly published. But the circulation climbed

[3] For this ad, the young printers naively set up the last paragraph, reading, "N.B. Newspaper proprietors who will give the above three insertions, will be entitled to five dollars in such articles as they may select from our specimen."

steadily, for the rollicking tone of many of its items must have appealed to its readers. For example:

"A duel took place yesterday afternoon which resulted in the death of the principals, each firing through the other's body. This is pretty sharp shooting, and, we think, very fair play—at least neither can say it was otherwise."

After two issues Lumsden quit working half the night as pressman for the paper and the presswork was done by the *True American*. By the third issue the front and back pages were filled with advertisements and there was an additional column and a half on the third page. The publishers boasted, "Already are our thoughts turned toward a double cylinder Napier press! If there is a paper in the city, whose circulation would warrant the purchase, ours is the one."

Riding high on the crest of success, Kendall and Lumsden decided to go after the Sunday market during their first week of publication. On Saturday they announced, saucily enough, "We have no other motive for publishing our paper on Sunday than self-interest."[4]

When the city's factions argued over the construction of a new canal, the *Picayune* applauded the speed with which this improvement was being completed. It could not refrain from twitting the opponents, however, and asked, "Will it not materially facilitate the intercourse between the crawfish and such like in the river and those in the swamp in the rear of the city? And will it not afford fine opportunities for carrying on the catfishery in the very heart of our city, which now employs a large number of individuals?"

Even its complaints gave the *Picayune* readers a chuckle. When Kendall rescued one of three pretty girls from the mud on

[4] Not all of the staff members approved the Sunday publication. On Tuesday the editors complained, "Our edition of Sunday (1,500) was *entirely* sold with the exception of 140 or 50, which were left in the office of one of the carriers until it was too late to dispose of them. He came to the office this morning and said his conscience would not allow him to sell papers of a Sunday. Were we afflicted in that manner we would exclaim, with Richard, 'Conscience avaunt.'"

Notre Dame Street, she lost her shoes and he lost one boot. He wrote, "Thanks to the glorious mud hole, thou has introduced to our acquaintance, three pretty women!"

An iron pipe in the gutter brought forth a more serious protest, and the *Picayune* assumed credit for its removal afterward.[5] Not a town topic was overlooked, and the paper talked with the public as frankly as two of its readers might have gossiped along Camp Street. It prodded the mayor when complaints became widespread that the bakers were not baking their bread long enough, then admitted it was not sure where the jurisdiction lay.

Kendall went everywhere with his little black notebook. A contemporary wrote of him, "He never lost a joke, a bit of wit, or a scrap of humor or a ray of sunshine. . . . If a bright thought was uttered in his presence, he would 'take a note of it.' If a spark of wit flitted across his vision, Kendall would rescue it from oblivion. If any humor was in circulation in any social circle where he happened to be, he would treasure it up for future use. He became a Treasury of Wit."[6]

Bewhiskered jokes, thinly veiled as local happenings, dotted the pages of the *Picayune*. New Englanders claimed that some of these "stories" were versions of his boyhood pranks around Amherst. But along the levee, into the stores, warehouses, counting houses, theaters[7] and coffeehouses and into homes, up and down the Mississippi and then in a widening circle across the South the *Picayune* circulated.

[5] Kendall complained, "The rascal who deposited one of those infernal iron pipes in the gutter on Canal street, in front of Mr. Squire's store, deserves to be sent to Baton Rouge and locked up for ten years in the penitentiary. While walking hastily along, last night, we fell over this confounded iron pipe, flat on the paving stones, and cut through thick cassimere pantaloons, jeans drawers, and into one of our knees. We are quite lame. If we knew where to look for redress we would have it."

[6] Frederic Hudson, *Journalism in the United States from 1690 to 1872* (New York, 1873), 494.

[7] *Picayune,* February 22, 1837, recounts that a performance at the St. Charles Theatre included the reading, by one of the actors, of an outlandish account from its columns about a storm at Mt. Columbo.

It was inevitable that the rollicking tone of the little paper soon would cause the quick southern tempers of some of its readers to flare. Before the *Picayune* was three weeks old Kendall started a gossip column, as pointed and as saucy as any of those that ruffled the readers along Broadway a century later. Hardly had the ink dried on the first copy when an irate citizen stormed into the office demanding satisfaction.

The series began with a rhymed column entitled "The Devil's Walk in New Orleans," pointing out the vices of the pastor of a prominent church in Lafayette Square who was referred to as "Joel." A caustic verse singled out Alderman Bobby McNair with,

> *Bob's one of those Munzes*
> *Shocked at plays on Sundays,*
> *But would pocket his costs during sermon.*

McNair rushed into the office with a friend and threatened to settle the matter "tomorrow morning." Kendall refused to be drawn into any duels, having suggested in the issue of January 27 that in case the paper unwittingly offended, the affair of honor should be settled by a foot race instead of a duel.[8] So he laughed off McNair's threats and continued the column. Through the medium of "Old Nick," then "Mephistophiles, Jr.," then regularly through the "Gentleman in Black," Kendall received reports of many of the shady goings-on in the city. "Joel," who was singled out in the first impertinent poem, eventually cleared twenty-five thousand dollars in a stock market deal; a prominent New Orleans resident won fourteen hundred dollars at a gambling table, enough to pay off a huge wine bill; a noted actor squandered the receipts of a benefit performance in an evening; a prominent lady visited the gambling halls in disguise and a clerk gambled with his employer's funds. In his strolls with Kendall, this dark guide pointed out a temperance legislator reeling drunk, and a

[8] When J. Bayon, publisher of the New Orleans *Bee* attacked Lumsden "alone and unarmed," on his way to the post office, the *Picayune* of October 27, 1837, hotly declared, "The *Bee* is a rotten, abusive concern," and announced that the *Picayune's* other two editors were ready to stand back of every printed word.

French restaurant owner fighting with a bricklayer. He complained of the weather and of the muddy streets, and often they wound up their nocturnal jaunts at Elliot's restaurant for a plump woodcock or steamed oysters.

At first the *Picayune's* editors clipped liberally from exchanges; then the tables were turned and their own items were picked up far and wide. Readers of other newspapers were greeted so frequently with the credit line, "Pic.," on brief, breezy comments that Kendall soon was credited with the invention of the humorous editorial paragraph.

But if life was all a joke to the editors of the *Picayune,* so far as readers could see, it was far otherwise in reality. There were labor troubles, and in March the compositors, who made from twenty to thirty dollars a week, demanded a twenty-five per cent increase and walked out. For a day, New Orleans was without newspapers. Then the *Picayune,* in its issue of March 14, announced that other papers in the city would resume publication the next day.

There was constant trouble with the mail, and Kendall blamed his distant cousin, Amos Kendall, postmaster general in the Van Buren cabinet. When Richard Stephens, postmaster at Claiborne, Louisiana, reported that the "mail that arrived to-day from the east is so much torn and wet that it cannot go any further until dried, and the two thirds of it is entirely lost," the *Picayune* mourned "Amos, Amos, why don't you see to this?" It added, "Amos Kendall, from whom great things were hoped, treats us in the same scurvy manner as did his predecessor."

As the paper grew, Kendall and Lumsden had to give up work at the case and devote their efforts to handling the growing business of the firm. Within two months they got a new press—not the double cylinder Napier for which they hoped, but an old-fashioned Washington hand press. In announcing this improvement, the *Picayune* stated, "Hundreds of individuals have called at the office within the past week to purchase our paper, whom we have been obliged to disappoint."

Even in its serious masthead the *Picayune* could not pass up a joke: "Published at No. 38 Gravier Street, where our paper may be had, with good endorsers, at $6\frac{1}{4}$ per cent per day, Sundays included."

The matter of "endorsers" was a joke on a tender subject, for by the time the *Picayune* was three months old the European financial collapse of late 1836 had spread to the United States. New Orleans, as sensitive to the world fiscal barometer as any other city in the land, saw its levees and warehouses stacked higher and higher with cotton, grain and other commodities from the vast Mississippi basin. Everywhere business and banking houses closed with staggering losses. Men walked the streets in search of jobs. When they found none they begged for food.

Earlier, when the *Picayune* had reported bank failures in England, these seemed so remote that New Orleans was not alarmed. When news came of food riots in New York, the paper scoffed, "Why the devil don't some of these needy editors, who are always grumbling about their destitute circumstances, &c. &c. leave off their foolish ways, and go into the all cash business like ourselves." By March, when money grew scarce in New Orleans, the *Picayune* boasted that it had money to lend to the needy. But within another month it was warning other business centers that there was no relief for the national emergency to be found in New Orleans. "Our principal business men find it extremely difficult to take care of themselves without rendering assistance elsewhere," it reported.

Cotton dropped within a few weeks from fifteen to six cents. The New Orleans correspondent for the New York *Courier and Inquirer* wrote that interest of "from five to six per cent a month is required to negotiate the best paper. . . . Business has entirely ceased, if we except the grocers, tavern keepers and market people—for our citizens must eat and drink even in these distressing times, which begin to affect the theatres and other places of amusements, usually so well attended."

It was difficult for two young businessmen who, in spite of

their boast of capital to lend, were having a hard struggle with their new venture, to sympathize with the losses of great capitalists. "Business will revive again," they said, "and on a much more stable footing. The wild dreams of monopolists and speculators, thank God, are destined never to be realized." With the people in the streets, they shared the distrust of "the partial, humbugging banks," and argued that "in the way they are at present carried on, they are the greatest curse ever entailed upon us."

As money disappeared, hats and pockets were stuffed to overflowing with personal notes and IOUs for one, two or three bits, issued by hotels and barkeeps throughout the city. The *Picayune,* deciding it was better to laugh than complain, stated, "We get just as much to eat, and somewhat more to drink, than we did in what were called prosperous times. A man can now issue any kind of a card or slip of paper, mark there 'good for' one, two or three bits, just as he pleases, and it passes current anywhere and everywhere."

In spite of the panic, the young partners still were dreaming of better times. They promised customers who had made "numerous requests," that they would have a job printing shop by September, though neither Lumsden nor Kendall knew how it could be financed. Meanwhile they had far outgrown the little room at 38 Gravier Street. They rented a building at No. 5 Camp Street and moved, but the owner came and said that a print shop would affect his insurance, and they had to move back to 38 Gravier. In July they moved to 74 Magazine Street, but already were looking ahead to still larger quarters. Kendall wrote, "We shall have the first of October a splendidly furnished editorial office on Camp Street, in the neighborhood of the theatres and the court of fashion. We shall have 26 chairs, one for every State, and a big black ottoman for loafers."

When the heat of August settled down on New Orleans, and sultry mists hung over the swamps or swept lazily up the Mississippi, the city turned from worry over the depression and watched

with growing concern the beginning of its annual siege of pestilence. The plague of cholera and yellow fever had combined in the
terrible scourge of 1832 and 1833 to take a toll of nearly ten
thousand lives, but in 1837 only the yellow fever came.

The first cases began to appear and multiply in August. Citizens who could, fled from the city to nearby plantations or to
those along the higher shores of the river beyond Baton Rouge,
while some sought refuge in other states. Nor was this a simple
thing to do. One man, sending his wife and baby up to Louisville,
sent a slave along as nursemaid and another to take care of the
cow, which had to be shipped aboard the boat so the infant could
have food for the long trip.

Daily the toll increased. The population was reduced by almost half as refugees crowded into boats headed up and down
the river, or choked the roads leading out of the city. Those who
remained grew accustomed to the constant clang of hearse tires
on the cobbled streets. Smoke from pitch fires darkened the skies
as the harassed residents sought some means of combating the
disease. Cannon were fired in the vicinity of the foundries where
the toll was worst, in an effort to drive off the malignant mists.
Ten thousand were afflicted, and nearly half as many died before
the epidemic subsided in October.

Kendall went north—not to escape the fever, for he was im-
mune through earlier illness, but to do something about the much-
needed job shop. In New York he explained his needs to Horace
Greeley, and Greeley, himself in sore financial straits, took him
to the foundry of George Bruce. He told Bruce that if Kendall
lived he would pay for the type, and Bruce fitted him out with the
job office equipment on six months' credit.

The worst of the epidemic settled on New Orleans during
Kendall's absence, and Lumsden faced the most critical situation
that had yet confronted the *Picayune*. His staff dwindled as the
fever struck one after another, and the funds saved during the
first lush days of the paper's existence disappeared. He was on
the verge of suspending publication when Wilhelmus Bozart, a

31

New Orleans businessman, stepped in and advanced funds to keep it going. This help enabled Lumsden to go ahead with the plans he and Kendall had made for removing to Camp Street. On Saturday, September 30, he wrote that the *Picayune* would not appear "until Tuesday next . . . we have to move on Monday, and our fatigue for the last week, added to the sickness of our assistant, is too great to admit of a publication sooner."

When the new job shop equipment arrived late in October, the partners skipped an issue of the *Picayune* again while rearranging their new plant at 72 Camp Street and preparing a new type dress for the paper. Then the *Picayune,* which had gone to press at four o'clock in the afternoon during the summer months, resumed its morning publication and watched New Orleans slowly recover from the summer's illness.

The paper had appeared daily throughout the summer, which was a real triumph for the young partners, since the other journals in the city had slowed down to semi- or tri-weekly appearance. By the end of the year advertisements filled fifteen and a half of the paper's twenty-four columns. In spite of panic and pestilence, the *Picayune* had survived its first year, and its future was well established.

4

Twenty-four hours ahead of the mail

THE YEAR 1838 was one of steady growth for the *Picayune* and hard work for its owners. Lumsden, then thirty-eight years old, rushed his little bay pony up and down Camp and Magazine streets, his long legs dangling almost to the ground, searching for spicy bits of news. He and Kendall had more freedom after Alva Morris Holbrook joined the staff.

Holbrook was a New Englander from Townshend, Vermont, a year older than Kendall. He trained for a business career by working in a country store, and went to New Orleans in 1835 as clerk and accountant for a large shipping firm. When the *Picayune's* increasing business affairs threatened to bury Kendall and Lumsden under a mountain of office details, Holbrook was induced to come in and take charge of the books. He soon became business manager, then purchased an interest, and in his last years was sole owner of the paper.

Kendall now turned his attention to the shipping news. This was an item of vital importance to New Orleans and particularly to the newspapers, since almost all trade and a large portion of communications were carried on by water.

Since the first Fulton boat had steamed into New Orleans in 1812, and chugged back up the river at the rate of three miles an hour on her way to Louisville, speed had become important. In 1838 the *Diana* won the prize of five hundred dollars in gold offered by the Post Office Department for the first boat to make the trip from New Orleans to Louisville in less than six days.

Three boats had been in service in 1814, and despite the depression this number had grown to four hundred and fifty by 1844. Down the Mississippi this flotilla swept, aided by hundreds of flatboats in bringing livestock and cotton and corn and wheat, hides and hemp and whiskey—produce from a third of the continent to be consumed in the South or reshipped to the Atlantic seaboard or on to the far markets of the world. Through the gulf the lanes of traffic converged at the Balize, and ships from a hundred scattered ports sailed upstream to deposit and pick up cargoes.

There was news in a ship's cargo, in the mailbags it carried, in the information brought by its officers, its crew, its passengers. The local market rose or fell as new quotations arrived by ship from London or Birmingham, New York or Boston or Philadelphia. The newspaper that could send its newsboys out with fresh editions, yelling "One day later from Louisville," or "Two days later from New York," or "Ten days later from London," found excited customers waiting for copies. It was worth money if the newsboy could cry, "Twenty-four hours ahead of the mail!"

Postal service had improved greatly since colonial days, but not enough to satisfy traders or enterprising newspaper publishers. A government express mail, authorized July 2, 1836, was slowly organized and put into operation, and by late 1837 had reduced the time between New York and New Orleans, by way of Nashville, to between nine and ten days. An ordinary journey, by stage and boat, still required twenty days. But letters sent by government express mail cost three times as much as by the slow mail, and at first could be sent collect. Newspaper editors complained that much worthless matter came to the office to be paid for. The *Picayune,* impatient at the delay in getting the express mail started, arranged its own private express which it announced in October, 1837, with a cut of "Our Horse."

It boasted, "Just look at him—see how he bounds o'er hedge and stile . . . observe how the *Bee* and *Bulletin* are in pursuit of him . . . as he lets fly the streamer bearing the words 'you're all too late—my news is for the *Picayune* . . . It will be the first to publish all news, commercial, political and foreign . . .' " Even when the government express was functioning well in 1838, the *Picayune* continued its struggle to get the news first by using its own as well as the postal express. In January, 1838, it boasted, "Our animal got in last night about half past 12 o'clock, leaving Cousin Amos' horse nowhere."

Sometimes it was half-past two o'clock in the morning before the expressman came in with the precious slips.[1] Often they arrived in bad condition, and the paper was forced to say, "Owing to the great storm on the lake . . . the wallet is completely soaked through, but we are able to make out all contained in the Uncle Sam slips. The packages beyond that are altogether unintelligible."

The *Picayune* delighted in a chance to boast, "Three of Amos' express boys were passed—one was fastened in the ice of the Roanoke—another was joining in a coon chase in South Carolina —and the other was perfectly swamped in the bottoms of the Chattahoochee."

The postal express worked smoothly during 1839 and the *Picayune* discontinued "Our Horse" for several months; but the government failed to renew its express contracts and newspapers again complained at what the Louisville *Journal* called "non-intercourse beyond the Potomac."

Even when the fast express was functioning, New Orleans newspapers found it necessary to meet every incoming boat. Not unlike New York publishers who in 1826 had organized the

[1] These slips were proof sheets of shipping and other important news which exchange newspapers ran off in advance of the regular edition and dispatched by express mail or special courier. The length of each slip was regulated, and the *Picayune* often requested its exchanges not to send an inch over the amount permitted by law, as the postmaster was strict about the matter.

For establishment of the postal express, see Richard Peters (ed.), *The Public Statutes at Large of the United States of America* (Boston, 1854), V, 88.

35

harbor news service to go out and meet sailing vessels from Europe, Kendall sailed up the Mississippi to meet the downstream traffic.

However, he went one step farther than the New Yorkers had gone. He loaded a case of type and a small press on the northbound boat, transferred to a big river steamer at Baton Rouge or Natchez or Memphis, and started gathering news. In the huge stateroom set aside for men passengers, or under the cool awnings above deck, he met and interviewed scores of passengers headed for the Crescent City. When the boat docked he had handbill extras of the *Picayune* ready for immediate street sale, and his paper hit the streets with detailed news from the North while his rivals still were trying to get their stories.

The newspaper scoop was not born in New Orleans, but it grew tall in stature along the levee, in the counting houses and on the flags of Carondelet where the exchange later was located. Newspapers put extra editions on the street with surprising speed, despite their handicap of setting type by hand. In some instances important news was sent out as a brief bulletin in an extra, to be followed by two or three editions as fast as printers could set up additional details.

In a little more than a year Kendall and Lumsden were ready to publish a weekly edition of the *Picayune*, which they launched on February 24, 1838. Their next step was to arrange for circulation in Texas, where there were only five newspapers, published weekly.[2]

Already the *Picayune* carried correspondence from Texas, and Kendall and Lumsden watched with great interest the emigrants who passed through New Orleans. Boats called every five days, carrying settlers' families with their negroes, wagons, plough horses, dogs and guns. Too much attention had been paid to speculation in Texas, the paper asserted, while a fortune

---

[2] *Niles' National Register*, February 10, 1838, listed the Houston *Telegraph*, the Matagorda *Bulletin*, the Velasco *Herald*, the Nacogdoches *Chronicle* and the Brazoria *Signal Star*.

The Founder of the Picayune

From an oil portrait by Thomas Hicks, about 1837

awaited the farmer who took along his agricultural implements and vigorously drove the ploughshare.

Lumsden went to Galveston and Houston on a circulation trip late in 1838, and made a trip inland to Austin in 1839. The journey was difficult, but he found consolation in his report to the *Picayune,* "By December I have little doubt our circulation will come to 2,000 in the republic."

Almost from the start of the paper, its publishers had been concerned about the fate of Texas. They joined in the clamor for annexation in 1837, and early in the following year Kendall was writing a humorous column, chiding England for turning covetous eyes on Mexico, and asserting that the Louisiana Purchase actually made Sam Houston not a squatter but an overseer of the Republic of Texas for the United States. War with Mexico would grow out of the Texas dispute, Kendall felt sure, but he had no inkling of the effect such a conflict would have on his own career. This war was not to break out until eight years later, and in the summer of 1839 Kendall was more concerned with a trip north, when he missed a wedding because a trip of less than two hundred miles required more than thirty-six hours, than with possible complications in Texas.

He was by this time an exceedingly eligible bachelor, whose friends were eager to see him married. The *Picayune* denied rumors that the wedding was to be his own. The rumor persisted through the winter and Kendall appealed, "those editors who have been instrumental in getting us into the *scrape* will please help us out by giving our flat denial of the charge publicity."

During his journeys Kendall sent back long, chatty letters to the paper. On this trip he picked up a copy of the New York *Herald* and confided to his readers, "Bennett can say more about nothing, spin a longer yarn with less of the raw material to commence with, than any other editor in the country."

In Kentucky he saw the races with his good friend William T. Porter, editor of the New York *Spirit of the Times,* and attended the Episcopal church where he heard a "good sermon" and noted the "pretty and well dressed women." He visited Henry Clay's home, Ashland, and spent some time with George D. Prentice, editor of the Louisville *Journal*.

Prentice wrote the *Picayune*, "Kendall comes to attend the races. We have not the slightest confidence in the prevailing report, that one of the turfmen, whose horse is familiar with Kendall's looks, has engaged that young gentleman to show his face at a particular point of the race track, and thus cause the other horses to fly the track."

Sparring between these two friends in their editorial columns continued for a quarter of a century, and Kendall admitted that Prentice "was sometimes hard in his hits." These personalities which editors published concerning themselves and each other helped to spread their fame widely. Although Kendall and Prentice were rather handsome young men, distant readers often thought otherwise. Catherine Kendall Rix, George's sister, once wrote him of meeting a mother with a very homely little boy on an excursion steamer. When she asked the child's name its mother replied, "Kendall Prentiss, after the two great editors, who besides being the homeliest men in the world are particular favorites with my husband."

The *Picayune* gave extra publicity to comments upon its spicy reputation. Kendall quoted the Philadelphia *Saturday Evening Post* as having called the *Picayune* "a chronicle of iniquitous accomplishments, pot-house witticisms, horse racing, elaborate indecencies, and the annals of a gambling community," whose writers used such filthy phrases as "Give us a light gin toddy."

"Straws," the office poet, compiled the following in retort:

> *Oh George! I've always bin afraid*
> *Of something like this 'ere,*
> *While looking at the wicked course*
> *In which you persevere.*
> *You stand up for the-a-tres, George,*
> *A shame to any body,*
> *Horse racing, wit, and worst of all*
> *You like a light gin toddy!*

"Straws" was J. M. Field, who retired temporarily from the stage to write for the *Picayune,* and who went to Europe in 1840 as the paper's first foreign correspondent. Newspapers often picked up his jingles, frequently with credit, sometimes without. Once the *Picayune* chided, "The editor of the Philadelphia *Ledger* lately cut his finger in an awkward attempt to split a straw in two."

When Fanny Elssler, the famous danseuse, came to New Orleans, the *Picayune* joined in the furor of enthusiasm which greeted her. Its "Sonnet to Fanny Elssler" was copied in the New York *Mirror* with the comment that the *Picayune* was one of the cleverest journals in America, and Kendall replied, "we are proud to see ourselves reflected in the *Mirror.*" Two years later Kendall wrote from Texas that he had met a man "who had never *even heard* of Fanny Elssler! . . . I think I can put him down as evidently insane."

As the new decade got under way the *Picayune* editors continued to search their exchanges "all day looking for something to laugh at and to make our readers laugh," and they went to the theater at night to laugh, and their paper and their job shop continued to make money.

Much to the resentment of the older papers, the *Picayune* was awarded the contract for the city printing for the Second Municipality. The *True American* had done the work previously, and it complained that the *Picayune* was "notorious for its viperlike enmity to the great Harrison cause, under the specious plea of neutrality." It called the newer paper "insignificant," and the *Picayune* roared that it had ten times the circulation and more headlines "by more than one half," than the *True American.*

Refusal to give its columns over almost wholly to politics was one of the causes of the *Picayune's* success. The paper prided itself on its prompt and accurate election returns, but aside from an occasional serious comment, it usually poked fun at politicians and politics along with the other follies of the age.

Nowhere were human frailties more apparent than in the

39

police court, or "Recorder's Court," of New Orleans. All the problems that a later period has treated with solemn, furrowed brow, appeared there in the garb of poverty, drunkenness, greed and inhumanity.

There came the beautiful mulatto whose white master had promised for years to educate their children in France, but postponed the separation because he could not bear to part with them. After his death she and her children must be sold to settle his estate.

There came the worn and aged negress whose skill with the fluting iron made her a valuable possession, so that three times she had almost earned her freedom—only to be sold, to start again the toilsome, heartbreaking road toward earning her market price. The jealous wife, the drunken vagabond, the abandoned mother, quarrelsome cabmen and rival suitors, aired their grievances in the Recorder's Court.

Among these scenes of tragedy and comedy Denis Corcoran, police reporter of the *Picayune*, spent his nights. His sketches, often credited to Kendall in later years, were published in a little volume which was advertised as popular reading material in 1843.

Another *Picayune* feature, widely reprinted in newspapers including the St. Louis *Gazette*, the Philadelphia *Post*, the Boston *Times*, the London *Satirist*, and many others, with or without credit, was the series entitled "Prairie Sketches," or "Scenes from Santa Fe." M. C. Field, brother of the office poet, "Straws," went to Santa Fe with a group of traders in 1839 to improve his health, and brought back glowing accounts of the trip across the prairies, which he contributed to the *Picayune* under the pen name of "Phasma." The paper ran these accounts irregularly during 1839 and 1840, especially when the mails failed, interspersed with the growing volume of news from Texas which also was being picked up by other newspapers all over the country.

Field made another excursion to the far West in 1843, as "historiographer" for the expedition that the wealthy Scotch baronet, Sir William Drummond Stewart, took on an exploring trip to the headwaters of the Platte and Yellowstone rivers. Fifty men, including the famous artist, John James Audubon, made up the party.

Both in his editorial capacity and as a matter of personal interest, Kendall considered the "Prairie Sketches" important. The section of country they described was increasing in general interest; emigrants were going to California; travelers to the mountains were becoming more numerous; Santa Fe was attracting traders from up and down the Mississippi, and all information about the Great Plains region was news.

In the spring of 1839 a hundred Mexican traders came overland from Chihuahua to New Orleans and returned with three hundred thousand dollars worth of American goods in wagons and on the backs of their five hundred pack mules. They traveled three hundred miles up Red River, then southwest across the plains to the border.

More and more frequently the *Picayune* carried news items about the overland trade between Missouri and Santa Fe, about the scientists and explorers who were heading westward, and the tourists who found excitement and adventure and good hunting in the comparative safety of the well-guarded trains of prairie schooners.

In the summer of 1840 Kendall made his customary journey north to buy paper and new type, but it was not an adventurous or satisfactory trip. He went by way of Chicago, Saratoga, New York, Boston, and Philadelphia, but the food at the post taverns was bad, and stages and trains were crowded. Even during his visits to theaters he kept hearing the call of the open country.

His hat, stuffed with papers and letters, blew out of the train window. The engineer refused to stop, but slowed long enough for Kendall to run back and rescue the hat and catch the train again while passengers popped their heads out the windows and laughed.

Kendall's next journey was to be filled with greater troubles than a lost hat, badly prepared food, and crowded trains.

5

Texas finds
a press agent

MIRABEAU BUONAPARTE LAMAR, president of the Republic of Texas, lay on his sick bed in New Orleans early in 1841 and dreamed of a vast empire—a dream which was to plunge Kendall into one of the most dangerous and exciting adventures of his career.

Scarcely five years earlier, Lamar had passed through New Orleans on his way from Georgia, one of the many hundreds of venturesome young men answering the Macedonian cry of Sam Houston and his little band of Texas patriots for help against the invading hosts under Santa Anna. A kind fate landed Lamar at San Jacinto in 1836 just before the retreating Texans determined to turn on their pursuers. A fellow soldier was winged and unhorsed in a brush with the enemy, and Lamar, with the flourish that had marked his entry into Texas, dashed back and brought the wounded man to safety. He became the hero of the camp. Sam Houston demoted his cavalry leader and handed the captaincy to Lamar, and on the next day watched his handful of mounted Texans support the right wing of the patriots' attack that shattered the Mexican defenses and turned the battle into a rout. Out of this engagement the Republic of Texas was born.

Lamar became one of the immortal heroes of San Jacinto. This popularity carried him to the vice-presidency of the Republic on the ticket with Houston, and, in 1838, to the presidency.

Many of the angry Texans clamored for a quick and thorough

hanging of Santa Anna when the Mexican leader was brought in with the prisoners on the day after the Battle of San Jacinto. But Houston intervened to save his prized captive. Before he started home by a circuitous route, to brew more trouble for his impetuous countrymen, Santa Anna had signed a treaty acknowledging the freedom of the Texans.

Lamar dreamed of this treaty when he lay on a hospital bed and looked out on the busy streets of New Orleans.

While thousands of eager Texas settlers clamored for annexation, he had maintained that Texas should stand alone. The United States accorded recognition in March, 1837, but annexation of the vast area meant adding to the Union that much slave territory, just as surely as it would have led to war with disgruntled Mexico. New England and the northern states would have none of it.

So Houston, in his short term, set to work to weld the few sparsely inhabited and widely scattered settlements into a nation. He borrowed sparingly and spent reluctantly, hoarding resources and nursing credit. He wrote soothing notes to the restless Cherokees who waited in vain for titles to the land they had farmed around Nacogdoches since the days of Spanish rule. With one ear toward Washington, in the hope that Texas might one day be a state in the Union, he courted diplomatic recognition from England and France. But affairs at home kept him busy. He was far too occupied, for instance, to worry about the western boundary of the Republic which stretched on out to somewhere beyond the unsettled, uncharted prairies.

But not so Lamar. He built up a formidable army and scowled in the general direction of Mexico. He whipped the Cherokees and sent them scampering across the Red River and on into Arkansas, and chased the Kiowas and Comanches far back into their hunting grounds. He bought four small ships and called them the Texas navy. When no enemy appeared in sight on the gulf he sent his fleet off to Yucatan to help the natives foment a revolution against Mexico. He moved the capital from the muddy

43

banks of the Brazos to the hills above the Colorado River on the western frontier and named the new site Austin. True, the citizens had difficulty in communicating with each other across the fabulous expanse of its main street, for it was laid out in the grand manner. And it was the same with his program of education. Lamar dreamed of schools throughout the Republic, with a great university as the capstone.

But while he planned and debated and painted rosy pictures of Texas as it would be in ten, twenty, or fifty years, Kendall was writing in the *Picayune* that the Texas national currency was sliding down to fifty, to thirty, and then to twelve cents on the dollar.[1]

The navy was ordered mustered out. Isolated settlements again fell prey to sudden attacks of Indians from the plains, while marauding bands of Mexicans sneaked across the Rio Grande to murder and pillage and then melt away in the chaparral. Hard money was scarce. Congressmen and other officials found it difficult to subsist while serving the Republic.

Lamar's head ached when he saw the empty treasury and the puny exchange rate of the Texas currency, the hungry congressmen, the poverty and distress abroad in the land. It ached worse when he heard again and again of the rich harvest that enterprising Americans were reaping through overland trade with New Mexico, of the long wagon trains that crawled over the Santa Fe Trail with loads of merchandise to be exchanged for Mexican gold, of the fabulous cargoes of pelts assembled at Bent's Fort on the Arkansas and freighted across to St. Louis. This, he insisted, was trade which belonged to Texas, which could be diverted from Santa Fe through Austin and down to the gulf by a route much shorter than the long haul from New Mexico to St. Louis. It was this vision that Lamar took with him to New Or-

[1] In its issue of February 22, 1840, the *Picayune* stated Texas treasury notes were discounted 76 per cent. By the following April 22 it reported that they were "passing at the rate of 25 cents on the dollar," and on April 13, 1841, after Texas had secured a loan, it stated that the notes "were selling yesterday at 38 and 40 cents—but a week since and 12 could hardly be got for them."

leans when he asked leave to recuperate from illness late in 1840.[2] And it was tied up with the treaty Santa Anna had signed with Sam Houston on the battlefield of San Jacinto.

News of this treaty filtered slowly back through the Texas settlements. The thirty thousand residents who cheered over their independence from Mexican rule were scattered between the coast and a line extending roughly from Nacogdoches southwest through San Antonio de Bexar and on to the Rio Grande.

Almost a thousand miles west of this line a chain of villages— Santa Fe, San Miguel, Albuquerque, El Paso del Norte, with their neighboring agricultural settlements—marked the northern thrust of the Spanish conquistadors along the course of the Rio Grande. Between this chain of villages and the line of the Texas frontier there stretched a vast area, unknown to white explorers and unpeopled except by occasional hunting parties of the plains Indians. Far to the north the traders from St. Louis had blazed trail across the plains to Santa Fe. But no traders had traveled from the Texas settlements westward to New Mexico. Yet all this vast stretch of the southern end of the "Llano Estacado," even including a part of the western settlements of the Rio Grande Valley, was claimed as Texas territory—by the Texans.

When Texas became free, Houston and his followers assumed the Rio Grande to be the boundary between Texas and Mexico. Since the earliest settlement, the river had been the accepted line between the Department of Coahuila and the Department of Texas, and when Santa Anna signed the treaty recalling the Mexican armies, the troops withdrew to points below the Rio Grande.

[2] Lamar, president of the Republic of Texas from 1838 to 1841, was ill on leave of absence in New Orleans from December 12, 1840, to February, 1841. He went to Texas to write its history after his wife had died and he had been defeated in the race for Congress. His profits from the sale of the Columbus (Georgia) *Enquirer,* which he had established in 1826, permitted him to indulge his desire for historical research. In October, 1837, an old associate on the Columbus *Enquirer* was expressing the hope that "your Press may promote the cause of Liberty and Truth in Texas and that you may shortly occupy the highest station in the State." See Sam Acheson, *35,000 Days in Texas* (New York, 1938), 6–8.

With recognition of the Republic of Texas by the United States, the matter of boundaries again was agitated. John Quincy Adams, as secretary of state under President Monroe, had built up a diplomatic barrier against southwestward expansion when he negotiated the Florida purchase in 1819. In this treaty the United States agreed with Spain that the boundary of the Louisiana Purchase ran along the Sabine to its source, then north to the Red River and along its course to the one hundredth meridian, north along that parallel to an east-west line at 42°, and along this line westward to the Pacific. This fixed the north and east boundaries of Texas.

Stephen F. Austin, first secretary of state of the Republic, instructed William H. Wharton, the Republic's envoy at Washington, to explain to the United States that Texas claimed possession of all the land up to the Rio Grande. The first Congress backed up Austin's contention by an act asserting civil jurisdiction over this same area, and for good measure added the islands in the river channel. Austin pointed out that the river served as the boundary up to its headwaters.[3] This, however, was a point of bitter dispute with Mexico, a dispute not to be settled until the United States annexed Texas and thereby plunged into war, until Zachary Taylor had fought his way into Monterrey and occupied the desert stretches below the Rio Grande, until Winfield Scott had chased Santa Anna through Mexico and into exile, until Stephen Kearny had marched across the plains to capture New Mexico and on to the Pacific to take over California as well.

From the Gulf of Mexico the Rio Grande winds northwest until it reaches El Paso, then its course swings north into the mountains. Santa Fe, the converging point of all the early western trade, lay fourteen miles east of the river, and according to Texan claims was within Texas territory. Mexico, however, refused to listen to the argument which asserted that this and the other settlements were included in Santa Anna's treaty.

[3] For the Texans' claims, see George Pierce Garrison (ed.), "Diplomatic Correspondence of the Republic of Texas," I, 132, in *American Historical Association Report*, 1907, II.

But how was Lamar to assume the ownership of this territory? How was he to enforce the Congressional act extending civil administration to the Rio Grande, including its islands? And how was he to capture this rich trade and divert it down to Texas ports on the gulf? President Lamar pondered these questions as he lifted his eyes from the dark and discouraging scenes near at hand and gazed at the light of adventure blazing so brightly for him in the general direction of the future. He believed that New Mexico hung ripe and ready for the picking, that the commerce of the prairies could be rerouted easily to pour millions into the ever-so-gaping treasury, and that the New Mexicans were eager to throw off the Mexican yoke and become a part of Texas.[4]

To this end Lamar talked an expedition to Santa Fe. His enthusiasm spread through the Republic, and by August 4, 1840, Kendall was writing in the *Picayune,* "Our Texan neighbors have been talking lately about making a dash into the Santa Fe trade. It will not do for them to waste much time in debating the matter, if they wish to secure this branch of the trade. . . ."

Not only was Kendall interested in the efforts of Texas to dip into the prairie commerce, but for some time he had been toying with the idea of joining an exploring party into the wild country. He thrilled over the graphic tales Charles Augustus Murray wrote after his trip through the hunting grounds of the Pawnees on the prairies west of St. Louis. He talked with Josiah Gregg, and learned of the reports of Zebulon Pike after his journey into the Rockies.[5] He considered joining a number of young men on a

[4] In 1837 the Texans were discussing the fate of Colonel Albino Pérez, who in 1835 had been sent to take over the governorship of New Mexico under the same central government in Mexico City from which Texas seceded. His methods of tax collection irked the natives. He called out his army, but the troops deserted to the mob and Pérez was slain. Manuel Armijo had suppressed the revolution and installed himself as governor in January, 1838, but the Texans did not learn of this until long afterward.

[5] Zebulon Pike, *Account of an Expedition to the Sources of the Mississippi and through the Western Parts of Louisiana* (Philadelphia and Baltimore, 1810) ; Josiah Gregg, *Commerce of the Prairies* (Philadelphia, 1844). For recently discovered Gregg material, see Maurice G. Fulton (ed.), *Diary & Letters of Josiah Gregg: Southwestern Enterprises, 1840–1847* (Norman, 1941).

trip through the buffalo range, stopping at Fort Towson or Fort Gibson on the route into the Osage country. Then Colonel Pierce M. Butler, former governor of South Carolina, organized a party to leave from a point high up on the Red River for Santa Fe, and Kendall decided to go along. But the party failed to assemble in time to be sure of plenty of grass and water on the prairies.

All during this time he was watching developments in Texas, where the Santa Fe mirage was visible to all the settlements.[6] Texas newspapers took up Lamar's project, and there was widespread discussion over estimated distances across the plains to the Rio Grande. The editor of the Austin *Sentinel* guessed that the route would cover four hundred and fifty miles through a "rich, rolling, well watered country." Fifty men, he wrote, could guard the expedition against the Comanches, and, "the Texan traders would have every advantage over those from St. Louis."[7]

Lamar discussed the matter with the Texas congress, then sent an address to the settlers of the upper Rio Grande whom he still believed to be in revolt against Mexico. After detailing the heroism of Texas in throwing off the "Thralldom of Mexican domination," he stated, "We tender you, a full participation in all our blessings." He proposed, if nothing intervened, to send one or more commissioners, "gentlemen of worth and confidence to explain more minutely the condition of our country, of the seaboard and the co-relative interests which so emphatically recommend and ought perpetually to cement the perfect union and identity of Santa Fe and Texas."[8] A military escort to keep off the hostile Indians would accompany the commissioners, he promised, and they would arrive "about the ninth of September, proxima." But before September a number of events had inter-

[6] See *Lamar Papers*, No. 1049, W. J. Jones to Lamar, February 8, 1839, in which Jones wrote that the trade would net twenty millions in gold and silver bullion and rich furs of the mountains. Also *Lamar Papers*, No. 1162, for Lamar's address to a Harrisburg regiment "which was to be placed under Colonel Kearnes in the anticipated expedition to Santa Fe."

[7] Austin *Sentinel*, April 8, 1840.

[8] *Lamar Papers*, No. 1773, Lamar to the Citizens of Santa Fe, April 14, 1840.

48

vened. The Comanches grew troublesome and before they could be chased to a safe distance the season for launching expeditions was past and winter was coming on. The people had elected a congress pledged to economy and it was preparing to meet. Lamar's venture had to wait, but the Texans did not quit talking about it.

While the Texans talked and Lamar planned, the specter of a gaunt and empty treasury stared at them. Beside it stood the sardonic figure of old Sam Houston, who had taught the Republic its first lessons of national economy, had guarded Texas resources far more jealously than his own, and had boosted Texas currency up to par and kept it there while he was president. Houston hooted at the Santa Fe bubble.[9] And when he spoke, his voice was one to be heard, for he thumped his bared breast in harangue for votes and had been elected to congress. He was now leader of the lower house.

But despite Houston's opposition and the haunted treasury, the pressure of public opinion swung congress into the Santa Fe controversy. Opponents of the westward expansion program supported the famous Franco-Texienne bill for a colony on the plains, but this eventually was defeated.[10] Lamar became ill and went to New Orleans to recuperate and when he returned in February, 1841, he found that both houses had passed separate bills favoring a Santa Fe expedition, but had adjourned without concurrent action on either bill. The senate had voted to open communications and inform the settlers east of the Rio Grande of their privileges as citizens of Texas; the house, over Houston's protests, substituted a measure authorizing the president to raise

[9] Marquis James, *The Raven* (New York, 1929), 317. "Sam Houston said that to attempt it now would be foolhardy. He whittled sticks during the speaking and crushed the orators with ridicule."

[10] The Franco-Texienne bill would have granted three million acres of land midway between Austin and Santa Fe to a French company. A. K. Christian, *Mirabeau Buonaparte Lamar* (Austin, 1922), 113, states that this bill was "ardently supported by the French minister, Count Alphonse de Saligny, and the opponents of the administration led by Sam Houston. . . . It is likely that it would have passed except for the opposition of Lamar."

49

volunteers to make an expedition to Santa Fe. Lamar followed both suggestions.

The capital took on a new hurry and bustle with Lamar's return. He started immediate plans for the expedition. Again he greeted the people of Santa Fe in a long proclamation. He urged them to accept Texas rule peacefully, and reminded them of the guarantees of privileges noted in his letter of April, 1840.[11]

He selected an expedition commander, General Hugh McLeod,[12] and opened the rolls for volunteers. Since no appropriation had been made for the expedition, Lamar on his own authority instructed the comptroller to open an account for its cost.[13] He bought lavishly in Texas and sent Major George T. Howard to New Orleans to purchase supplies.

There Howard met Kendall. He told him of the proposed expedition and invited him to go along, and thereby the expedition gained its historian and Texas gained a champion who for a quarter of a century was to be her first and most vigorous press agent.

[11] William C. Binkley, *The Expansionist Movement in Texas* (Berkeley, 1925), 44, quotes the address Lamar sent with the expedition, which stated in part, "The only change we desire to effect in your affairs, is such as we wrought in our own when we broke our fetters and established our freedom. . . ." Thomas Falconer, F. W. Hodge (ed.), *Letters and notes on the Texan–Santa Fe Expedition* (New York, 1930), 38, stated that members of the expedition had no knowledge of its political nature until August 11, after the caravan was well on its way across the plains.

[12] McLeod resigned from the United States Army June 30, 1836, to fight in the Texas struggle for independence. He was in the Texas congress in 1842–43, served through the Mexican War, and was colonel of the First Texas Regiment in the Confederate Army. He died at Dumfries, Virginia, June 2, 1862.

[13] *Lamar Papers,* Lamar to Chalmers, secretary of the treasury, March 24, 1841; Henderson Yoakum, *History of Texas* (New York, 1856), II, 323n. James, *The Raven,* 317, states: "When congress declined to sanction the expedition the President ordered half a million dollars from a New Orleans printer and proceeded on his own responsibility."

6

The trail
to San Antonio

HOUSTON RESIDENTS were astir early on the morning of May 21, 1841, when a little coastwise steamer puffed up to the landing and Kendall made his first stop on his way to Austin to join the Santa Fe Expedition.

As he trudged through the mud of the settlement's main street, frontiersmen hurried in and out of stores. Heavy transport wagons were being loaded and horsemen dashed along leading pack mules. Through the open doors he saw saddlers busily making bullet pouches, overhauling harness, and repairing saddles. Gunsmiths worked feverishly and almost everyone, it appeared, was heavily armed. Houston's company of young "Santa Fe Pioneers" was being organized under Captain Radcliff Hudson and lieutenants Lubbock and Ostrander. All was hurry, preparation and excitement.

The livery stable was the busiest place of all. A crowd gathered to watch intently as traders led out their horses, praised their fine points and haggled with bidders. Here Kendall bought a pack mule and a horse named, for no obvious reason, "Jim the Butcher." He passed over the lighter, speedier horses to select "Jim the Butcher" for his weight and endurance.

Kendall might have passed unnoticed in the crowd. He wore a brace of pistols, a bowie knife and other knives, and he carried powder and lead and a rifle that later was to prove the best gun on the expedition. It was a short-barreled, heavy piece, accurate for a great distance, throwing a ball weighing twenty-four to the pound. He had purchased it from the well-known gunsmith, Dickinson, of Louisville, and had boasted to *Picayune* readers that it had reached New Orleans in the unprecedented time of thirteen days after his order left that city.

He had questioned Major Howard closely about the purpose of the expedition and was assured that its only purpose was commercial. Traders with wagonloads of merchandise, accompanied by a military escort as protection against the Indians, would cross the plains to exchange their goods for bullion and furs. Lamar's dream was not mentioned.

Since he planned to leave the expedition before it should reach Santa Fe, Kendall had gone on May 15 to the office of the Mexican vice-consul in New Orleans and secured a passport giving him permission to enter, as an American citizen, "Any place in the so-called Republic of Mexico." His program was to include an extensive tour of Mexico, with stops at Chihuahua, Durango, Zacatecas, San Luis Potosí, and Guanajuato on the road to the capital.

As he made plans for the trip from Houston to Austin, Kendall already had begun to gather about him new friends. On the steamer over from New Orleans, the captain confided to him that "a piece of raw hide, placed in the mouth while suffering from thirst, would impart much moisture and consequent relief." At Galveston he met Frank Combs, son of General Leslie Combs of Kentucky, who remained his close companion in the months ahead.

When they reached Austin, Colonel William G. Cooke and Dr. R. F. Brenham, two of the commissioners Lamar had named to treat with the New Mexicans, informed them that the expedition would not leave for ten days. This gave Kendall an opportunity for a side trip to San Antonio, a journey eventful because it provided further schooling for the hardships of frontier life he was to endure, and because on this jaunt he made the ac-

MAP SHOWING ROUTE

OF THE

FIRST SANTA FE EXPEDITION

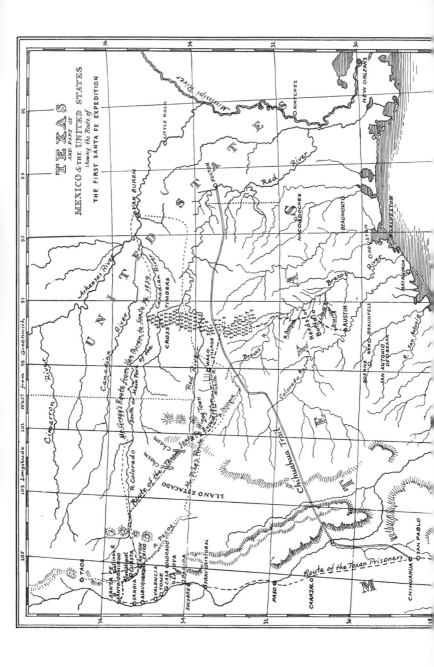

TEXAS
AND PART OF
MEXICO & THE UNITED STATES
showing the Route of
THE FIRST SANTA FE EXPEDITION

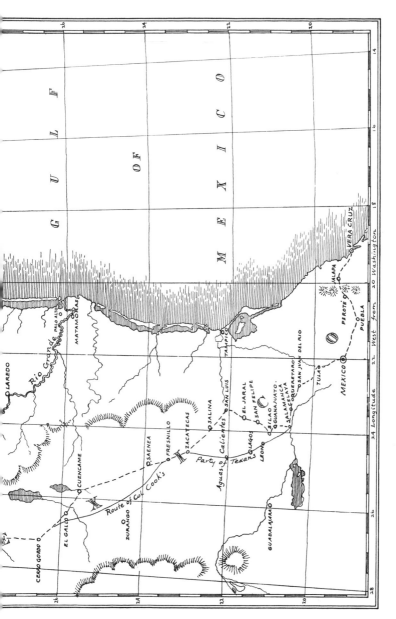

Redrawn from the map in

Kendall's Narrative of the Texan Santa Fe Expedition, 1844

quaintance of Thomas Falconer. More important, he found the land where he chose to spend his last years.

Falconer was a young Englishman who later became famous as a judge advocate of the Edinburgh bar. He already had attained a reputation as an able young barrister when he came to America late in 1840, and he was considered an important addition to the expedition. His "high literary and scientific attainments" and his remarkably amiable disposition attracted Kendall at once.

Falconer already had arranged for guides and appointed himself provisioner for the trip to San Antonio, when he invited Kendall and Combs to go along. They started in the afternoon, their departure hurried by the guide who insisted on getting under way in the face of a glowering black cloud. Scarcely had the party left the village and reached the banks of the nearby Colorado River when the deluge set in. Kendall and Falconer had difficulty swimming their mounts through the flooded stream. Late in the afternoon Kendall stalked and shot his first deer on the trip, and was repaid only by a disgusted grunt from the guide. He had lugged the whole carcass back to camp when only a small portion of it was needed for supper.

The night was dark, damp, and disagreeable, and a fog rose from the creek on whose banks they were camped. Kendall's clothes were wet, his blankets were wet, the grass was wet and mist hung in the air. Never before had he faced a night without bed and shelter. As the newest tenderfoot, he was the butt of many jokes around the campfire, and he hesitated to ask how one slept under such handicaps. But, with the others, he spread out his sodden blanket and rolled up, and was surprised to awaken refreshed next morning from sound slumber.

Kendall laughed over Falconer's mount. The Englishman, tall and ungainly, rode a crippled mule that hobbled along lazily, usually headed about a quarter south of her line of advance. Her chief virtue was endurance, but she often stumbled and sent her rider sprawling. As cook and purveyor general of the party, Falconer had left Austin well equipped. About his mule he had hung a teakettle, a half-dozen tin cups, a gourd, a pistol, a coffeepot, a ham, and "something like a bushel of fresh baked biscuit" which Mrs. Bullock, their landlady in Austin, donated for the trip. "In addition, Falconer had with him a number of books and scientific instruments, and these were arranged, here and there, among the hardware and groceries." When he mounted, with a double-barreled smooth bore upon his shoulder, the distinguished young barrister looked like a "gipsy or a travelling tinker."[1]

In the eighty miles between Austin and San Antonio there was not a single habitation. Bleaching bones of unfortunate travelers along the way served as grim reminders of recurring Indian raids, and Kendall's party was not surprised to see several large clouds of smoke ahead which the guides identified as Indian fires. A body of horsemen galloped over a roll on the prairies. "Indians," the cry went around, and Kendall and his companions dashed for cover in the nearby timber—all but Falconer. With kicks and whacks he had got his mule into some semblance of a gallop when she stumbled, "strewing the road, for some ten feet, with mule, Falconer, and sundries." The horsemen proved to be one of Lamar's scouting parties returning from a chase after Comanches. Two of their number had been ambushed the day before; one of them escaped, badly wounded.

Falconer's habit of festooning his mount with gadgets resulted in a one-horse show on the prairies weeks later, after he had abandoned his mule for a mustang. When the expedition "nooned" near a spring, Falconer took the bridle from his horse to let it graze. The pack galled the animal and he started a solo stampede. Falconer's precious quadrant was shattered by an accurate kick, and sauce-pans, books, thermometer, and finally the saddle flew off. Then the mustang quietly resumed its grazing, while the Englishman followed along, sadly collecting his battered equipment.

[1] G. W. Kendall, *Narrative of the Texan Santa Fe Expedition* (2 vols., New York, 1844), I, 42, 43.

Falconer may have appeared ludicrous in his costume "somewhat resembling a New England washing-day dinner, inasmuch as it was picked up here and there," but he came out of the expedition lean, bronzed and healthy when many had fallen by the way. He knew his limitations, and he foresaw more clearly than the rest the chance of misadventure on the journey. Before leaving he hired Tom Hancock, a picturesque leatherstocking who was best tracker and one of the most famous Indian fighters on the frontier. Tom was not a servant. He would have scorned waiting on any man. He simply was to go along on the expedition to Santa Fe, and "his obligations to Mr. F. extended this far—he was to find him if lost, and to keep him in provision should other supplies fail."[2]

Kendall was fascinated with the landscape that stretched out before him on the way to San Antonio. The "St. Marks" spring that gushed from the foot of a cliff and immediately became a deep, swift-running river, amazed him. He exclaimed over the wide valleys and the rolling hills, the drier climate that was free from "the bilious fevers and debilitating agues so prevalent upon the Colorado, the Brazos and other muddy and sluggish rivers of Eastern Texas." If settlers but "enjoy facilities for getting their produce to market, no finer or more healthy openings exist in America," Kendall confided to Falconer.

Late the next night, after two days and a half of riding, the party reached San Antonio. Passing by the all-but-deserted Alamo on the outskirts of town, Kendall noted that only two or three Mexican families still lived in the buildings surrounding the old church-fortress. Already the spot was revered by Texans, who pointed out the exact places where Bowie and Crockett fell in the massacre five years before. The most impressive greeting

[2] Kendall, *Narrative*, I, 54; also Hodge, *Falconer*, 12. Falconer and Kendall remained steadfast friends, and when Kendall was preparing the seventh edition of his two-volume work, the narrative of the expedition, Falconer provided him with notes on events during the interval when the two were separated in the latter weeks of the trip across the western prairies. These notes, which are among the Kendall papers, Kendall used as the basis of an additional chapter in his narrative. This chapter is not included in the earlier editions.

the late arrivals received was the chorus of barking dogs. The town, whose former population of twelve thousand had dwindled sharply during the years of fighting, had barking dogs to spare. Kendall watched the natives bathing in the winding, limpid San Antonio River "like so many Sandwich Islanders." But again he was impressed with the surrounding country. "The prairies in the vicinity afford the finest pastures for cattle and horses to be found in the wide world," he wrote, "and so mild is the climate that they thrive at all seasons."[3]

He chuckled in recording San Antonio's boast of its healthy climate: "If a man wants to die there he must go somewhere else," but while he laughed the spell of the land was upon him. Many times in the weeks that followed he was to remember the clear, cool streams and the fertile valleys and the breeze in the rolling hills, as he toiled across the parched western prairies. He carried the picture with him through months of privation and imprisonment when Lamar's grand gesture of political expansion turned into a tragic fiasco. He remembered the springs and the peaceful landscape through the campaigns of the Mexican War, through the years of adventure that made him famous in both America and Europe as war correspondent and author.

And when he brought his young Parisian wife and their little family to America for the first time, they paused only briefly in the comfortable surroundings of New Orleans. Then they headed west for this land of his dreams in the hills above San Antonio where he was to gain new fame as a frontier rancher, where he was to die while still fighting against the obstacles that Nature builds in the pathway of every pioneer.

[3] Kendall, *Narrative*, I, 48.

7

Bound for Santa Fe

THUNDER RUMBLED in the hills above the village of Austin, and the steamy, sticky heat promised a rain before the black night ended. Kendall had spent a busy day on his return from San Antonio, and now lounged with a group of friends in his room at Mrs. Bullock's boarding house. As a relief from the stifling early June weather he suggested a swim in the Colorado River before bedtime.

The approaching storm thickened the pitch darkness of the night. Kendall, walking ahead, missed the fork of the road that led down to the water's edge. Instead, he followed the turn that led along a high bluff overlooking the river. Before he realized his mistake he had walked off the precipice "all standing." He yelled as he hurtled through the air. He braced himself rigidly, still upright, feeling for all the world as if he had been dropped from a third- or fourth-story window to a sidewalk.

His right foot struck a boulder and sickening pain shot up his spine. He lay crumpled at the foot of the cliff while his friends fumbled for the trail down to the river.

He was unconscious when they reached him, but revived when they dashed a hatful of river water in his face. Then he started the painful trip back to Mrs. Bullock's on the shoulders of his companions. Doctor Brenham, Santa Fe commissioner and fellow-boarder, took charge of the patient. He found that Kendall's right ankle was shattered and his back was paralyzed from the fall. And the expedition to Santa Fe was to start in three days.

57

As the numbness left his spine and he was able to move his limbs, Kendall wondered about his chances for a trip out to the plains and down into Mexico that summer. Twice, earlier, expeditions he had planned to join were cancelled. Only the previous week, at San Antonio, he had been tempted to join a party of Mexican merchants who were returning below the Rio Grande.

Visitors flocked to his room. They joked with him about the accident, assured him of speedy recovery, and all talked about the expedition to Santa Fe. President Lamar came by to see him next morning. Shortly after the President left, Kendall received a letter written by the secretary of state of the Republic of Texas on Lamar's instructions, inviting him to go with the expedition as a guest. He was to eat at the commissioners' mess in the civil division, to be free of military or civil control, to stay on the excursion as long as he wished, or to leave when he saw fit.[1] More than that, the Republic of Texas placed at his disposal a "Jersey wagon," high of wheel to clear the stones and bumps, and with a top and curtains to shut out sun and rain. While still unable to walk, Kendall accepted the invitation.

June 18 found Austin hysterical with excitement. Government agents went about offering a thousand dollars in currency of the Republic for horses for last-minute replacements.[2] Teamsters yelled and swore as they hitched unruly oxen to the traders' wagons. The commissioners, the merchants and the rest of the fifty civilians tightened cinches, checked saddlebags, buckled

[1] Twenty-seventh Congress, second session, *Executive Documents,* Vol. 5, *Doc.* 266, pp. 35–36. Waddy Thompson, special envoy to Mexico, during his efforts to get Kendall released from prison, wrote to Daniel Webster, secretary of state, in a letter from Mexico City dated April 29, 1842, ". . . A most important . . . fact, in the case of Mr. Kendall had never been alluded to in the correspondence of my predecessor with the Mexican government, to wit: that when he was captured he had in his possession, and there were taken from him by the Mexican officials, letters from Texas officers inviting him to join the Santa Fe expedition, and his letters in reply, containing unqualified refusal to do so; and also, a letter after addressed to him by the acting secretary of state of Texas, inviting him to join the expedition as a guest until he had passed through the Indian country, and that on his arrival at Santa Fe he could leave the party, and a copy of his letter, assenting to the proposal."

[2] James, *The Raven,* 317.

on small arms. Down in front of Mrs. Bullock's, friends lifted Kendall into the Jersey wagon, along with Commissioner Antonio Navarro[3] who also was unable to walk. Many tried to dissuade Kendall, but he stubbornly refused to stay behind.

The caravan included sixteen ox-drawn wagons of merchandise, a wagon for the sick, and a baggage wagon for each of the military companies—twenty-four vehicles in all. President Lamar rode up and down the street. A bugle sounded. The President wheeled his horse and led the procession out of the village. The expedition of the Republic of Texas to Santa Fe was under way.

Up on Brushy Creek, twenty miles northwest of Austin, six companies of soldiers, two hundred and seventy men in all, waited for the last unit of the expedition. For a month these volunteers, many of them youths ranging in age from fifteen to nineteen years, had been drifting into Austin from all quarters. As soon as each had satisfied the government as to his arms and equipment he was sent up to the rendezvous. It was a long wait, and they ate government beef and other rations faster than the Republic could afford to supply them. Meanwhile, in the precious month that passed, water holes were drying up, and the fresh, green grass of the spring was turning brown and tough.

On the march to Brushy Creek, Kendall's little black notebook had a busy morning. Every rise in the prairie unfolded a scene of interest, every turn in the trail suggested newspaper copy. He jotted down notes of a massacre that had occurred here, of an ambush there, and the legend of a dreamer who had laid out a city of Athens on the Colorado bluffs.[4] At the noonday stop,

[3] Antonio Navarro was one of the natives of San Antonio who took an active part in the Texas revolution. Because of this he was singled out for particular punishment by Mexico after the capture of the Santa Fe Expedition, and was imprisoned until 1844. He returned to Texas in 1845 and spent his last years in San Antonio.

[4] Kendall, *Narrative*, I, 71. Captain Frederick Marryat, in his *Narrative of the Travels and Adventures of Monsieur Violet*, which was published after Kendall's sketches appeared in the *Picayune*, picked up this reference to the city of Athens. See *Violet*, Illustrated Sterling Edition (Boston, n.d.), 148. Marryat also used the incident of the stampede of Falconer's horse on the prairie, recorded in Kendall, *Narrative*, I, 99–100. See *Violet*, 151.

Lamar unsaddled and staked his horse and cooked his own meal over the campfire. Another good item for the notebook: "There was a specimen of Republican simplicity—the chief magistrate of a nation cooking his own dinner and grooming his own horse!"

After sleeping on the ground overnight, Lamar reviewed and addressed the troops next morning and rode back to Austin to wait eagerly, and then with grave concern, for news of his dream of empire. But this enthusiasm aroused by his appearance in camp held on as the men spent another two days repacking the wagons and making last minute preparations to start. Even then, the preparations they made were all too few.

Never had there been an expedition like this one. Santa Fe traders from St. Louis drove their wagons in the wake of hunters and trappers and every foot of their trails had been crossed and recrossed before them. Ahead of the Texans lay an unknown, uncharted expanse, clouded with guesswork and pipe dreams. In their enthusiasm they estimated the distance at less than half the actual mileage, and limited their supplies and equipment accordingly.

The twenty-seven-year-old commander of the expedition, General Hugh McLeod, must have thought he was in command of an army of youngsters on a holiday picnic, as the march got under way on June 21, 1841. Drivers sweated and swore and prodded, and the unruly young oxen slowed down the whole unit. By midday the first camp site was still miles ahead and the sluggish pace continued without a stop. Younger and more adventurous volunteers scampered for the San Gabriel River, when a halt was finally made, to fish and shoot alligators. But most of the men gathered around while a beef was butchered for the evening meal. Their fare was simple enough, the beef cooked on ramrods before the fire, with salt, coffee and sugar, and a small amount of rice. Afterwards troops gathered around campfires along the banks of the San Gabriel, while old-timers spun tall yarns of buffalo hunts, Indian scrapes, and narrow escapes on the prairies. Kendall listened, but not for long. He was tired from his bumpy ride, and his ankle throbbed. He rolled himself in his blanket and went to sleep early, on the ground.

Within three days the party neared the buffalo range, and at night the campfire talk was all about buffalo. Early one morning the cry, "Buffalo, Buffalo!" passed down the line. First they saw a stray cow or a tough old bull, then small droves. Soon the horizon was dotted with black objects that looked like stumps in the distance. But as the line forged steadily ahead these grew and moved and multiplied until the whole landscape was covered with huge, grazing beasts.

General McLeod gave orders that the volunteers should not break their double file ranks, but the temptation was too great. Every few minutes an excited horseman dashed from the ranks to single out a buffalo and pour shot after shot into its shaggy sides as the race continued. Momentarily the rider was engulfed in a mild stampede and then the frightened animals calmed down and started grazing. Twenty-eight were slain near Kendall's Jersey wagon, but this caused little turmoil in the vast herd. Nearby animals snorted and galloped away, the old bulls reminding Kendall of loads of hay in motion. But the plodding column left only a slight impression—like eddies in the wake of a boat on a placid lake.

Unable to mount a horse, Kendall had to content himself with watching the sport from his carryall. He laughed when a rollicking Irish soldier of fortune, Archibald Fitzgerald, spurred out to join the chase.[5] The rider lost his hat, then his blanket and his saddle bags, and abandoned them in the excitement of his first buffalo hunt. Falconer, too, took a hand, though his old double-barreled gun was loaded with bird shot. But his mount was so laden down with paraphernalia that he could only gallop along at a trot.

[5] Kendall *Narrative,* 81. See *Picayune,* June 17, 1842. From this account Marryat (*Violet,* 149) used the name "Fitzgerald," and related the incident almost in Kendall's words. Fitzgerald was a trader from San Antonio who was closely associated with Kendall from the start of the expedition until the prisoners reached Mexico City, and Kendall made numerous references to him in the *Narrative.*

In awe, Kendall wrote: "I have stood upon a high roll of the prairie, with neither tree nor bush to obstruct the vision in any direction, and seen these animals grazing upon the plain and darkening it at every point. There are perhaps larger herds of buffalo at present in northern Texas than anywhere else on the western prairies." They appeared as "numerous as the sands of the seashore."[6]

That night, upon reaching camp on Little River, the party feasted on choice buffalo meat, tongue and marrow bones, and there were excellent veal steaks from some of the butchered calves. Yet, in the face of an endless supply of game, a beef was slaughtered as usual. Some of the men complained that buffalo meat was tough and stringy, and the regular allotment of three pounds of beef was distributed to each man—to be thrown aside by scores who had eaten their fill of game.

Perhaps no other incident illustrates so clearly the haphazard and foolhardy management of the entire expedition. Buffalo swarmed over the prairies, and trout and catfish made the streams a fisherman's paradise. Herds of antelope followed in the wake of the buffalo. Wild hogs and bear roamed in the wooded valleys, and there were innumerable "sign" of deer on the hillsides. Quail and prairie chickens were thick in the open meadows along the brushy ravines, and the notes of the bugler's reveille often brought defiant calls from the gobblers keeping watch over their flocks in the roosts high over the stream banks. Yet, when the cattle were counted, it was found that in the month's delay the estimated supply for the trip had dwindled. There was not enough beef to finish feeding the expedition; so the volunteers and the civilians and the merchants and the officers—President Lamar's messengers of goodwill for the extension of his empire —sat on the banks of Little River and waited for more beef. Five days they loafed and fished and hunted and amused themselves as best they could, while a detail hurried back to Austin

[6] *Ibid.,* 78, 84. See *Picayune,* June 17, 1842. Marryat (*Violet,* 149) used Kendall's words to describe the chase of a buffalo.

for thirty more beeves. They remembered this delay when the water holes on the prairies vanished and they plodded through dry streambeds with parched and aching throats. And they cursed their prodigal waste when provisions gave out and they ate Falconer's mule and shot half-starved Indian dogs and stalked wary prairie dogs for small morsels of food.

Sundown brought a flying visit from a drove of wild mustangs. "They were first seen ascending a hill at the distance of half a mile, and as they were coming towards us were taken for Indians. When seen on a distant hill, standing with their raised heads towards a person, and forming a line as is their custom, it is almost impossible to take them for anything but mounted men. Having satisfied their curiosity, they wheeled with almost the regularity of a cavalry company and galloped off, their long thick manes waving in the air and their tails nearly sweeping the ground."[7]

That night Kendall heard for the first time the legend of the white steed of the prairies, which has been retold so often since. This fabulous animal was very large, and had speed and endurance to outrun three race horses in succession. He was never known to gallop or trot, but paced faster than any horse ever sent out after him could run. Later Kendall heard that a big white horse, resembling this legendary pacer, finally had been captured between the headwaters of the Trinity and the Brazos rivers, but died from exhaustion of the chase.

Shortly afterward, General McLeod became ill, and Major Howard took charge. But the expedition marched into further trouble and delay. Ill-advised selection of the route led the line in a general northwesterly direction from Austin, instead of directly west through the open prairies. Seeking a sure water supply, officers hoped to reach the Red River, follow its course through the present Panhandle region and then strike directly

[7] *Ibid.*, 88; *Picayune,* June 21, 1842. Used by Marryat, (*Violet,* 149). Marryat's description follows Kendall's almost word for word, except that Marryat's mustangs departed "with their tails erect" like well trained English cob horses.

west to the mountains. But the country was unknown and the party never got far enough north to find this stream.

Instead, difficulties began to multiply when the first of the troops started diagonally through the "cross timbers." This timbered strip, from thirty to fifty miles wide, extends north and south along the eastern fringe of the plains country. It appeared to Kendall as "an immense natural hedge dividing the woodlands of the settled portions of the United States from the open prairies which have ever been the home and hunting-ground of the red men." The thin soil is covered with underbrush, brambles, and stunted blackjack oaks, and its hillsides cut by innumerable ravines and streams. A march could have been made directly across the cross timbers without unusual delay, but the diagonal route kept the expedition floundering for nearly two weeks of tedious, heartbreaking toil.

Their start into the timber was ominous. They had their first dry camp. Striking a few prairie stretches, they made twenty miles, a long march for the wagons, but found no water at nightfall. The day had been hot and breathless. Canteens were emptied before noon. An early start next morning enabled them to reach a spring by late afternoon.

The party marched on stubbornly into the timber, but almost met defeat in crossing the Bosque River. The fatigue party spent a day cutting a road through the trees and brush, and digging away the high, steep banks of the stream. Troopers with ropes pulled the first wagon to the precipice, its brakes locked to slow down its plunge into the channel. After they dragged it through the water, ascent up the opposite bank started. Twenty yoke of oxen were hitched on, and fifty or sixty troopers manned the lariats. "Finally," wrote Kendall, "all the drivers would be called into requisition, and when all was ready for a start such a jumping, whipping, cracking, yelling, pulling, cursing and swearing would arise as to set all description at defiance."

This scene was repeated over and again, with variations. Hardly a day passed without an overturned wagon. The column halted for hours while the fatigue companies hacked a passage through dense underbrush, and often a strenuous march of twenty miles would bring them only a fourth of that distance from the starting point.

Occasionally, the monotony was broken. Well into the timber there appeared the first signs of Indians. General McLeod, recovered from his illness, caught up with the expedition and passed word along that a large party of Cherokee, Caddo and scattered members of other Indian tribes occupied a fertile bend of the Brazos River, ahead. The expedition camped by a mineral spring; there "the skull of a white woman, but recently killed, was found in the vicinity, and large and fresh Indian trails were discovered running in the direction of the Brazos."[8]

The march led through an Indian village apparently deserted in haste a few hours earlier. A practical joker slipped into the village ahead of the troops and hastily decorated the wigwams with sketches of men and beasts, and signed in Roman letters "the crack-jaw name of some Indian brave." The Texans were amazed until they discovered the hoax.

One of a detail assigned to gather wood for campfires foolishly tied a limb of down-timber to his horse's tail and started a stampede of horses.[9] One volunteer shot himself, and another died of eating too many unripe grapes. On July 14, after a particularly difficult passage through the quicksands of the Brazos, the party had a narrow escape from a prairie fire. The blaze, started by accident, roared through the high, tinder-dry grass, singeing the beards and eyebrows of all who tried to fight it. But when the struggle was abandoned the wind swept the blaze away to the left, and that night, from camp by a mudhole, the troops watched the

[8] Kendall, *Narrative,* I, 106. See Marryat, *Violet,* 152. Marryat had his hero camp near the mineral spring, in Kendall's own words, but changed the incident in a way which showed his animosity toward the Texans.

[9] Kendall recounted this incident in the *Picayune,* June 22, 1842, and changed the wording slightly in *Narrative,* I, 96. Marryat took it from the *Picayune* and included it in *Violet,* 150.

flames licking their way up through the river bottoms. This should have been a warning of the parched prairies ahead.

Another camp without water left the entire expedition in distress. Stock suffered and was difficult to herd at night. Without breakfast the march started again, and not until late afternoon did one of the "spies" ahead bring back news of a big spring of water. Teamsters lashed their oxen and troopers raced for the spot. They found a spring gushing from a rock, with a pool below it ten or twelve feet deep. As the thirsty groups straggled in they drank eagerly and then enjoyed a general swimming party. Kendall hobbled to the pool and got tremendous relief by holding his battered ankle in the cold spring water.

When the expedition had been on its way a month, it reached the heart of the cross timbers. It floundered on until July 23, when a three-day halt was called for a general repair and reloading. Many of the wagons, old and too heavily loaded even for the level prairie stretches, were almost worn out from being dragged over the hills and gullies. Traders dumped some of the goods destined for the Santa Fe trade. General McLeod examined the dried beef, brought from Austin as emergency rations, and found it partly spoiled. The remainder was issued and consumed immediately. In order to lighten the loads, all tents were burned. Thereafter Kendall slept with the rest, out under the stars, regardless of the weather.

Worst of all, the morale of the party began to give way. When, after buffeting about during the day, cutting away trees, crossing deep ravines and gullies, and turning and twisting some fifteen or twenty miles to gain five, they finally camped by a mudhole of miserable water, men were heard to say they had "seen the elephant." Kendall explained this expression: "When a man is disappointed in anything he undertakes, when he has seen enough, when he gets sick and tired of any job he may have set himself about, he has 'seen the elephant.' "

While the party waited by the mudhole, spies sought a way out. They returned with a report that the only possible route lay over twenty miles of thickly timbered hills and dry stream beds, without water anywhere along the way. They believed a road could be cut, and a fatigue party went ahead to hack away at the trail. The expedition moved out early, but at the first gully they crossed, not more than half a mile from the starting point, two of the wagons upset. Repairing and repacking took two hours, and by noon not a fourth of the twenty-mile drive had been covered. Navarro, in preparation for the forced march, abandoned the Jersey wagon, and Fitzgerald, who had earlier lost his hat in the excitement of his first buffalo chase, volunteered to drive the mules for Kendall, who had to remain in the wagon. Unfortunately they pulled out at the tail end of the wagon train. Every delay ahead brought them to a standstill.

They hoped for a downpour when thunder clouds piled up at nightfall, but the few drops that fell only added to their tantalizing thirst. By midnight there was a long delay, and word was passed back that an artillery carriage had stuck in a gully half a mile ahead. Most of the fatigue men had mounted their horses and started off in the darkness in search of water. There was no moving on until daylight. Fitzgerald unhitched the mules, tied them to a blackjack and crawled under the wagon to sleep, while Kendall bedded down on an inside seat.

At dawn they found that their mules had broken loose and strayed off. They were caught only after a long search, and meanwhile the wagons moved on. By noon Kendall and Fitzgerald were out of the timber, and after a short ride across the prairie they found their companions camped by a spring of fresh water.

There were many causes for the failure of the Santa Fe venture, but among them that last night in the cross timbers cannot be overlooked. The expedition was whipped when it emerged on the prairies. Kendall never forgot the experience.

8

Through hell—
to prison

ISOLATION AND THE WOODED BARRIER just behind kept the Santa Fe Expedition from breaking up on the western edge of the cross timbers. Discipline was gone, and the men broke from line repeatedly to hunt, to forage for wild plums or gallop on toward the next water hole. But ahead lay the unknown expanse of prairie and when three thin, mangy dogs came whimpering to join the marchers, scouts said there must be an Indian camp near.

Even this warning failed to keep the men in ranks after a night in camp without water. When word came that spies had discovered a small stream, those on good horses dashed ahead. The advance guard left the wagons, and soon the command was scattered for miles.

Kendall and Navarro, disabled, were jogging along with Fitzgerald in the Jersey wagon out of sight of their companions, when a buffalo cow dashed madly down the hills within a few yards of them. Close behind raced a mounted Indian, his long lance poised. Hardly had he passed when another raced by, so close that the earth thrown by his horse's hooves rattled against the curtains of the Jersey wagon.

"¡Los Indios, los Indios!" cried Navarro.

"Comanches," yelled Fitzgerald, lashing the mules into a gallop.

"The whole tribe," added Kendall, looking through the back curtains at a third mounted Indian bearing directly down upon them.

Kendall's rifle was buried beneath their luggage in the bottom of the wagon. The three could only hold onto their seats and watch the exciting chase, feeling frightened and uneasy until they caught up with the company. There they learned that the buffalo had dashed into camp and been brought down by Texas rifles. The Indians gave up their quarry and rode away.

General McLeod sent out several parties, each with a white flag, hoping to find friendly Indians and secure a guide, but found none.

Kendall grew more and more irritated at his confinement behind the slow, plodding mules. He still could not bear much weight upon his foot, or walk without great pain. But on August 3, after six weeks on the trail, his friends helped him into the saddle. Three days later he joined the spy company and thereafter ranged ahead with this picked group, searching for water holes, bringing in game and pondering over the best route to New Mexico.

Eagerly the *Picayune* staff awaited Kendall's letters. His first from Austin, dated June 1, was published June 17. Three weeks later the paper told its readers of his accident, saying "The worthy editor grumbles excessively, as well he might, over his annoyances and misfortunes." And on July 17 appeared a letter almost a month old, dated from Camp Cazneau, June 19. After that, silence. And as silence lengthened, rumor and apprehension grew.

None of the rumors was as bad as the reality.

By August the weakness of slow starvation slackened the pace of the expedition on the march. The sugar was all gone and little coffee was left. There was still an allowance of three pounds of beef a day, but the cattle had not enough water or grass, and the meat was tough and stringy. The men became inured to camping without clear water, to eating half-cooked meat without salt.

Officers and scouts sat around the fire for a long time one

night, talking over their plight and trying to determine their location. In the belief that the New Mexico settlements could not be more than seventy or eighty miles to the west, they selected Samuel Howland, Baker, and Rosenberry to push ahead. They were to get sugar, coffee and bread, and to sound out the people, particularly the officials, about the possible reception of the Texans. Howland and the others took provisions for three days. Because of hostile Indians they planned to travel at night and lie concealed by day.

Fortunately for Kendall, friends persuaded him to stay with the expedition. His pack mule and heavy baggage would have slowed down the march, and he hesitated to abandon them. He saw Howland and Baker once after that. They were led out in the plaza at San Miguel and shot, while he watched through a prison window.

Rosenberry also was killed, but the Texans were not forced to witness his death.

Before the three started their dash for the settlements, Carlos, a Mexican, was added to the spy company. He had carried mail between Austin and San Antonio and was considered trustworthy. He claimed to know the country. But when they had traveled hundreds of miles, the suspicion grew that even Carlos was lost. One morning he and a companion slipped away, and the Texans did not hear of them again until they reached the Rockies.[1]

The expedition came to a village of the Wakoe tribe, and the men were amazed at the comfort and "not a little style" of the dwellings. The inhabitants fled at the sight of the travelers. Corn and pumpkins from the Indians' fields provided a brief change in diet, then the daily beef ration continued, with an occasional deer brought in by the spies.

---

[1] Carlos reached the settlements a few hours ahead of Captain Sutton's advance party of Texans on September 13. Binkley, *op. cit.*, 87, said, "Early in September, Carlos and his companion arrived in Taos, and the information which they gave concerning the expedition was immediately conveyed to Armijo." A letter from Armijo to General García Conde, the governor of Chihuahua, stated that Carlos was in the expedition for the purpose of giving information to the Mexicans.

Kendall, with "Old Paint,"[2] an experienced hunter, left the line of march to explore a level, grassy prairie in search of deer or antelope. They frightened a drove of deer. "Old Paint" knew better than to follow after being seen, but Kendall could not resist the temptation. Soon he was thoroughly lost. The sun was high and he had no idea which way to turn.

Filled with a despair which he later described as maniacal, with "the rudder and compass of . . . collective faculties gone," he wandered for half a day. Then, soon after climbing a hill that rose sharply above the broken grasslands, he saw the advance guard of the expedition, followed at snail's pace by the white-topped wagons.

To Kendall, it was a beautiful sight, so beautiful that he spurred his horse impetuously down the steep, rocky hillside. Old "Jim the Butcher," ordinarily sure of foot, sprang suddenly aside as a rattler coiled and struck, and leaped again as his hooves churned a dozen or more of the snakes sunning among the rocks. The whole hillside seemed alive with the whirring, coiling, squirming reptiles, as horse and rider dashed madly downward through the confusion of snakes and rocks.

Safe in the valley, Kendall looked back and saw the mouth of a cave, the refuge of untold hundreds of the rattlers.

A half-dozen snakes were killed inside the camp lines before dusk, and even after he dropped off to sleep, Kendall could not escape them. First he dreamed he was ringed about by a ravenous wolf pack. Next he was racked with hunger and thirst, his powder was soaked and the clouds poured out a torrent of bitter, brackish water. Then, alone, he was chased by a gang of bloodthirsty Indians, and his horse slowed down to half speed. Fire swept the prairie on all sides, roaring toward the little knoll where he had fled in vain. Finally, the prairie was covered in every direction with rattlesnakes.

[2] This was the familiar name which members of the expedition used for Captain Matthew Caldwell, of the Fifth (Gonzales) Company of Volunteers. Caldwell was given this name because he had a piebald beard, jet black with white patches. His fourteen-year-old son, Curtis, accompanied the expedition.

Morning brought relief to his tortured nerves, but never afterwards could he see a rattlesnake without an uncontrollable fit of trembling.

Game was scarce as the expedition moved into a region dotted with mesquite trees, and the hunters redoubled their efforts. Kendall was so desperate that when he found deer, he had an attack of "buck ague," and was so nervous at the sight of game close at hand that he missed several shots. Tom Hancock, who left camp shortly after Kendall, came in with three deer. Though they had fresh venison for supper, they had no water. Through another hot morning and until midafternoon the company moved on, making fair progress through the tall, parched grass that covered a high plateau. Then without warning the advance guard came to a steep precipice overlooking a valley three hundred feet below, its floors four or five miles across, dotted with burned, dead cedars. Off to the side, the turn of a river was visible.

While Kendall and a hundred of his companions pushed into the valley to drink from the brackish stream, a fire started accidentally in the tall grass of the plateau and burned some of the wagons. The last of the coffee was burned beyond use, and Kendall's carpetbag containing his boots and rough clothing was destroyed. Fortunately, friends saved the trunk in which he had stored his money, watch and papers. Pots and kettles, knives and forks were melted down to useless scrap iron, but the company now was down to half-rations of stringy beef and this loss did not seem important.

They left the river valley, and two days later found a spring of sweet water, but their next stop was at a water hole so brackish that it acted as a powerful cathartic. Kendall and several companions rode back ten miles to their previous camp for a drink of fresh water, and scouts spent four days searching for a route the wagons could follow through the broken country.

When the scouts reported their way led through a large prairie-dog town, Kendall and two friends rode ahead to see this curious animal commonwealth and also to get food. They spent several hours watching the antics of the prairie dogs and shot nine for their evening meal.[3]

After days of hunger and thirst and marching, after nights when Indians stole horses and mules, the expedition camped by a stream which Kendall called the Quintufue,[4] and a hunting party brought the news that there were Indians nearby.

Captain Strain set out immediately with twenty men to bring in some of the Indians, and Captain Hann with ten men went to look for a route to the northeast. The others pushed slowly to the west, but found the country too rough for even a mule to cross. When Captain Strain had been out thirty-six hours, and no report had come in from Captain Hann, animals and men faced death from thirst. They decided to retrace their road to the Quintufue. Before the march got under way, a young man dashed up with news of an Indian attack upon Lieutenant Hull and four companions, out on a scout for water. Guided by the sound of gunfire, fifty men spurred their horses to the rescue. They were too late. The Texans had been overtaken, slain and scalped and their bodies mutilated. The Indians cut out the heart from one man before they retreated.

Captain Strain met the company before it reached the Quintufue. He had found neither Indian guides, water, nor a way out of the broken country. Captain Hann came in on the following day. Horsemen, he said, could skirt the ravines to the northeast, but there was no route for wagons.

A number of men failed to answer roll call; the Indians had begun systematically to pick off small parties of stragglers. Desperately it was decided that a hundred chosen men, mounted on

[3] Kendall, *Narrative*, I, 183–84; *Picayune*, July 16 and 19, 1842. Marryat related this incident in *Violet*, 156. Kendall's letter to the New York *Courier and Enquirer*, bitterly protesting this plagiarism, was reprinted in *Niles' National Register*, December 2, 1843, 214–15.

[4] Falconer also called this river the Quintufue, "a branch of the Palo Duro, a tributary of Red River." Another important contemporary account of the expedition was written by Franklin Combs, whose "Narrative" appeared in *Niles' National Register*, March 5, 1842, 2–3. He began his report with the arrival of the expedition at this camp, designating the stream as the Palo Duro.

the best horses in camp, should push on and not return until they found the settlements of New Mexico. They were to send back guides and provisions immediately.

Captain Sutton commanded the advance party of eighty-seven officers and men, and these included Captain Lewis, and lieutenants Lubbock, Munson, Brown, and Seavy. Kendall, Van Ness, Fitzgerald, Combs, Dr. Brenham, Colonel Cooke, and Major Howard, civilians with the expedition, and a few merchants increased the total to ninety-nine.[5]

The men butchered several oxen and dried the meat. Each man cleaned and adjusted his rifle and pistols. They shod horses and molded bullets. At sunset on August 31, riding in double file and close order, the picked horsemen started their dash for New Mexico. Saddlebags bulged with five days' provisions, and each man carried a canteen or a gourd filled from the Quintufue.

They found a zig-zag trail up the side of the hills, and followed it to a high plateau that was like a level prairie. They rode westward across it for three days. "We were going forward at a rapid pace," Kendall wrote, "when suddenly, and without previous sign or warning, we found ourselves upon the very brink of a vast and yawning chasm, or *cañon,* as the Mexicans would call it, some two or three hundred yards across, and probably eight hundred feet in depth!"[6]

[5] Kendall, *Narrative,* I, 212. Falconer gave the number as 95. The report of Cooke and Dr. Brenham in *Texas Diplomatic Correspondence,* II, 778, gave the total as 97. Combs's "Narrative," *Niles' National Register,* March 5, 1842, p. 2, stated that the force included "about a third of the armed force, and two of the commissioners . . ."

In any case, it was a small command to be carrying out such orders as Lamar had issued to Cooke and Brenham, who were given the authority belonging to a governor. Cooke was expected to remove all officials who were not elected but held their positions direct from the Mexican government, to supervise the courts, and put the country in a state of defense. Brenham was to remain in Santa Fe as collector of the customs, and finance the return of the expedition.

[6] Kendall, *Narrative,* I, 221, and *Picayune,* July 22, 1842. Marryat, *Violet,* 160, followed closely: ". . . we had not gone half a mile, when our progress was suddenly checked by a yawning abyss or chasm, some two hundred yards across, and probably six hundred feet in depth."

There was no place to cross. They examined their supplies and found that most of the half-dried beef was spoiled. They cooked and ate what they could, and threw the rest away. A sudden violent rainstorm during the night increased their suffering.

Kendall and Combs, who were sleeping in a sandy hollow, salvaged their belongings and moved to higher ground. They watched the lightning playing about in the chasm far below them, bringing out, in wild relief, its bold and craggy sides.

That was another night Kendall never forgot, but when morning came, the sight of his companions gave him a chuckle:

When . . . we crawled out from under our wet blankets, I doubt whether a more miserable, wo-begone set of unfortunates, in appearance, could have been seen since the passage of the Red Sea . . . I verily believe that we could have "passed muster" even in the ragged and renowned regiment promiscuously pressed into service by one Sir John Falstaff years before the Santa Fe expedition was thought of.[7]

They followed the rim of the canyon, reached a place where trails across the prairie converged in a path down the steep bank of the gorge, and made the crossing with great difficulty. A day and a half brought them to another canyon, deeper and more awe inspiring than the first, with an upward trail so steep that the men had to carry their rifles, ammunition and saddlebags.[8]

Deer and antelope dashed ahead of them on the prairies, but pursuit on jaded horses was out of the question. They killed some blackbirds, and when they camped beside a shallow prairie lake, Kendall tried to shoot some curlew. They were poor targets for a heavy rifle and he went to bed without supper.

Late the next afternoon they saw a buffalo. Tom Hancock, the veteran hunter, went ahead to stalk the animal, while Kendall and three others prepared for the chase. Each man had a pair of heavy belt pistols, and a Colt's revolving pistol with a cylinder

[7] Kendall, *Narrative*, I, 222–23.

[8] *Ibid.*, 227–38, and *Picayune*, July 24, 1842. Marryat follows Kendall's description almost word for word in *Violet*, 163–68.

75

containing five shots. Kendall also had a heavy Harper's Ferry dragoon-pistol, besides a short bell-muzzled gun loaded with two or three balls, and some twenty-five or thirty buckshot. Kendall chased and fired until the barrel dropped off his Colt's pistol and he had to dismount to hunt it.[9] Lieutenant Lubbock rode up, took Kendall's horse and remaining pistols, and chased the buffalo until he had discharged all the ammunition into its side. Then a third man mounted "Jim the Butcher," and fired broadside at the fast weakening buffalo. He returned, saying their quarry stood at bay, bleeding profusely from many wounds. They did not find the animal until morning, but his coarse flesh kept the party from starving.

"Jim the Butcher" was covered with foam and dangerously worn from the chase. Trotting ahead, Kendall led him the entire five miles back to camp and rubbed him down vigorously with coarse grass, then tied one of his own blankets over the animal to prevent its chilling.

In the dusk, as he leaned over to drive Jim's stake in the ground, he failed to see a large rattlesnake coiled in the grass. It struck him violently above the elbow but the fangs failed to penetrate his coarse, Attakapas cottonade jacket, red flannel, and linen shirt.

They traveled in the rain next day, each with a portion of buffalo meat hanging at his saddle horn, but with no way to cook it. At night they tried to make fires with damp buffalo chips, but could do little more than warm a part of the meat before they swallowed it.

By the tenth day the men were desperate. "Every tortoise and snake, every living and creeping thing was seized upon and swallowed . . . Occasionally a skunk or polecat would reward some one more fortunate than the rest; but seven out of ten of us were compelled to journey on without a morsel of anything

[9] Both Kendall and Violet dashed after the animal with equal abandon. They even cut so closely across his course that his horn grazed their boots. Finally Violet dropped his rifle on the prairie, but unwilling to give up the chase he slew the buffalo with his bow and arrow.

to appease our sufferings."[10] They shot a horse formerly belonging to Howland, and distributed the flesh.

At the edge of the plains an icy wind swept down as they climbed over the first range of foothills. Two men were lost in the descent, and the others were too spent to search for them. But there were fish in the valley stream, and they caught enough catfish for a meal.

Next day they found a wagon road, and by nightfall overtook a group of Mexican traders, who told them that San Miguel was eighty miles away. At the little village of Antón Chico, said the traders, there were large flocks of sheep. Three traders were hired to go back to the wagon train and guide it to the settlements. By a direct route, they said they could cover in four days the distance for which the Texans had required thirteen.

Four men went ahead to arrange for provisions, and sent back word that they had bought enough sheep for the command. Kendall spurred his horse with the rest. The advance scouts had made camp on the bank of the Rio Gallinas, where they dressed twenty large, fat sheep. Soon every ramrod, every stick that could be found, held sizzling portions of mutton over the campfires. Fortunately, the meat was fresh and an ample supply of salt had been purchased. Otherwise, Kendall observed, the men might have died of overeating. The Mexicans, finding the Texans excellent customers, went to their village during the night and brought back a supply of flour, and the company had mutton stew for breakfast.

American traders in Santa Fe had heard of the approach of the expedition from Austin, and word traveled slowly back over the Santa Fe Trail to the Missouri newspapers. On October 16, more than a month after the expedition reached New Mexico settlements, *Niles' National Register* quoted from the St. Louis *Bulletin* a letter dated at Independence, Missouri, September

[10] Kendall, *Narrative*, I, 253. Combs wrote ". . . the rations provided for the troops were exhausted before they accomplished a third of the road to Santa Fe . . . they were compelled to live upon snakes, horned frogs and other reptiles . . . which constituted their principal and for a time, their only food."

21, 1841, saying "A ready submission on the part of the inhabitants is to be anticipated, but the number sent from Texas, without further reinforcement is entirely too small to retain possession of the country."

The shepherds told the Texans that Howland, Baker and Rosenberry, the first to leave the expedition, had been taken prisoners. More ominous still was their report that the residents were arming under Governor Armijo to drive the invaders back.[11]

Captain W. P. Lewis and George Van Ness, secretary to the commissioners, now went ahead to confer with the Mexican authorities. Van Ness took along letters to the alcalde and copies of General Lamar's proclamations, printed in English and Spanish, to distribute to the inhabitants. Two merchants, Major Howard, and Fitzgerald decided to go along, and Kendall made a fifth member of the party.[12]

Increased hostility of the inhabitants of the country through which they passed prompted Van Ness to send back by his Mexican servants most of the letters he had brought along. As they approached Antón Chico, heavily armed men watched their passing. Villagers quit work at their community mill and scampered to their huts, and the Texans had a hard time buying fodder for their horses. When they asked for lodgings they were given a

11 Binkley, *op. cit.*, 82–86. Armijo had been preparing to receive the expedition since he learned, in May, that it was organizing. General Mariano Arista, in command of Mexican forces on the lower Rio Grande, kept agents in Texas, who reported the plans. Five thousand dollars a month was set aside for defense, and one hundred dollars was offered the first man who brought Armijo definite information of the expedition's approach.

12 Combs wrote, "From this place, Van Ness, Lewis, Howard and Fitzgerald, accompanied by Mr. Kendall, were sent on to Santa Fe, to hold an interview with the governor, explain the pacific object of the expedition, obtain stores for the troops and permits to bring the merchandise taken out by the traders within the province."

This was on September 14. But Mexico had already made provision for closing her ports to Texas goods. The consul at Matamoros announced that the Mexican government considered the ports of Yucatan, Tobasco, and Texas closed, and forbade the introduction of any articles coming directly or indirectly from these countries, which Mexico considered to be in a state of rebellion. The decree was enforced from August 25.

place to sleep on the dirt floor of a large room, along with almost thirty of the inhabitants of the dwelling, most of whom were suffering from whooping cough or influenza. In the night a Mexican came to give the expedition a warning. He told Captain Lewis that a party was gathering in the valley to capture them, and added that the Texans would be shot. He wanted a dollar for the information.

Though he discounted the warning, Kendall concealed his valuables. His gold coins, which he had worn in a linen belt, he hid under the buttons on the sides of his riding pantaloons. He put a valuable breastpin under a waistband button, and concealed his gold watch and chain, and other pieces of jewelry, under the folds of his shirt bosom. Halfway to San Miguel they were met by a hundred armed men under the command of Dimasio Salazar.[13] This officer, when they said they were on their way to see the governor, insisted that they must leave their arms in his keeping. Surrounded, they had no choice.

Kendall showed Salazar his passport, issued by the Mexican consul at New Orleans, but the officer still insisted that the mission could not proceed under arms. He took them to the nearby village of Cuesta and ordered them to stand in line and be searched. He took Kendall's letters and passport, his arms and his horse, but did not find his concealed valuables.

Salazar then turned his prisoners over to a subordinate, Don Jesús, and marched the main body of his troops toward the Texans' camp. Kendall and his friends were now afoot, unarmed, and guarded by natives armed with clubs and bows and arrows. Don Jesús, mounted on a mule, with an American rifle resting on the pommel of his saddle, waved a rusty sword to direct the column along the mountain road.

[13] This was on September 17. Three days before, Manuel Alvarez, the United States consul at Santa Fe, asked the governor to protect American citizens, in case of trouble. He was warned that neither he nor other foreigners could leave New Mexico on any pretext, and on September 16 his house was attacked by Mexicans led by Armijo's nephew. Thirteen Americans appealed to their government to interfere. After the capture of the expedition, Alvarez returned to the United States to report to the government his treatment at the hands of the Mexicans.

79

After five miles of marching, Kendall's lame ankle began to tire; after ten miles it began to swell. When they had to ford the Rio Pecos, he dared not remove his boot, knowing he could not get it on again. They traveled fifteen miles before they came in sight of the church spire at San Miguel, and Kendall was weak and ill when they were herded into a small room off the plaza and locked up for the night. His ankle throbbed, and the bread he had recently eaten gave him an acute case of colic.

The prisoners sent word to the alcalde of their plight, but he replied that he could do nothing. A woman in the crowd who peered in at them through the barred window went to her home and returned with a buffalo robe. Kendall managed to buy a blanket from a man in the crowd for an English sovereign. This was the bedding for the five of them.

9

Herded across Mexico

WHILE KENDALL and his four companions huddled behind prison walls, treachery blotted out the last hopes of the Santa Fe Expedition. The governor had not arrived in San Miguel, and Don Jesús announced that the prisoners must march toward Santa Fe, sixty miles away, for the interview. Through the good offices of some of the citizens they purchased a sheep, part of which they cooked for breakfast. The priest sent in a pitcher of coffee. As they were driven with merciless haste over the rough road to meet the governor, they felt certain that the appearance of Armijo would be the signal for their immediate execution.

Late in the afternoon a blast of trumpets announced the approach of the Governor General Armijo and his troops. Armijo rode to where they stood and addressed the prisoners politely, asking them who they were. Lewis, although he was wearing his captain's uniform, replied immediately that they were merchants from the United States, and Van Ness interrupted to say that with the exception of Kendall they were Texans. Armijo furiously grasped Lewis by the collar of his dragoon jacket and dragged him to the side of his mount, shouting that no merchant from the United States traveled in a Texas military jacket.

Howard and Van Ness explained the commercial nature of the expedition, pointing out that Kendall came with a passport from the Mexican consul, and stayed with the party for protection from Indians. Don Jesús produced the passport, Armijo examined it and said that Kendall must be held until more could be learned about him. Then he asked for an interpreter who could speak Spanish fluently, and Lewis eagerly volunteered. Armijo accepted his offer, ordered him released, and sent for a mule for him to ride.

Before riding away, Armijo ordered the other prisoners to march back to San Miguel, over nearly thirty miles of rough road, so that he might question them further the next day. If they faltered, or pretended to be sick on the road, Don Jesús was instructed to shoot them and bring in their ears.

The sun had set before the last of Armijo's troops trotted past and the exhausted Texans started back. They halted at midnight in a rainstorm, resumed their march at dawn, and were taken before Armijo for a brief interview. Then from their cells overlooking the plaza of San Miguel they watched while Baker and Howland, emissaries whom General McLeod had sent on ahead of Kendall's party, were led out and shot. They had been captured upon their arrival, escaped, and almost reached Colonel Cooke's party before they were retaken. Rosenberry was killed in the encounter.

At sundown a soldier rode up with the news that the other Texans had surrendered, and the villagers plunged into a night-long orgy of celebration.

Three days later, when Kendall saw Colonel Cooke's troops march through the village on their way to Mexico City, he suspected that treachery had contributed to their capture. Lieutenant Lubbock afterward told Kendall of their surrender. While Cooke was camped across from Antón Chico, Armijo came up with three hundred and fifty men and camped nearby with apparent friendly intent. When the alert Texans prepared for possible attack, Captain Lewis rode up and urged that they lay down their arms. They would be permitted to come in as traders, and their arms would be returned at the end of eight days, under the custom of the country, he told them, but if they resisted they faced annihilation by an army of "four thousand of the best equipped men he had ever met."[1]

After they had submitted and realized that Armijo had only a poorly equipped rabble, the Texans were furious.[2]

Months later, from Falconer and others, Kendall learned the fate of the main body of Texans who had remained on the plains. They had suffered repeated sniping attacks from the Cayugas (Kiowas) and were on the verge of burning their wagons and returning home, when guides came in from Colonel Cooke's party. They were led by a route around the deep canyons, but their sufferings were so great on the last days of the march that many of the men threw away their rifles. Only ninety could be mustered to resist Armijo's troops. Promised food and protection, they surrendered.

When their wagons and stores were brought into San Miguel for distribution, Kendall watched Lewis receive a share.

General Lamar's expedition to capture the rich Santa Fe trade for Texas had failed, and he was to receive bitter criticism from men who had been enthusiastic over the venture. But news was slow to reach the States.

The *Picayune* of August 29 quoted the Louisville *Gazette,* which expressed fear for Kendall. The *Picayune* explained, "we do not expect to hear from him again until his return from Santa Fe." The issue of September 11 quoted the New York *Tribune's* opinion that "not one man in ten will ever return alive. . . .

[1] Kendall, *Narrative,* I, 324–25. Much has been written about the treachery of Lewis, which Kendall described as the "blackest piece of treachery on record." See Hodge (ed.), *Falconer,* 53, 54, 86, 87; also Combs, "Narrative," *Niles' National Register,* March 5, 1842, p. 2, and Binkley, *The Expansionist Movement in Texas,* 88.

[2] *Short Ravelings from a Long Yarn, or Camp and March Sketches of the Santa Fe Trail,* from the Notes of Richard L. Wilson, by Benjamin F. Taylor (Chicago, 1847, reprint Santa Ana, California, 1936), 151. This contemporary account of Armijo's soldiers says they "were uniformed in cloth round-abouts and miserable little carbines, the most ferocious thing about them being their mustaches. It is certainly a wonder that the flower of Texan chivalry should have surrendered to a troop that Falstaff would have been ashamed of, and Don Quixote would have looked upon with contempt." The writer, who went with a trading expedition from Independence, could have had no idea of the sufferings the Texans experienced before meeting Armijo's soldiers.

Heaven guard our friend Kendall of the *Picayune* who accompanies this expedition with a crushed ancle [*sic*] on a litter! A Comanche onslaught at midnight, would leave a poor chance for him." On November 7 the *Picayune* quoted the *Galvestonian* of October 26, quoting the Austin *Gazette* which stated that "Monteray [*sic*] papers reported the safe arrival of the expedition."

Lumsden wrote to the *Picayune* on November 10 from St. Louis, where he had been selling subscriptions to the paper: "I shall not be at all surprised if Kendall would reach here by the great prairie route from Santa Fe before I leave, and come down along with me." On the next day the *Picayune* again quoted Galveston papers of November 1, telling of the safe arrival of the expedition.

Although Kendall had been captured September 16, first vague rumors of disaster were mentioned in the *Picayune* of November 30. Issues of the paper for December 5 and December 11 quoted Texas papers as disbelieving the reported capture of the Texans, but on December 21 the news was confirmed by a letter which Colonel Cooke and Dr. Brenham sent, through a friend in Chihuahua, to Dr. John G. Chambers, Texas secretary of war.

News of the disaster soon came by a more direct route, over the Santa Fe Trail to St. Louis. The *Picayune* called attention to its front page story on January 4, with "a letter copied from the St. Louis *New Era,* giving a melancholy picture of the sufferings of those belonging to the late expedition from Texas to Santa Fe. Our heart sickens at the bare contemplation of their miseries. . . . G. W. Kendall, we feel assured, was among those whose capacities of endurance enabled them to pursue their perilous journey to the end. If spirit and determination would carry him through, he is safe. God grant it!"

Many gave Kendall up as lost, but the *Picayune* stoutly kept insisting that he must come through unharmed.

Meanwhile, Kendall was on his way to Mexico City with the other prisoners. On October 17, when he was confidently expecting release, he was ordered to join the march. The early New Mexico winter was setting in. Two thousand miles to the south, across barren stretches and beyond formidable mountain ranges, lay Mexico City. There Santa Anna, the military despot, was riding high on the wave of popularity that periodically swept him into the presidency. It was to him the unfortunate Texans were being sent, on foot, so that he might see and know of the valor of his governor, Manuel Armijo. It was for this reason only that the Texans were not executed when they were taken.

Except for worry over the fate of the last party of the expedition, Kendall and his companions had not fared badly during their imprisonment. They were far better prepared to start than those recently captured. Kendall's ankle again was mending, and Major Howard was able to travel, while many of McLeod's men were ill and spent even at the start of the long march.

After the one hundred and eighty prisoners were paraded in the plaza of San Miguel, and the ceremony of counting them off was completed, they learned to their dismay that the notorious Salazar—"the greatest brute among Armijo's officers"—would have charge of them.[3] They were guarded by two hundred soldiers, some armed with muskets, others with bows and arrows or clubs. From the start it became evident that Salazar's plan was to drive the prisoners so hard that they would not have the strength to resist. In their first march they plodded over thirty miles of the rough trails that Kendall had crossed and recrossed on the way to meet Armijo in those first days of captivity.

[3] Kendall wrote in his "History of the Mexican War" (unpublished manuscript), 269, that Salazar "has not hesitated to add wanton murder to his other heinous crimes. Salazar had charge of the Texan prisoners on the march from San Miguel to El Paso del Norte . . . and neglected no opportunity to display his heartlessness and brutality." During this trip Salazar rode Kendall's pack mule, which had been confiscated upon his arrest. "She was a strong, powerful animal, but an extremely hard one to ride, having, in addition to a trick of throwing people over her head, a jolting and most uneasy and unsteady trot . . . he complained, on several occasions, of the gait of the animal, and said that he was disappointed in her."

This manuscript is in the possession of the University of Texas, and a copy is in the Kendall papers.

85

By nightfall they reached the former settlement of Pecos, crumbling in decay.[4] Salazar herded them into an enclosure amid the ruins. They had no food or water. Each rolled up in his thin blanket on the damp ground and tried to sleep.

The days and nights stretched into a nightmare which Kendall was never able to erase from his mind. From dawn until dusk the Texans were driven until they scarcely had energy enough to eat their scanty rations, while the frost or the snow that swept down from the mountains on a biting wind made the nights a torture.

One night, as dusk was settling and the men already were numb with cold, they trudged into the little settlement of Algodones. They begged for shelter, and the whole party was herded into two small rooms, hardly large enough for twenty men. The front room had one window about two feet by eighteen inches; the rear had none. There was not space in which to lie down, or even sit down. Soon after the heavy door was barred, the single window was blocked by the mass of men crowding around it, and the Texans faced suffocation.

Half-stifled cries came from the rear, begging that the door be broken down. A human wedge crashed against it, but it held. Guards, hearing the commotion, called Salazar, and he granted permission that fifty sleep outside in a barnyard for the remainder of the night.

Reeking with perspiration, Kendall crawled under the lee of a low mud wall. The cold wind penetrated his blankets and chilled him through, yet he was thankful to have escaped suffocation.

Occasionally the villagers gave melons, cakes or corn to the pitiful caravan. Even as he hobbled along on blistered feet, Ken-

[4] Pecos, about thirty miles southeast of Santa Fe, was once a fortified town, with about 2,500 inhabitants when Coronado visited it. Its two pueblos, each four stories high, contained over eleven hundred rooms. Not far away were the remains of a Catholic church, and of an Aztec temple where the sacred fire was kept in underground vaults. This fire was believed to have been kindled by Montezuma himself, and when it was accidentally extinguished in 1838, the seventeen remaining inhabitants abandoned the village, believing that fate had turned against them.

dall could not help admiring the beauty of the native women who came to offer food to the Texans.

"It was at Albuquerque that I saw a perfect specimen of female loveliness," he wrote. "The girl was poor, being dressed only in a chemise and coarse woolen petticoat; yet there was an air of grace, a charm about her, that neither birth nor fortune can bestow."[5]

Hunger and the rigors of the trip took the first toll that night. One of the prisoners, named Ernest, sank down with the others to sleep at the end of a particularly long march; when his companions tried to awaken him in the morning he was still and cold. Salazar ordered his ears cut off, as evidence that he had not escaped, and his body was thrown into a nearby ditch. Later in the day John McAlester, a volunteer from Tennessee, sank down in exhaustion. He was shot, and the party marched on.

Through Casa Colorado, Parrida, and Joya the prisoners were driven southward; then across the Rio Grande into Socorro. After a day and a half spent in levying food for the long, uninhabited stretch that lay ahead, Salazar started them off again. At Parrida, Kendall managed to buy a pair of heavy shoes to replace the soleless moccasins he had been wearing.

They pushed on forty miles the next day, recrossed the Rio Grande, and after another long march reached Fray Cristobal. This was the last camp before they entered the barren stretch across the bend of the river, known as La Jornada del Muerto, "the journey of death."

[5] Kendall, *Narrative,* I, 383–85. Susan Shelby Magoffin, who traveled in New Mexico with her husband in 1846, was not so impressed by the beauty of the Mexican women. She wrote, "We have passed through some two or three little settlements today. . . . It is truly shocking to my modesty to pass such places with gentlemen. The women slap about with their arms and necks bare, perhaps their bosoms exposed (and they are none of the prettiest or whitest) if they are about to cross the little creek that is near all the villages, regardless of those about them, they pull up their dresses, which in the first place but little more than cover their calves—up above their knees and paddle through the water like ducks. . . . Some of them wear leather shoes, from the States, but most have buckskin mockersins, Indian style." *Down the Santa Fe Trail and Into Mexico,* the Diary of Susan Shelby Magoffin, 1846–1847 (New Haven, 1926), 95.

From Fray Cristobal the Rio Grande loops to the west in a winding crescent, a distance of one hundred and sixty-five miles. Across this bend, through a dreary waste dotted with coarse tufts of vegetation which the Texans called "bear grass," lay ninety miles of the most difficult trail the prisoners had yet faced. There was no water, and no shelter from the wind that continuously swept down from the mountains.

Salazar let them rest overnight and most of the next day before they marched on, in a snowstorm. Kendall started out with a two-quart gourd filled with water, but it slipped from his numbed fingers and spilled on the frozen ground.

Through the night they trudged on, and were marching again at dawn, after a short rest. The twenty-four hour march so exhausted the horses, pack mules and guards that Salazar called a halt of four hours at nightfall. Two exhausted Texans, Golpin and Griffith, met death at the hands of the guards, and their ears were added to the buckskin thong.[6] By eight o'clock on the second morning they sighted the Rio Grande, and the tired prisoners ran to the stream. For forty hours they had marched without food or water. It was a nightmare they never forgot.

Fearing another search before they reached El Paso, which might reveal money and valuables Kendall had sewed beneath the ornamental buttons on his pantaloons, he and Falconer and Van Ness hastily made their ration of meal into small cakes, concealing coins and jewelry. Van Ness wrapped Kendall's expensive watch and chain in the scarf around his neck.[7]

[6] Marryat's treatment of the Golpin incident in *Violet*, 196–97, made Kendall more furious than all of the plagiarism of material from his articles in the *Picayune*. Marryat pictured Golpin as a murderer who had escaped from Louisiana, and cited an alleged article in the New Orleans *Bee* of "January, 1840" as his authority. (Neither the French nor the English side of the *Bee* during January, 1840, mentioned Golpin). He charged that Golpin's execution followed his murder of a Mexican woman who had given some of the Texans shelter in her home on the previous night.

[7] At the time of Kendall's death, a contemporary wrote in the Farmersville (Louisiana) *Record*, November 2, 1867, of an incident Kendall did not mention in his *Narrative*: "We became acquainted with Mr. Kendall on the Santa Fe expedition, in 1841. . . . We had a companion, a Mr. Morris, a brother typo, who was

When they reached El Paso, Kendall was surprised to see Dr. Whittaker and several Texans who had marched among the captives of Colonel Cooke's command. They were standing on the street, apparently at liberty. He was further surprised, when Salazar turned over the prisoners to the command of the new district, to find that they were divided into small squads and billeted in the homes of residents, where they were treated with kindness and respect.

One of Kendall's particular benefactors was Ramón Ortiz, the young curate of El Paso. When the Texans marched on again, Ortiz loaned him a saddle horse for the three-hundred-mile march to Chihuahua.[8]

Their marches now became noticeably shorter and food was plentiful. The men began to lose the pallor stamped on their faces in the nighmare drive from San Miguel under Salazar. Their

---

afflicted with the rheumatism, and during that two nights and one day's weary march seemed to be doomed to the Mexican's cowardly shot in the back, as it was in this manner they dispatched most of the broken down during our march from Santa Fe to El Paso. We had selected one of the kindest looking mexican's [sic] who was well mounted, in order to solicit a ride for our dying friend, but our appeal was about to prove unavailing, when Mr. Kendall chanced along weary and sorefooted himself. Mr. Morris' situation was explained, and the Mexican yielded to some small change though he turned a deaf ear to the calls of humanity. How Mr. K. had managed to retain any money was a mystery, as every one had been thoroughly searched and robbed of every cent. We mention this little circumstance to show the kindness of his heart, and this act showed forth in that selfish crowd as refreshing as an aosis [sic] in the desert to the famished traveler. Mr. Morris before reaching Puebla became a sound and healthy man, and we have often heard him recount how 25 or 30 cents in small change saved his life." A notation on the clipping which is included in the Kendall papers, reads, "Mr. Mims of this paper says:"

Morris later visited Kendall at his ranch in New Braunfels, and again received help "along his way."

[8] A portion of Hervey Allen's *Anthony Adverse* (New York, 1936), 1175–1208, includes incidents related in Kendall's *Narrative,* although Allen did not use Kendall's words. Anthony was captured by the New Mexicans, and with a party of Indians and Texans, including "Van Ness." "Griffith" and "Falconer," was marched cruelly over the route to El Paso by "a rascal by the name of José Salezar." "A young priest," Ramón Ortiz, also was revealed as the benefactor of Anthony, although Allen's tale was laid in 1816 and Kendall's experiences took place in 1841, when Ortiz was little more than twenty years of age.

cheeks filled out and developed a healthy tan. After this considerate treatment by their guards at El Paso, they were surprised when they were confined closely in the Jesuit hospital at Chihuahua.

A young merchant from Massachusetts offered his services to Kendall, who had him buy chocolate, sugar, and clothing for the next part of the trip to Cerro Gordo. Here, too, Kendall sent the first letter he had been able to write his friends in New Orleans since the expeditioners marched from the camp above Austin the previous June. The letter, dated November 27, was published on February 2.

Though he stoutly asserted his innocence, a letter dispatched from Chihuahua for other members of the party mistakenly referred to Kendall as one of the commissioners of the expedition. This letter, to his sorrow, reached New Orleans six weeks in advance of his own, and was promptly printed.[9] Later the Mexican government was to pick out a sentence from this letter and use it as an excuse for his imprisonment. The damaging statement read: "A Captain Lewis was one of the commissioners, and the other was Mr. Kendall, editor of the New Orleans *Picayune*."

When Kendall read the letter in his paper after he reached Mexico City, he was furious. That it was to cost him months of imprisonment shows that he had good reason to be angry.

When the march from Chihuahua was resumed, Kendall started out on foot, but after a day's journey he sent word to his Yankee friend from Massachusetts to purchase a horse and saddle for him. For his purchases he gave drafts payable at New Orleans.

The prisoners pushed on steadily, through El Ojito, San Pueblo, Saucillo, La Cruz, Santa Rosilia, Guajuaquilla. Larrabee, one of the volunteers, died of illness in a cart at Saucillo after

[9] This letter, unsigned, was sent to the Texas secretary of war, apparently at the request of Colonel Cooke and Dr. Brenham, and was printed in the *Picayune,* December 21, 1842. It was referred to in Webster's letter to Thompson, April 5, 1842, in Twenty-seventh Congress, second session, *Executive Documents,* Vol. 5, *Doc.* 266, pp. 25, 26.

he had ridden many miles. The guard courteously asked Dr. Whittaker to examine the body to see "if he was dead enough to bury."

"It was Christmas day that we reached San Sebastian," Kendall wrote, "and anything but a 'Merry Christmas' did we spend in the wretched hole. Many of us had intended to 'keep' the day and night somewhat after the manner of our country, but we could not procure eggs and milk enough in the town to manufacture even a tumbler of egg-nog."[10]

Smallpox of the most virulent type appeared among the prisoners at Zacatecas, and seven were left in hospitals as they moved on out of San Luis Potosí. As they marched on through El Jarel, San Juan de los Llanos, and Silao, more men became sick. Then at Guanajuato, Fitzgerald, Captain Caldwell and sixteen of the volunteers were sent to hospitals. Curtis Caldwell, the captain's son, was left ill at Celaya.

When they reached the old palace of San Cristobal, fourteen miles from Mexico City, they were marched inside the crumbling ruins and locked up. Hardly had the key turned when Lumsden and three American friends rode up and were admitted by the guard. Kendall was overjoyed at meeting his associate, and cheered by his friends' assurance that he would be liberated shortly. Lumsden had made a plea to the Mexican government for Kendall's release, and had presented affidavits of his citizenship. Brantz Mayer, secretary of the United States legation, and John Black, American consul at Mexico City, called and asked for details of Kendall's passport and his connection with the expedition. Lumsden and his companions left with assurances that Powhatan Ellis, American minister to Mexico, would do everything he could to secure Kendall's release.

When physicians called to examine the prisoners, Kendall was suffering from cold and fever. Along with seventeen others he was ordered to the city for hospitalization, while the able-bodied men were marched off to the castle of Perote at Puebla,

10 Kendall, *Narrative*, II, 122.

in the direction of Vera Cruz. Just inside the city Kendall and his companions were halted in front of a large building adjoining the church of San Lázaro. Hideous faces peered out at them from grated windows. After a consultation, the door was unlocked and they were marched into a sort of anteroom that was to be their quarters. Through an arched doorway they looked into a long hall, filled with cots, where wretched creatures were hobbling about. It was not until then that they realized they were confined in a leper hospital.

Despite his disgust and loathing at such a place, Kendall felt better after a night on the floor. Mayer and a number of Americans called during the day, but the hours dragged. The prisoners were free to wander about the hospital, but the sight of the hideous, wasted faces kept the Americans close to their little room.

Four days later, Kendall and ten of his companions were marched to another prison, a room in a mud building. Its appearance was cheering. Clean mattresses were spread on the floor for them, and each man was given two blankets. This was a great improvement—until nightfall. Then, scarcely had they stretched out on their mattresses than the place became alive with chinches.

They begged to be taken back to San Lázaro, but their request went unheeded. After that they slept by day and stayed up at night, talking, and reading by candlelight.

On February 18 Lumsden left by stage for Vera Cruz. He urged Kendall to escape by bribing the guard, and this might easily have been accomplished. But Kendall decided to wait until his partner was safely out of the country, since Lumsden's movements were closely watched and he would have been implicated in the prison break. Then, on the day after Lumsden's departure, Kendall became ill with smallpox. He suffered for four days and had started to recover when the guard took the men back to San Lázaro. Five of his companions were marched off to join Colonel Cooke's party, but Kendall was given a cot in the big hall with the lepers. He remained there two months.

10

Locked up with lepers

KENDALL laid aside his book and watched the procession file from the hall, while the interminable chant rose from kneeling groups of San Lázaro inmates.

Since nightfall the ceremony had been in progress. It was March 18, 1842, just a week before Good Friday, and to Kendall, unschooled in the religious practices of the prison, the performance seemed to consist of a prolonged chorus.

At dusk the women inmates, dressed in all their finery, began to assemble in the huge room where the men were quartered. Then came the hospital attendants and their families, the priests attached to San Lázaro, and a few visitors.

All the lepers joined in the chorus, their harsh, croaking and discordant voices creating an effect horribly grating to Kendall's ears. They did not sing through their noses, for many of them had none to sing through; but they gave utterance to screams and screeches which seemed unearthly. Their appearance, too, kneeling about in groups with their disfigured and hideous faces lit up by the glare of numerous candles, combined with the strange and most unnatural chorus to give Kendall the impression that he was part of a monstrous dream.

As the last of the procession passed from the hall, the note of a harp rang out sharply. The kneeling prisoners hobbled to their feet and gathered around the musician, who sat near Kendall's cot, and then a wild, strange dance started. Alternately singing and dancing, the couples whirled round and round. Some of them were on crutches, and all of them were lame and disabled in some way. The singing was even more harsh and discordant than the chant had been.

"The weird sisters around the magic cauldron never made a more grotesque or frightful appearance than did these lepers," Kendall wrote, "and had Macbeth encountered the latter on the heath he would have run outright, without even exchanging a word of parley. No midnight revel of witches or hobgoblins, or of the misshapen dwarfs could compare with the horrible manifestations of mirth that fell upon our ears."[1]

They were well supplied with liquor, and the wild revel grew louder and more boisterous until, one by one, the exhausted dancers dropped aside. Finally all was quiet, save for the groans of the suffering lepers who were on the threshold of death.

Kendall had been locked in San Lázaro nearly a month. With six of the Texans he spent the gloomy hours reading, writing letters, or playing euchre. When time hung too heavily on their hands, one of them would deal cards and open a monte bank, a game which they had learned from the inmates, who were inveterate gamblers.

In time he became accustomed to the hospital routine. But he never forgot the hideous sight of the faces that leered at him from nearby cots, the croaking whispers and the screeching laughter, the groans of the doomed or dying patients.

The hospital fare was wretched. Patients were served in tin cups, each marked with the number corresponding to the one on his cot. Kendall raised an uproar when cups with other numbers were brought, and thereafter subsisted as nearly as he could on fruits which women peddlers sold at the door.

The day after he had been returned to San Lázaro, a little girl came to the window and slipped Kendall a note from his companions who had shared his chinch-ridden prison. They were now

[1] Kendall, *Narrative,* II, 224.

with Colonel Cooke's party at Santiago, and in chains. They hinted that Kendall would not mind chains when he got used to them. Later he was to wear them, and joke about it, but now the idea was revolting. All the disappointment and suffering he had endured, all the distressing memories of his butchered companions, combined with this final humiliating prospect and blazed into a burning hatred of Mexico and all things Mexican.

A priest came to administer last rites to a dying man. Kendall and his companions stopped their card game, but others paid little attention. A group joked and laughed as they warmed their tortillas over a little charcoal furnace. One leper strummed his guitar with withered fingers, and another struck light repeatedly to his small black *cigarritos*.

Disgusted as he was with his surroundings, Kendall determined not to join the chain gang that was marched out daily to work the streets. He "got up" symptoms of chronic rheumatism and complained each morning of his illness when the prison physician made his rounds.

Henry E. Lewis of New Orleans, who arrived as bearer of dispatches to Judge Powhatan Ellis, the United States minister, came to visit the prisoners, assuring Kendall of his early release. But Kendall by now was convinced that his freedom must come through his own efforts.

On St. Lazarus' Day the prison was opened to visitors, and from morning until night the place was thronged. Some came to visit relatives who were confined there, others to dispense charity, the remainder were drawn by curiosity. Almost all brought gifts. Frequently during the day Kendall left his bunk to accompany the crowds through the building, hoping to walk out unobserved. Each time an alert guard turned him back at the door.

These sympathetic visitors stopped to see the Santa Fe prisoners. By nightfall Kendall's cot was piled high with "several bushels" of cakes, fruit, sweets, cigars, cigarettes, and flowers.[2]

[2] Mexican indignation at the treatment of the Santa Fe prisoners found expression in the newspaper *El Siglo XIX*, December 14; "We have the pain to an-

Later he distributed the gifts to less fortunate inmates. But out of this day there came one gift he enjoyed thoroughly. Among the visitors was a Mexican *señora*, the wife of an American resident who had come from Kendall's own boyhood Yankee country. She asked what he would like most of all.

"New England boiled codfish and potatoes," he replied, laughing.

Little did he hope that his remark would bring a response, but next morning a big bowl of boiled codfish and potatoes was delivered to him.

"Nothing the fair señora could have sent me would have been more acceptable," he recalled. "I warmed and rewarmed the savory compound, morning, noon and night, day after day, for it lasted more than a week."[3]

Mayer called from the legation bringing books and a bundle of American newspapers. He returned later with a box of cigars and several bottles of wine, a gift of Judge Ellis. Falconer also brought an armload of books. The prison was barred to visitors, but Kendall's friends found it easy to bribe their way in.

Meanwhile Kendall was busily writing letters, explaining his plight to Judge Ellis. He pointed out the circumstances under which he had joined the Santa Fe Expedition, and told in detail how his regular passport into Mexico had been taken from him.

Judge Ellis started negotiations for the release of the Ameri-

nounce to the public an act of barbarism, committed by Captain D. Damaso Salazar, who escorted the Texian prisoners to Chihuahua. Captain Salazar had the iniquity to kill three of these prisoners in cold blood, because they had become wearied. It was reserved for Salazar to eclipse the triumphs of Señor Armijo by this cruel and brutal action. Every one is indignant at such an atrocious act, peculiar only to a cannibal. Don Jose Maria Elias, colonel of the army, and commandant of Paso del Norte, is preferring charges against this barbarous captain, and Señor Conde, Governor of the Department, is very much mortified by such an event, which does so little honor to Mexicans, whose humanity is their principal device."

This newspaper comment, which Ellis enclosed in his letter to Webster on December 16, was republished widely in the press of the United States.

3 Kendall, *Narrative,* II, 246.

cans in the party before the Santa Fe prisoners arrived.[4] Sir Richard Pakenham, the British minister, had secured the immediate release of Falconer, but Judge Ellis met only delays and evasions. With the first news of the surrender of the expedition, the New Orleans *Bee* explained to its readers the status of Kendall and Combs, and called for the intervention of the United States.

Kendall's indignation at the prolonged delay in his release was echoed vigorously by his newspaper friends throughout the country, and this storm of protest found quick reaction in Congress. The *Picayune* reported on January 19, "Mr. D. K. McRae, bearer of despatches from President Tyler to Judge Ellis, the American Minister to Mexico, arrived in this city yesterday from Washington. We are much gratified to learn that the instructions to Mr. Ellis are to demand preemptorily [*sic*] the immediate release of Mr. Kendall and Young Combs, and a young man named Howard, belonging to the District of Columbia, and likewise of such others as have proof of American citizenship."

Kendall's friends in New Orleans came to the *Picayune* seeking information and offering assistance, so that the paper expressed "sincere satisfaction" in the generous warmth of their interest, and its own belief that he would be home "in a fortnight at the farthest. . . ." Citizens met at Banks' Arcade to consider means of liberating the prisoners "and to assist such of the citizens of Texas, who have been taken prisoners through duplicity and official treachery, and treated with a rigor and cruelty without parallel in the annals of civilized nations."[5] At this meeting

[4] Ellis wrote to Webster on December 16, "I beg you will be pleased to inform me how far I can proceed, in my representative character, to serve the Texian prisoners." Webster replied on January 3, "You will press this case with the utmost earnestness on the Mexican Government . . . Any reasonable expenses which may be necessary to defray the charge of a special messenger from the Mexican capital to the place of captivity of young Combs and his American associates, or for any other proper purposes necessary for their safety and liberation, will be borne by this Government. . . ." Twenty-seventh Congress, second session, *Executive Documents*, Vol. 2, *Doc.* 49.

[5] *Picayune*, February 3, 1842.

resolutions drawn up by A. C. Bullitt were carried by acclamation, and several eloquent addresses were made.

Another storm of protest followed Falconer's return to New Orleans a month later. His letter, published in the New Orleans *Bee* of March 11, gave details of the imprisonment of the Americans and the Texans. He included a statement from Dr. Brenham and Colonel Cooke asserting that Kendall had his passport at the time of his capture. The *Bee* commented: "If the country requires any exhortation . . . to rise as one man and demand exemplary and swift redress, it will prove that the spirit of the Revolution has evaporated in Fourth of July declamation."

By the time Lumsden returned from his unsuccessful trip to Mexico City, New Orleans was seething. The *Picayune* issued an extra edition giving Lumsden's version of the capture and imprisonment of Kendall and his friends, and his own failure to effect their release.

"Our opinion is," the New Orleans *Bulletin* commented, "that nothing but force, or their death, will release those men from their state of abject servitude."[6]

On March 11 the *Picayune* stated:

. . . Our minister in Mexico had made a preemptory [*sic*] demand for the release of Mr. Kendall, in reply to which shuffling and evasive answers had been received. . . . Mr. Falconer, an Englishman, was liberated at the polite *request* of the British minister, before he reached the Mexican capital. . . .

But the demand of the accredited agent of the United States Government, for a citizen who never forfeited any of his rights, and who produces the most triumphant evidence of that fact, is treated with scorn!

Has the United States become so utterly contemptible as to permit itself to be trodden under foot by Mexican officials?

News that Mexico was preparing to recapture Texas was considered important enough for an extra, which sold so readily

6 New Orleans *Bulletin,* March 11, 1842.

that the paper was unable to print enough copies to meet the demand.[7]

Citizens of New Orleans held a second mass meeting at Banks' Arcade to draft resolutions and to raise funds to aid Texas. Alexander Bullitt again was a member of the committee, which resolved that the detention of the Americans was an act insulting to the honor and dignity of the nation.

On every hand agitation over the detention of Kendall and his companions was linked with support of the Texas cause. Embers of indignation, which were to flame up into the war with Mexico four years later, were now glowing to white heat. A mass meeting was held at Mobile, Alabama, and a committee of twenty-one appointed to take subscriptions for the Texans.

An appeal was sent to President Tyler to strengthen the Army and Navy. He replied that the requisitions from those departments could not be met, for want of delayed appropriations.

However, United States cruisers in the Gulf of Mexico steamed for Vera Cruz and stood menacingly offshore. Santa Anna found in this another excuse to hold the Americans.

The "committee of five," which the New Orleans citizens appointed at their mass meeting of March 19, announced that residents would be called on personally to contribute powder and lead to send on the steamer *Neptune,* which was being loaded for a Texas port.

Two days later the *Bulletin* reported that the *Neptune* sailed "last evening for Galveston, with 2 or 300 passengers, mostly emigrants. In her assorted cargo were several heavy articles of

[7] There was a sudden increase in the amount of news published in the *Picayune* and other papers regarding Texas and Mexico. Its issue of April 10, 1842, quoted the New York *Tatler,* which had expressed surprise that Santa Anna's letters were written in such good English. The *Picayune* stated: "Our contemporary has been betrayed into a bit of blunder . . . there is no proof that 'Santa Anna is an accomplished English scholar.' Certainly the proof is not found in the letters to Mr. Bee and Gen. Hamilton. Those letters were 'written in choice' Spanish, and published in Mexico, in the Spanish language alone. They were translated expressly for this paper, where they were originally published in this country. Half the journals in the United States have copied them from us without credit. . . ."

various calibre, besides some of our surplus produce, Missouri lead, etc. etc."[8]

Texas at this time had a peculiar definition for the word "emigrant." Governor Sam Houston wrote to P. Edmonds, consul to New Orleans, from Galveston, March 11, 1842, stating:

If any should be anxious to volunteer in rendering assistance to our republic . . . it will be required for such emigrant to bring with him a good rifle or musket, with a cartouche box, or shot pouch and powder horn, with at least one hundred rounds of ammunition, a good knapsack and six months clothing, and enter service for six months, subject to the laws of Texas.

General Waddy Thompson, an active South Carolina Whig, was named United States minister to replace Judge Ellis in Mexico City.[9] Early in January, Senator Preston of South Carolina urged that Thompson be sent in a frigate to Vera Cruz with special instructions, but these were not given until April 5.

The State Department based its demands for Kendall's release upon the fact that he was unaware of the ulterior purpose of the Santa Fe Expedition. In his letter of instructions, Webster wrote Thompson:

Mr. Kendall is a man of letters, a highly respectable citizen of New Orleans, and was the editor of a literary publication carried on at that place. He was fond of travel at those seasons of the year when most of the persons who are able leave the city; and having, in all previous tours, made himself acquainted with all parts of his own country, and learning, early in the spring of 1841, that a TRADING expedition would start from Texas to Santa Fe about the first of May, he resolved on joining it, as a pleasure excursion of a novel and interesting character. . . . Mr. Kendall was no soldier, no revolutionary adventurer, but a man of respectable connections, engaged in prosperous business,

8 New Orleans *Bulletin,* March 28, 1842.

9 Waddy Thompson had been a nullifier and a brigadier general in forces organized to defend South Carolina against Federal interference. In 1835 he was the successful Whig candidate to fill the vacancy in Congress created by the death of Warren R. Davis, where he remained until 1841 despite Calhoun's opposition.

and fond of the enjoyments of intellectual and social life. It is hardly possible that such a gentleman should have left such a condition to form a part of a military expedition, subjecting himself to all its hazards and all its results, in an attempt to subjugate by force a Mexican province five hundred or a thousand miles from his home and his connections . . .[10]

Meanwhile, in San Lázaro Kendall talked openly with his companions and visitors of his plans for escape. One morning in the outer yard of the prison he found a long pole by the back wall. When the guards were gathered around a monte game conducted by one of the lepers, he slipped out and carefully placed it against the corner of the wall, where he could readily climb out. He planned to go over the wall at dusk, just before the doors were locked for the night.

That day Mayer called from the legation again, with news of negotiations for his release. Judge Ellis had interviewed Santa Anna, and the release was promised as soon as a few points were cleared up. The dictator had heard that young Frank Combs, recently released, had raised a hostile force which was advancing against Mexico. Texas, he said, had proclaimed a blockade on the eastern coast of Mexico, and this action had followed arrival in Texas of a messenger bearing dispatches from the United States. American war vessels were standing off Vera Cruz, and this worried the dictator. He was concerned because stories and editorials in American newspapers were unfriendly and inflammatory.

These objections were relayed by the minister of foreign relations to Mayer, and he passed them on to Judge Ellis who entered into patient correspondence to refute the statements. Mayer strongly urged Kendall to stay away from the pole in the corner of the prison yard until diplomatic proceedings had advanced a bit further.

[10] Webster to Thompson, April 5, 1842, Twenty-seventh Congress, second session, *Executive Documents,* Vol. 5, *Doc.* 266, pp. 25, 26. Falconer, in his widely circulated letter, had been explicit in his statement: "Mr. Kendall joined the expedition as a guest. He was not enrolled and was not subject to any military orders. . . ."

Kendall demurred, but decided to postpone his attempted flight when he learned that Thompson had been named to succeed Ellis and was then on his way to Mexico City.

Kendall's mother became greatly exasperated with the delays that Ellis faced. From Vermont she wrote to her daughter, Catherine, and her son, Thaddeus Richmond, in Sumterville, Alabama:

... we heard of the capture of the Santa Fe expedition we had all sorts of news but nothing definite until they arrived chihuhua and from there we receivd an extract of a letter from him we thought if he only livd to get there he would immediately be liberated but seems Old Santy don't give him up we received a letter from Mr. Elis our Minister stating he should do all he could officially and that was nothing more than he was obliged to do I consider him an Old Granny and always shall until I know better. he wanst to keep in on both sides he pretends he don't know what to do it is generally thought Tomhson will accomplish something more favorable you mentioned our writing to Mr. Webster we had thought of it but he had written to Mr. Elis particular for Georges release at the time Mr. Cooms sent in a petition for his sons releas he directed Elis to demand it as soon as he got there Mr. Holbrook rote to us soom after Mr. Lumsdale left stating we mite rest assured that there had and were still doing every thing that could be done. . . .[11]

General Thompson called on Kendall the morning after his arrival in the city, but the sight of the diseased inmates was too much for him. He obtained permission for Kendall to accompany him to the front door, where they discussed the editor's case.[12]

[11] Kendall papers, A. W. Kendall to Thaddeus Richmond Kendall, dated Burlington, May 11, 1842.

[12] Waddy Thompson, *Recollections of Mexico* (New York, 1846), 51: "I arrived in Mexico on Saturday evening, and early on Sunday morning I went to see Mr. Kendall and the Texan prisoners. Although I had not then any personal acquaintance with Mr. Kendall, I felt a deep interest in his sufferings, an interest which was heightened by the terms in which many of his friends in New Orleans had spoken of him to me." Also Thompson's letter to Webster, April 29, 1842, in Twenty-seventh Congress, second session, *Senate Executive Documents*, Vol. 5, *Doc.* 266, pp. 34, 36. Also, Kendall, *Narrative*, II, 266, 267.

The new minister promised to do everything he could to get Kendall released unconditionally, and if that failed, to get him paroled or sent to some other spot than San Lázaro for safekeeping while his freedom was being considered.

Lieutenant Pounce of the United States Revenue Service, Mr. Perrin of New Orleans, and Mr. Coolidge of Massachusetts, who accompanied General Thompson, urged Kendall not to attempt to escape. A Yankee friend even urged Kendall to remain in prison, hoping his detention would bring on a war with Mexico which would give United States citizens recognition equal to that which Mexico accorded English subjects and French citizens.

During March the tone of the press was warlike, and statements in Congress reflected this spirit. Senator Barrow of Louisiana introduced a resolution stating that the United States government had tolerated long enough the insolence of other nations and that it was time to terminate these evils. The Washington *Madisonian* warned that Santa Anna soon might find himself and his ragamuffins more severely peppered than they had been either at San Jacinto or San Juan d'Ulloa. In his bitterness, Kendall declared that had Andrew Jackson been in office, the prisoners would have been released within twenty-four hours after the news reached Washington.

The war spirit died down, however, as the long series of disputes with England almost crowded Kendall and his companions out of the spotlight. The perplexing question of the Oregon boundary, which was to be settled four years later in the Webster-Ashburton Treaty, the quarrel arising out of English search of United States merchantmen off the coast of Africa, and the demands for restoration of the slaves who captured the brig *Creole* and escaped to a British port, echoed through the nation.[13]

Then there was the irritating question of England's pressure on Texas diplomacy, and her domination of the situation in Mex-

[13] Twenty-seventh Congress, second session, *Senate Executive Documents,* Vol. 4, *Doc.* 278. News of the brig *Creole* was carried in the *Picayune,* December 3, 1841.

ico. The *Picayune* asked, "If England seeks Texas, is she not also likely to seek Cuba?"[14]

"Old South-West," writing from Washington to the *Picayune*, concluded that Kendall's imprisonment might last until there was a showdown in the troublesome disagreements both with England and Mexico.

Kendall finally was brought directly to Santa Anna's notice by Thompson's exertions. On the night after the minister's visit Kendall was awakened by the tramp of soldiers, and looked up to find ten armed men surrounding his cot. He was ordered to dress and pack his carpetbag in preparation for leaving. His leper friends crowded around in deep concern. None of the inmates, either Mexican or Texan, expected ever to see him again.

He asked where he was to be taken, but the guard said, "*¿Quien sabe?*"

Outside the soldiers formed on either side of Kendall and prepared to march. He asked permission to ride, and the commander ordered a litter brought up. It was so filthy that Kendall refused to enter it. His books and bag were dumped inside it, and the march began down the middle of the cobbled street that led toward the heart of the city.

After half a mile his ankle began to pain him, and when he had hobbled a mile over the rough stones he was suffering terribly. Finally he sat down on the curb and refused to move until a cab was called. The officer complied, and got in beside him, the soldiers marching alongside as they went on through the darkened city.

Eventually they arrived before a prison gate, Kendall was registered, and the guard led him across a courtyard and unlocked a heavy door. As the key grated in the lock there rose the sound of sudden clanking of chains. Kendall was shoved inside and the door slammed behind him. A shout went up and his name was called by many voices—he was in the midst of Colonel Cooke's party at Santiago.

[14] *Picayune,* March 31, 1842.

Immediately after breakfast next morning the Mexican in charge of the chain gang told Kendall to select a partner among the prisoners—someone to help him carry the fetters which were now to decorate his ankles for the first time. He chose Major Valentine Bennett, because the major had confided that he had a secret way of slipping off the chain.[15]

They were led off to the blacksmith shop amid the banter and jests of their friends. There Kendall slipped a dollar into the hand of the blacksmith, and submitted to the operation. The chain was some eight feet in length and extremely heavy. After cutting the straps from a pair of fashionable French pantaloons which he had bought at Zacatecas, he placed his foot upon the anvil.

The Mexican hammered away with as much zeal as though the chain were to remain in place for life. However, Kendall's dollar proved a good investment. Thereafter, when the door was locked at night, he removed his boot and easily slipped the manacle from his ankle. The clanking he had heard upon entering the prison that first night was made by the Texans scrambling to replace their chains when the door was unlocked.

When the road-working crew marched out for the day, Kendall found that he would be permitted to stay inside, since Major Bennett was detailed to work in the kitchen. Kendall again laid plans for escape. Since the building was closely guarded at all times and locked securely at night, he decided that his best chance lay in securing the costume of one of the priests in attendance at the adjoining convent. Thus he could walk out during the daylight hours.

General Thompson learned of Kendall's transfer next morning, and although he had not yet been received as the accredited

15 Major Bennett had been quartermaster of the expedition. Kendall wrote that he was a Scripture-quoting Quaker "some fifty-five or sixty years of age," a native of Massachusetts and a descendant of the Puritans. He was a young man at the time of the War of 1812, and was a lieutenant at the "celebrated and hard-fought battles of Bridgewater and Lundy's Lane." He had been engaged in the earlier conflicts of Texas, and was wounded at the battle of Victoria.

minister of the United States, he hurried to the legation. He urged Judge Ellis to write immediately protesting the placing of Kendall in chains, but the retiring minister believed this would do no good. Thompson then addressed a note directly to the Mexican minister of foreign affairs and reported this move to Daniel Webster.[16] As this correspondence was being dispatched, Kendall decided to delay his plans for escape until after San Jacinto Day.

While Santa Anna, perhaps, was remembering that April 21, eight years previous, when Sam Houston and his handful of Texans routed the Mexicans and wrung from the captive general the treaty of freedom for Texas, the prisoners decided to celebrate the event with a great ceremony.

American friends in Mexico City had sent the prisoners a half-dozen turkeys and other foodstuffs, and a generous supply of wines and liquors. Now their objective was to secure permission from the gruff old *comandante* to remain indoors for the feast. A committee of those who could speak Spanish was assigned to this task. In respectful and courteous address, they requested the privilege of celebrating the day as that of their "patron saint."

Their piety impressed him. He granted their request.

They asked only for the afternoon, since they were anxious that the morning road-working detail go out as usual. These men were commissioned to buy additional refreshments.

All who could paint or draw cartoons feigned illness and remained in the prison that morning. When the guards left they unearthed paint and crayon and decorated the walls with Texas flags and scenes of sea and land battles—with the Texans victorious over the Mexicans.

Dinner was served at three o'clock; not such a dinner as the St. Charles or the Astor House might have served—"but we had roast beef, turkey, and good appetites."

[16] This series of letters is included in Twenty-seventh Congress, second session, *Senate Executive Documents,* Vol. 5, *Doc.* 266, pp. 21–36.

Then the oratory and merriment really got underway. Major George W. Bonnell and Dr. R. F. Brenham were drafted from among the prisoners to make addresses. A survivor of San Jacinto, then living in Mexico, was invited in to tell anecdotes of that famous battle. They sang all the Texas patriotic songs they knew and then turned to "Hail Columbia" and "The Star Spangled Banner." They took time out to drink to the memory of George Washington, with everyone standing uncovered. Wild snatches of song and uproarious merriment came from the room long after the prisoners had been locked in for the night.

In the midst of the celebration word came from the embassy that Kendall and seven others claiming United States citizenship were to be released. By now this was an old story. Kendall refused to believe it.

"As the hours sped along, the prisoners, one by one, rolled themselves in their blankets upon the floor, and soon fell asleep," Kendall wrote. "Suffering from a cold and slight headache at the time, I had followed their example and was already in half a doze, when a sound was heard at the door as of a key slowly turning in the lock."[17]

The prisoners scrambled to replace the chains about their ankles, thinking the old *comandante* had decided to pay them a late visit. However, it was Judge Ellis, Mayer, and three of the Mexican officers on duty at the prison.

They confirmed the earlier report of Kendall's release, but there was a bitter taste for him in this cup of joy. Santa Anna had released the Americans to Judge Ellis as an act of benevolence —not as a right accorded them out of respect to their government.

The officers had brought along a blacksmith to remove the prisoners' chains. Kendall waited until the anvil was dragged to his side, then he kicked his chain off in contempt.

After seven months of captivity, he was free.

---

[17] Kendall told of this celebration in *Narrative*, II, 306–12.

11

Troubles brew
in Texas

THE SOLEMN VISAGE of Henry Clay, chiseled in marble, looked down on the disordered editorial office of the *Picayune* at 72 Camp Street. But now the famous old Kentuckian looked anything but stern and solemn, for a red fireman's hat slanted cockily over his brow, tossed there for want of a nail in the wall.

Beneath the bust, at one of the three round tables, George Wilkins Kendall sat writing. The noise from the business office beyond the green curtain that partitioned off the editorial "sanctum," and the clatter of the composing room upstairs, rose above the scratching of his pen as he wrote, for the issue of May 20, 1842:

Mr. Kendall, on returning once more to his home, cannot let the occasion pass without tendering his sincere thanks to his fellow citizens for the kind solicitude manifested for his welfare while suffering imprisonment in Mexico, and also for the warm welcome he has received from all since his return. . . .

If there is anything that would recompense him for the sufferings he has endured, it is the reflection that his firm personal friends, as well as those upon whom he has had no particular claim, have manifested towards him, upon all occasions, the kindness of brothers rather than the courtesy of countrymen; and that indignities offered the American name have been amply sufficient to arouse in the breasts of the people of the United States all that should distinguish the American character.

The sharp contrast between the treatment of Americans by the Mexicans and that accorded the British remained a matter of bitterness with Kendall. After his release he had returned to Mexico City to make leisurely preparations for the trip to New Orleans. He prowled among the markets selecting presents for friends and members of his family. He bought a pony for Catherine's little boy, George Kendall Rix, and chose an elaborately trimmed Mexican saddle to replace his own which he had lost with old "Jim the Butcher" at San Miguel.[1]

He spent a sleepless night trying to get used to the comforts of a luxurious hotel room in Mexico City, with clean sheets and a soft mattress. Roaming the streets in the late hours, he tried to get accustomed to his new-found freedom. On one of these nocturnal jaunts he was accosted sharply by an armed sentry.

"I am British," he answered.

The words almost stuck in his throat, and he was disgusted at the prompt and courteous way in which he was passed. Had he revealed his identity he might have suffered further abuse and annoyance.

He remembered this humiliation when he wrote his editorial of gratitude in the *Picayune's* sanctum, under the stern eye of Henry Clay, shaded by the jaunty fireman's hat.[2] He remembered it again and again as he sat in the office interpreting the

[1] This saddle caused him some embarrassment later. In 1843 he permitted a Cincinnati saddler to display the saddle in a case before his store, and the Cincinnati *Gazette* reported that the saddle cost $600 and had been presented to Kendall by his fellow Santa Fe Expedition prisoners in return for his services in securing their freedom. He denied this story in the *Picayune* of June 15, 1842, saying that he had not been able to help the other prisoners and had secured his own release with difficulty, and that he had paid $160 for the saddle and $75 more for the bridle, spurs, "and other appurtenances."

[2] Kendall had been made a "captain" in one of the volunteer companies which formed the city's only protection against frequent and disastrous fires. These companies, with their uniforms, their parades, and their rivalry that was not always friendly, formed an important and picturesque part of civic life in New Orleans. Kendall endured much good-natured jibing because of his title, on the part of other editors, but it stuck, and he was often called "Captain Kendall."

The description of the editorial "sanctum" was carried in the *Picayune,* March 13, 1842. It adjoined the business office on the ground floor of the building, and

news from Texas and Mexico, or piecing together from memory the vivid pictures of his adventures on the Santa Fe Expedition.

For Kendall lost no time plunging back into his newspaper work. He wrote the story of his own homecoming for the issue of May 19, 1842, inserting so much additional news of political turmoil in Mexico that the article filled more than three columns. With his return the stream of news and comment on Texas and Mexican affairs in the columns of the *Picayune* swelled noticeably.

Although he had been away from New Orleans only a year, Kendall learned that news events which were to have tremendous effect on his career had been published in the paper during 1841. Before he left for his western excursion the Whigs had inaugurated their first president, William Henry Harrison, who died suddenly and was succeeded by John Tyler. By now the discontent at Tyler's course of action had split the Whig ranks, all his cabinet except Daniel Webster, secretary of state, had resigned, and the President was discredited in the eyes of his own party leaders.

In England the Melbourne ministry had fallen on August 30 and Aberdeen had replaced Palmerston as Peel's foreign minister. This brought Aberdeen and Guizot, Louis Philippe's prime minister, into the close relationship that cemented good feeling between England and France and caused these two nations to act together in their policy regarding affairs in the western hemisphere.

In Mexico the periodical revolutionary storms had swept Santa Anna into office again, this time as provisional president. He was to go into temporary eclipse again in 1844, but not until he and his cabinet had muddled relations with the United States beyond hope of settlement.

---

was "one fourth division of a larger apartment, shut off by a framework hung with green curtains, and a door. . . . It is the propensity of everybody to get into our special corner, for, generally, no other reason but because there is a curtain around it."

Down in the Republic of Texas, the prodigal and quixotic administration of Mirabeau Buonaparte Lamar ended in December, and Sam Houston became president a second time, with Anson Jones as secretary of state.

This significant turnover of four administrations in 1841 was to have a far reaching effect on the destiny of the United States. For the annexation of Texas and the acquisition of a vast domain extending to the Pacific coast were at stake, and Kendall and the *Picayune* were in the vanguard of the crisis which involved the diplomatic forces of Great Britain, France, Mexico, the Republic of Texas and the United States.

In the early 1840's, the *Picayune* grew to man-size stature, expanding to six columns. It insisted over and over, in a serious tone that contrasted strangely with its earlier hilarious comment, that Texas should be annexed to the United States. Its staff combed the Texas and Mexican press for significant comment, and its correspondents in Texas, in Mexico, in Washington, and in the northern and eastern states poured in news of developments, of comment, of opinion bearing on this question which was so close to Kendall's heart. Soon the *Picayune* was recognized far and wide as the authority on developments in Texas and Mexico.[3]

Its dispatches were picked up and copied widely in other papers, often without credit, which the *Picayune* resented. One such protest is typical:

If the editor of that popular and most respectable sheet, the *National Intelligencer,* knew the trouble and expense we were at in obtaining Mexican news, we believe that he would be more ready in giving us credit whenever he draws upon our columns for accounts from that quarter. The leading article under the head of that journal of the 20th inst., with the exception of the first line or two, was copied from this paper; and if it was sufficiently interesting to ensure for itself a

[3] Justin H. Smith, *The War with Mexico* (2 vols., New York, 1919), I, 120 In its early years the *Picayune's* bright editorial paragraphs were copied widely. Now it was quoted almost as extensively on its news from Texas and Mexico.

place in that print, the source from whence it was derived should also have been given.[4]

There were also significant and exciting events to record at home. On the day of Kendall's return from Mexico citizens rioted and wrecked the offices of several exchange brokers at Canal and Camp streets because of a dispute over municipal currency. In the depression that began a few weeks after the *Picayune* was founded in 1837, the councilmen of the different municipalities in New Orleans had issued small notes which passed at current exchange rates. In the waning months of this depression in 1842, the banks of the city resumed specie payments on their notes, and this sent the municipal currency into a slump that almost wiped out the small note holders.

The *Picayune* urged that these notes be refunded to prevent loss, and had the satisfaction of publishing the ordinances which provided for the refunding.[5] But this did not end the financial turmoil in New Orleans. By May 28, 1842, bankruptcies had become so numerous that the *Picayune* commented, "The epidemic of insolvency is every day sweeping off its victims."

The banks were in trouble again. Runs were started on the Citizens Bank and the Louisiana State Bank. Both suspended specie payments until December. Three more followed on June 2, then others. In another month only four of the city's sixteen banks were making specie payments, and the other twelve were discounting their own notes from fifteen to eighty per cent.[6]

Finally the *Picayune* turned to joking about the matter, as it

[4] *Picayune,* June 28, 1844.

[5] The First Municipality had more than $300,000 in outstanding notes, and the Second Municipality more than $360,000. See *ibid.*, May 10, 11, 15, 19, 20, 21, 22, 25, 28, and 31, and June 2, 1842, for news of this financial difficulty.

[6] *Picayune,* June 2 and 29, and July 1 and 6, 1842. The *Picayune* reported: "A note drawn in the name of the Gas Bank of this city, and signed by its then president, Thomas Barrett, in favor of the Bank of the United States, payable to Mr. Jandon, and now overdue, was yesterday sold by auction in the St. Louis Exchange, by the sheriff of the District Court. Its amount was $650,000. It was set up at $50, and the bidding went on till it was finally knocked down for $7,070."

had in the first months after its founding. It announced on June 2:

ANOTHER SUSPENSION—Stevenson's soda fountain encountered a tremendous run yesterday, and for a time was compelled to suspend, but resumption of the soda quickly followed, and consumption of the soda is still going on.

The paper joked of other matters, too. In connection with mail delays, it commented in the same issue:

It seems some of the mail riders in Wisconsin have lately been chased by Wolves. It might not be a bad plan for the government to employ a pack of wolves to chase its mail carriers upon a good many routes throughout the country.

On July 6 it added this item:

CAPTAIN, COOK AND ALL HANDS.—An Editor out West, in giving an account of the bursting of the boiler and blowing up of a steamboat while racing, says that every *soul* on board was more or less injured; also a large number of cattle and hogs among whom was the *captain* of the boat.

And then it roared:

Lord Byron calls a daily editor "an unquenched snuffing of the midnight taper."—D--n Byron!

However, it seldom joked about Texas or Mexico.

Kendall's immediate task upon his return was the writing of the detailed story of his adventures on the Santa Fe Expedition. The first article, devoted to his preparations for starting on the expedition, and his voyage from New Orleans, appeared June 1. Many newspapers reprinted the installments.[7]

7 Kendall wrote in the *Picayune* of August 14, expressing "thanks to the many journals throughout the country which have copied these sketches and kindly commended them to notice."

Falconer's *Narrative,* which the *Picayune* had published May 3 to 8, differed from Kendall's only in a few details, particularly in dates of events on the march

When he went to Washington and New York on a business trip in August, 1842, the *Picayune* ran four articles Kendall had prepared, and did not resume publication of the series until his return in the fall. Captain Frederick Marryat at Langham Manor, Norfolk, rewriting them as his own for *The Strange Adventures of Monsieur Violet,* could not wait for the completion of the series. His plagiarism of the Kendall material ended with this first group of articles.[8]

Business and the stress of work at the office delayed Kendall, but he kept steadily at the job of revising the sketches through the early months of 1843. The paper announced on January 12 that the story of the "Texan Santa Fe Expedition starts again, having been crowded out by the report of the State Legislature."

In June the editor went north to visit his parents in Burlington, and then on to Long Branch, New Jersey, where for a month he wrote steadily. But while he was completing final details for the publication of his book, Marryat's manuscript was being rushed through the presses. Kendall saw a copy of it in November and was furious to find many of his own adventures, written in his own words, in a volume which reached the public months ahead of his own. Not only had his sketches been stolen, but he had been denounced as a liar for his account of Golpin's murder on the march to El Paso. The Texans had been pictured as robbers and brigands, and the whole expedition branded as a marauding venture.

Kendall's fury boiled over. To the publisher of the New York *Courier and Enquirer* he wrote a letter pouring out his protests. The New York *Tribune,* started two years previously by Kendall's friend, Horace Greeley, ran the letter in full, with the com-

when both were relying on memory. On May 12 the *Picayune* announced the publication of the Falconer *Narrative* in pamphlet form, saying, "Supplies of the pamphlet will be forwarded from our office to St. Louis, Louisville, Mobile, Galveston, and other places immediately, while we shall retain such a number on hand as we suppose may meet all calls made upon us." A copy of this pamphlet is in the University of Texas library.

[8] See notes on chapters 7, 8, and 9 for details of this plagiarism.

ment, "The gross humbug, so far as it poaches upon his manor, is thus effectively demolished by Mr. Kendall."[9]

While Kendall was writing his Santa Fe sketches, he kept a close check on his companions who had been left behind in prison when he was released, with John Howard and T. A. Sully, on April 21, 1842.

On the following June 13, Santa Anna announced that in honor of his birthday all of the remaining prisoners should be released—all except Antonio Navarro whose connection with Texas and the expedition was considered treasonable. Navarro was confined in the Acordada, "the vilest hole in Mexico," and one of Kendall's last acts before leaving Mexico City had been to visit his old friend.

Joy over the release of the prisoners was dimmed, however, by the plague of yellow fever which struck them when they arrived in the low country near Vera Cruz. Dr. Francis A. Whitaker, surgeon, and Theodore Seavy, adjutant, were among the first of many victims. John Holiday, listed as "assistant-commissary in charge of supplies" on the expedition rolls, died aboard ship on the way home.

"By the first of August," Kendall wrote, "nearly all the survivors of the ill-fated expedition had reached Galveston or New Orleans, most of them without means, and many in broken health."[10]

[9] The *Tribune* letter began, "Our friend of the New Orleans *Picayune* exposes a small portion of the atrocious larcenies by which Capt. Marryat has fabricated his pretended 'Travels of Monsieur Violet,' a work in the manufacture of which the Captain has laid Farnham, Lewis and Clark, and almost every other writer on our Western Prairies and Wilderness under heavy contribution. . . ."

Kendall's letter with the *Tribune's* comment, appeared in *Niles' National Register,* December 2, 1843, p. 214.

[10] Kendall papers, "Rough Notes of Additional Chapters to Santa Fe Expedition." This apparently is the first draft of the additional chapter included in the 1856 edition of Kendall's *Narrative.* Fourteen of the Texans had died of yellow fever at Vera Cruz. The *Picayune* of August 21, 1842, reported the return of Captain Caldwell and his fourteen-year-old son, Curtis. They shipped from Vera Cruz for Galveston by way of Key West, Pensacola, and New Orleans. The *Picayune* of September 4 announced that "Col." [*sic*] McLeod and the rest of the men had arrived in Galveston.

After their return he recorded their adventures during the years from 1842 to 1845, through the recurring clashes between Texas and Mexico which grew out of the Texas expedition to Santa Fe.[11] For, though the expedition was over, its impact was to be felt through the following four dramatic years.[12]

These definite results of the expedition were evident:

It helped cause a renewal of hostilities between Mexico and Texas and revived the dispute over contested territory.

It brought the Texas question again before the people of the United States. The feeling of resentment over the treatment of the expedition prisoners did not subside until after the Mexican War.

Its failure was interpreted in Europe, and particularly in France, as evidence of the inability of Texas to occupy territory which she claimed, and raised the question as to whether she could maintain her independence. This doubt impaired her credit abroad and checked the stream of settlers from Europe.[13]

The continued clashes between Texas and Mexico caused England and the United States to exert pressure to stop hostilities, and England's interest in an independent Texas aroused the United States to propose annexation.

England and France joined in the diplomatic maneuvering to build Texas into a strong buffer nation that would prevent expansion of the United States to the southwest and to the Pacific coast, and for an interval during 1844 these nations strongly considered armed intervention. In the end, through British pressure, Mexico reluctantly agreed to recognize the independence

[11] Kendall's work as correspondent in the Mexican War brought him in frequent contact with his old comrades. Occasionally he saw one of the survivors during his years on his ranch on the Texas frontier. Numerous entries in his diaries from 1857 to 1867 record these meetings.

[12] Binkley, *op. cit.*, 96, stated: "From the point of view of territorial activities in Texas, the four years from the failure of the Santa Fe expedition to annexation to the United States may be characterized as a prolonged effort to overcome the effects of that failure."

[13] However, Houston's appeals during 1842 brought many armed "settlers" from the Mississippi Valley for Texas' defense.

of Texas, but Texas voters rejected the proposed peace and chose instead to become a part of the United States.

This led to war between the United States and Mexico. From 1842 to 1846 events moved steadily toward this conflict, and Kendall recorded the successive steps in the *Picayune*.

Hostilities between Texas and Mexico had been resumed before the Santa Fe prisoners got back to the Republic. The actual outbreak was preceded by threats on both sides, and throughout the struggle the verbal barrage was far more intense than the fighting.[14]

Widespread agitation for the recovery of Texas had swept through Mexico following Armijo's report of the capture of the Texans near San Miguel, and Santa Anna issued a statement threatening to take over the territory as far as the Sabine.

Preparations began for the first of three sorties across the Rio Grande which were to take place during 1842.

On March 5, General Rafael Vaquez led seven hundred men in an attack on San Antonio. The defending force of a hundred Texans withdrew, the Mexicans took as much loot as they could carry and fled across the Rio Grande.

Three thousand Texans armed and proceeded to San Antonio where General Edward Burleson, Texas vice-president, went to take charge. But when President Houston gave the command to General Alexander Somerwell the troops refused to follow him. The force disbanded on April 2.

Kendall recorded in the *Picayune*, June 7, "San Antonio Abandoned.—The Matagorda *Gazette* of the 21st ult. conveys information that the Americans have evacuated San Antonio, and that the place is now in possession of Agatore, with 400 Mexicans. This fellow, it should be recollected, is a celebrated robber."

Houston's earlier appeal for American "settlers" to rendezvous at Corpus Christi had been well timed, for in July General

[14] An exchange of correspondence between Bernard E. Bee, Texas agent in Washington, and Santa Anna, was carried in the *Picayune*, March 10, 1842. Bee warned Santa Anna that he would never be able to conquer Texas, and the dictator replied that he believed war to be "indispensable to the salvation of Mexico."

Canales attacked that place and was repulsed by the Texas forces.

Mexico struck again in September when General Adrian Woll captured San Antonio by surprise, despite the scouting activities of Colonel Jack Hayes.[15] Fifty-five men, including judges and court officials, were made prisoners and marched off to Mexico, where some of them were kept for two years.

Woll marched on north of San Antonio, but was turned back on the banks of the Salado River by rallying Texas volunteers.[16] This attack led to an unauthorized counterinvasion when Texans stormed the town of Mier on December 25. There, after standing off superior numbers under General Ampudia, two hundred and twenty-six volunteers surrendered under flattering terms and were started off toward prison in Mexico City.

En route, however, they surprised their captors and escaped, broke up into small parties and attempted to make their way back to the Rio Grande, only to be recaptured. Seventeen of their number were shot and the rest marched to prison.[17]

Meanwhile, in 1842 and 1843, the Texans turned their attention to the Northwest again, with a view to the capture of New Mexico. Under the heading "Important from Texas," the *Picayune* announced:

[15] Jack Coffee Hayes (1817–84), world-famous scout and Indian fighter and first captain of the Texas Rangers, was a Tennessean who emigrated to Texas and joined the army of the Brazos shortly after the Battle of San Jacinto. He was engaged in surveying lands after Texas gained her independence, but already had become widely known as a frontier fighter. In 1840, when Texas was too poor to support a regular army, a company of "Texas Rangers" was organized as a protection against Mexican and Indian forays, and Hayes, although he was only twenty-three years old, was made captain. Later he was promoted to major in charge of two ranger companies, and during the Mexican War was colonel in charge of the Texas scouts. After the war he emigrated to California and was elected the first sheriff of San Francisco. In his second term he resigned to take the office of state surveyor.

[16] Kendall's "Rough Notes" includes a dramatic account of this battle on the Salado. See also *Jack Hayes, the Intrepid Ranger* (Printed by the *Frontier Times*, Bandera, Texas, n.d.), 10.

[17] There are many dramatic accounts of this, a lottery where 153 white beans and 17 black beans were placed in a jar and each man required to take one as he marched by. See Thomas J. Green, *Journal of the Texian Expedition against Mier* (New York, 1845).

One of the most important items is the published fact that a large force left Texas early in the spring on another Santa Fe expedition, although this time their object is war and not trade. . . .

The whole thing has been kept a secret in Texas—and in this the editors of that country have pursued the wiser policy. The calamities which befel the former Santa Fe expedition were in part caused by the too great publicity given its movements.[18]

Before the last of the Santa Fe Expedition prisoners had reached home, Texas had commissioned Charles A. Warfield as a colonel and authorized him to raise a force as part of the Texas army. He was to move against the New Mexico settlements and the Santa Fe Trail where it was unguarded.

He wintered in Missouri, secured twenty-four recruits, and in May engaged in two minor brushes with Armijo's forces near the New Mexico town of Mora. Before leaving Missouri he had commissioned John McDaniel to raise more troops and follow.

McDaniel's men captured a wagon train on the Santa Fe Trail at a point which the Mexicans declared to be within the United States, and Antonio Chávez, member of an old Santa Fe family, was killed. American dragoons were dispatched to protect the traders, and the Missourians later were captured and punished in the United States after their act was disavowed by Texas.

During the year following Warfield's departure, Texas officials heard nothing from him, and President Houston was persuaded to launch another campaign against the Santa Fe trade. But when Major Jacob Snively marched out of Georgetown in July, 1843, with two hundred men, Warfield's force already had disbanded and McDaniel was a fugitive.[19]

---

[18] *Picayune,* May 19, 1843.

[19] These futile ventures caused a tremendous stir in the United States and Mexico at the time. Santa Anna, believing the Texas attacks were inspired by the United States, closed the customs houses at Taos, Paso del Norte, and Presidio del Norte. Thirty-second Congress, second session, *Senate Executive Documents,* (Series 660), *Doc.* 14, pp 113–18; Garrison, *Diplomatic Correspondence,* II, 189, 215–17; Binkley, *Expansionist Movement in Texas,* 104–10, 114, 115; *Niles' National Register,* LXIV, 235, 290, 323, 354, 386, and LXV, 166, 167; Gregg, *Commerce of the Prairies,* II, 169–70.

Snively was hardly on his way when Texas and Mexico, under the urging of Captain Charles Elliot, British chargé d'affaires, agreed to a temporary cessation of hostilities.[20] Before this news reached Snively, he had been captured by United States troops as he lay in wait for a prairie caravan, and his men sent home. The last effort of Texas to take over the New Mexico settlements and capture the rich prairie commerce ended as dismally as had President Lamar's grand gesture of 1841.

[20] General Adrian Woll, in command of the Mexican army of the north, demanded that Texas either recall her expeditions or renounce them, in which case they would be treated as outlaws. Since they were unable to communicate with Warfield or Snively, Texas officials gave Woll a cancellation of Warfield's orders, and endorsed on a copy of the armistice proclamation an order to Snively to return to Texas. See Ephraim D. Adams (ed.), "Correspondence in British Archives Concerning Texas," *Southwestern Historical Quarterly,* XVII, 85–87.

12

The Picayune
smokes out a plot

After the failure of the Santa Fe Expedition and the furor aroused through efforts to release United States citizens from Mexican prisons, it was inevitable that interest in the annexation of Texas should be revived.

For a brief, stirring period before the outbreak of the Mexican War in 1846, the intrigues carried on in Texas by English, French and Mexican diplomats, and the mysterious meddlings of the "Man with the White Hat," were discussed in cabinet meetings, were debated in Congress, were bandied on street corners, and were told and retold in news and editorial columns of hundreds of newspapers throughout the country.

And in the vanguard of this strife the *Picayune* galloped with all the audacity of its earlier years. But it was a more serious *Picayune*. Before Kendall went on the Santa Fe Expedition and wound up in a Mexican prison, the paper went its happy-go-lucky way, paying little attention to international affairs. While he was in captivity his colleagues scanned the Washington news eagerly for a hint of progress in the negotiations for his release. After his return the *Picayune's* perspective was entirely changed, for in that year of his adventure it had grown to maturity.

Thereafter, its correspondents trailed French and British diplomatic representatives in Texas and Mexico, and sent in lengthy reports of events in Galveston, Washington on the Brazos, Houston, Tampico, Vera Cruz, and Mexico City. Its editorial columns bristled with demands for firm handling of the diplomatic problems that grew more and more perplexing below the Rio Grande.

Fifteen years after the memorable diplomatic struggle that finally added the great southwestern domain to the Union, Kendall recalled his part in the drama which in 1845 was swiftly drawing to a climax:

If any man worked hard for the annexation of Texas to the United States, it was your humble servant; Whig that I was, in '45 I toiled with coat off, and sleeves rolled up.

Sitting upon the same log upon the banks of the Brazos, you might have seen as many men as the log would hold: it was a shady spot, the spot where that old log slumbered, and there in diplomatic conclave might have been seen Anson Jones, Sam Houston, Capt. Elliot, the Count de Saligny, and Major A. J. Donelson—perhaps not all at one and the same time, but one time and another all felt the log.

And I was there too, watching every movement, and especially watching Elliot, a long ways the smartest man in the crowd. I dogged him to Galveston, and when in every grocery and bowling alley he proclaimed that he was going to Charleston, in the British Frigate *Eurydice,* I suspected that he was going to the City of Mexico, to prevent annexation if in his power. I was right, came out in the *Picayune* with the mysterious movements of the "Man with the White Hat," and perhaps did as much as any man to thwart and break up his game.[1]

The fate of Texas was in the balance. Great Britain, long alarmed at the rising power of the United States, was keenly interested in seeing Texas remain as a buffer state to block further expansion of the Union to the Southwest and the Pacific Ocean.[2] With the connivance of France, England sought to block annexation, and early in 1844 the two agreed to go to war, if necessary,

[1] Unfinished, undated letter in Kendall papers, apparently written in 1860 when he was disturbed over the approach of disunion.

[2] The *Picayune* of March 1, 1845, charged that at the time of Santa Anna's capture at San Jacinto in 1836, a treaty was being drawn up ceding California and New Mexico to Great Britain.

in order to prevent Texas from becoming one of the United States. The London *Times* spoke frankly: "In maintaining the independence of Texas, they [England and France] may hope to establish an important element in the distribution of powers over North America. There, as well as in Europe, an universal domination is impracticable."[3]

The *Picayune's* broadened editorial vision was due in no small measure to Alexander Bullitt, one of the publishers of the New Orleans *Bee,* who joined the *Picayune* as a partner in 1844 and remained there until his death in 1868. He was widely known for his civic enterprise and his resounding editorials.[4]

Bullitt had presided over city-wide meetings demanding Kendall's release from imprisonment in Mexico, and his editorials in the *Bee* had insisted on immediate government intervention in behalf of the Santa Fe prisoners.

Extension of the telegraph lines to New Orleans was almost five years in the future, and out of the North and East news came to the *Picayune* slowly by boat and overland stage. But regardless of the difficulties of getting domestic news, the paper had an advantage in collecting information about the turmoil brewing in the West and across the Rio Grande. It might take a week, or two weeks, to get news from Washington, Baltimore, Philadelphia, or Boston, and the *Picayune* railed at even an extra day's delay. But the press of these eastern cities had to wait for newspapers from New Orleans in order to learn about the latest developments in Texas and Mexico.

"Heretofore the Texas accounts via New Orleans, both as

[3] Quoted in the New Orleans *Bee,* May 30, 1845.

[4] Bullitt, a Henry Clay Whig, was born in Louisville in 1802, practiced law there, and came to New Orleans in 1833. He joined the *Picayune* staff on November 25, 1844. He served in the state legislature in 1846 and 1847 as a representative from the third district of New Orleans, and was a member of the city council in 1847 and 1848. He was one of the early supporters of the boom of Zachary Taylor for the presidency in 1848, and after the General's election Bullitt went to Washington to edit the Whig organ, the *Republic.* He retired from the management of that paper in May, 1850, to be succeeded by Allen A. Hall, of Tennessee, and returned to the *Picayune* on January 31, 1851.

regards Texas and New Mexico, have been wild in the extreme," wrote the Cincinnati *Gazette*. "We have generally waited until the *National Intelligencer*, the best informed on these subjects, informed the public how far these reports were true or false."[5]

"What wisdom to wait," jibed the *Picayune*, "until the *Intelligencer* republishes the information from the New Orleans papers."

From the time of its establishment until in the 1870's, when the telegraph finally lowered the barriers of time, the *Picayune* assumed the leadership of the nation's press in collecting and relaying Texas news.[6] Kendall established correspondents in all of the important Texas settlements and Mexican ports. Newspapermen, merchants, travelers, officers in the Texas navy and army and captains of coastwise vessels sent in a stream of letters which were published or made the basis of editorial comment.

All shipping to and from Galveston, Matagorda Bay, and Houston cleared through New Orleans, and often many boats put in at New Orleans on their way from New York, Boston, or Charleston to Mexican ports. Occasionally boats from Mexico bound for Europe sailed across the gulf to Havana, but often these stopped at New Orleans. Most of the overland routes to the Southwest cleared through the city. The *Picayune* reporters and editors prowled the wharves and the hotels, gleaning bits of information.

So completely was the paper a sounding board for events along the western end of the Gulf of Mexico that officials in Washington, in the years 1842 to 1846, frequently got their first inkling of diplomatic maneuvers of England and France through the *Picayune's* columns.

The activities of traders and adventurers and diplomats made up only one phase of the news. Others were in the incessant domestic difficulties of Mexico, its frequent revolutions and coun-

[5] *Picayune*, January 9, 1845, quoting the Cincinnati *Gazette*.
[6] The Houston *Morning Star*, September 23, 1839, told of Lumsden's visit to Texas, and from that time until Kendall's death in 1867, the *Picayune* editors emphasized news from Texas.

ter-revolutions. The *Picayune* also recorded the strained relations between the United States and Mexico, increased after 1842 by the growing pressure for annexation, which in turn brought France and England into the picture. Exposure of the diplomatic maneuverings of these European powers in 1844 and 1845 probably was the high spot of the *Picayune's* activities before the outbreak of the Mexican War.[7]

Santa Anna, in the *Picayune's* opinion, was the archadventurer among the many opportunists who had made Mexico's experiment in self-government a tragicomedy. He began his activities as a captain in Hidalgo's uprising in 1810. Three times he had risen to the presidency or dictatorship, and each time he had been overthrown. Now in 1845 he was in exile, plotting another coup that would place him at the head of the Mexican government.

Difficulties between the United States and Mexico began when the Republic started out under its first constitution in 1825. Many United States citizens still resented bitterly the bargain John Quincy Adams made with Señor de Onís in the Florida purchase settlement in 1819, acknowledging Texas as Spanish territory. Consequently Joel R. Poinsett, first United States minister to Mexico, left Washington with instructions to offer to buy Texas. Failing in this he finally negotiated a treaty of limits in 1828, but before it was approved in 1832 and provisions made for a boundary commission, Mexico had demanded his recall.[8]

Poinsett soon learned, in 1825, that his task of developing peaceful relations with Mexico was a difficult one, for the British, immediately after the revolution of 1821, had assumed commercial and diplomatic ascendancy below the Rio Grande. A large

[7] Justin H. Smith, *The War with Mexico*, I, 120, states that "The *Picayune* was widely recognized as the best informed authority on Mexican affairs among our newspapers."

[8] Poinsett was followed by Anthony Butler, who in turn was recalled in 1835 at Mexico's request. Powhatan Ellis, the mild-mannered Democrat, followed him and was the minister on whom Kendall placed futile reliance for his release from prison in Mexico City in 1842. Ellis in turn was succeeded by General Waddy Thompson, who assumed credit for the eventual release of the prisoners.

part of the Mexican debt was held by British bondholders. Britain's traditional policy of supporting barriers to the extension of the United States had centered in Mexico in 1825, and for the next twenty years Mexico and Texas were used by British statesmen as pawns to stem the increasing tide of our westward expansion.

One of Poinsett's early assignments was to secure settlement of claims against the Mexican government growing out of acts of violence to citizens, and confiscation and loss of their property. Negotiations dragged on until 1842, and payments were started, but these stopped abruptly in 1843 after diplomatic relations between the countries became tense.

Bitterness of Mexicans toward the United States increased after the Texas revolution, and political leaders made capital of the widespread feeling that this country was responsible for Mexico's loss of Texas. They repeatedly promised to recapture the lost province, and when Texas and Mexico arranged an armistice in June, 1843, Santa Anna accepted with the insistence that final peace would come only through Texas' acknowledgement of Mexican sovereignty.

This alarmed advocates of annexation in the United States, and the alarm turned into a sectional dispute when England revived agitation for abolition of slavery in Texas. Aberdeen met a delegation of American and Texas abolitionists who had convened in London in July, 1843, to promote freedom of slaves in Texas. This incident raised a storm of protest in the South.

The United States had recognized Texas as an independent nation in 1837, but refused her request for annexation, partly because of the feeling that annexation at that time would have brought on an open conflict with Mexico. The matter of annexation, however, never was far beneath the surface of politics. Southern newspapers and expansionists in Washington brought it up again and again, particularly after England's interest in Mexico and Texas came to light.

England's foreign office repeatedly refused to recognize the independence of Texas, insisting that recognition on the part of Mexico should come first. However, in 1840, Palmerston started negotiations which led to the ratification of treaties in 1842.[9] The signing of these treaties brought to Texas Captain Charles Elliot as chargé d'affaires for Great Britain, a man whom the *Picayune* was to single out as the archenemy of its cherished annexation program.[10]

Elliot arrived in Galveston on August 23, 1842, three months after Kendall's release in Mexico and at a time when many newspapers were reprinting his articles on his experiences. The United States still seethed over the whole Santa Fe Expedition episode. Before the end of the year Elliot was working on a fantastic dream of making Texas a strong free-soil republic, with Great Britain's aid, and with a permanent inside track for British interests there.

Through 1842 repeated Mexican forays across the Rio Grande, coupled with the ill-advised attempts of Texans at retaliation, led many Texas newspapers to clamor for annexation to the United States as a means of peace and safety. This agitation, together with the widespread concern over British abolitionist activities and the growing hostility between the United States and Mexico, led President Tyler's administration in 1843 to make a definite proposal to Texas to join the Union.

The treaty was drawn up, but on June 8, 1844, the United States Senate rejected it. Tyler immediately announced plans to submit to Congress a proposal to annex Texas by joint resolution.

Through 1844 Aberdeen was perfecting his plans to unite with France in preventing annexation through armed interven-

[9] Three treaties had been signed in 1840: November 13, regarding commerce and navigation; November 14, on arrangements relative to the public debt; November 16, regarding mutual rights of search.

[10] Ephraim Douglas Adams, *British Interest and Activities in Texas* (Baltimore, 1910), 106–108. Elliot, born in 1801, was the son of Hugh Elliot, minister to Saxony and intimate friend of the younger Pitt. Captain Elliot had been in Guiana and China, where he participated in the "Opium War" and had arranged for the treaty which followed in 1842. This was later disavowed and Elliot was recalled, discredited.

tion. His proposal was that Mexico should recognize Texas' independence, and England and France then would guarantee territorial limits of Texas, together with her independence.

However, time and again an energetic New Orleans press upset Aberdeen's plans. The *Picayune,* followed by its contemporaries, unmasked his agents at a critical point in their operations. These disclosures aroused the United States and infuriated the Texans, who rejected the British-inspired Mexican offer of recognition. The move for annexation turned into a stampede.

Time was an important factor in these developments. Messages and instructions went from the Secretary of State in Washington to his agents in Texas in three weeks. It took two months, sometimes longer, for the British foreign office to communicate with its representatives in Mexico and Texas, and all the while Kendall and the *Picayune* correspondents dogged their footsteps, relaying news that often changed the course of events while the slow British communications were on their way.

Early in 1842, the *Picayune* criticized the administration of President Sam Houston and suggested that Texas should find some means of getting rid of him "if he is trying to sell the liberty of his country, and there are those who think he is. . . ."[11] It watched the activities of Captain Elliot and M. de Saligny, French chargé d'affaires in Texas, and late that year reported English and French collaboration in mediation for peace between Texas and Mexico.

When Tyler proposed the annexation treaty, the *Picayune* turned loose its pent-up enthusiasm: "The question of the annexation of Texas to the United States—ever deemed grave, momentous and pregnant with far-reaching consequences—has sprung into sudden and startling importance." People of the South, it pointed out, long had insisted on the justice, policy and absolute necessity of adding Texas to the Union, "to recover back for the United States a magnificent territory . . . to do away with the necessity of protecting a long line of frontier from smugglers;

[11] *Picayune,* May 20, 1842.

to defeat the insidious policy of England, for it is believed by many that she is aiming to attack us in our slave property by adding another Canada upon our borders; in fine, to prevent Texas, now that many of her first men find it impossible to support a government with so small a population, from either throwing herself into the arms or falling into the clutches of Great Britain. . . ."[12]

The *Picayune* admitted that in the North the question was generally viewed in a different light, but was gratified that the matter was not considered a party issue. "Texas will become a great commercial depot for the trade of England and other European powers," it warned. "English emigration, English capital, English commerce, English enterprise and English influence will overwhelm and swallow up everything that is American, and estrange the people of Texas from their loyalty to the United States."[13]

The paper reported that Elliot and Saligny had conferred in Galveston, and pointed out that the British Anti-Slavery Association had proposed to pay Texas the sum of six million dollars on condition that she emancipate her slaves. It quoted both the Clay and the Van Buren letters on annexation, and gave considerable space to the fact that Senator Barrow of Louisiana opposed the ratification of the treaty.[14] But even before the treaty came up to a vote the paper was looking ahead to Tyler's next move. "The English and the Abolition Party will yet be defeated," it predicted on July 16. "Texas will yet be annexed to the United States before the adjournment of the present session of Congress. Immediately upon rejection of the treaty the President will unquestionably (we think) annex Texas by joint resolution."

After the Senate rejected the treaty, and while the country was discussing Tyler's joint resolution proposal, the *Picayune*

[12] *Ibid.,* March 26, 1844.

[13] *Ibid.,* April 11, 1844.

[14] Henry Clay, outstanding candidate for Whig nomination for the presidency, and Martin Van Buren, the popular Democratic candidate, both agreed in open letters not to make the Texas question an issue in the coming campaign.

kept on pointing out Mexican military moves. Santa Anna had ordered General Adrian Woll to proclaim the end of the armistice with Texas, and the immediate renewal of hostilities. Woll was to advance into Texas. Santa Anna had called on the Mexican Congress to furnish him with thirty thousand men and four million dollars for use against Texas.

The *Picayune* quoted the report of an Englishman, a friend of Elliot, indicating "that England had advised Mexico under no circumstances to acknowledge the independence of Texas, but keep up an armistice with her as long as possible; and in case a successful attempt at annexation between the United States and Texas took place, then to go to war, and England would back her in the contest."

All during this interval messages between Aberdeen and his agents in Mexico were trailing back and forth across the Atlantic at a snail's pace, far too slowly to keep up with events on this hemisphere.

By June, 1844, Aberdeen had his plans well shaped to step in with France and prevent annexation by the use of their combined armies and navies. On June 2 he tried to get from Ashbel Smith, Texas minister to England, a definite pledge that Texas would not permit herself to be annexed to the United States in case Mexico should make peace. Smith replied that he believed Texas would prefer independence if her boundaries were guaranteed, peace assured, and if a treaty of commerce with Spain enabled her to trade with Cuba.[15]

The New Orleans press reported England's plans for enlarging her naval squadron in the Pacific so as to be in position to seize ports in Oregon in case of a rupture between Great Britain and the United States.

Aberdeen, had the plans for armed intervention matured, could call on the British Navy, which at this time had six hundred and eighty ships of war, carrying from one to one hundred and twenty guns. One hundred and twenty-five of these were armed

[15] For Aberdeen's correspondence, see Adams, *op. cit.*, 155–95.

steam vessels. Their forces included "23,000 able bodied sea-men, 2,000 stout lads and 94 companies of royal marines."[16]

The Washington *Union* reported that the United States Navy included ten ships of the line, one razee, twelve frigates, first class, and two second class; seventeen sloops of war, first class, and six second class; eight brigs, eight schooners, eight steamers, and four store ships—a total of sixty-eight.[17]

In Washington, Tyler was moving promptly. Three days after the Senate rejected the Texas treaty, he outlined his plan for se-curing annexation by joint resolution. Sir Richard Pakenham, British minister in Washington, urged that the time was not ripe to disclose Aberdeen's plan of combined French and English in-terference. The French minister agreed, and Guizot withdrew French consent to the plan for joint action.

Meanwhile the Texas question had been made the issue of a presidential campaign. The Democrats shelved Martin Van Buren for a dark horse candidate, James K. Polk, and wrote an annexation platform that carried Polk to the presidency in the November elections.

When Aberdeen's peace plan of May reached his minister, Bankhead, in Mexico late in August, the program of joint inter-vention had long since been discarded. But Bankhead did not know this. He discussed the matter with Santa Anna, but the lat-ter's reactions were exactly opposite those hoped for in the original scheme. He proposed to raise all the troops possible and plunge immediately into the reconquest of Texas, which course he had been agitating since June, as the *Picayune* had reported earlier.

In September Bankhead's report of the threats Santa Anna made in June reached Aberdeen, and he replied that if Mexico attempted to recapture Texas, England would not help her. Both France and England were watching the American presidential campaign. In December, after Polk's election, a revolution drove

16 New Orleans *Bee*, May 29, 1845.
17 New Orleans *Tropic*, May 22, 1845, quoting the Washington *Union*.

131

Santa Anna into exile and Mexico was freed from his bombast for another year and a half. However, the succeeding administration was thoroughly committed to the recapture of Texas, even at the cost of a war with the United States.

Late in December, 1844, Aberdeen wrote Elliot in Texas, Pakenham in Washington, and British agents in California that if possible annexation of Texas and California must be prevented, but they must pursue a passive course.

In uncovering this resistance, Kendall and the *Picayune* made perhaps their greatest contribution to the annexation of Texas. Polk's election and the apparent certainty of annexation discouraged Aberdeen, but his hopes were revived by Elliot's report that the new Texas president, Anson Jones, favored independence. He sent Elliot detailed instructions urging that Texas resist pressure from the United States.[18]

When news of the passage of the joint resolution for annexation reached New Orleans, the *Picayune* published an extra edition, then shook its fist in editorial triumph at England:

"We trust that it will become the settled policy of the Nation not to allow any further appropriation of the soil of America by European powers. The Western Hemisphere should be ruled by Western people . . ." Passage of the resolutions, it insisted, was "the triumph of American power over European arts; the triumph of republican energy over royal finesse; the triumph of free minds over the diplomacy of foreign taskmasters . . ."[19]

But the *Picayune* could not refrain from discussing Elliot. On March 25 it told of a letter he had written a year earlier to Jones, then secretary of state of the Republic of Texas, referring to a conference between these two and President Houston resulting in a pledge against Texas annexation. Four days later it was snapping at his heels again, when the steam packet *New York* brought news from Galveston. Just before she left, the paper stated, a British man-of-war brought a vast amount of money

18 Adams, *op. cit.*, 202.
19 *Picayune*, March 8, 1845.

with instructions to Elliot to offer to guarantee the national independence of Texas, provided the annexation resolutions were rejected. It further reported that the French government offered the same guarantee on the same conditions. Elliot set out immediately for the capital. Saligny was already there.

As Aberdeen had feared, expansionists were now looking toward the Pacific. The *Picayune* in April referred to the New York *Courier and Enquirer's* assertion that if Mexico declared war, the United States would also take California, adding that Mexico scarcely would declare war unless she wanted to get rid of more territory than was included in the Texas Resolutions.

The situation in Texas was becoming tense. Kendall went there to handle the news himself. His dispatches confirmed reports of Elliot's activities, and the *Picayune* published another extra. He reported Elliot's hurried trip to Washington on the Brazos and his return to Galveston with Saligny on April 1. He quoted the Galveston *News* as stating, "Now again our government is to be plied with English gold, and power, and influence, and with all the riches of her commerce."[20]

When Kendall's letters came in a week later, the paper issued still another extra. He insisted that the Texas government had been listening to the flattery of foreign ministers, "that Capt. Elliot and Mr. Saligny, between them, have poured the 'leprous distilment into the porches' of President Jones' ear by the quart. ... We much mistake the spirit of the Executive of the Republic, if Capt. Elliot and Mr. Saligny together can smother the will of the nation. . . ."

Before long Elliot had left the scene. "On Saturday last," Kendall wrote, "the Eurydice, British frigate, sailed from this port for Vera Cruz, with dispatches for Mr. Bankhead—on the same day the Electra, British sloop of war, sailed for Bermuda, with Capt. Elliot on board. He was to be left at Charleston. . . . When he left Washington, it was with the understanding that as much delay as possible might be used by the President in calling

20 *Ibid.*, April 8, 1845.

Congress together, so that he might ascertain what terms Mexico could be induced to assent to through the influence of his government."[21]

Kendall went on to Houston, to sound public opinion there. "Were it not for the half promises made by the agents of the English and French governments," he wrote, "of the unconditional recognition of Texan independence by Mexico, the opening of the ports of that Republic to the free admission of Texas cotton, and all that sort of thing, I am induced to believe that nine-tenths of the inhabitants would go in for the resolutions as passed by the United States Senate at once."

Kendall reported that Dr. Ashbel Smith, Texas secretary of war, had left Houston for Galveston on his way to the United States. A *Picayune* reporter met him at the wharf in New Orleans and found that he was accompanied by Saligny who "asserted, in terms rather more peremptory than are usually employed by diplomatic agents, that annexation will not (shall not) take place."[22]

Smith was in a mellow mood and jokingly said that he was "about to go to England, to get the money for which Texas was to be sold."[23] Many persons believed he was in earnest, and the *Picayune* warned that if Elliot had so far subdued President Jones that the people were to be denied the right of expressing their minds on annexation, "the Executive of the United States would be sustained in using the military force of the country in freeing the Republic from the tyranny of foreign dictation."[24]

When the Mexican minister of foreign affairs addressed a note in April to the ministers of England, France and Spain, announcing Mexico's preparations for war in case of annexation, the *Picayune* urged the United States to take proper precautions. The United States had 7,200 men under arms at this time, and already the bulk of these, under General Zachary Taylor, had been moved to Fort Jessup in western Louisiana. Three months

[21] *Picayune* extra, April 14, 1846.
[22] *Picayune*, April 15, 1844.
[23] *Ibid.*, April 17, 1844.
[24] *Loc. cit.*

were to elapse before he moved this force to the mouth of the Rio Grande.

A *Picayune* correspondent in London wrote to warn against a war fever that had suddenly broken out in England, and urged citizens to prepare cotton bales for a bombardment.

Then the *Picayune* levelled its editorial artillery in the general direction of England, pointing out that the British seized, month after month, an island here and an island there, yet said to us "Thus far shalt thou come, and no farther. . . . It is not to be endured that Great Britain should hem us in on three sides with her military posts and naval stations, and then threaten war because we will not allow her to complete the cordon." The people of the United States, it asserted, would not submit to this accumulation of insolence and wrong, and the stand "may as well be taken now."[25]

This agitation began to bear fruit. On May 13 the paper published resolutions passed by Texans at Matagorda, resolving that they had heard with astonishment and indignation of the appointment of a minister from Texas to England and France, which with the delay in calling Congress, "is well calculated to excite our distrust in the action of the President." They resolved further "that delay is useless, as we wish to see no overtures from any government save that of the United States." Resolutions also came in from Colorado County echoing the *Picayune's* criticism of Elliot and Saligny, "The circumstances connected with their busy meddling in the annexations are . . . notorious," and "Ashbel Smith was despatched to England upon a mission hostile to Annexation."[26]

[25] *Ibid.*, May 3, 1845. This was no new protest for the New Orleans press. As early as April 19, 1842, the *Bee* had stated that "a letter from Vera Cruz of April 7th, speaks of rumor prevailing there and generally credited that Santa Anna was negotiating a loan of $7,000,000 with the British government on a pledge of the peninsula of California. It is to be hoped for the preservation of the peace already threatened between Great Britain and the United States, that it is not true. The United States feel already enough of the encroachments of that power upon every border of her country."

[26] *Ibid.*, May 13, 1845.

The *Picayune* editors watched for comment in the London *Times,* which they called "The anointed thunderer of the 'swell heads' of Great Britain." They pointed out its comment that in case of war between Mexico and the United States, Mexico would surely win.[27]

The results of the frenzied activities of Elliot and Saligny in late March and early April, at the time Kendall went over to take a hand in Texas news coverage, came to light in May with news that Luis G. Cuevas, Mexican minister of foreign affairs, had presented to the chamber of deputies "Texas's plea for recognition."

The New Orleans *Tropic* was surprised, but the *Picayune* was not.[28] Its editorial columns pointed out that a few more such developments would convince even the most skeptical that "a deep, not to say disgraceful, intrigue has been long on foot, in which the British Minister to Texas, the President of Texas, and probably Capt. Elliot's shadow are implicated." Although proof did not come to light for some time, Elliot had secured the signatures of Smith and Jones to a document agreeing not to accept any proposals for ninety days.[29] But the *Picayune* was hot on the story. It boasted, "The next time the parties engage in a traffic of the sort, they ought to put this motto on the lentils [*sic*] of their doors:

> *A chiel's amang ye takin' notes,*
> *An' faith he'll prent 'em.*[30]

Then without warning, all of the *Picayune's* drudgery in gathering news around the Gulf, all its investment in planting

27 *Ibid.,* May 17, 1845. This was the widespread opinion, expressed frequently in British, French, and Mexican papers. Smith, *op. cit.,* 106–109.

28 *Ibid.,* May 20, 1845, and *Tropic and American Republican,* May 20, 1845. The *Picayune* claimed that the communication "settles the matter beyond all 'ifs and buts' and proves very conclusively that President Jones and his cabinet have been pestering Mexico to acknowledge Texian independence in the hope that such acknowledgement by gratifying the national pride of the Texians might induce them to reject annexation. We entertain no such belief."

29 Adams, *op. cit.,* 210. The *Picayune* of July 6, 1845, carried a digest of the proposed treaty between Texas and Mexico, and pointed out that the conditions of this treaty were signed by Ashbel Smith on the previous March 29.

30 *Picayune,* May 21, 1845.

watchful correspondents in out-of-the-way places suddenly paid dividends in a spectacular way. Its "chiel amang ye" in Vera Cruz spotted Elliot in that city when he was supposed to be on the high seas bound for Charleston.

The *Picayune* stormed. Was it possible that President Jones had secretly sent commissioners to Mexico under the patronage of England? Had Elliot sneaked off to Mexico to get a sly advantage? Was the President attempting to sacrifice the people of Texas?

So excited was the paper that contemporaries believed it doubted its own story. But confirmation came three days later, with details. Then the *Picayune* snapped its fingers and boasted of its widespread news dragnet. Since the United States was to be made the victim of iniquitous purposes, and Texas sacrificed to the policy of foreign governments, "It behooved us to establish extensive means of information in such quarters as were likely to be the scenes of operation, and in a manner so systematic as to be scarcely liable to mistake or imposition. As yet we have not been led astray by a single error when we relied upon these means for the whole truth."

Then it enlarged upon the Elliot trick: "The intrigues which we have felt it our duty to expose, the secret negotiations and mysterious movements of official conspirators that we have been compelled, from a sense of the obligations which our relations to the public impose upon us, to lay bare to the gaze of the world, have been so fraught with crime, so marked with duplicity, so overcharged with baseness, that we have not been surprised that some of our contemporaries have hesitated to put full faith in the revelations we have made."[31]

The report from Mexico stated that the bill authorizing the foreign minister to negotiate a treaty with Texas for her independence, with the proviso that she should not be annexed to the United States, had passed the Mexican house of representatives and was being debated in the senate. The paper later was to learn

[31] *Ibid.*, May 21, 1845.

137

that Elliot had been in Mexico City for several weeks and was then in Vera Cruz waiting word from the senate before sailing for Galveston. The *Picayune* wasn't sure what Polk would do about it, but it was sure what Monroe or Madison would have done in the face of such unfriendly and insulting interference. It added, "The mention of Monroe's name in this regard makes the air have a gunpowder odor."[32]

It was revealed later that Elliot left Galveston on the *Electra* and was transferred to the *Eurydice,* bound for Vera Cruz. From there he traveled in great secrecy to Mexico City, where Cuevas promised quick approval of the recognition scheme. Three weeks elapsed, however, before he was able to start back, his identity still a secret.[33] It was on his return trip that the *Picayune* correspondent identified Elliot. When confirmation of the first report came in, the New Orleans *Tropic* and the *Courier de la Louisiane* took up the story, the *Bee* ignored it for a time, and the *Republican* scoffed at the importance the *Picayune* attached to it.

Elliot's mysterious companion was mistaken by the *Courier* for Ashbel Smith, but the *Picayune* said no, Ashbel was due to return to Texas soon from England with considerations "identical with those for which Judas Iscariot betrayed the Savior of the World."[34]

Soon this elusive diplomat was referred to as "the man with the white hat." The *Republican,* in defending President Jones, ridiculed the *Picayune* for its "mysterious bugaboo of the *man with the white hat*—a sort of diplomatic raw-head-and-bloody-bones, who seems to have been conjured up just to set people to guessing and gossiping . . ."[35]

[32] *Ibid.,* May 24, 1845.

[33] Adams, *op. cit.,* 214, states that "when the report of the Mexican mission appeared in the public press in the U. S. it aroused the greatest indignation. Here was a capital opportunity to charge Great Britain with 'secret' designs, it being known that Elliot had had a 'secret' part in it."

[34] *Picayune,* May 25, 1845.

[35] *Ibid.,* May 31, 1845. Denis Corcoran, popular police reporter of the *Picayune,* wrote one of his police court gems about a "man in the white hat," a prisoner

President Jones announced an election for the convention that actually was to consider both the Mexican proposal and annexation, but the furor in the New Orleans press continued. The *Bee* and the skeptical *Republican* took up the cry, and Elliot found his name on every hand linked with "the man in the white hat."

He returned to Galveston on May 30, then made a hurried trip to the seat of government and back to Galveston, but the ridicule of the *Picayune* and its contemporaries made him so unpopular that he gave up his office and came on to the United States. The *Picayune* presumed that he was content "for having produced confusion in Texas as he did in China."[36]

When the fact became known that Elliot returned to Galveston, not in the *Eurydice,* but in the French war vessel *La Perouse,* the *Picayune* pointed out that he had two navies to carry him on his missions. The barrage continued until the Texas convention met in Austin. Galveston was excited and many Texans throughout the Republic were infuriated at Elliot's actions.

Kendall's dramatic unmasking of the "man with the white hat" had its effect. When the delegates assembled they quickly rejected the Mexican proposal and voted overwhelmingly for annexation.

---

in the Recorder's Court, with mysterious documents regarding annexation which proved to be only letters pertaining to his "reannexation to his estranged wife."

[36] *Ibid.,* June 18, 1845. The *Courier* announced Elliot's arrival on June 2, but at that time he was in the Texas capital. He got to New Orleans on June 18. Adams, *op. cit.,* 223, states, "Elliot . . . was reproved and ordered to return" to his post "at once, to close his office when the formalities were concluded and return to England. In the last month or so of his stay, however, Elliot was more occupied in meeting the American attacks occasioned by his secret mission than he was with the dignity of England or the affairs of Texas."

The *Picayune* chuckled when it learned that Elliot had been held up and robbed by the notorious *ladrones* on his trip from Mexico City to Vera Cruz. He was stripped of his possessions and left standing by the highway in his shirt. Governor Wilson Shannon, United States minister to Mexico, was also held up and beaten by these brigands. See *Picayune,* July 4, June 21, 1845.

13

War with Mexico

THERE WAS AN UNUSUAL STIR, little connected with the momentous proposals for Texas annexation, in the City Court of New Orleans on the morning of September 9, 1845. Through the hot summer an argument had raged up and down Camp Street, because the *Picayune* had printed the account of a master beating his slave.

Denis Corcoran had picked up the story in May when Sylvester, a mulatto boy, sought refuge in the city jail after a terrible whipping. The *Picayune* was indignant that there was no law in Louisiana that might bring the owner to justice. There had been a case in the Felicianas where an owner beat a slave so that she died, and he was sentenced to the penitentiary for life. But Sylvester had not died. Also, in Kentucky the law took a slave away from an owner who abused him.

Clement de Neufbourg, Sylvester's master, threatened suit, and the French side of the *Courier* criticized the *Picayune* as not being prudent and proper in calling the case to the attention of the public. The *Picayune* insisted that it was the business of the press to try to correct abuses, and the *Tropic* agreed, and when Sylvester's master filed suit against the two papers, the *Picayune* warned, "He will have a great deal of lawing to do before he deters men from expressing their opinion upon a transaction that was a disgrace to our city, an outrage against humanity, and a stain upon the law of the land." The case was called in June, then postponed until the fall term. Corcoran was called to the stand, and his testimony won the verdict for the paper.

Corcoran by this time was among the most popular of the *Picayune's* staff of reporters. His humorous sketches of scenes in the Recorder's Court helped build up the circulation of the paper shortly after its establishment. Taking a hint from the New York *Sun* and the New York *Herald,* whose police court reports were read eagerly by the poorer subscribers, Corcoran poured all of his native humor into his stories, occasionally turning in a pathetic essay or one that burned with satire.

For an interval in 1843 Corcoran was the *Picayune's* correspondent in Cuba, sending back a column of "Hieroglyphics on Havana." But when he took the stand to testify in the libel suit against the *Picayune* he already had made plans to leave its staff and start a rival paper, the New Orleans *Delta.*[1]

When the *Delta* started, it began a rivalry with the *Picayune* that did not cease until the *Delta* shop was confiscated by federal troops in 1862. Its correspondent, James L. Freaner, who wrote under the name of "Mustang," was Kendall's strongest competitor in covering the Mexican War. Four *Picayune* staff members took part in the *Delta's* establishment. Corcoran and M. G. Davis, also of the editorial staff, were listed as publishers, and Alexander H. Hayes, a *Picayune* compositor, and J. E. "Sam" McClure of the circulation department were partners in the venture. John Maginnis soon left the *Picayune* business office to join the *Delta,* and Alexander Walker, a rising young New Orleans attorney and strong southern Democrat, joined Corcoran's editorial staff.

These new partners, however, failed to take with them the spirit of harmony that they might have learned from their years with Kendall and Lumsden and Holbrook. Within a short time they failed to agree on policy, probably because of Judge Wal-

---

[1] The *Delta* started publication October 12, 1845. Corcoran's sketches, which have been erroneously credited to Kendall himself, were published in 1843 under the title *Pickings from the Portfolio of the New Orleans 'Picayune.'*

ker's strong Democratic leanings, and in 1848 Hayes and Mc-
Clure left the *Delta* to establish the New Orleans *Crescent*, which
was to become one of the strongest papers in the South in the late
1850's. The *Delta* staff split again in 1849 when Maginnis and
Davis withdrew to establish the New Orleans *Daily True Delta*.

The *Picayune* was taking other losses in its early staff, paying
the toll of old age though it had not yet reached the stature of ten
years. With grief it recorded the death of William H. Flood, only
thirty years old, "who set up the first stickful of type that went
into the columns of the *Picayune*."[2] It had already recorded the
death of M. C. Field ("Phasma") whose sketches on western ex-
ploration had proved so popular.

Kendall, who later wrote to his wife, "I am glad that I know
so many ways to make a living," valued versatility among his staff
members, and knew the value to his paper of everything its mak-
ers did to draw the spotlight. The quality was exemplified in the
person of "Phasma's" brother, "Straws" (J. M. Field), not only
a "favorite actor and popular editor," but poet and playwright as
well. His play, "Such as It Is," opened at the Park Theater, New
York, on September 11, 1842, with Field playing the principal
part, and the *Picayune* reported that it proved a hit with New
Yorkers. When he returned to New Orleans with Mrs. Field in
1846, after an absence of two years, to play an engagement at the
St. Charles Theatre, the *Picayune* gave him much publicity.[3]

These losses in staff were partly offset by the work of George
Porter, another young man with a most varied background. He
was the younger brother of William T. Porter, Kendall's friend
who edited the New York *Spirit of the Times*. A native of Vermont, young Porter entered Dartmouth College at the age of
fourteen and was graduated with honors, studied law in the offices
of George Brinkerhoff in New York City and entered into part-

[2] *Picayune*, April 23, 1846.

[3] *Ibid.*, Sept. 11 and 17, 1842 ; January 6, 1846. Field was later editor of the
St. Louis *Reveille*. Their daughter, Kate Field, was widely known in newspaper
and theatrical circles.

nership with Brinkerhoff and Edward Curtis. He gave up his practice to become coeditor with his brother of the *Spirit of the Times,* where he learned sports reporting and dramatic criticism, joined the *Picayune* as associate editor in November, 1842, and remained until his death in May, 1849.

The prolonged depression which paralyzed New Orleans shortly after the *Picayune* was founded had finally run its course, and in 1845 the city was entering upon a great period of expansion.

Twenty-six nations had resident consuls there at this time. Besides the chief European countries and the neighboring Brazil, Montevideo, Mexico, and Texas, the list included the smaller countries of Belgium, Holland, and Portugal. There were also representatives from those states which later were to be merged into Germany—Baden, Bremen, Hamburg, Hanover, Prussia, Saxony, and Wurtemburg—and from Rome, Sardinia, and Sicily, which were to form the nucleus of united Italy.

As trade boomed down the Mississippi, demand for space in the *Picayune,* both for news and advertising linage, became so great that on October 28, 1845, the partners reluctantly expanded its size to seven columns, stating that the change "has almost literally been forced upon us." The paper thus remained four pages, but increased its space one-sixth. However, on that morning the *Picayune's* press, which had served for years "with very remarkable fidelity," broke down and the paper had to be printed on the *Delta's* press.

In these years the *Picayune* prospered tremendously. In the thirteen months from November 19, 1844, when Bullitt became a partner, until the end of 1845, income from advertising and subscriptions totalled $44,797.44, and unpaid advertising accounts and expenses of running the paper amounted to $17,-163.08, leaving a cash income for the period of $26,365.64. In this interval the job shop did a gross business of $16,733.28, with $6,640.70 net. Active accounts in this statement showed that "book accounts," probably advertising and uncollected bills for job printing and notes, amounted to $23,477.51. There was due for *Weekly Picayune* subscriptions $29,454.00 and for the daily, $6,612.00.[4]

The weekly edition was made up from type picked up from the daily, and carried no advertising. The subscriptions in arrears indicate its wide circulation. The large amounts of the bills receivable at that time—more than $50,000 for subscriptions and advertising—is explained by the prevailing custom of settling accounts annually or semiannually. On January 1 the *Picayune* announced, "Mr. J. E. McClure is our authorized agent for the collection of debts due the *Picayune* in Mississippi and Alabama," and on February 11, "Mr. J. B. Weld, our regularly authorized agent, is about starting on a tour through this state for the purpose of collecting all subscriptions and other debts . . . we do not trouble our friends in the interior but once a year, and trust they will cheerfully settle up arrearages . . . which we now stand in need of."

During this thirteen months' interval the partners had drawn out $16,729.57 as their share of the profits, distributed as follows: Kendall, $6,018.04; Lumsden, $4,868.33; Holbrook, $2,-994.27, and Bullitt, $2,848.93.

A composite statement of earnings of the paper, filed with the inventory of the property after Kendall's death, showed that during the five-year period prior to Bullitt's joining the firm, Kendall's portion of its earnings was $29,900.00 and that Lumsden and Holbrook each drew half of this amount. This shows clearly why, in its early years, Kendall was called "the principal editor of the New Orleans *Picayune*." It also is a tribute to the energy of these three young men that a small four-page daily, a job shop, and a weekly that carried no advertising could have earned for them $59,000 in little more than five years. During a part of that

[4] This statement of "copartnership affairs of Lumsden, Kendall, Holbrook and Bullitt in the Daily and Weekly 'Picayune' " and the composite statement of affairs of the firm from the time Holbrook joined it in May, 1839, until May 31, 1867, are included in the Kendall papers.

time, too, the nation was wallowing in the worst depression it had known.

From 1844 until 1855, when S. F. Wilson joined the firm, the four partners shared equally in the profits of the paper. The 1845 financial statement shows, "We have Book Accounts, Notes & Viz." a total of $76,291.33, and included among these were "Slave Sam, $608.00," "Slave Oliver, $506.50," and "Slave Sandy, $703.68."[5]

The *Picayune's* earnings were to increase during the next ten years, but its expenses, particularly the cost of covering the Mexican War, mounted to a high figure. Already, in 1845, the cost of securing news was a heavy item. So the paper agitated for reduction of the letter rates from twenty-five cents to ten cents within the three-hundred-mile zone, and pointed out that "the freight on a letter weighing an *ounce* from New York to New Orleans is one dollar, but a *pound* of cotton is carried from this city to Liverpool for one halfpenny."

The *Picayune* looked to the telegraph to break down the stranglehold which the government had placed on efforts to get news quickly. In connection with its stories of the Democratic national convention at Baltimore it reported that the "magnetic telegraph was now kept in continual operation during the day, so that editors in Washington were apprised of what was going on, almost instantaneously after anything transpired." A week later, after a wire breakdown, the paper reported, "The telegraph has been put to work again, and Baltimore and Washington are chatting together as cosily as two old gossips over their tea."[6]

Then too, Kendall and other editors were looking to the railroads to bring them the speed of travel that the North already

[5] Apparently each of the three partners had an office slave in the early days of the *Picayune,* for on Kendall's return from a trip to Texas in 1852 he wrote his wife, "Were it not Sunday I should go immediately to the office . . . Mr. H. has the keys, and Sandy could not get at my letters. Speaking of Sandy, you should have seen him when I first got home, should have witnessed his happiness on seeing Master George once more. He is the best colored man alive—true and faithful as steel—and as long as he lives he shall have a good home."

[6] *Picayune,* June 7 and 15, 1844.

enjoyed. The South depended largely on river travel, which could be had at a bargain if one were not in a hurry—only ten dollars for a cabin passage from Cincinnati to New Orleans, a distance of 1,600 miles. This included board, "and," boasted the *Picayune,* "at tables as well and profusely filled, as can be found at any hotel in the country, and in as splendid boats as can be found afloat."

But when Kendall went north in 1844 he longed for the South to achieve the miracles that fifteen years of railroad building had accomplished in southern New England. He made the trip from Boston to New York in one day, by taking the "train of cars" from Worcester to Norwich, then a two-hour boat ride across the sound to Greenport, Long Island, "resuming the cars" there.[7]

Not only by trips to the North and West, but through his exchanges, Kendall and his staff kept in close touch with all that was going on in the whole of North America. But Kendall's greatest interest was never far from Texas, where his eyes were turned toward the future. At this early date the *Picayune* was waging a serious campaign for subsistence farming rather than the one-crop system in general use in the South.

This matter was dear to Kendall's heart; he was beginning, in 1845, the program he carried out in practice and agitated through his years as a farmer in Texas, and which the paper has continued through almost a century. "When it is known," the *Picayune* argued editorially, "that a crop of seventeen hundred thousand bales will fetch more money than one of twenty-four hundred thousand, it seems strange that planters do not employ their labor in producing other products than cotton . . . that planter will do well who converts his estate into a farm, properly so called, producing every thing that he needs at home, and send-

---

[7] Kendall was much disturbed, on this trip, over the growing excitement which he found concerning abolition. His boyhood neighborhood was a hotbed of anti-slavery activity. He wrote the *Picayune* that Northampton, Massachusetts, was "tainted with abolitionism to an extent greater, perhaps, than any other town of its size. . . . The great misfortune of the inhabitants appears to be, that they have no business of their own to attend to, and hence their great zeal in endeavoring to regulate the affairs and domestic institutions of their Southern brethern."

ing to market only the surplusages raised upon it. . . . No agricultural country can prosper, where the producers buy all they use and sell all they raise."

Much of the early migration to Texas had cleared through New Orleans, but now a great many wagon trains were going westward through the settlements in northern Louisiana. The *Picayune* quoted the Shreveport *Gazette* reporting a "stream of Texas emigrants—men, women, and children. The latter abounded but their faces were so dirty it was impossible to count them."

Almost any item about Texas or Texans was news. It was worth mention when Sam Houston, on his way to Washington as United States senator from Texas, walked down Camp Street wearing a Mexican blanket and attracting the attention of the crowds.

Although the Texas convention had approved the annexation proposal, formal ratification was not completed until February, 1846. But even before the convention had acted, the *Picayune* warned of Mexican troops on the Rio Grande and stated, "It behooves our Government at once to march an efficient force to the frontiers of Texas. So long as the negotiations are pending . . . not a single Mexican should set foot on this side of the Rio Grande."

Looking forward to the acceptance of the annexation proposal, and concerned with the warlike attitude of Mexico, the War Department ordered General Taylor to an embarkation point to be ready to sail for Texas. Taylor moved his infantry to New Orleans, sailed for Aransas Bay, Texas, in July, 1845, and moved on to Corpus Christi. Mexico already had broken off diplomatic relations. John Slidell was sent to Mexico City as minister, with authority to make a substantial payment to settle boundary disputes, but when news came in January, 1846, that Slidell was not received, Taylor was ordered to march for the Rio Grande. By April 7 he had started construction of a fort opposite Matamoros.

By this time another menace to the United States was rearing its head below the Rio Grande. Earlier, the *Picayune* recalled, there had been a plan afoot to place Louis Philippe's son on the Mexican throne, and failure to prevent annexation of Texas had caused taunts across the English Channel. Now the proposal had been revived, with variations: "The idea of reducing Mexican states to Colonial dependencies upon old Spain has met with favor in many quarters; the proposal of the Bourbon family has again been discussed; and a triple alliance between France, England, and Spain for the direction of Mexican and Central American affairs proposed and considered." The delay, in the opinion of the *Picayune,* was due to quarrels over the booty. The administration of Herrera, which succeeded Santa Anna's overthrow, was swallowed up in another revolution, and Paredes now was in power. Kendall believed that this shakeup was of foreign inspiration, to cripple relations with the United States.[8]

Coincident with this threat of monarchy, England was sending thirty ships of the line to the Gulf of Mexico. The Oregon dispute, the crisis in our relations with Mexico, the frequent marauding expeditions of Mexicans in southern Texas—all these, in the opinion of the *Picayune,* were a part of the continued intrigue directed against the United States from European capitals.

When Taylor with his command was on the march from Corpus Christi, an open outbreak of hostilities was narrowly averted at the Arroyo Colorado. There General Mejía, commander at Matamoros, confronted the American column, but withdrew when Taylor sent his advance guard across despite Mejía's warning.

With the opening actual warfare now only a matter of time, Kendall moved closer to the scene of action. He went to Torrey's station on the Brazos, north of Austin, to report a council the United States government was holding with the Indians who

[8] *Picayune,* January 25, 1846. The overthrow of the Paredes government on the following August 4 was due partly to widespread opposition to its well-known monarchial policy.

ranged the vast western stretches of the new state. Kendall never had seen the Comanches in camp, and he swore he would not have missed the sight, even though his journey took more than two weeks and wore out a fine team of horses. The Indian chiefs filed in in regular order, old Mopechocopee, their civil chief, in the lead, followed by a host of mounted women and children. The old chief was dressed only in a coarse tow shirt, but the younger chiefs were rigged out in all their finery and painted in fantastic colors. "The wild night dances of the Tonkoways and Lipans, carried on for twelve, sixteen or twenty hours at a time without cessation, would excite most especial wonder in those who had never seen them before," he wrote the *Picayune*.

While Kendall was arranging to send his friend, Porter of the *Spirit of the Times*, a gift of a bearskin, Comanche bows, arrows, and a tomahawk, and was watching the ceremonies that preceded the signing of the treaty, General Taylor's force on the bank of the Rio Grande was virtually surrounded. General Ampudia had assumed command and ordered Taylor to remove beyond the Nueces River. Taylor replied by having the United States Navy blockade the mouth of the Rio Grande. As the Americans worked to complete their fort, parties of Mexican lancers frequently were seen in the nearby mesquite thickets. On April 10, Colonel Truman Cross, acting assistant quartermaster general, failed to return from a ride back of the camp. Lieutenant H. T. Porter and a detachment searching for a clue to the disappearance of Cross were ambushed on the nineteenth, and Porter was killed. The body of Cross was found the next day, badly mutilated, about a mile and a half from the camp. Still General Taylor waited.

General Arista arrived in Matamoros on April 24 to supplant Ampudia, and one of his first acts was to send General Torrejón across the Rio Grande with a force of sixteen hundred men. Taylor heard a rumor of this move and sent Captain Thornton up the river with sixty dragoons to investigate. This little band was ambushed the next day, several were slain and the remainder captured. American troops had been attacked in force north of the

Rio Grande. The war, which had been brewing so long, had started.[9]

News of the outbreak of hostilities swept back through the Texas settlements slowly, because of the difficulties of travel. Reports of the ambuscades reached the camp on the council grounds on May 8, eighteen days after the body of Cross was found. On that afternoon General Taylor had fought his first pitched battle with General Arista at Palo Alto.

"I had anticipated remaining here until the great Indian treaty came off, which will take place probably next week," Kendall wrote the *Picayune,* "but an express has come in from Austin with the exciting intelligence of the murder of Col. Cross on the Rio Grande and the commencement of hostilities with the Mexicans, and I am off tomorrow in the direction of Matamoros."

The adventure which was to make Kendall the first modern war correspondent and the most widely known reporter in America in his day, had begun.

[9] Taylor's dispatch telling of Thornton's capture reached President Polk on Saturday, May 9, and this news led to the declaration of war by Congress on the following Monday. Kendall and his friends in Texas considered that war had broken out when news of the slaying of Colonel Cross arrived. He described these events in detail in his manuscript, "History of the Mexican War," 84–90.

14

First modern
war correspondent

NEWS OF THE WAR sent Kendall hurrying to the border, more than four hundred miles away, in company with a single rider. He left coverage of the treaty negotiations to one of his correspondents, "Buffalo Hump," whose story reached the *Picayune* six weeks later, and with a "Dr. Beard," one of his party on the trip up through the buffalo range, rode southward out of the Indian encampment on May 9.

One hundred and fifty miles north of Houston Kendall left Dr. Beard behind and galloped on alone until he caught up with other Texans headed for the conflict. He paused at "Bucksnort— you cannot find it on the map—near the falls of the Brazos," then at Lagrange, to write hurried notes to the *Picayune*, and was off again.

He reached Corpus Christi May 25 and hired a Mexican guide to take him to Point Isabel by a shorter route than the one that had taken Taylor's cavalry sixteen days during the excellent March weather. However, spring rains had flooded the whole Rio Grande valley and turned every dry arroyo into a lagoon or a dangerous torrent. He and his party had to travel at night because during the hot days swarms of prairie flies tormented the horses.

By now the party had grown to nearly three hundred. Major Jack Hays, noted Texas Ranger and Indian fighter, Albert Sidney Johnston, Colonel Reuben Brown and Captain Chevalier rode into their camp at Agua Dulce, and a company of mounted men from Montgomery County joined them.

When the tide receded they got their horses across the muddy banks of the Arroyo Colorado, where they saw the bodies of seven settlers, one of them a woman, who had been massacred in a border raid several weeks earlier.

Kendall reached Point Isabel on June 6, thin from hard riding, but "well conditioned." The party camped at the outskirts of the settlement, and during the night a rainy norther drenched them and stampeded their horses, but he commented, "these things, however disagreeable, we are used to." The next night he reached Taylor's camp.

During this month when Kendall was riding for the border, General Taylor and his little army had won two brilliant victories north of the Rio Grande. When the Mexicans retreated into the interior, he had crossed the river to take over the city of Matamoros. The capture of Captain Thornton on April 25, following General Arista's ultimatum that he would fire on the Americans unless they abandoned the fort in thirty-six hours, convinced Taylor that he could no longer delay the calling of volunteers from the nearby states. He dispatched Colonel Charles Doane to Washington with reports of the outbreak of the war and with messages to the governors of Texas and Louisiana calling for four regiments from each state.

Arista's next move was to send two thousand troops across the river below the fort to cut Taylor's communications. When Taylor learned that his depot at the mouth of the river was threatened, he left a small detachment at the fort and hastened to Point Isabel. There he began to load supplies and recruit additional men for the return up the river. In the night Captain Walker, a Texas Ranger, came in with news that the fort had been attacked after Taylor's departure. Walker had made his way through the lines of the Mexicans who surrounded the fort. On May 8 Taylor finished loading supplies and ammunition, collected every man who could be spared from the depot, and with a train of three hundred wagons started back to the relief of the fort and the battle with the Mexican forces which he now knew was inevitable.

This month of May put the New Orleans newspapers on a wartime basis. At first, news of the approaching conflict came by the increasing flotilla of coastwise steamers plying between that city and Brazos Santiago, the island just off Point Isabel. On April 21, the *Picayune* reported that Ampudia had warned Taylor to abandon camp opposite Matamoros, and that Taylor had refused. The story was based on a "report of Capt. Windle of the Alabama, who got it from Col. Harney."

It stated on May 1, "The brig Apalachicola, Capt. Smith, arrived at this port yesterday from Brazos bay, whence she sailed on the 24th ult., and reports that on the 22d she left Point Isabel, where Major Thomas the acting Quarter Master informed Capt. Smith that the body of Col. Cross had been found about four miles from Gen. Taylor's camp on the Rio Grande. From the wounds upon the body it seems evident that he was killed by a lance. . . ."

The *Delta's* issue that morning carried the report from "The schr. Cornelia, Capt. Stark," that Arista had delivered his ultimatum to Taylor, and that the express rider who brought this news down to Point Isabel reported that two thousand Mexicans had crossed over the Rio Grande below the fort.[1] New Orleans

---

[1] "We do not believe this story," the *Delta* countered. Taylor's supplies were ready to be dispatched to the fort under a small escort, and would have fallen easy prey to the Mexicans had not the messenger got through to the depot.

The *Delta* missed this angle of the story, which appeared in the *Commercial Times,* and explained sourly in its issue of May 2, "The U. S. transport schr. Gen. Worth, Capt. Atwell, arrived opposite the *Picayune* landing yesterday morning at half-past 1 o'clock, but was anchored so far off, that no one could board her.— Capt. A. had been confined to his berth for seven days previous and did not wish to be disturbed. Upon calling on Capt. Atwell, at daylight, he fully corroborated the report made by Capt. Stark and Smith.

"The *Times* report, said to have come from Capt. Atwell, is the production of Mr. Marks, former U. S. Consul at Matamoros, who came up on the Schr. Ella, and got aboard the Gen. Worth at the English Turn, and being very anxious to communicate his information to the *Times,* hired a boat by some means, and landed, no one knows where. For the truth of these reports, though made in good faith, we do not wish to be held responsible."

now knew that Taylor's situation was precarious. Then, on Saturday morning, May 2, the war news broke in full force.

Colonel Doane arrived on the steamer *Galveston* with news of the ambush of April 25, and with the requisition for Louisiana volunteers. Every newspaper in the city picked up the story and presses turned out extra editions throughout the day.

"The war has begun in earnest," the *Picayune* shouted in a ten-point headline. "The Enemy is upon our soil!! Louisiana Volunteers, the Hour has arrived!!! For fuller details, see letters, etc., inside."

J. F. H. Claiborne's conservative *Jeffersonian* carried the ten-point headline, "Late & Important from Texas!" and followed with an eight-point line, "War! War!!"[2]

Every news story and editorial column echoed the call for volunteers. The aged general, E. P. Gaines, commanding the southwest region for the United States Army, became so excited that he sent requisitions to all the southern and Mississippi Valley states, calling for unlimited enlistment of volunteers for a period of three months.[3]

War fever rose to a high degree. The Louisiana legislature promptly sanctioned the plans of Governor Isaac Johnson by voting one hundred thousand dollars for enlisting and equipping volunteers. Tents were pitched in Lafayette Square, where officers recruited their companies, and the whole square between Canal and Poydras streets was turned into a great encampment. As detachments volunteered, they marched up and down the streets with bands, soliciting others to join. The *Jeffersonian*

[2] In a day when headlines were almost unknown, and when even the most important news was set in five- or six-point type, these outbursts must have seemed to the readers little short of colossal. The *Tropic* published two extras during the day and the *Delta's* presses ran until evening supplying copies to the crowds that thronged its offices.

[3] This led to confusion almost approaching chaos, when these troops began to pour through New Orleans on their way to the front. Many of them were unseasoned and poorly equipped for the tropical weather of the border, and the toll of death from disease among them was frightful. Their enlistments expired before they saw service in any engagements, and those who took part in the war later enlisted for longer periods.

started a campaign to raise the pay of soldiers.[4] Senator Marks, of St. Francisville, and Bailie Peyton, prominent New Orleans attorney and Whig leader, volunteered as privates but were given commissions to raise companies.

Captain Lumsden of the *Picayune* started organizing the Orleans Regiment. However, when the Gaines Rangers, a mounted company from Georgia which equipped itself and traveled at its own expense, arrived in the city and elected Lumsden captain, he quit recruiting and shipped for the border.

Among the first to respond to the call for volunteers were the New Orleans printers who set in type the news from the front and who dashed off the patriotic handbills which plastered the walls and fences throughout the city. When Senator Marks opened the rolls for enlistment in Company A of his regiment, twenty printers were included. Among these were J. H. Peoples, J. L. Freaner, and J. G. H. Tobin of the *Delta*, and Charles Callahan of the *Picayune*, all of whom later were to be widely known for their letters from the war front.[5] Other companies also included printers in their ranks.[6]

At a time when every newspaperman was generally referred to as "a printer," and when almost every typesetter was experienced not only in working at the case but in collecting and writing news, the front was soon to be swarming with potential war correspondents. Anyone who had any information, or an opinion about how the war should be conducted, might pour out fact or criticism in letters to newspapers, signing initials or pen-names of classical or regional flavor.

[4] Pay of enlisted men was as follows: first sergeant, $16 per month; second, third and fourth sergeants, $13; corporals, $9; musicians, $8; and privates, $7. The *Jeffersonian* insisted that privates should receive at least $10 per month, with a guarantee of homestead land after service. New Orleans *Jeffersonian*, May 14, 15, 25, 26, and June 10, 12, 1846.

[5] The list of printers in this company appeared in the *Picayune* and *Delta*, May 6, 1846.

[6] The *Tropic* reported on May 21, "we have lost many of our printers," and on June 13, "We understand there are fifteen printers in one company of the Tennessee Volunteers, and eight in another." H. S. McFarland, editor of the Plaquemine *Gazette*, came in with a hundred volunteers from the parish of Iberville.

However, before these newspapermen got to the front, New Orleans journals continued to rely on reports from incoming ships' crews and on letters sent in voluntarily by army officers. On May 11, both the *Picayune* and the *Delta* received accounts, written by officers, telling of the bombardment of the American fort on the Rio Grande after General Taylor started his march for Point Isabel. Although the fort was shelled from May 3 until Taylor's return on May 9, only one man was killed. American batteries returned the fire of Mexican batteries across the river at Matamoros, with negligible effect, but on the strength of their vague reports both the *Picayune* and the *Delta* reduced the town to ashes.[7]

Ships' captains again brought in the news of General Taylor's first crushing victory. On the afternoon of May 8, after he had marched out of Point Isabel, he met the Mexicans under General Arista, drawn up across the plain at Palo Alto. The two armies engaged in an artillery duel that lasted until dark, and during the night Arista withdrew to a ravine known as Resaca de la Palma, farther along the road to Matamoros. Taylor followed and routed the Mexicans in a brilliant charge on the next afternoon, and chased the remnants of Arista's army across the Rio Grande.

All New Orleans newspapers got the story eight days later. The *Picayune's* extra, rushed off at 10:00 P.M., May 16, carried the headline in eighteen-point capital letters:

GREAT BATTLE!

GEN. TAYLOR VICTORIOUS

[7] The *Picayune*, on the strength of "a letter from an officer at Point Isabel," signed "S.S.F.," on May 11, and another two days later signed "W. S. Henry, Lieut. U.S.A.," reported: "The Americans hotly returned the fire. The attack in the rear was immediately repulsed, and in less than thirty minutes the Mexican batteries were silenced and the City of Matamoros battered down. . . . The town of Matamoros is a complete ruin; there are scarcely houses enough left standing to serve as hospitals for the wounded." The *Delta's* "Capt. S." wrote, "The U.S. batteries knocked down Matamoros, killing two or three hundred Mexicans . . ." and in another story in the same issue stated, "Our batteries were opened on Matamoros, and reduced the place to ruins, or nearly so." Neither paper corrected these reports.

The story began: "By the extreme kindness of Capt. Eddy of the Schooner Louisiana who left Brazos Santiago on the 11th inst., and arrived at the English Turn[8] this evening, we are indebted for the following important and interesting account from Point Isabel up to the evening of the 9th inst."

Captain J. D. Wood of the United States steamer, *Col. Harney,* brought the news next day that Arista had been routed at the Resaca de la Palma. On May 17, General Taylor had sent a detachment across the Rio Grande to occupy Matamoros, after the Mexicans had retreated. This news reached New Orleans on May 29 by the steamship *Telegraph,* and newspapers stated that the information was provided "through the politeness of her obliging clerk."

Meanwhile the first of the letters from volunteer printers were arriving in New Orleans newspaper offices. The *Picayune* on May 20 received a letter from "L." at the camp opposite Matamoros, and from "A.B." at a camp down the river. On the same day the *Delta* published its first letter from a correspondent at Point Isabel, signed "S," and three days later its first dispatch signed "Tom," from its former reporter, now Captain Thomas Stringer, paymaster of the regiment of volunteers who sailed on May 15. He reported that there were two women and twenty servants accompanying the troops. Other *Delta* contributors from the front signed their letters "H.F.," "Z.," and "J.T.D."

Buried among the other contributions in the *Delta's* issue of May 20 was a letter telling of the troops' arrival at Point Isabel. There was little news there, so the correspondent dug up the story that General Taylor had started out on the morning of May 8 to meet the Mexicans, dressed "in a simple farmer's apparel," and riding in a light wagon driven by a Negro servant. He signed his letter "Corporal," but added a postscript which was signed

[8] The "English Turn" is a bend in the river below New Orleans where an English frigate in 1699 turned back after French settlers informed its captain that the land adjoining the river was claimed by France. See Alcée Fortier, *A History of Louisiana* (New York, 1904), I, 43, 44; John Francis McDermott (ed.), *Tixier's Travels on the Osage Prairies* (Norman, 1940), 36.

"J. L. F." This identified him as James L. Freaner, who on June 3 began signing his letters "Mustang," and who was to gain fame approaching that of Kendall as a war correspondent.

While Kendall was riding south to the border, while Lumsden was organizing his company, and before the great number of New Orleans printers had reached the front, the *Picayune* sent C. M. Haile to the Rio Grande to serve as the first of the elaborate staff of correspondents who worked under Kendall's direction.[9]

Other newspapers soon began sending their staff members to the front. On May 13, the *Delta* announced "our assistant editor," M. G. Davis, was leaving for the Rio Grande; and a week later the *Tropic* stated, "Our associate, T. B. Thorpe, Esq., has gone to the Army as bearer of dispatches from Gen. Gaines. Mr. Thorpe will, while at Camp, furnish the latest war news for the *Tropic*."[10]

While this army of printers was converging on the Rio Grande, Kendall reached Matamoros to find it converted into "an American City." Stores, coffeehouses, restaurants, billiard rooms and hotels reminded him of New Orleans. Ice had been introduced, and mint juleps, which he considered "a long step towards civilization." He and Haile set up a systematic program of news gathering. In their rounds they ran into Freaner and two other former *Delta* printers, J. H. Peoples, who already was writing under the name of "Chaparral," and J. G. H. Tobin, who con-

[9] Haile, a native of Rhode Island who was appointed from that state as a cadet at West Point in 1836, left the academy at the end of one year and went to Louisiana where he became editor of the *Planter's Gazette* at Plaquemine. He joined the *Picayune* staff and became widely known for his humorous letters, signed "Pardon Jones," which were patterned after the style of Artemus Ward.

[10] Thorpe was the author of two books, *Tom Owen, the Bee Hunter,* and *Mysteries of the Backwoods,* which enjoyed wide popularity. He was a partner on the *Tropic,* but on September 17, 1846, the paper announced he had left the firm and gone to Baton Rouge to publish the semiweekly *Conservator.* He was also the author of two books on the war, *Our Army on the Rio Grande* and *Our Army at Monterey.* The New York *Courier and Enquirer,* October 10, 1848, announced, "We commence today the publication of a brief life of Gen. Taylor by T. B. Thorpe, Esq., who is a resident of Baton Rouge, and of course, has had an opportunity of collecting materials for the work, not always in the reach of Gen. Taylor's Biographers."

tributed whimsical and humorous sketches to his paper under the heading, "From Captain Tobin's Knapsack."[11]

They found that while Matamoros was thriving in its mint julep modernity, deplorable conditions existed in the nearby camp of American troops. Tents were pitched near the river in ten inches of mud. Unseasoned troops fell ill by the hundreds, and the death rate was appalling. Taylor, without sufficient mules and wagons, or steamers small enough to navigate the treacherous Rio Grande, could move neither inland nor upstream.

With the whole military machine bogged down, and no exciting news available, Kendall wrote to the *Picayune* about Bill Dean, a ranger with Captain Chevalier's spy company. Dean had delighted Kendall's party with a tall tale about difficulties the rangers encountered in cooking food on their long marches. During one trip his troop had "lived eight days on one poor hawk and three blackberries—couldn't kill a prairie rat on the whole route to save us from starvation." On the ninth day a horse gave out and they shot it for food, but there was not a stick of firewood in sight. Bill lighted the prairie grass, stuck a chunk of meat on his ramrod and chased the racing flames a mile and a half trying to cook it. When he ran the blaze into a swamp he found that the meat was not cooked, but was barely crusted over.

Kendall saw many familiar faces on the streets of Matamoros. The Louisiana delegation gave a dinner in town, "in a style most magnificent," but this was tame compared to the excitement he had expected to find. The only soldiers who had any chance for excitement were the three companies of rangers who rode frequently into the region below the Rio Grande on scout duty.

The hardiest and best mounted of the Texans were organized under Captain Chevalier, whose men provided the advance guard

[11] Peoples was one of the three months' volunteers who stayed on with the troops after his discharge to write for the *Delta* and later for the New Orleans *Crescent,* and to publish army newspapers in the wake of the invading troops. Both he and Freaner served as *Picayune* correspondents in the California gold rush of 1849. Tobin was captain of one of the volunteer companies that sailed out of New Orleans on May 10. He wrote the *Delta's* story covering the battle of Buena Vista.

of Kendall's party from Point Isabel to Matamoros, and Ben McCulloch and Jack Hays, both noted Indian fighters and border leaders under the Republic of Texas. On the day he arrived in Matamoros Kendall joined McCulloch's company, and three days later they were off on a scouting expedition into the interior.

On the eight-day reconnaissance up to Reynosa, Kendall thought often of the St. Charles and the Verandah and Hewlett's and the other cool oases in New Orleans, for the party carried no tents. They had to wade, dig and flounder through the muddy road along the Rio Grande, turning aside into the thick chaparral of the higher ground a dozen times. No air was stirring.

Kendall left the rangers at Reynosa and went down the river on a boat to complete his news staff arrangements. He, Haile, and Callahan at Matamoros, D. Scully at Point Isabel, all were busy with the *"Picayune* office" which was to follow Taylor through northern Mexico and Scott from Tampico and Vera Cruz to Mexico City. Every employee picked up news, took subscriptions and transacted other business on the spot for the paper. Kendall remained at Matamoros until July 5, watching the almost constant arrival of volunteers, checking Taylor's plans for a push southward, and calling loudly through the *Picayune* for the speeding up of transports and mail.

He watched with disgust the argument which had broken out in Washington between the War Department and General Winfield Scott, commander-in-chief of the Army.[12] Immediately

---

[12] Scott was given command of the armies in the field, and Marcy and Polk expected him to leave immediately. After a week's planning of requisitions, supplies, troops, and transports, Scott still was in Washington, and the administration and the people became restless. Senator J. A. Dix of New York, a friend of Polk, advocated the appointment of two additional major generals for the army, and Scott wrote Marcy a letter so ill advised in tone and spirit that he was immediately relieved of command of the troops in the field, which a few days afterwards was conferred on Taylor. After complaining of the criticism in "high quarters," Scott stated that he was too old a soldier not to see the danger of placing himself "in the most perilous of all positions—a fire in his rear from Washington, and a fire in front from the Mexicans." His later letters of apology did not improve his case in the estimation of the public. He began his first letter of explanation with, "I had arisen from a hasty plate of soup," a line over which Kendall chuckled for years.

after war was declared, President Polk and his secretary of war, William S. Marcy, planned a campaign which included a push southward from the Rio Grande, an attack on Chihuahua, and another on New Mexico and California. The President urged immediate prosecution of each of these ventures, but Scott, in conference, argued that equipping and moving large bodies of men would require at least three months. The move on Monterrey could not be made during the rainy season, he argued, because the hooves of the horses would become tender, if not fall off entirely, during the wet weather of June and July. Kendall, back from hard riding in the hottest part of the rainy season, scoffed at Scott's plea on behalf of the horses. He groaned when General Wool at San Antonio began to outfit a column for a march on Chihuahua "to fight nothing more than starvation and fatigue." For this campaign, horses, mules, and wagons were requisitioned at a time when Taylor was crying vainly for transports at Matamoros.[13]

Kendall was on hand to witness the breakup of the volunteer companies which had enlisted with such patriotism and paraded the streets of New Orleans with such enthusiasm. While his army marked time, General Taylor realized that the enlistments of the three- and six-month volunteers would expire before they were needed for actual operations, and they were given the option of going home or enlisting for a longer period. Some re-enlisted, but many went home, having experienced only the discomfort of drilling in the mud, sweating under the blazing tropical sun, and fighting the swarms of mosquitoes which Kendall said were worse than those of New Orleans. A number of the printers remained to serve as correspondents for the New Orleans press, or to work on camp newspapers, which by now were flourishing.

13 For the Scott argument and delay on the Rio Grande, see *Picayune,* July 7, 8, 17, 1846; also Kendall manuscript, "History of the War with Mexico," 144–51. Kendall wrote, "Taylor might have sat down to his Fourth of July dinner at Monterey, and with little loss, had he been in possession of transportation after the battle of the Resaca. He had men enough for the enterprise, both cavalry and infantry, and the rainy season stood not in the way of his advance."

It was inevitable, when enough printers got together with time on their hands, that the urge to publish a newspaper would arise. This movement started while the troops were still at Corpus Christi. First came the Corpus Christi *Gazette,* issued January 1, 1846, by Samuel Bangs, a Bostonian who since 1817 had been a printer in Mexico and Texas. Working with Bangs was one of Taylor's troopers, Isaac N. Fleeson, who had suffered for years from pulmonary consumption, which caused his death in 1848.

When the troops moved on up the Rio Grande, Bangs, with Gideon Lewis, an editor of the Galveston *News,* loaded his equipment in an oxcart and headed for Matamoros. This was the beginning of the series of newspapers which sprang up like mushrooms in the wake of the moving troops. Bangs' press was turning out the Matamoros *Reveille* when Kendall caught up with him. At this time General Taylor was attempting to carry out orders from Washington to conciliate the people of Mexico whenever possible, and he closed the *Reveille* because objectionable material in Spanish was issued from the same press.

Hugh McLeod, who had led the Santa Fe Expedition, and who later served as editor of the San Antonio *Ledger,* secured the type and press of the Matamoros *Boletín* and started the *Republic of the Rio Grande and Friend of the People.* His purpose was to promote a republic of the four northern Mexican provinces, possibly looking forward to later annexation[14] to the United

14 *Picayune,* June 1, 1846, also *National Intelligencer,* June 25, 1846, which stated that the purpose of the *Republic* was "to convince the people of Tamaulipas, Coahuila, Nuevo León, and Chihuahua of the futility of resisting American arms, and to throw upon the administration of Paredes the responsibility of the war. A separation of the departments named above from the Central Government of Mexico is the distinct aim of this new paper." Also Lota M. Spell, "The Anglo Saxon Press in Mexico, 1846–48," *American Historical Review,* Vol. 38, 20–31. Issues of Volume 1, Numbers 2, 4, and 8 of the *Republic,* dated June 6, 16, and 30, 1846, are in the Library of Congress.

In the *Delta,* June 16, 1846, Freaner wrote of the *Republic,* "It is a 'small potato' affair. They attempted to use the 'typos' of Capt. Head's company, but in this they failed. The boys offered to take the materials to camp and publish a daily journal, and have it sold for the benefit of the regiment, but were not willing to be used by speculators. This Gen. Taylor was very willing to see them do, but the persons who had possession of the materials would not submit."

States. When McLeod retired as publisher of the *Republic,* the paper became the *American Flag.*[15]

July 4 was a noisy day on the Rio Grande, with American batteries on each side of the river burning quantities of captured Mexican powder in firing salutes to the other. Captain Ricardo gave a dinner for the rangers with whom Kendall rode; and the New Orleans press group planned another elaborate dinner, but Kendall could not attend it. He was busily making preparations for another ride with McCulloch's men.

This time they went directly to Reynosa, along the river road Taylor was to take in moving his troops to Camargo on their way to Monterrey, one hundred and fifty miles inland. The rangers were constantly on the alert for hostile attack, getting up shortly after midnight in order to travel during the cooler hours. They rested during the hot part of the day, sprawling about in the sun without shelter. One of Kendall's companions expressed wonder that anyone could ever sleep as they had to, fully dressed, "belted round with two pistols and a Bowie, boots on and spurs to boot." The trip was a quick one, for on July 8 Scully wrote from Fort Polk, "Kendall is back from his trip through mud and water."

Already Kendall was getting results through the system of expresses which dispatched his news from the border to the *Picayune,* a system designed to get vital news to New Orleans first. His letter of July 6 from Reynosa was published in the *Picayune* only nine days later. The time was to come when his dispatches from Monterrey in the hands of special couriers would reach New Orleans in the unbelievable time of eight days.

Even before war was declared, newspapers of the North and

---

[15] *The American Flag,* Matamoros, July 4, 1846, "Edited, Printed, and Published tri-weekly, by Fleeson, Peoples & Co." Fleeson had worked with Bangs at Corpus Christi, and Peoples now was becoming famous as "Chaparral" of the *Delta.* Fleeson and Palmer became publishers September 9, 1846, and on September 29 the paper issued an extra on the capture of Monterrey. In January, 1847, it was enlarged to a good-sized tabloid, and on June 7, 1848, it carried a line on its masthead, "Issued simultaneously in Matamoros, Mexico, and Cameron County, Texas." Scattered copies up until July 29, 1848, are in the Library of Congress.

East had found it highly desirable to co-operate in the speeding of news between the troublesome Mexican border and the Atlantic seaboard. Relays of pony express riders were established on the route not covered by rail, from the *Picayune* office in Camp Street to the office of the Baltimore *Sun*. The pony express riders carried *Picayune* regular and extra editions, leaving copies with newspapers along the way.[16] From New Orleans the riders galloped to Lake Pontchartrain, where they met fast boats that skirted the coast around to Mobile. There the express riders picked up the news and took it on its way to Montgomery, to Charleston, to Richmond, to Baltimore. Papers beyond Baltimore also benefited by this fast-riding express.[17]

Not only did the express riders take news from New Orleans northward, but in returning they brought copies of newspapers and "slips" of their commercial news to the *Picayune*.[18] Since the thriving New Orleans cotton, grain, and produce markets were affected by prices in New York, Liverpool, and London, the

[16] *Picayune,* May 24, 1846. News of the battle of Palo Alto on May 8 reached New Orleans on the seventeenth, and a copy of the *Picayune* reached Mobile in time for publication in the *Register* and *Journal* on the eighteenth. On the route to Montgomery a fifteen-year-old boy carried the papers one hundred and eighty-six miles in thirteen hours, "he having to saddle all the horses himself, as he was not expected at the stations." So great was public interest in the news that citizens of Montgomery raised a purse of seventy dollars for the boy and "got up a petition asking the P. M. General and Secretary of War to run an express that could gain two days on the regular mail."

[17] It took fourteen days for Kendall's letter of May 8 from the Indian council ground on the Brazos to reach New Orleans. It was published May 22 in an extra of the *Picayune,* and was reprinted in the Boston *Advertiser and Patriot* on June 1. His letter of July 16 from Camargo was published in the *Picayune* of August 1, and in the Boston *Daily Advertiser* of August 13.

[18] In the *Picayune,* October 24, 1885, an old-timer recalled these early days of the pony express. "When a President's message was delivered to Congress," he wrote, "the *Picayune* met its expresses at Mobile with a steamboat, on which were a set of type, cases and other material, with compositors to do the work, and the message was put in type on the boat, locked up in the forms, and was ready to go to press on arrival in the city. Some amusing stories are told of the attempts of rival papers to beat the *Pic.* by getting its printers intoxicated on occasions when these expeditions were made."

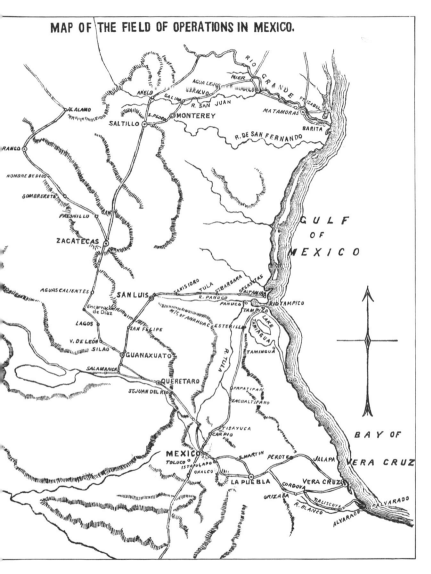

MAP OF THE FIELD OF OPERATIONS IN MEXICO.

RIO GRANDE

AGUA LEVOS
SERALVO
MIER
REINOSA
ISABEL
ANELO
SALINA
R. SAN JUAN
S. PEDRO
MATAMORAS
MONTEREY
SALTILLO
BARITA
EL ALAMO
R. DE SAN FERNANDO

DURANGO

NOMBRE DE DIOS

SOMBRERETE

FRESNILLO

GULF
OF
MEXICO

ZACATECAS

AGUAS CALIENTES
SAN ISIDRO
STA BARBARA
TULA
OCASITAS
R. PANUCO
ALTAMIRA
SAN LUIS
PANUCO
RIO TAMPICO
Encarnacion
de Diaz
MTS OF ANAHUAC
ESTERILLA
TAMPICO
LAGOS
SAN FELIPE
LAKE
TAMINGUA
V. DE LEON
SILAO
R. TULA
TAMINGUA
GUANAXUATO
SALAMANCA
QUERETARO
PAPATIPAN
ST. JUAN DEL RIO
ZACUALTIPANO

TISAYUCA
CARPIO
BAY OF
MEXICO
TOLUCO
S. MARTIN
PEROTE
JALAPA
VERA CRUZ
ISTAPULAPO
CHALCO
LA PUEBLA
CORDOVA
VERA CRUZ
ORIZABA
TALISCOYA
ALVARADO
R. BLANCO
ALVARADO

From a contemporary newspaper

Picayune spent great sums to get the latest market quotations after the arrival of a steamer from Europe.[19]

New Orleans competitors of the *Picayune,* less enterprising in getting commercial news from the North, insisted that the paper was using its advantage for its own financial profit in the market.[20] But the *Picayune's* columns gave no hint that these charges worried its publishers. Its readers continued to get the news "in advance of the mail," and newspapers from Mobile to Boston published letters written by Kendall and Haile and Scully and Callahan, and by August were beginning to reprint letters from Lumsden.

The Gaines Rangers, under Lumsden's command, had sailed from New Orleans for Galveston, then marched overland to the border. The steamer carrying their baggage and ammunition sank in a storm, and shortly after they reached Matamoros their period of enlistment expired and they were discharged.[21]

In the meantime Haile finished his work at Matamoros and

[19] *Picayune,* February 28, March 1, and March 29, 1846, had stories of the spectacular races from Halifax and Boston to New York with news from the steamers *Cambria* and *Hibernia.* The *Sun* and *Tribune* of New York joined with the *North American* and the *Journal of Commerce* of Philadelphia in picking up the *Cambria's* news at Halifax, but their rider lost four hours in a snowstorm, and came in two hours behind the rider whom the New York *Herald* and the Philadelphia *U. S. Gazette* had hired to get the *Cambria's* news at Boston. In March, 1846, seven papers co-operated in speeding the *Hibernia's* news from Halifax, and the news had been in Boston six hours before the *Hibernia* put in at that port. The *Picayune,* through its express connections, was able to print the news from both ships a day ahead of its competitors.

[20] New Orleans *Tropic,* May 8, 1846, declared, "The government has the monopoly of carrying the mails. It should therefore be above competition. Yet this is not the case: private expresses are running everywhere over the great routes, and by excelling the mails, large profits accrue to the speculation of the few, at the expense of the many. In consequence of the enterprise of the private express, cotton and other produce was purchased in our city by individuals, of holders who had no knowledge the news was in the city." New Orleans *Commercial Bulletin,* May 7, 1846, insisted that the papers from which the *Picayune* of April 4 took its news were in the city a day earlier, "and suppressed throughout that day to subserve private ends."

[21] Lumsden, after a short scouting trip with Jack Hay's rangers, returned to New Orleans and did not rejoin the troops until Scott's move on Tampico and Vera Cruz during the following year.

went home, "during the inactivity of the army," but his stories had been so popular in New Orleans and had been reprinted so widely in the northern papers that the *Picayune* persuaded him to return to work under Kendall's direction.

Matamoros had long since grown too crowded for Kendall. With the rangers at Camargo on July 16, he reported that one division of the army was preparing to move on toward Monterrey, while scouting parties were working toward Mier, up the river. Reports that Captain Seguín was nearby with a force of lancers sent McCulloch shuttling back and forth along the river and far inland. The rangers dashed down to the village of China, arriving at half-past one in the morning after a forced march of fifty-five miles, but Seguín had fled. McCulloch occupied Seguín's head-quarters for a day and left a saucy challenge with the village alcalde to be delivered to the lancer captain. They missed Seguín again at San Francisco, and suspected he had laid a trap for them at Paso de Sacate, but they entered the town without resistance.

These trips brought Kendall back to Camargo again and again during the interval from July 16 to August 27. There he picked up incidents and proclamations and statistics on Taylor's strength— all the while sending voluminous letters to the *Picayune*.

At Camargo Kendall was seen often in the company of Forbes Britton, a Virginian who was captain of the Seventh Infantry, and who later was Kendall's partner in a ranching venture in Texas. On convivial occasions they joined with Mirabeau B. Lamar, Edward Burleson, who had been vice-president of the Texas Republic, J. Pinckney Henderson, then governor of Texas, and Lumsden, "to drink warm champagne together out of a tin cup."[22]

There, also, Kendall finally located Tom Hancock, the Indian scout who had looked after Falconer on the Santa Fe Expedition. While they were prisoners together at Santiago, Kendall had promised Hancock a gun made to his order, if the two should get home safely, a promise he kept. He searched for Hancock in

[22] For these reminiscences, see Kendall's letters to the *Picayune* from Boerne, November 4, 1859, and February 23, 1861.

Camargo, but Hancock kept out of sight until he had redeemed the rifle, which he had pawned.[23]

By late August, Kendall had completed his express system down the river from Camargo, cutting the time to New Orleans to ten days, and was ready to start inland with McCulloch's rangers again. The rangers had served as scouts for the engineers sent ahead on reconnaissance, and for the troops repairing the roads for the advance. When, on August 20, General Worth's division started in the direction of Cerralvo, McCulloch's men again led the way. Detachments combed the wasteland of chaparral along the road for possible ambush, and with them Kendall shuttled back and forth.

He wrote the *Picayune* from Cerralvo, from Camargo, from Mier, from Punta Aguda and again from Cerralvo. All through these letters ran the growing conviction that the Mexicans would put up a strong resistance at Monterrey, that the delay in getting transportation for Taylor would cause tragic loss in the American ranks.

Haile saw Kendall for a short time at Cerralvo on September 8, but the rangers were soon pushing ahead again.[24] The

---

[23] Kendall papers, manuscript of "Rough Notes." Hancock and his bosom friend, Fitzgerald, were captured in the Texan invasion of Mier in 1842, and Fitzgerald died of wounds while Hancock endured a second long imprisonment in Mexico. After this experience, Kendall stated, "Tom's habits, previously a little irregular, grew more wild . . . When out on a hunting or surveying party, or on a scout after Indians, he was himself—no better woodsman, spy or hunter, or fighter could be found than Hancock. But on the first night of his return to San Antonio the bar-room and the monte bank would swallow up his earnings, and as a last resource the rifle I had given him would be pawned. Not one of the rangers of Jack Hays would purchase it outright, nor would they allow the weapon to be sold out of the company: there among them, by a compact into which they entered, it should always be found when Tom was ready to redeem it, which he did over and over again."

[24] Haile wrote the *Picayune* from Cerralvo, "I hunted him as soon as I arrived, but could not succeed until I happened to espy *Spriggs,* his favorite charger, standing near the door of a dwelling. I have never seen Spriggs and his doting master very far apart in Mexico, and knew very well that my search was at an end. Mr. K. is as robust as his best friends could desire to see him, and seems to be in his element while dashing around the country with the spy company."

Texas ranger company of R. A. Gillespie now was attached to Worth's division, and both his and McCulloch's companies were kept busy bringing in information. They learned that Ampudia was receiving reinforcements from San Luis Potosí and that every approach to Monterrey was being fortified.

On September 6, Lieutenant George G. Meade of the topographical engineers and ranger escort returned from a reconnaissance in the direction of Monterrey, having penetrated as far as Ramos where they were turned back by a strong force of Torrejón's cavalry.

Five days later Kendall started with McCulloch's rangers again, on the route to Marín to cover the road repair detail. They were followed on September 13 by General Twigg's division, and two days later by those of General Worth and General Butler. On September 14, between Papagayas and Ramos, McCulloch's rangers had another brush with three hundred of Torrejón's cavalry, in which three Mexicans were killed. The Texans pushed on, though they numbered only thirty-five men, and were six miles ahead of the main force. The Mexicans made another stand at the stream near Ramos, and after an exchange of volleys the Texans set an ambush in the chaparral to draw a Mexican charge, but Torrejón withdrew. At Marín they caught a glimpse of him again, but he dashed out of the city in a cloud of dust and the Texans occupied the town without firing a shot.

During the next exciting week, Kendall wrote the *Picayune* repeatedly, from "Camp near Marin," from "San Francisco," from "Camp near Monterey, 12 o'clock noon, Sept. 19," from "Camp opposite Monterey, 8 a.m., Sept. 20."

On the night of September 20, all of Taylor's available troops were massed before the Mexican stronghold, which bristled with artillery. Kendall lay beside a campfire with a group of Texans who talked idly of the glamorous days of border fighting, who recounted the Texan attack on San Antonio ten years earlier, when the advancing columns captured the city by burrowing their way through the adobe houses. His own plans for covering the coming battle were complete. His couriers were ready to dash to New Orleans with his dispatches.

He listened as the men talked of the amazing amount of ammunition fired in Napoleon's wars—approximately one hundred rounds for each casualty that resulted. One of McCulloch's rangers spoke up, "I have got just twenty bullets in my pouch, and if I don't kill or cripple just twenty greasers, it will be because they are licked before I have had time to load and fire twenty times, or else because I have been 'sent under' early. I can't afford to pack lead, and tire down my horse, like they do in the old world."[25]

During the next three days Kendall was to record that the sharpshooting of these riflemen, and their knack of burrowing through the walls of houses when the streets were raked with artillery, had won the battle of Monterrey.

[25] Kendall papers, manuscript of "Rough Notes."

15

Reporting under fire

K ENDALL AWAKENED on the morning of September 20 in a drizzly rain, but as the sun came up he looked southwest across the city where during the next three days he was to witness and record his first pitched battle.

Monterrey, with ten or twelve thousand inhabitants, lay at the foot of the Sierra Madres, along the little stream which the Mexicans called "Río San Juan de Monterrey." Taylor's six thousand troops, encamped at the grove of Walnut Springs, north of the city, found their road blocked by the fortified citadel, which the soldiers named "the black fort." Reconnaissance of the army engineers and the topographical engineers under Lieutenant George G. Meade had revealed strong fortifications, particularly along the eastern edge of the city centering around the cathedral and the municipal palace. Breastworks and gun emplacements lined the brook that ran out of the town and joined the river a short distance to the east.

Two fortified hills guarded the Saltillo highway on the west. The Loma de Independencia rose about six hundred feet above the plain, and on its eastern slope stood the Bishop's Palace, an unfinished structure now heavily fortified. South of this, across the highway and beyond the river, the Loma de Federación was fortified with gun emplacements on the west and with a small fortress on its eastern slope. Back of these fortifications Ampudia had slightly more than six thousand troops, and was gradually gaining strength through reinforcements from the interior over the Saltillo road.

Persistent rumors that Santa Anna was marching up from San Luis Potosí with a strong force worried Taylor. Late on the night of September 19 Meade reported that this western approach might be gained by a wide detour beyond the fortified hills. For this purpose, Taylor divided his army, retaining command of the forces before the city for movements against its northern and eastern fortifications, and sent about two thousand men under General Worth on the swing around to the west.

On the eve of the battle, Governor J. Pinckney Henderson of Texas arrived with his division of rangers, and the consolidated Texas force was divided for scout duty with Taylor and Worth. McCulloch's company, with the men of Hays and Walker, led Worth's march to the west, and in its ranks rode Kendall on his favorite horse, Spriggs. The column swung out of range of the guns of the citadel, took possession of the roads leading to Monclova and Pescaria Grande, and late in the afternoon turned south at the foot of the mountains beyond the Bishop's Palace toward the Saltillo road.

General Burleson, with twenty men, advanced down a byroad while General Worth, Captain McCulloch, and other officers rode up on the brow of the hill to the right to reconnoiter. General Burleson hurried back to report to General Worth that he had met the enemy's pickets and that a large body of cavalry and infantry was drawn up across the road. "Our position at once became very critical," one of McCulloch's men wrote, "and the presence of Gen. Worth was immediately required. Mr. Kendall here volunteered his services, and proceeded after Gen. Worth, who by this time had disappeared far to the right."[1]

Worth sent McCulloch's company in advance, with the rest

[1] Samuel C. Reid, Jr., *The Scouting Expeditions of McCulloch's Texas Rangers* (Philadelphia, n.d.), 153. This is the first record of Kendall's serving on the field as an aide. He served as General Worth's aide during the campaign from Vera Cruz to Mexico City in 1847, and was cited in official reports.

of the Texans and a body of infantry to support them. As the rangers pushed forward, scouts scrambling up the hill to the right warned that a company of cavalry had dismounted and lay in ambush in a cornfield ahead. The next moment a rattling fire of *escopetas* opened on the scouts, followed by round shot and shell from the battery on Independence Hill. Dusk was falling, and since Worth had no means of returning the fire of the fortress, he ordered his men to fall back and bivouac at a group of jacales, or small peasant huts.

Throughout the day Kendall had been with the troops in the advance. Now he learned that Haile, too, had accompanied Worth's column, and thus the *Picayune's* dramatic stories of the battle of Monterrey were to be devoted mainly to Worth's attack from the west.

The Texans marched without blankets or supplies, and when Kendall and his companions rode into a small farmyard they immediately began to scramble after the chickens, pigs, and kids they found there. But hardly had they started when a sharp fire was opened on them from three or four hundred Mexican cavalrymen who had trailed the retiring Texans and occupied a nearby hill. Captain C. B. Acklen's company went out as skirmishers in the chaparral, while the remainder, behind the cover of a fence, awaited attack. A cold rain set in at dark, and the Mexicans drew off. The Texans were annoyed that they were not permitted to build fires to cook the fresh meat they had foraged. At dawn, under fire from the guns on the hill, they set out. When they had advanced a mile and a half, a turn in the road brought them in view of the enemy again. Mounted lancers were drawn up across the road, while the avenue in the direction of the Bishop's Palace swarmed with lancers and foot soldiers.

McCulloch's and Acklen's companies deployed into the chaparral at the right and were ordered to dismount and await a lancer charge. A few began to fire at the enemy, but as the distance was more than two hundred yards they were ordered to remount and advance within rifle-shot, then take cover in a nearby cornfield. The lancers charged before McCulloch's men had received the order to dismount again, and Kendall and his companions opened up from the saddle, "pouring in a perfect storm of lead from their rifles, double-barreled guns and pistols." Fire from the deployed rangers also swept the Mexican ranks. "The lancers tumbled from their saddles by dozens; yet with uncommon daring the survivors dashed onward, engaging, hand to hand, with the rangers still mounted."[2]

The accurate shooting of the Texans' rifles was too much, even for the daring lancers, and they retreated in disorder, "carrying with them a portion of McCulloch's men, who had fought their way nearly to the enemy's centre, and seeing their peril, were fighting their way back. Then it was that the hardest struggle took place. . . . McCulloch had been twice borne back with the Mexicans, and making a desperate struggle to gain his company, he put his horse to his speed, running every thing down in his way, and regained his command without a scratch."[3]

Kendall counted a hundred and fifty of the enemy dead and wounded. Only one Texan was killed, although several of McCulloch's men suffered from lance wounds.

Worth quickly took possession of the Saltillo road and turned his light batteries against the breastworks on Independence Hill. However, when masked batteries of heavier guns from Federation Hill, across the river, opened up, he retired farther west to a sugarhouse down the road.

Heavy firing from the opposite side of the town indicated that Taylor had moved against Monterrey from the east. Since his movements were constantly harassed by the batteries of Federation Hill, Worth at noon decided to storm this point. Captain C. F. Smith's regulars led the attack, assisted by Major Chevalier's Texan companies of McCulloch, Tom Green, R. A. Gillespie, Daniel T. Chandler, John P. McCown, and Ballowe.

Again Kendall moved into the thick of the fighting. The

[2] *Picayune,* November 19, 1846.
[3] Reid, *op. cit.,* 157–58.

storming party deployed through a cornfield, and was pouring across the stream into the chaparral when it was greeted by the fire of the batteries. General Worth then sent Captain Miles with the Seventh Infantry in support and soon ordered General P. F. Smith to advance with the Fifth Infantry and Blanchard's Louisiana Volunteers. When the two supporting detachments found the first party storming the hill, they united and attacked the small fortress on the east. Swarms of infantry and sharpshooters moved down to check the first rush of the attackers. Regulars and rangers pressed forward under a galling fire, yet not until they were within good rifle distance did they open up.

The enemy could not withstand the shock. The dreaded Texans, who had unnumbered wrongs to avenge, were savage fighters. Each picked off his victim, often with a single shot, while the more open and regular discharges of the infantry guns staggered the Mexicans. The victors dashed furiously into the earthworks, the enemy fled, and before they were out of range, Lieutenant Deas had one of their own cannon turned upon the retreating columns.

General Smith's men carried the lower fort with a similar drive and turned the captured pieces on the Bishop's Palace, across the road to the north. The palace guns answered, and the cannonading continued until nightfall.

While Kendall watched this duel he observed, "perhaps the history of war affords few instances so full of grandeur and sublimity as this. Every discharge of cannon seemed to have its thousand echoes in the otherwise quiet and secluded valley. Hemmed in by the huge mountains of the Sierra Madre, the reverberations would crash and re-echo across the valley; and as the latter narrowed in width towards the gorges of Santa Catarine and the noted Rinconada, the reports would follow each other in such rapid succession that it seemed as though a thousand cannon were engaged in man's destruction instead of the half dozen so vigorously plied."[4]

[4] *Picayune,* November 19, 1846.

A chilly rain set in at dusk, and the Texans went back to care for their horses. The men were hungry, wet, and worn out, but still eager for more fighting. Worth had dispatched a courier to Taylor's headquarters after the brush with the lancers in the morning, and again in the late afternoon, but no news came over the hazardous eight-mile detour.

With the capture of the southern fortified hill, Worth, in order to hold it, faced the necessity of storming Independence Hill and the Bishop's Palace. At three o'clock on the morning of September 22, Colonel Thomas Childs started the move toward this hill. Two hundred Texans under colonels Hays and Walker were detailed as sharpshooters with three companies of artillery and three companies of infantry. Again McCulloch's rangers were included, along with the companies of captains R. A. Gillespie, Green, Acklen, James Gillespie, C. C. Herbert, and Ballowe.

The morning was dark, damp and drizzly, and a fog hung over the landscape. The rattling of the soldiers' tin canteens warned the Mexicans of their approach. Skirmishers poured out of the breastworks and started a random fire in the darkness, but dawn exposed them to the sharp fire of the storming party. On up the heights the attackers fought their way, taking the breastworks with a shout that sent the defenders scurrying down to the Bishop's Palace. Although Worth's losses were slight, Captain R. A. Gillespie and Lieutenant Herman B. Thomas were among the slain.

A party of regulars and rangers under Captain J. B. Scott followed the Mexicans and deployed as an outpost, to be reinforced by troops who had occupied the hill across the river. Throughout the morning they faced terrific fire from the Bishop's Palace. Worth ordered Lieutenant J. F. Roland forward with a twelve-pound howitzer, and after incredible exertion the piece was dragged and lifted up the jagged and precipitous cliff, and soon was dumping shell into the Bishop's Palace. Unable to withstand its accurate fire, the Mexicans resorted to cavalry and infantry attacks. The front ranks of the Louisianans held their fire until the cavalry was within thirty steps, then opened with a shocking volley that sent the horsemen riding back pell-mell over their supporting infantry. The Americans followed them back and swarmed into the works before the gates could be closed, and within a few minutes Colonel Walker and one of McCulloch's men were cutting the signal flags from the cross in front of the Palace. Their own cannon were turned on the Mexicans as they fled into the city.

Worth's exhausted men, who had fought two days and nights without food, shelter, or bedding, now had complete command of the Saltillo road and the fortresses guarding the city's western entrance. Worth ordered the wounded brought up to his new headquarters in the Palace, and his tired troops lay down to rest while he dispatched messengers to Taylor. Kendall was busy with Haile, checking operations of different detachments and jotting down the details that were to fill nine columns of the *Picayune*.[5]

Worth had no positive instructions to attack the city of Monterrey itself, but he could see, from the Palace front, that the other divisions of the attacking force had advanced on the eastern side of the city. He now determined to advance with his whole force toward the cathedral. Colonel Childs was ordered up with two columns, one to advance through each of the parallel streets that led from the cathedral square. Kendall watched this advance from Worth's headquarters on Independence Hill. Guns of the Palace, trained on the city, had driven the defenders from its western edge. Thus Worth's columns advanced to within four blocks of the cathedral before they met a raking fire from the housetops and salvos from field pieces behind barricades.

Colonel Childs' column had reached the Plazuela de Carne when his men were forced to take cover behind a high wall. "This street," wrote one of the officers in the column, "was swept by

[5] *Loc. cit.* Kendall's detailed story was run in a supplement which the paper published for its daily and weekly issues, when he returned to New Orleans on November 19. However, his first dispatches reached the city on October 3.

Mexican guns, and while bullets and shells were flying thick, so thick that it seemed impossible for a man to live amidst the flying missiles, Mr. Kendall suddenly appeared on horseback at the gate and delivered an order from Gen. Worth to the officer in command in the yard, then turning his horse rode back along the street to headquarters."[6]

In the conference that followed, Worth sent Hays and half of the Texans to the right with instructions to make their way toward the Grand Plaza by digging through the houses. The other half of the rangers, under Walker, was dispatched to the left to aid Colonel Childs in the same way. Kendall and McCulloch's men fought with the column on the left.

Here was fighting such as the Texans had known in San Antonio in their struggle for independence in 1836. Above the incessant rattling of small arms and the heavy boom of cannon from the enemy barricades there rose the sound of pickaxes, crowbars, and battering rams, as the troops burrowed through house after house. "As the regulars or rangers reached the top of some new house, a fresh shout of exultation would rise, striking terror into the hearts of the assailed," Kendall reported. "If the head of a Mexican appeared above a parapet some rifle ball would instantly pierce it—if but a hand was shown at a loophole, the owner of it was at once a cripple."[7]

General firing ceased at nightfall, but the burrowing continued. The column nearer the river had advanced to within two squares of the cathedral when it captured a bakery, and Lieutenant Hansen immediately put it to work turning out batch after batch of bread for the famished soldiers.

Kendall's companions of the northern column crossed the street near the post office and started digging through a wall. A number of Mexican infantrymen, concealed inside, tried to escape through the door but were mowed down as they poured

[6] Incident related by General H. P. Bee to Henry C. King, and included in a letter from King to Mrs. Fellowes, San Antonio, Texas, November 22, 1903.

[7] *Picayune*, November 19, 1846.

into the street. With the first morning light Texans were picking off housetop defenders twenty feet away. At sunrise, however, a white flag was sent out from Ampudia's headquarters, and fighting ceased. The parley which led to the surrender of the city was soon under way.

Kendall now learned that, in the fighting since the morning of September 20, Taylor's men also had advanced deep into the city from the opposite direction. When Taylor noted that reinforcements were moving toward the Bishop's Palace to oppose Worth he made a demonstration against the eastern works. Here, again, the tragic lack of transportation to bring in heavier guns from the Rio Grande was evident, for the pieces Taylor brought up during the night to play on the citadel made little impression. His attack from the east had to be carried on mainly with foot soldiers.

Early on the morning of the twenty-first, Taylor received Worth's note, written after his first brush at nightfall with the lancers, in which he urged a strong demonstration from the east. Taylor moved against the fortified tannery, and only after repeated attacks and with heavy losses were his forces able to take this single outpost. He lost heavily in three unsuccessful attempts to take the nearby Diablo Lunette.

Late on the night of the twenty-second, after Worth had taken the Bishop's Palace, Ampudia withdrew his forces from the outer works on the east, and Taylor sent Quitman into the city. These troops also resorted to burrowing tactics, and had penetrated to within one square of the Plaza when Taylor withdrew them awaiting a conference with Worth. At one time on the twenty-third, the troops of Taylor and Worth were within a short distance of each other, without either general's realizing it.

Taylor at first demanded unconditional surrender, but in the parley that followed he allowed surprisingly liberal terms and a two-month armistice, generosity which was to bring widespread criticism from Washington.

But Kendall had little time to gather even the details of the fighting on the eastern side of the city. He had taken part in, and he and Haile had hastily written the details of, the glorious action from the west which he considered the turning point in the engagement. His courier was waiting to speed the news to the *Picayune*. Back through Marín and Cerralvo and Mier the rider galloped, then down the river road through Camargo to Matamoros and on to the waiting steamer at Point Isabel. The news spread rapidly, but now for the first time Kendall's rider was dashing on ahead of the spreading news rather than following in its wake.

When the steamer *James L. Day* tied up at a New Orleans wharf on the night of October 3, its crew and passengers repeated rumors that Taylor had captured Monterrey, and all the morning papers carried the story. But the *Picayune* did not have to wait for further news as it had after Palo Alto and Resaca de la Palma and the occupation of Matamoros. This time the accounts dispatched by Kendall only eight days earlier were in its hands.

Although "Mustang" of the *Delta* fought through the battle of Monterrey with McCulloch's rangers, his paper, like the others in New Orleans, had to rely on the news from the officers of the steamer *James L. Day*.[8]

The *Picayune* rushed a story into type for its regular Sunday morning edition, then announced in eight-point capital letters, "An extra Picayune will be issued this morning at 10 o'clock, with ample details of the Battles of Monterey and the previous movements of the army." Compositors who had worked through the previous afternoon and evening stood at their cases and set up column after column from inspired dispatches. Crowds filled the office. Others stood along the walk and swarmed over the flagstones up and down Camp Street.

[8] After he became famous through his dispatches covering the battles in the Valley of Mexico, the *Delta*, November 6, 1847, said of Freaner, "At the battle of Monterey, where, it is said, he killed in single combat an officer of the Lancers and captured his Mexican horse, he gained the familiar cognomen of 'Mustang' over which signature he has since been a regular correspondent of the *Delta*." This version also is reported in J. F. H. Claiborne (ed.), *Life and Correspondence of John A. Quitman* (New York, 1860), I, 399 n.

Freaner, however, had been using this signature since June, 1846.

"Rapidly as our press works," the paper commented on October 6, "throwing off between five and six thousand sheets an hour, we began to despair of ever satisfying the demand for it. Vast numbers bought copies to forward by the mails and the boats which left that day, as well as to read; and several hours elapsed before our office and its vicinity resumed their usual Sabbath quiet and decorum."

And while the crowd along Camp Street was scrambling for the extras, the pony express was rushing copies to the North and East. In Mobile, Montgomery, Charleston, Wilmington, and Richmond, the *Picayune* carried the first news of the victory, with all the details that Kendall had witnessed. The staid old *National Intelligencer* got its copy in time to give the news to Washington, in four columns of type, on October 12, but already the *Picayune* had been rushed on up the seaboard.

"If we were able to lay before the citizens of New Orleans and the country at large full particulars of the three glorious days at Monterey in advance of our contemporaries," the *Picayune* stated, *"it was owing to no happy chance,* but was due entirely to the foresight and prudence of our associate, now with the Army. Appreciating the vast importance of the news, and prompt as he ever is to incur any expense which may contribute to the interest of the columns of the *Picayune,* Mr. Kendall determined to forward the despatches of our correspondents by express, cost what it would. Circumstances favored his design, and our packages reached us by private hands in *eight* days from Monterey."

"Mr. Kendall's express," later to become famous with the troops in central Mexico, had got its start. For some time the paper had considered plans for speeding its news from Mexico. Kendall's arrangements at Monterrey had settled the matter. Now, its editors boasted, "these plans shall be consumated without regard to expense."

The Battle of Monterrey

From a contemporary wood engraving

16

With Scott
at Vera Cruz

THREE DAYS after the surrender of Monterrey, Kendall rode in the escort that accompanied General Ampudia out of the city. The defeated Mexicans, released under General Taylor's generous armistice, marched along the Saltillo road between the frowning fortifications of the Bishop's Palace and Confederation Hill which Worth's men had taken in the first two days of reckless attack. When he rode past the Texans, still encamped by the sugarhouse down the road, Ampudia feared some of the rangers would shoot him from the roadside.

"The base and lying wretch—for every page of his black history proves him such—looked crest-fallen, nervous, and timid . . ." Kendall told the *Picayune* readers in his dispatch of September 29.

Two miles out of the city, the escort pulled up and watched the troops file by, followed by a pathetic host of camp women who trailed after their men on horseback, on burros, or trudged along on foot. Kendall chuckled over the misfortune of Don Ignacio, captain of the Guanajuato cavalry, whose pack mule the Texans had captured in the push on Monterrey. Not only did he lose his richly ornamented uniforms, but the prying rangers found among his baggage a half-dozen green, red, and figured petticoats, a dozen pairs of beautiful little satin slippers, and a number of linen *camisas*—all the wardrobe of some pretty Poblana girl who had followed him off to the wars.

With the evacuation of the city, the burial of his dead, and the care of his wounded, Taylor settled down to write his official reports of the battle and to await additional troops for his push deeper into Mexico. Since no immediate hostilities were expected, he released the Texas volunteers subject to recall on short notice, and Kendall's companions, who had performed such notable service as scouts, started back home. Leaving Haile and S. D. Allis, a former *Picayune* staff member now with Taylor's troops, to cover the military news, Kendall left for New Orleans.

Haile's final list of those killed and wounded at Monterrey reached the *Picayune* on November 4, filling three and one-half columns of tabulation of names, ranks, places, and dates. He also listed all arms and munitions captured, and sent an exclusive copy of Ampudia's proclamation telling of his "victory" at Monterrey. Afterwards Haile turned to writing humorous sketches, giving official reports of "Col. Pardon Jones" to General Taylor and President Polk. Then he followed Kendall to New Orleans.

With Taylor's troops concentrated at Monterrey, communication to and from his posts along the river was slowed down by the guerrillas who swarmed through the chaparral. Haile wrote the *Picayune* from Matamoros on November 1, "At Reynosa I saw for the first time your *extra* containing the account of the capture of Monterey. It was copied into the New York *Herald*, but there was only one copy of it in the place, and we had no time to read it and could not *borrow* it."

At home Kendall found interest in the battle of Monterrey still running high, and compliments on his and Haile's graphic stories of the campaign were pouring from newspapers all over the country. His first task was to write a detailed narrative of the activities of Worth's division, beginning with the skirmish between McCulloch's rangers and Torrejón's cavalry at Ramos on September 14. This account, running more than ten thousand words, filled nine columns of a supplement to the daily and weekly issues of November 19. Like the dispatches in the *Picayune's* memorable extra of October 4, this story was reprinted again and again in newspapers over widely scattered areas.

Worth, who had gone to Washington to submit his resignation because of a petty quarrel over seniority at the outbreak of hostilities, and thus missed the first battles of the war, now found himself a national hero. The names of Duncan, Childs, Hays, Walker, McCulloch, and other officers praised by Kendall and Haile became household words. The *Delta* complained, "The *Picayune's* account of the battle was copied and enlarged on until Generals Taylor, Twiggs, Butler, Quitman, etc., were forgotten. . . . The American people in the absence of all official accounts huzzaed for Worth's division, nor cast a thought upon those at the east end, who worked incessantly, day and night, to subdue the strong redoubts that opposed them. This is the greatest error that ever was committed, and owes its origin altogether to accident."[1]

This "accident" was coverage of the attack from the west by both Kendall and Haile, who had time to gather only a few facts about the fighting on the eastern side before their courier started his race for New Orleans. When Haile gathered data for his list of casualties, he found that only eighty out of five hundred and nine killed and injured were of Worth's division.

The *Delta* was voicing a complaint that was being expressed even among army officers, but it is doubtful that Kendall could have realized how widely his stories would be circulated in the interval of nearly three weeks before Taylor's official reports were released.

There was widespread disappointment in the United States over the armistice terms, and Kendall did his best to explain Taylor's effort to carry out the government's conciliatory policy toward the Mexicans. Soon after the battle of Monterrey, President Polk and his cabinet began to criticize Taylor and to assert that he was not qualified for the chief command. Kendall was caught in the crossfire of this criticism from Democratic leaders.

[1] *Delta*, May 2, 1847.

Polk confided to his diary on November 14 that Taylor "had been recently controlled, particularly in his expedition to Monterey by Bailey Peyton, Mr. Kendall, editor of the *Picayune* of New Orleans, and ass't adjutant Gen'l Bliss, who were cunning and shrewd men of more talents than himself, and had controlled him for political purposes. . . ."[2]

Criticism mounted as plans were made to invade Mexico City by way of Vera Cruz. Instead of getting reinforcements for his thrust down beyond Monterrey, Taylor found large numbers of his troops drawn off to aid General Winfield Scott in his campaign from the coast.

Polk's determination to push this campaign grew out of the realization that he had been duped by the wily Santa Anna. The exiled dictator had talked his way through the United States blockade with peaceful promises, and now was vigorously leading the war party. Plainly there was more hard fighting ahead.

Naval forces which had blockaded Tampico and Vera Cruz since the outbreak of hostilities, moved in on November 17 to attack Tampico, only to find the Mexicans had abandoned the city. General Scott passed through New Orleans in December, and early in 1847 set up headquarters on Lobos Island, off the Mexican coast, to direct the campaign against Vera Cruz. This time Lumsden went along to cover the big news for the *Picayune,* and at Tampico he was appointed aide on the staff of General Shields. Haile was sent back to the Rio Grande, while Kendall remained in the home office.

The war moved slowly, however. Taylor, after the battle of Monterrey, pushed on down to Saltillo, then withdrew to Monterrey. He marched southeast to Victoria, then back again, but the main forces of the Mexicans were far inland. Only elusive bands of guerillas hung around his flanks to harass his supply lines and pick off dispatch riders.

---

[2] Milo M. Quaife (ed.), *The Diary of James K. Polk* (Chicago, 1910), II, 236. Bailie Peyton, prominent Whig attorney in New Orleans, later was appointed minister to Chile by President Taylor.

Confusing orders from Washington and from Scott, together with his own bitterness at being stripped of so many of his forces, led Taylor to continue his maneuvers. Scott attempted to confer with him on the Rio Grande early in 1847, but slow communications found him on the march. He moved from Monterrey down to Saltillo again, then southward to the village of Agua Nueva, where he made contact with General Wool's force that had started from San Antonio to Chihuahua.

Haile was ordered to follow the coast campaign, and Kendall, impatient at office routine, joined Lumsden at Tampico. There both were alarmed at persistent reports that Santa Anna had struck in the north. They relayed these rumors to the *Picayune* and sailed for Vera Cruz with Scott's forces, but while they were writing their dispatches Santa Anna's beaten army was fleeing in disorder from the battlefields at Buena Vista.

While Taylor's little force was encamped at Agua Nueva, Santa Anna advanced up to San Luis Potosí and took charge of Ampudia's army which had marched out of Monterrey in defeat. He recruited vigorously, and in February marched northward to intercept Taylor, sending a strong cavalry force through the mountains to cut Taylor's communications at Saltillo. McCulloch recruited another company of rangers and hastened to join Taylor. He penetrated the Mexican picket lines and slipped out with the information that Santa Anna's force numbered more than twelve thousand, at least three times as many men as Taylor could muster.

Now for the first time Taylor realized his enormous disadvantage. He started northward to Saltillo, moving his troops and supplies as fast as possible, and leaving a rear guard to burn the last of his wagons and retreat at the first approach of the enemy. Santa Anna reached Agua Nueva on the night of February 21 to find wagons and buildings ablaze. Although his men were tired after the forced march from San Luis, he pushed on without rest, hoping to trap Taylor's retreating forces.

Taylor marched as far as the hacienda Buena Vista, in the

narrow pass through the mountains, and there turned to face the enemy on the morning of February 22.

The road to Saltillo followed the deep river canyon along the west side of this pass, and the plain was cut diagonally by deep gullies which grew shallower as they led into the foothills of the mountains to the east, more than a mile from the river. Taylor planted batteries commanding the road and sought to stop the enemy here and on the adjoining plains. Santa Anna, however, made only a demonstration in front of the well guarded road and threw heavy detachments into the foothills on the east. When night fell after the first few hours of fighting, Taylor rushed back to Saltillo to organize his defenses against a possible cavalry attack at the rear, then on the following morning marched back to Buena Vista with all the men who could be spared from his depot.

During the night Santa Anna strengthened his heavy columns in the foothills on the east, and when Taylor reached the field he found that his left flank was being slowly turned under the sheer weight of the Mexican attack. He pulled in artillery support from the detachments of Bragg, Sherman, and Washington on the west, and sent Jefferson Davis' Mississippians to the rescue of the faltering Indiana regiments. This checked the Mexican thrust and saved Taylor's little army from annihilation.

Throughout the day the battle raged from the river to the mountains on the east, and when darkness ended the struggle Taylor had regained the positions he had held that morning. When the next day dawned, Taylor found that Santa Anna had withdrawn his weary troops for the long march back to San Luis.

There was not a *Picayune* reporter within hundreds of miles to report the victory, but Kendall's friends in the army came through with another scoop for the paper. On the night of March 22, a month after the battle started, the *Picayune's* reporter, who had been stationed down the river to meet incoming boats, galloped down Camp Street and rushed into the office, and compositors began frantically to set type for an extra.

Paymaster Coffee had brought the news from the battlefield

to Monterrey, and sent it on by Mexican courier to Camargo. The rider was nine days on the road, making a detour of five hundred miles in order to escape the Mexican forces and rancheros who swarmed in the valley.

From Camargo "Dr. Turner, U.S.A." started for Washington to report the battle to the President, and Lieutenant J. J. C. Bibb got the news from him at Matamoros. Bibb wrote the story for the *Picayune* and it reached New Orleans two days before Doctor Turner came through. Long before he reached Washington, the *Picayune's* pony express had carried the news to the nation.

Determined not to be caught short again, the *Picayune* sent J. E. Durivage to cover the news along the Rio Grande. Anything Taylor did, after his astounding victory at Buena Vista, was news. Even before his official accounts of this battle were received in New Orleans, the *Picayune* was launching the boom that carried him to the presidency on the Whig ticket in 1848. Its issue of April 8 insisted, "It is not for the party press to snatch him.... He belongs to the country."

Although he had found little war news to report from Tampico, Kendall was impressed with the changes the invaders had made in the city. "Here," he wrote, "we have an American newspaper, the American theatre, the United States Hotel, the Union Restaurant, and an American court of justice."[3] Both Kendall and Lumsden served as judges in the court which was established to preserve order in the city and punish the numerous offenders among the volunteer troops.[4]

J. R. Barnard and William Jewell, New Orleans newspapermen, had established the Tampico *Sentinel*, and during his stay

[3] *Picayune,* March 19, 1847.

[4] *Ibid.*, February 25, March 9, 1847, relate Lumsden's serving during the trial of Louis Paulina Seron, who was found guilty of the murder of "Young Bowlin," a volunteer, and was executed. Kendall papers, H. C. King to Mrs. Fellowes, San Antonio, Texas, November 24, 1903, recounts a story of General Henry R. Jackson, who visited court in Tampico and reported, "Occupying the bench as trial judge was George Wilkins Kendall, dispensing justice with a dignity and dispatch which might have served as a model for a more formal court of law."

there Lumsden had helped edit the paper. By the time the troops moved on, they were ready to pack their type and establish a new paper in Vera Cruz, upon the surrender of the city.

When the advance on Vera Cruz got under way, Kendall and Lumsden sailed on the steamer *New Orleans,* one of more than a hundred vessels which carried twelve thousand troops. Within sight of the towering castle of San Juan de Ulloa, which guarded the entrance to the harbor of Vera Cruz, the invading forces landed on March 9 and began the investment of the city.

Thirteen days later, when Scott had his siege guns in place, he called on General Morales to surrender, but when Morales refused, bombardment started. By March 25 the poorly supplied city was starving, and the Mexicans ran up the white flag. They accepted Scott's terms two days afterwards.

Lumsden had written the *Picayune* on March 9, "I was unlucky enough to miss the sport at Monterey, and do not feel willing to be absent when the 'ball' opens at Vera Cruz." But while the operations before the city were under way, he was thrown from his horse and received a broken leg.

After he had checked on the widespread damage caused by the siege, Kendall picked up bits of human interest for *Picayune* readers. He wrote of the crowd of camp women and army retainers who, along with many inhabitants of the city, followed the evacuating troops.

"Among others in this motly throng," he wrote, "was a seedy looking priest, with grave but resigned expression of face. His entire stock of worldly effects seemed to consist of a fiddle and a fighting chicken, which he carried carefully, one under either arm. Immediately behind him stalked a young woman, barefoot and bareheaded yet wearing one of the gaudy petticoats of the country, who bore a cage containing a macaw of gayest plumage."[5]

During the siege of Vera Cruz, Haile, who had attended the United States Military Academy, was commissioned a first lieutenant of infantry, leaving Kendall to carry the full load of cover-

[5] *Picayune,* April 14, 1847.

ing the war news for the *Picayune*. He appointed D. Scully as the paper's agent in Vera Cruz, to receive dispatches from the interior and forward them to New Orleans along with copies of camp newspapers.

By now the tradition of newspapers springing up in the wake of the troops had become fixed, and a series of these papers was to trail Scott into Mexico City. Less than a week after the occupation of the city, the Vera Cruz *Eagle* appeared. It was published semiweekly by Peoples of the American *Flag* of Matamoros, and Jewell and Barnard, who had started the Tampico *Sentinel,* and was the first of a series of such papers.[6]

Scott, fearing the yellow fever along the seaboard, ordered his troops inland before the United States flag had been flying over Vera Cruz three days. Leaving Lumsden on a hospital bed, Kendall joined the march on April 14. On the morning of April 17 he wrote from Plan del Río that Worth's division had come up during the night. Just before noon he sent off another letter saying, "The division of Gen. Twiggs started two hours since, and a heavy cannonade has already commenced on his line from the fartherest of the Mexican works . . . I am going out . . . to the scene of action, and will return here at night to report the progress of the fight."

He did not return, however, until the next afternoon, when he wrote his dramatic story of the victory of Scott's troops in the mountain pass at Cerro Gordo.

---

[6]Spell, *op. cit.,* 29; *Picayune,* October 5, 1847; *Delta,* January 15, 1848, and *Weekly Delta,* June 28, September 6, 1847, mention these papers. One issue of the Vera Cruz *Chronicle* appeared, April 26; from June 15 to August 15, 1847, the *Sun of Anahuac* was published by a Cuban, R. Valdéz Alfonso. The *Genius of Liberty* was started September 25 by R. Matthewson and M. J. Quin, but was suppressed by military authorities. It was replaced, from December, 1847, to June 9, 1848, by the *Free American,* published by F. A. Devilliers, another New Orleans printer, and J. A. Epperson. Devilliers also had difficulties with military authorities and was ordered to leave.

17

March to Mexico City

FROM VERA CRUZ the road to the interior ran through coastal dunes, and for most of the forty miles to the Puente Nacional it was deep with sand. Fifteen miles further on in the hills lay the little village of Plan del Río, and beyond this the winding road led up sharply through the mountains to the higher plains of the "tierra templada" and thence on to Jalapa and Puebla. In April, 1847, it was incredibly hot in the lowlands.

The army's advance began when the division of General Twiggs moved out on April 8, followed by General Patterson with the volunteers of Shields and Pillow, then by Worth's division. Because of lack of transportation, baggage was cut to the minimum. Each company had only three tents for sick and arms, and each man carried full equipment, in addition to four days' rations, in his haversack.

Twiggs passed the Puente Nacional without opposition, but frequently saw small parties of the enemy to the right or left of the road. These increased as he neared Plan del Río, and he had to brush aside a mounted detachment before he could occupy the village. He pushed on two miles up the road into the mountains, but as the defile narrowed he found every commanding position in front strongly fortified and swarming with the enemy. He fell back to Plan del Río and sent word to General Scott by two separate detachments of dragoons, one of which was cut to pieces.

While he waited for Scott, Twiggs sent out reconnaissance parties. He found that a series of peaks rose to the right of the road, which ran close to the river through the pass and then turned sharply to the right behind these peaks. These elevations were heavily fortified, and the highest, Cerro Gordo, commanded both the approach from Plan del Río and the road behind it leading on to Jalapa and Puebla.

Lieutenant William T. H. Brooks, acting adjutant on the staff of Twiggs, pushed his reconnaissance far to the right and found that a difficult passage might be made beyond Cerro Gordo. Two young first lieutenants, Robert E. Lee and Peter G. T. Beauregard, followed this up with a thorough investigation and traced the route which the troops later followed. Fatigue parties started cutting down trees and removing heavy boulders from the route early on April 16, and by the next morning had opened the way to the ridge on the flank and partly to the rear of Cerro Gordo.

Twiggs moved his men in and took possession of this ridge by noon, and the cannonading began shortly afterward when the Mexicans discovered their position. It was this cannonading that Kendall heard as he was writing his letter to the *Picayune* on April 17, and rushed out to witness the fighting.

During the afternoon Santa Anna sent a column down from Cerro Gordo to dislodge the invaders, but Colonel William S. Harney's Second Dragoons drove it back, and Lieutenant Colonel Thomas Childs, with the First Artillery coming to his support, moved up the hill to within one hundred and fifty yards of the first Mexican breastworks before he was turned back.

Kendall sat in on the conference that night when Scott made his general plan of attack. Strong artillery reinforcements were moved up to the ridge under cover of darkness, and a howitzer battery was placed on top of the cliffs to the left of the river. Riley was to advance on the right of Cerro Gordo to gain the Jalapa road in the rear, while Harney was to storm the hill, with Shields in support. Pillow was to move over ground he had previously examined and to threaten or assail the batteries on the left of the main road. Meanwhile Worth was to march at sunrise, following the new road, in support of Twiggs.

At dawn the howitzer across the river opened fire on the Mexican fortification, while from their position on the flanking ridge the storming parties moved up the hill in three columns. They scaled one parapet after another, and sent the defenders scampering down the Jalapa road in disorder. Riley and Shields had moved down on the Mexican left, turning the enemy's position, while Twiggs pursued the fleeing reserves down the road.

"Santa Anna himself," Kendall wrote, "cutting the saddle mule from his travelling coach, fled through the chaparral and escaped. The victory in this quarter of the field was complete, all the artillery of the Mexicans, an immense amount of ammunition, military stores, and provisions fell into the hands of the Americans, with several wagonloads of specie. Even Santa Anna's tent, private papers, and all his camp equipage were among the spoils."[1]

By four o'clock Kendall was back in Plan del Río writing to the *Picayune,* "the rout of the Mexicans was total—complete." There, also, he learned of a futile and costly attack which General Pillow had ordered the volunteer brigade of Tennesseans and Pennsylvanians to make against the strong batteries at the left of the main road while Harney was storming the peak. More than a fourth of his column of four hundred men had been killed or wounded.

"A bold feint or demonstration sufficient to have held the enemy in this quarter and prevent them from sending reinforcements to the Cerro and the batteries on the extreme left was all that was required," he wrote.[2] "But Pillow was craving distinc-

[1] Kendall, *The War Between the United States and Mexico, Illustrated* (New York, 1852), 25.

[2] *Loc. cit.* Kendall's failure to praise General Pillow later was to bring complaint in Democratic newspapers that he had deliberately refrained from giving credit to the exploits of any but officers who were members of the Whig party. See Boston *Post,* October 4, 1847; Washington *Union,* October 22, 1847, and the *Picayune's* reply, November 25, 1847.

tion, his men eager to have a hand in the conflict, the position and great strength of the batteries and intrenchments imperfectly understood, and an unnecessary outlay of life followed an ill-advised and profitless attack."

This attack was echoed in the *Picayune* when the officers of the Second Regiment of Tennessee Volunteers addressed a letter to the public explaining their reversal. Editorially, it added that "the assault miscarried solely because they were commanded to do an impossible thing by an officer who enjoys the exclusive credit of having ever ordered a regiment from that gallant State to make a charge which necessarily resulted in failure." It ran Pillow's reply to the charges made by the Tennessee regiment, adding "we thought it but fair to General P. to republish it."[3]

Already Pillow had the *Picayune* worried. He was no military man, but a political appointee who had served as chairman of the Tennessee delegation which led the stampede for Polk's nomination in 1844. Now, as major general, he ranked above every other officer with Scott's column except Scott himself, and, the paper stated on June 2, "if Gen. Scott should meet with an accident, the command of the army would devolve upon him."

Kendall's letter reached the *Picayune* on the night of April 30, in time for its issue of the next morning to carry the headline,

ANOTHER GLORIOUS VICTORY!!!
BATTLE OF CERRO GORDO

A brief summary of the highlights, apparently prepared in the office, was followed by four columns of Kendall's letters from April 16 through April 18, all dispatched by courier from Plan del Río. Its issue of Sunday, May 2, was expanded to eight pages instead of four, and included a four-column cut showing a "Sectional and a Bird's eye view of the pass at Cerro Gordo." On May 7, it carried a detailed story on the battle, by Kendall, with-

[3] *Picayune*, June 9, 1847. Private correspondence between Bullitt and Kendall indicated that the editors wished to print as little as possible concerning this quarrel between officers.

out date line, with two columns of his list of the dead and wounded. This issue also carried his letter of April 20, telling of his arrival in Jalapa.

When the troops moved past Cerro Gordo to Jalapa, enterprising printers were close on their heels. Jewell stayed on in Vera Cruz to publish the *Eagle,* while Peoples and Barnard moved inland to start the Jalapa *American Star.* The editors had taken over the press and type of a former Jalapa paper, and issued the *Star* there until May 13.[4]

From Jalapa Kendall continued to send long letters to the *Picayune,* which it repeatedly referred to as "the very latest news from Mexico." He enclosed copies of the *Star* and such Mexican papers as he could secure, and hired his own couriers to get these dispatches through to Vera Cruz. The pony express continued to carry regular editions from New Orleans eastward, bringing back market quotations and commercial news which was now bulletined, "Extraordinary Express."

This express had brought in news of successes on other fronts. Before the battle of Monterrey, Colonel Stephen W. Kearny made a hurried march across the prairies and on August 18, 1846, took possession of New Mexico. Colonel Sterling W. Price early in 1847 put down the only serious attempt of Mexico to recover this territory. California surrendered to the United States by the Treaty of Cahuenga on January 13, 1847, and on the following March 1 Colonel Alexander W. Doniphan took possession of Chihuahua.

The accumulated enthusiasm of New Orleans rose to a high pitch with news of the victories at Buena Vista, Vera Cruz, and Cerro Gordo. To celebrate the recent triumph of arms the city arranged a mammoth public demonstration centering around Municipal Hall. There were placed transparencies which were

---

[4] *Ibid.,* May 6, 1847 Long afterward, when the troops were being moved back through the city from the capital, John Shea started another American paper, the *Watch Tower.* Volume 1, Number 1, February 12, 1848, is in the Library of Congress.

full-length likenesses of Scott and Taylor; Taylor on the field of Buena Vista with glass in hand and anxious expression; Scott, after the victory of Cerro Gordo, ordering a forward movement upon the city of Mexico. Between these two was a tablet which recorded the battles of the Revolutionary War, another with the victories of 1812, and a third with the victories already achieved in a single year. A bust of Washington surmounted the whole. Colored lights surrounded the square before Municipal Hall, and hung in festoons between the trees. Stores, shops, and private homes were decorated and lighted. Bullitt's house on the square had a transparency which represented the Kentucky regiment passing through the craggy ravine at Buena Vista.

The newspapers along Camp Street competed with each other in the matter of transparent illuminations in their windows. The *Delta* had three transparencies, one representing the conquest of New Mexico and California, a second illustrating the victories of General Taylor, and a third with a likeness of General Scott. The *Times* had full length transparencies of Scott and Taylor; in the *Price Current* windows were illuminated likenesses of every hero, military and naval; the *Bulletin* gave every pane in its windows to a hero or to an event in the war, and the *Picayune,* in line with its growing presidential boom for Taylor, had a huge illuminated likeness of him on display. The levee blazed with lights, and every ship along the river was lighted.

Scott could not follow up his victory at Cerro Gordo because of lack of transportation and because of the approaching end of service of the twelve months' volunteers. The *Picayune,* summing up Kendall's dispatches, had stated on April 27:

It is not supposed here that a single regiment can be formed out of all the twelve months' men now in Mexico. . . . The officers are as little desirous as the men of remaining in the service. . . .

The reason for this universal desire to quit the service has been explained to us. The men of Monterey and Buena Vista assert, and with good reason, that the laurels that have been won by them have been garnered by the Government to decorate other brows. They say, and with truth, that no valor, no sacrifice, no victories of theirs can insure their promotion or protect them against . . . inexperienced officers and . . . the command of political appointees. . . .

From Jalapa, Scott sent back to Vera Cruz the volunteers who were not willing to re-enlist. Sickness cut his effective strength still further. Kendall insisted that the American commander could not have marched upon the Mexican capital with over five thousand reliable troops; while had he taken even this number he would have been compelled to leave insufficient garrisons in his rear, and cut himself from all hope of support from any quarter in case of reverse.

Scott was further exasperated by the arrival of Nicholas P. Trist, a clerk in the State Department at Washington, with Polk's authority to suspend hostilities and negotiate for peace. He arrived in Vera Cruz on May 6, three days later wrote Scott announcing his mission, and then followed on to Jalapa.

Meanwhile the commanding general had determined to move on to a better location at Puebla, one hundred and eighty-six miles to the southwest on the road to Mexico, and sent Worth ahead to occupy the city. Worth advanced and fought a brief engagement with three thousand mounted Mexicans before Santa Anna retired from Puebla along the road to Mexico City. For once, Kendall did not ride out with Worth's command as had been his custom since the troops landed at Vera Cruz. This time he stayed in Jalapa nursing a cold, and moved up to Puebla with the headquarters staff. Once there, he still was too ill to write, and his friend Captain Forbes Britton of the quartermaster corps served as correspondent. Signing his letter of June 3 "Man in the White Hat," Britton wrote:

"Gen. Scott and staff, with the dragoons, a train of about forty wagons, Mr. Kendall, your humble servant and no particular quantity of *adventurers,* reached Puebla on the 27th ult., and on the 28th Gen. Twiggs' division, with the big train; all of whom and which combined with previous arrivals, give us a force of about 6,000 men, 600 wagons and near 5,000 horses and mules.

... Two days ago it was thought Gen. Scott would move immediately on the capital, but I think this morning he will remain here three or four weeks, at the expiration of which time he will not only have slightly increased his army but will have all his horses in good condition."

Kendall resumed his correspondence two days later, explaining "Thanks ... to starvation, to hot mustard foot baths, and to quinine—especially to quinine—I have been enabled to weather the attack ..."

News from home brought echoes of the administration's continued criticism of General Taylor, and Kendall was furious, particularly when Taylor was censured for not pursuing and annihilating Arista's army after the battle of Resaca. Taylor did pursue Arista into the Rio Grande, Kendall insisted, but it would have been expecting too much, even of American soldiers, to strip and pursue the enemy across the river with their bare hands. Furthermore, Taylor's march deep into Mexico with such a small army would read in aftertime like a romance; and Worth's entrance into Puebla had no parallel since the days of Cortés.

Kendall broke another lance in Worth's behalf in the matter of provisions and supplies. The government's policy contemplated payment of good prices for everything purchased from the Mexicans, and since the previous April the quartermaster's department had sent requests to Washington for more than three hundred thousand dollars, but not a cent had been received.

Kendall had a reliable news source for these facts close at hand in L. S. Hargous, army agent, who formerly was consul at Vera Cruz and who had interceded in Kendall's behalf during his imprisonment in 1842. Hargous and other provisioners for the troops had great difficulty in securing cash to make purchases. The only men from whom money could be borrowed on any terms were the gamblers who followed the armies. They were ready each morning to turn over the previous night's winnings to the quartermasters, receiving drafts on the United States treasury. The Mexicans were well aware of the financial plight of the

Americans, and made capital of it in their newspaper propaganda by publishing letters which had been intercepted by *leperos* on the route back to the coast. Long before Kendall moved to Puebla these roadside bandits, operating between Jalapa and Vera Cruz, had made the sending of news to New Orleans a serious problem. When Worth marched out of Jalapa for Puebla, Kendall made arrangements for news and Mexican papers to be sent back from the column. However, on May 23, he complained, "I am fearful that an express man, who must have left Puebla with newspapers and letters for the *Picayune,* has been cut off."

One of the most vicious of the guerrilla leaders was Padre Jarauta, who ranged all the way from the hot lowlands to the mountain passes between Jalapa and Perote. Large numbers joined his band during the summer of 1847. They were well mounted, knew every part of the country and the best points for ambuscade and attack. They struck quickly, retreated to secret strongholds, and harassed even the largest detachments of Scott's soldiers. After the war Jarauta attempted to overthrow the Mexican government and was captured and shot.

Another bandit leader, Rebolledo, collected a group of minor guerrilla bands and attacked a large military train between Vera Cruz and Jalapa on June 5 and 6. One hundred and twenty-seven wagons had moved out from Vera Cruz on June 4, to be joined shortly after by a train of between five and six hundred pack mules, probably the property of United States merchants and adventurers who sought the protection of the troops along the route.

On its second day out the train was strung along the sandy road for miles, many of the teams having broken down. While it was still scattered along the first ground which afforded ambush, the command suddenly was attacked on every side by swarms of guerrillas. The attackers eventually were pushed back out of musket range, but twenty-four men belonging to the escort, and a large number of frightened teamsters and muleteers, were killed or wounded.

Guerrilla attacks were nothing new; for many years bandits had made the transporting of dispatches difficult. The most successful dispatch rider over this route was Raphael Beraza, a native Spaniard who had served under Wellington in the Peninsula and who had become a British citizen. He was often referred to as "the best express man in the world."[5]

In spite of all efforts, couriers with messages to Scott repeatedly were intercepted. On June 11 Kendall wrote that Mexico City newspapers were publishing these letters, but except for one from Secretary Marcy to Scott, they were of little consequence to the military operations. Kendall read in the Mexican papers several letters addressed to himself, otherwise he never would have known their contents. To meet this difficulty in his own operations, Kendall organized a courier staff made up of Mexicans, and the *Picayune* began to run explanatory lines over his stories, "Sent entire by special express from Puebla."

Shortly afterward the paper reported that one of General Scott's Mexican messengers had been murdered on the road. One of Kendall's express riders, also a Mexican, arrived in Vera Cruz on July 16 badly wounded and without his dispatches. Near Orizaba he had been attacked by five bandits, robbed, stabbed repeatedly, and when he feigned unconsciousness he was left for dead. After they left he found a letter from Kendall to his Vera Cruz agent, torn to bits, lying nearby. He gathered up most of the pieces and made his way to the coast.

Such hazards sent wages of expressmen soaring. Kendall wrote in the *Picayune* of August 7, "I despatched a man to Vera Cruz with letters, and after his departure I was obliged, by virtue of a verbal contract, to pay all the expenses of his family during his absence, to keep a candle continually burning and have a function performed in one of the churches for his safety and *buen viaje*. I have just learned that the fellow was captured on the road by the guerrillerios, stripped, beat most unmercifully,

[5] Kendall manuscript, "History of the Mexican War," 733; Rives, *The United States and Mexico,* II, 495; and *Picayune,* August 24, 1847.

his horse—I paid for the animal—taken from him, and was then turned loose to make the best of his way back to Puebla."

Kendall was disappointed about his letters, but added, "I will only say that I thought the family made too much fuss from the first."

But the *Picayune* continued to get his letters; it had now become a game of wits, and newspapers in the east began to comment on his success in eluding the bandits. "Mr. Kendall perseveres in sending couriers to Vera Cruz," *Niles' National Register* stated on August 21, "though he has had three captured. One was killed."

Early in August Captain Ruff with a squadron of cavalry gave the guerrillas a severe drubbing at San Juan de los Llanos, but this provided only short relief and the bandits continued to be a menace to couriers as long as Scott's force remained in Mexico.

Except for the excitement of getting his letters through to Vera Cruz and the long dispute between Scott and Trist, life in camp at Puebla was monotonous for Kendall. He was incensed by Scott's treatment of Worth, which led to estrangement between the two. Worth, in accord with Scott's written instructions, pursued a policy of conciliating the inhabitants, yet Scott found fault with the terms given. Kendall watched this unfortunate situation, and listened to camp gossip about Scott's plan to bribe Santa Anna into peace with ten thousand dollars down and a promised three million,[6] while between times he wandered about the city noting the way of life of a population that seemed little concerned over the presence of an invading army.

The same merchants, barbers, restaurant keepers, bartenders, and theater companies that had followed Taylor's army of occupation through northern Mexico and trailed Scott to Vera

---

[6] Elliott, *Winfield Scott*, 497, states that "a million dollars had been earmarked from the secret service funds, to be paid to the Dictator as soon as the treaty was formally ratified." Camp gossip increased the amount, and garbled accounts of the transaction appeared in different newspapers in the United States.

Cruz, now moved up to Puebla and set up their places of business. Kendall went to Spanish theaters and was much impressed with the dancing. He wrote the *Picayune* that the "Bolero" and other Spanish dances were never given with proper effect in the United States, but that in Mexico one saw the "Jota Arragonese" danced by women who labored "under no particular restraint that can be discovered."

Throughout the camp, as Scott and Trist argued back and forth, there was talk of peace which Kendall discounted thoroughly. "I do not know that any one has reflected much upon this subject," he wrote to the *Picayune,* "but to me it seems that this thing of making peace is to be a more difficult matter than making war upon the Mexicans, and will be surrounded with greater perplexities. Texas has to be brought into question, other boundaries taken into consideration, California is to be a bone of contention, indemnifications and costs of war are to be called into account, and a thousand other matters will be found in the catalogue of stumbling blocks in the way of an amicable arrangement of difficulties. The 'three millions' after Santa Anna has helped himself—for he must be thought of first—will not go far, in way of salve or cordial for the many wounds under which poor Mexico is suffering, and there will be other provisos than Wilmot's for increasing the sum."[7]

Weeks later, he wrote home that peace again was being talked, but that he had no faith in the prospects for settlement. Santa Anna's sole aim, he warned, was to gain time.[8]

Peace rumors continued so strong in Vera Cruz that the *Picayune* felt justified in calling attention to them. Few thought that Scott would meet much opposition if he were to march on Mexico

[7] *Picayune,* July 8, 1847. The Wilmot proviso, ultimately defeated in both houses, attempted to bar slavery in territory acquired from Mexico, and was the chief subject of debate in Congress through the early months of 1847. Preston King of New York tried to introduce a bill appropriating three million dollars, with the proviso as one of its clauses, but failed in the attempt.

[8] This much was deciphered from fragments of the letter recovered by Kendall's wounded courier, and published in the *Picayune,* July 23, 1847.

City. "Mr. Kendall thinks differently, and gives his reasons," it added on August 7.

With his letters Kendall now was sending current issues of the *American Star No. 2,* published twice a week in Puebla by Peoples and Barnard and Charles Callahan, former *Picayune* staff member. The paper was tabloid size with three columns to the page, containing official orders and sentences, reports of courts martial, and a few news items from the United States. They still used type from a Mexican shop, and substituted two 'v's' for a 'w.'[9]

Slowly reinforcements came in and the health of the troops improved. Brigadier General Franklin Pierce arrived with a detachment of twenty-five hundred newly recruited regulars, and Scott, after sixteen weeks of delay at Puebla, determined to abandon his communications at Vera Cruz and march on Mexico City, ninety miles away. According to Kendall's tabulation, the entire force which set out on this hazardous enterprise included ten thousand seven hundred and thirty-eight men, barely three-fourths of whom were tried regulars.

Then followed weeks when an anxious nation wondered if this little army would return.

[9] Two issues of this paper, July 1 and July 8, 1847, are in the Library of Congress. The *Picayune,* July 8, 1847, announced receipt of copies "from the 12th to the 27th June."

18

Armistice—
"we're humbugged"

AS HE RODE out of the mountains with Worth's column and looked down on the valley, Kendall got a much more pleasant view of Mexico City than he had five and a half years earlier when he was paraded in as a prisoner.

The ancient lake of Texcoco which surrounded the city in the days of Cortés had dried up considerably by 1847, yet it remained a fairly large body of water on the right of the road from Puebla. South of this road lay two other lakes, Chalco, which was the larger and lay farther to the east, and the Laguna de Xochimilco, a long narrow body of water extending almost to Mexicalcingo, just southeast of Mexico City.

To the north, the rough hills of Guadalupe Hidalgo guarded the city, but on its other sides approach was gained through a half-dozen causeways leading over boggy, marshy ground. Each of these causeways entered the city through a *garita,* or fortified customs house. The strongly fortified hill, El Peñón, frowned down on the Puebla road. A branch road turned left of this hill and led directly to the heavy defenses of Mexicalcingo, while another route led to the north and around Lake Texcoco, into the hills north of the city which were bristling with guns.

The only other route lay south of the city, around Lake Chalco, following a little-used road which eventually led into a ring of fortifications that guarded the southern and western approaches. These defenses included the village of Mexicalcingo, a fortified bridge, the church and convent at Churubusco, and the Molino del Rey with the towering castle of Chapultepec on a hill nearby.

By August 15 all four divisions were encamped in the vicinity of Lake Chalco. They had expected opposition in the strong mountain pass at Río Frío where defense works had been started, but the pass was deserted. Small parties of lancers, seen on the distant mountainside, fled when Harney's men approached.

Kendall reported a meeting of the general officers at Ayotla on the morning of August 14, when Scott announced his plans of advancing by the direct road to Mexicalcingo, which turned to the left of El Peñón. Twiggs, Pillow, and Quitman were to follow this way, while Worth was to take the difficult road around Lake Chalco, sending his heavy baggage up the lake in boats, in an effort to turn the village from the rear.

After these orders were issued, Colonel James F. Duncan, who had been dispatched by Worth on a reconnaissance to the south of the lakes, returned with the information that, despite earlier reports, even the heavy baggage and artillery could be transported over this route. The Americans were lucky, however, because, save for the light rainfall of 1847, parts of this road would have been entirely under water.

Scott immediately cancelled his earlier orders for the dangerous direct attack on Mexicalcingo, and ordered the movement south of the lakes.[1]

[1] Kendall, in his manuscript "History of the Mexican War," 658–67, devotes much space to the argument that Scott had not previously selected the southern route; Rives, *op. cit.*, II, 457–58, agrees; Smith, *op. cit.*, II, 96, leaves the question open, while Elliott, *op. cit.*, 503–505, points out that Scott at Puebla "had pre-determined to use the Chalco–San Augustin route should it prove practicable for the trains and artillery," but available information caused him to abandon the plan, then to choose it after Duncan's reconnaissance.

Shortly afterward, Duncan wrote to an acquaintance in Pittsburgh, discussing the choice of the route around Lake Chalco, a choice upon which Scott's later successes depended, taking from Scott the credit for this decision. The letter was published in Pittsburgh and at other points, and later appeared in the Tampico *Sentinel*. When Scott eventually saw it at the close of his campaign, he interpreted it as a scheme to rob him of credit for the victorious conclusion of the war. The arrest of Duncan, one of the disagreeable episodes in Scott's quarrel with his officers, followed immediately.

Worth moved out, and on the night of August 17 occupied the large village of San Agustín. The invaders were now nearly ten miles south of Mexico City, and two miles south of the important settlement of San Antonio, an outpost of the southern fortifications. To their left rose a mass of volcanic rock, known as the Pedregal, so rough and sharp that foot soldiers could make their way over it only with the greatest difficulty. Running north and west from San Agustín, the road led through Coapa and San Antonio, while beyond the Pedregal another road ran north and east from the village of Contreras through the rancho of Padierna, and the settlements of San Gerónimo, San Angel, and Coyoacán. Both roads converged in a rough triangle at Churubusco. A lateral road skirted the northern rim of the Pedregal, connecting Coyoacán and San Antonio.

Scott came up on the morning of the eighteenth and ordered Worth to move on San Antonio. This approach, however, could be made only over a causeway swept by cannon, and after the first contact with the enemy Worth halted for reconnaissance into the Pedregal on his left. This reconnoitering party met and turned back a body of Mexicans in the lava beds, and learned that General Valencia had a strongly fortified camp along the Contreras–San Angel road at Padierna. More important still, this party brought back the information that a passage for artillery could be made through the Pedregal, though with great difficulty.

Continuing the turning tactics that he had started with the swing around Lake Chalco, Scott now determined to attack the Mexicans at Padierna, rather than strike directly north over a route the enemy had chosen to defend so strongly. Worth was ordered to remain before San Antonio, while Pillow was sent to open the road through the Pedregal and gain possession of the Contreras–San Angel road, Twiggs following in his support.

By three o'clock on the afternoon of August 19 this advance met stiff opposition, and Scott, coming out on the Pedregal, sent his forces up toward the village of San Gerónimo in an effort to cut off Valencia's support from the capital. When the first of the troops reached the road they had a brief brush with Santa Anna, who was moving down to support Valencia. The Mexicans drew off, however, as a torrent of rain ushered in darkness, and left the invaders in possession of the village.

General Persifor F. Smith advanced to assume command of the troops at San Gerónimo, while General Pillow and General Twiggs, attempting to pick their way on foot through the Pedregal, got lost and returned to San Agustín in the darkness. During the night, while his soldiers lay unprotected in the drenching rain, Smith devised a plan of moving into the hills to his left and attacking Valencia's rear at dawn, and Captain Robert E. Lee made a dangerous trip back over the lava to arrange a simultaneous frontal attack by General Franklin Pierce's unit. Pillow's later claim that he planned these maneuvers in the night was one of the factors in his bitter dispute with Scott.

The rain continued, and Valencia was taken by surprise at daybreak on August 20. Cut off from retreat toward the capital, and attacked from front and rear, his command was cut to pieces and scattered in the hills. This inaugurated one of the most spectacular series of victories in a single day in the history of American arms. Twenty-two pieces of brass artillery, many of them of heavy caliber, a great number of muskets and other small arms, an immense amount of ammunition and military stores, besides nearly one thousand pack mules and horses fell into the hands of the invaders. It raised the spirits of the entire army under General Scott, so despondent when darkness and rain had closed in on them the previous night. It was a crushing blow to the Mexicans.

After Valencia's rout, Santa Anna withdrew his threatening column and retired to Churubusco. General Twiggs, who had come on the field at Contreras, moved the victors up and took possession of San Angel, where General Pillow, after crossing the Pedregal in daylight from San Agustín, now joined the column and assumed command. Scott ordered Pillow to follow the enemy cautiously, and soon directed him to halt his pursuit at Coyoacán.

While the battle of Contreras was in progress, Worth waited impatiently before San Antonio, fired on occasionally by the guns of the settlement. Kendall sat with Worth and his staff at breakfast in the hacienda of Coapa, that morning, when a ball from one of the enemy's batteries struck the window sill, passed through the room and entered the wall. It destroyed a tablet set in the wall, a memorial to a little child, and the Mexicans later accused Worth's staff of vandalism in desecrating a tomb. Kendall vigorously defended his companions against such a charge.

Worth's restless nature was ill suited to such waiting. With Scott's troops in possession of Coyoacán, the Mexicans would have found their position at San Antonio untenable, for a quick march across the lateral road would have placed the invaders in their rear. Before Pillow's advance had moved up to Coyoacán, however, Worth had sent a flanking column around to the left of San Antonio, at the same time attacking from the front. The Mexicans began to withdraw, and Worth swept through the village as his flankers cut the retreating column in two and captured General Perdigán Garay, whose troops were fleeing toward Churubusco.

Worth moved on after the fugitives, and when Scott arrived at Coyoacán he learned that Worth already had engaged the Mexicans at their fortifications at Churubusco. The invaders were now on ground that was entirely unknown to them, but there was little for Scott to do but support Worth in his attack.

As Kendall rode up with Worth's staff, along the highway lined with cornfields and into the village of Churubusco, he saw that the way was barred by a heavy *tête de pont* which the enemy had thrown up in front of the bridge across the river. Three hundred yards to the left in front of the bridge, the church and convent of San Pablo de Churubusco formed a square whose front was protected by a wall scaffolded for infantry. Behind this wall was a building crowded with sharpshooters; and farther in the rear rose the church, its windows, roofs and even belfry filled with men. Embankments lined the stream to the right as the invaders advanced from San Antonio. Beyond the convent, across a wet marsh, a heavy force of the enemy was posted to oppose any attempt to gain the road in the rear.

From his position at Coyoacán Scott ordered Pillow through the fields to support Worth, sent Twiggs up the road to attack Churubusco from the southwest, and detailed Shields and Pierce north of Coyoacán to cross the river and attempt to turn the fortifications from the west.

When Worth moved on the bridgehead, he met a vicious fire from its cannon and also a cross fire from the convent on his left. He pushed his column into the cornfields at the right, but this afforded little protection. Pillow now came up, and a detachment was sent to the left toward the road leading from the convent to the bridge, but it, too, met a devastating fire.

Twiggs then advanced from Worth's left and engaged the forces in the convent, and Shields and Pierce crossed the river and commenced the attack on the reserves in the rear. At every point the invaders met such resistance that their situation was critical. Shields's column was so severely shattered that Scott sent up his last reserve detachment in its support.

Scott now was compelled to move up to within range of the guns of the convent of San Pablo for safety, since numerous bodies of Mexican lancers were hovering in the rear, and he had not even enough men with him to beat off a single squadron. There were no idlers on this occasion—every camp follower was put to some use during the contest. While at Chalco all the sutlers' clerks, extra wagoners, circus riders, gamblers, and others in the miscellaneous crowd of camp followers enrolled themselves under Captain McKistry, and performed good service.

The first impression upon the enemy's lines was effected by Worth and Pillow at the *tête de pont*. The fire there was incessant for nearly two hours, then began to slacken as the first assailants reached a point within close musket range. They finally carried this work with the bayonet, turned one of its cannon on the retreating Mexicans and another on the rear of the convent. Duncan's light battery, which had been driven from the road and had found shelter behind some mud huts to the right, now opened at half range on the rear and flank of the convent. Throughout the engagement, Kendall was with Duncan's battery, and stood by the guns as they carried on this barrage.

Twiggs had found lodgment under the walls of the church and convent, but the defenders held on stubbornly, and the work was carried from the front only after its position was weakened by the fall of the bridgehead. The boldest in holding out were deserters from Scott's ranks who had formed the San Patricio Regiment, and who fought with desperation to the last, tearing down several of the white flags hoisted by the Mexicans.

As the enemy poured out of these defenses, Santa Anna attempted to organize a counterattack at the village of Los Portales, but this resulted only in a noisy demonstration. The troops of Worth, Pillow, and Twiggs effected a junction on the causeway and pursued the fugitives to a point within a mile and a half of the *garita* of San Antonio Abad, leading into the city. Here a halt was called, but Captain Philip Kearny, with a handful of mounted men, charged on into one of the batteries defending the gate. Kearny lost an arm in the charge, and was made a major for his "gallant and meritorious" service.

Kendall wrote that if Kearny "had been supported by a hundred resolute men, the garita of San Antonio Abad might have been held. A single infantry regiment, supported by a light battery, might even have entered the capital and taken possession of the grand plaza and National Palace, for Santa Anna could not have rallied a formation sufficiently strong to resist such a force."[2] However, Scott sent a staff officer forward ordering the troops to encamp for the night, and the push into the city which Kendall believed might have followed so easily on Santa Anna's headlong retreat was to be delayed until another series of bitter struggles crushed his final resistance.

As fighting ended at nightfall, Kendall hurried from tent to

[2] Kendall manuscript, "History of the Mexican War," 723.

tent, rounding up details of the series of engagements. James L. Freaner, the tall, rawboned, slow-talking correspondent of the *Delta*, who also was collecting news to send back to New Orleans by courier, called at the headquarters of General Pillow and asked for his version of the victories. Pillow prepared a statement which he asked be included with Freaner's dispatches, but Freaner insisted on reading it before he left the tent. It was so exaggerated in its praise of Pillow, and so different from Freaner's own observations during the two days, that he did not send it to the *Delta*, but kept it with his field notes. A short time afterward, however, Judge Alexander Walker, editor of the *Delta* opened a bundle of Freaner's letters from the front, and finding among them one signed "Leonidas," published it. This letter, which had somehow been smuggled into the dispatch bag, proved to be an almost identical copy of Pillow's statement to Freaner, the original of which Freaner still had. This original eventually reached General Scott's hands.[3]

This "Leonidas Letter" was soon to be branded as a hoax, but it was reprinted widely and proved one of the principal points of Scott's dispute with his officers, a quarrel which was echoed between the Whig and Democratic papers throughout the country as the presidential election of 1848 approached.

During the two days' fighting, Scott's casualties[4] had been terrific. While his tired soldiers were searching through the cold,

[3] *Delta,* September 9, 1847, and April 7, 1848; *Picayune,* September 16, 18, 21, 24, 1847; New Orleans *Crescent,* May 10, 1848; Thirtieth Congress, first session, *Senate Executive Documents, Doc.* 65, p. 14. "Leonidas" claimed that General Pillow had planned every move that led to the victories of Contreras and Churubusco, that he had issued every order except one of minor importance which he requested General Scott to issue to General Worth, and then soared to rhetorical heights in praise of Pillow's genius.

The *Picayune,* in reprinting the letter, included a fantastic paragraph which it insisted that the *Delta* had deleted, relating a mighty hand-to-hand combat between Pillow and a ferocious Mexican officer. Pillow vanquished him handily, while troops of both sides gazed in awe.

[4] Thirtieth Congress, first session, *Senate Executive Documents, Doc.* 1, p. 314. General Scott reported that his losses, killed and wounded, amounted to 1,053. This must have been more than ten per cent of his effective strength.

rainy night for their killed and wounded companions, a delegation from the British legation in the city arrived at Worth's headquarters to urge an armistice. The deputation included Edward Thornton, attaché of the legation; E. Mackintosh, consul general, and Raphael Beraza, the celebrated English courier. They visited in Worth's tent a few minutes while an escort to the rear was being arranged, and after they left, Kendall exclaimed bluntly, "It's no use, we're humbugged—Mackintosh is among them."[5]

He later wrote, "The appearance of Mackintosh, at the American headquarters beyond, betokened trickery; he was a man ever ready to do Santa Anna's dirty work, and had been so long in Mexico that he had become expert in every species of duplicity and deceit."[6]

Scott lent a willing ear to the suggestions of the Englishmen that peace could easily be brought about if he would halt his army outside the capital. His entrance at this time, they argued, would humble the vanity of a proud people, disperse the government, and scatter the legislature with its principal elements of the peace party. Kendall felt that Scott had previously determined to halt and negotiate for peace, hence his ready acceptance of the suggested armistice.

Years later, Kendall recalled the lives lost in the needless fighting that followed this armistice, and criticized Scott bitterly. "Gross blunders and mistakes have been made in war, but few as flagrant as this," he wrote. "Politics and Presidential aspirations and ignorance of Santa Anna's cunning and duplicity, were the cause. The death of many brave men followed the armistice signed at Tacubaya, and no one was to blame but Winfield Scott; he had his own way. He thought he was macadamizing a plain and smooth road to the White House at Washington. A peace

[5] This incident is related in Raphael Semmes, *The Campaign of General Scott in the Valley of Mexico,* Cincinnati, 1852, 300. Semmes, a lieutenant in the Navy, served as aide to Scott during this campaign, and had accompanied Worth during the operations at Churubusco.

[6] Kendall manuscript, "History of the Mexican War," 733.

with Mexico then so ardently desired in the States, would open a broad turnpike. . . . Winfield Scott missed the road."[7]

On the next morning Kendall finished his account of the events on the march from Puebla and the engagements of the two strenuous days of fighting, sending them off to the *Picayune* by a special courier. He then moved to Tacubaya where Scott had established headquarters, and from there watched while Quitman, P. F. Smith, and Pierce wrangled with the Mexican delegation over the terms of the armistice. He hastily compiled a list of the killed and wounded, and reported that teamsters from the camp sent into Mexico City for supplies under armistice terms were stoned by a mob. He wrote that Trist on August 25 had notified Señor Pacheco, Mexican commissioner of foreign relations, that he was ready to begin negotiations for peace, and had received word that Santa Anna's government was selecting commissioners.

After writing daily letters from August 22 to 28, as a matter of precaution he wrote another summary of the battles of the nineteenth and twentieth, with a map showing these operations. He bundled all these together and sent them off by another courier for Vera Cruz.

This was the first account of Churubusco that the *Picayune* received. In its issue of September 8 the paper carried the news of these victories, announcing, "By the Mary Kingsland we have rec'd our letters from Mr. Kendall from the 22d to the 28th of August, all dated from Tacubaya. A courier dispatched by him on the 20th with the first account of the battle fought that day was cut off."

The *Picayune* waited impatiently for further news from Kendall, complaining on September 22 that it had been fourteen days since a vessel had come from Vera Cruz. Meanwhile, at Tacubaya, Scott's army was growing restive. Many of the officers of the United States Army were opposed to granting an armistice.

---

[7] Kendall, letter to the *Picayune*, dated Boerne, August 28, 1867.

Pillow, Quitman, and Shields were perhaps the most strenuous in the opposition, Pierce was also antagonistic at the outset, and Worth insisted upon the possession of Chapultepec and its strong castle, which was within long cannon range of Tacubaya. "Wide spread feeling existed throughout the invading army that Santa Anna was not to be trusted," Kendall wrote, "and that if time were allowed him they would have to go through their bloody work again, thus losing all the dearly purchased advantages they had gained at Contreras and Churubusco. The sequel proved that they were right."[8]

Santa Anna apologized for the stoning of American teamsters in the city, and suggested that they come in for provisions only at night in order to avoid the wrath of the mob. This, Kendall suspected, was a carefully laid plan to prevent them from witnessing Santa Anna's frenzied efforts to build defenses in the city. He was convinced that these suspicions were well grounded when he later learned of the correspondence during this interval between Santa Anna and General Rejón, a former member of his cabinet.

Rejón had written to Santa Anna on August 20, "the war ought to be prosecuted. . . . Peace will destroy you," and Santa Anna replied two days later, "the suspension of hostilities would give my troops rest, re-establish their morale,—enable me to collect the dispersed, and adopt other measures to insure a reaction."[9]

From Tacubaya, Kendall watched Scott's growing impatience as the Mexican peace commissioners asked for delay in considering Trist's proposals, and the commander's slow realization that the armistice was a blunder. Tacubaya was packed with Santa Anna's spies and secret agents. He knew that General Scott was abiding by every article of the armistice, and he believed that Scott's sick list was increasing, while his offensive means must daily decrease. Finally, on September 6, Scott's patience was at an end. He notified Santa Anna that unless complete satisfaction

[8] Kendall manuscript, "History of the Mexican War," 739, 740.

[9] *Ibid.*, 770–72. These letters also are quoted in Semmes, *op. cit.*, 302–304.

was made by noon of the following day, hostilities would be resumed.

That evening Scott was told that Santa Anna was sending out all the numberous bells of the capital to the Molino del Rey, where they were being cast into cannon. While no smoke or other sign of foundry operations had been seen, General Scott seems to have placed implicit faith in the information brought to him.

The next afternoon Kendall rode out with Scott and his staff when they made a reconnaissance to determine the best means of attacking the Molino del Rey.

19

Into the halls
of Montezuma

ROM THE BELÉN *garita* the causeway led west two miles to the strongly fortified hill and castle of Chapultepec. A thousand yards farther on, through swamps and trees, stood the range of low, massive stone buildings known as El Molino del Rey, or the King's Mill.

From Scott's headquarters at Tacubaya, a narrow, winding road led to the southern end of the buildings of the Molino. The approach ran down a gradual slope through smooth, open land which extended half a mile to the west to a deep ravine. About halfway between the mill and this ravine stood a strong stone building known as the Casa Mata, which afterwards proved to be surrounded by an old Spanish breastwork. Intervening rows of magueys, with embankments thrown up to support the huge plants, occupied the space between the Molino and the Casa Mata.

Scott's plan was to attack the Molino suddenly and in the night, destroy the machinery and withdraw. He thought little resistance would be encountered, but Worth, who was assigned the task of reducing the mill, looked for a more strenuous engagement. Also, he urged, Chapultepec should be stormed immediately after the capture of the Molino and while the Mexicans still were shaken by this defeat. Scott permitted Worth to delay the attack until morning, but refused permission for him to move against the castle under any conditions.

Worth began his assault at dawn September 8, with Garland opposite the enemy's left, Wright the center, and McIntosh the right. Huger's battery was with Garland and Duncan's with McIntosh, while Cadwallader's brigade was held in reserve. Earlier shelling of the Molino had brought no response, but when the storming troops advanced within close range of the line the concealed batteries opened on them point-blank. Eleven of the fourteen officers and more than a fourth of the men in Wright's column went down. A thin line of attackers pushed on to take the guns, only to lose them in a counterattack. Smith's light battalion and the right wing of Cadwallader's brigade rushed to their support, and recaptured the guns.

Garland, meanwhile, with the aid of Captain Drum's guns, had carried the foundry after suffering heavy losses. McIntosh, however, was having difficulty with the enemy's right. Here again, despite Duncan's barrage, the Mexicans had held their fire until McIntosh's troops were within point-blank range. Half of the officers and a third of the men went down in twenty-five minutes, McIntosh falling mortally wounded, before the column was withdrawn to the shelter of Duncan's battery in the ravine on the left.

Duncan in this interval was shelling a detachment of two thousand Mexican cavalry under Alvarez that had moved up across the ravine to place Worth's flank in peril. Kendall, during the morning, watched the battle from Worth's side.

Now Worth, fearing for the safety of Duncan's battery in the face of such an avalanche of horsemen, sent Kendall to tell the artillery officer to retire with his guns from the ravine rather than run too great a risk. Duncan, rising in the saddle on his small dun mule, saw that the leading squadrons were wavering, and exclaimed, "Tell General Worth I can whip twenty thousand of them."[1]

When he had driven Alvarez out of range, Duncan turned his guns again on the Casa Mata. A detachment from the captured

[1] Kendall manuscript, "History of the Mexican War," 790. Also Semmes, *op. cit.*, 329.

Molino moved up to attack the Casa Mata from the rear, and its defenders fled. The weight of the struggle was over.

Firing had started at daybreak and the battle ended at 7:00 A. M. During this brief interval seven hundred and eighty-one officers and men were killed or wounded.[2] One member of Scott's staff said, ". . . we had more men killed or wounded in about forty minutes than had been killed or wounded in the two glorious days at Buena Vista."[3] Kendall called the battle "one of the most sanguinary ever fought on the American continent or in the world." The invaders had taken seven hundred and thirteen prisoners with fifty-three officers, and the total loss to the Mexicans, including killed, wounded and prisoners, exceeded two thousand. This did not include a great number who threw away their arms and deserted during the retreat.

When the fighting ended, Kendall galloped back to Tacubaya and wrote, "I have just returned from a battlefield—one on which the victory of the American arms was complete, and on which our troops contended against an enemy immensely superior in number. . . ." He told of the heavy losses, named a few of the officers who fell, estimated the Mexicans captured at one thousand officers and men, and added, "After the battle was over Gen. Scott came out accompanied by his staff, and also by Mr. Trist. The Mexicans at the time were throwing shells at some of the wagons Gen. Worth had sent out to pick up the dead and wounded. They had placed a howitzer in position on Chapultepec at the close of the action, and now, seeing no enemy within reach, the cowardly wretches opened upon the ambulances and those who were gathering the bodies of their wounded and lifeless comrades. On seeing this worse than savage outrage, one of our officers, with a sarcastic expression of countenance, asked whether Mr. Trist has any new peace propositions in his pockets."[4]

[2] Thirtieth Congress, first session, *Senate Executive Documents, Doc.* 1, p. 384.

[3] Semmes, *op. cit.,* 331.

[4] *Picayune,* October 14, 1847, Kendall letter dated Tacubaya, September 8, 1847.

He did not dispatch the letter at once, however, but kept it in his saddlebags with others which he wrote during the following four days. Since the armistice had ended, it seemed wiser to await the storming of Mexico City, which now appeared imminent, before sending another courier through the hostile country. The messenger whom he had sent out three days earlier got through only after a dramatic ride. He was shot in the neck, was robbed, made prisoner and escaped, got a mule and finally reached Vera Cruz.[5] Army officers by now were making use of Kendall's couriers to get news and dispatches through the bandit-infested country, and "Mr. Kendall's express" had become famous with the invading forces.[6]

No active foundry operations were discovered in the Molino —only a few worthless molds that had long since been discarded. Scott's plan of attack had shown that he anticipated no serious resistance at the mill, and that he was not aware that his cunning adversary was laying a trap for him.

Kendall blamed Mackintosh for prompting the false information that led to the attack, and wrote, ". . . he may have been the main mover in a scheme which had for its object the destruction of one of the regular divisions of the invading army, and such an end accomplished, the overthrow of the entire American force was counted upon as certain. It has been confidently asserted that, within two hours after the time General Scott's order for attacking the Molino was given, the substance of it was in Santa Anna's possession."[7]

After the Molino fell, Worth again urged that he be permitted to storm the castle of Chapultepec, but he was ordered to withdraw to Tacubaya. Here Scott immediately resumed his plans

[5] *Ibid.*, September 26, 1847. This issue carried Kendall's letters from Tacubaya dated August 30, September 2, 4, and 5, 1847.

[6] Robert Anderson, in *An Artillery Officer in the Mexican War* (New York and London, 1911), 305, wrote, "Yesterday, I sent a letter by Mr. Kendall's express," and again, 307, "I wrote hastily to you this afternoon, the letter to go by Mr. Kendall's express."

[7] Kendall manuscript, "History of the Mexican War," 798.

for the attack on the city. His situation was critical. The losses at Contreras, Churubusco, and the Molino, added to the sickness brought on by exposure and fatigue, had reduced his effective strength to seven thousand men. Of these nearly a thousand were needed for camp routine, guard duty and caring for the sick and wounded. Cut off as he was from all hope of reinforcements, a single failure would bring the Mexicans upon the invaders in overwhelming numbers. Kendall felt that Scott had courted such a disaster at Molino del Rey.

After several reconnaissances, Scott called a conference of his officers on September 11, and after a lengthy consideration of all the approaches to the city, determined to attack the western gates by way of the castle of Chapultepec.

The massive castle, used at the time for a military college, stood on a rocky hill which rose sharply to a height of one hundred and fifty feet. Its northern and eastern sides were too steep for troops to climb, while its western slope, rising from a growth of cypress trees, was precipitous enough to make its storming from this angle difficult. The southern side of the works was approached by a steep road that led to the west, then turned northeast to the castle. High stone walls leading from the buildings of the Molino to the hill formed a rough rectangle.

Pillow's division was chosen for the attack from the west, while Quitman was to guard his right flank and storm the southern face of the hill.

As soon as these plans were made, a small party moved in to regain possession of the Molino, and all during the day of September 12 a heavy bombardment was laid down on the castle. That night Pillow moved his entire division into the Molino. The shelling was resumed at dawn and continued until shortly before eight o'clock on the thirteenth, when Pillow and Quitman advanced to the attack.

Worth, assigned to support Pillow, sent Clarke's brigade to sustain the attack on the western slope of the hill, then moved along its northern flank from the Molino to prevent an attack from enemy troops posted on low elevations to the left. As Pillow's troops cleared the open fields and splashed through the marshy cypress grove near the base of the hill, Pillow was wounded by grapeshot, and Cadwallader took command. His troops spent an anxious period after they had pushed back the defenders on the hillside and reached the base of the castle walls, awaiting the storming ladders carried by slower detachments. The attackers, at this time, were lying on ground that had been mined, but they found and cut the fuses leading to the buried explosives.

Quitman's advance penetrated the lower defenses on the south and stormed up the hill just as the ladders arrived. With Pillow's forces, they raised ladder after ladder. The first were hurled back by the defenders, but eventually a lodgment was made, and the besiegers swarmed through the works. The most gallant among the defenders were a hundred or more cadets, from fifteen to eighteen years of age, who were stationed at the military college.

During this last dramatic assault, while Kendall was moving with Worth's staff along the road under the heights of the castle, they came upon one of Pillow's light batteries commanded by Stonewall Jackson who, with McClellan and other young officers, had just come out from West Point. A shell burst in the midst of the battery, killing or wounding eight or ten men and as many horses. A shoe from one of Jackson's men, with the foot still inside it, whizzed by Kendall and his companions, bounced off the wall, and fell beneath their horses.

"I never saw a man work as hard as young Jackson," Kendall wrote, "tearing off harness and dragging out dead and kicking horses."[8]

In the flurry of fighting at the base of the hill, Kendall was wounded slightly in the knee, but he rode on without stopping.

From the junction of the causeways in front of the castle, two routes led into the city. One ran directly east to the Belén *garita*,

[8] Kendall, letter to the *Picayune*, dated Boerne, August 2, 1867.

and on this, without waiting for orders, Quitman and Persifor Smith advanced, in pursuit of the fleeing Mexicans. They seemed to hurry on, Kendall observed, "as though they were anxious to get out of the hearing of General Scott's orders. They had not forgotten his *halt* at Churubusco, and the useless sacrifice of over a thousand men in consequence."[9]

The other route led northeast from Chapultepec, then east through the village and *garita* of San Cosme. Along this route, also without waiting for Scott's orders, Worth dashed after the retreating enemy.

Each of these causeways had a raised aqueduct running down its center, supported by heavy stone arches, and each was flanked by ditches and marshy ground. Midway in his advance, Quitman came upon a strong battery and had no other alternative than a costly frontal attack. At this point Worth sent Duncan's battery across on a lateral road to help dislodge the defenders. Quitman thus moved on and took the Belén *garita* before Worth had fought his way through that of San Cosme.[10]

With the fall of Chapultepec, Scott came up from Tacubaya and, ordering reserves to support both Worth and Quitman, followed Worth on to San Cosme. The garrison of this *garita* held out stubbornly, and Worth adopted the old plan of the Texans, boring and burrowing through the houses. A swarm of riflemen soon gained the housetops to help dislodge the defenders.

Worth then advanced into the edge of the city, but "darkness was fast settling down, dropping suddenly as it does in the tropics," Kendall reported.

Worth was no sooner inside of the Garita of San Cosme than, with his usual chafing and unquiet disposition, he thought of going ahead. But how and where? He was just as anxious as Quitman to shut the gate down on anything in the shape of another armistice—was determined on slamming the door in Santa Anna's face and jaws. He had

[9] *Loc. cit.*
[10] Both Semmes, *op. cit.*, 345, and Kendall in the *Picayune*, August 2, 1867, recalled this delay to assist Quitman.

around him Pemberton, Bowyer, Wood, Mackall, Semmes the pirate, (so-called but not by me) Solon Borland, and your humble servant, all belonging to his regular or volunteer staff, with Huger, Hagner, Stone and several ordnance or artillery officers.

There, lying idle, but anxious to work, were two 10-inch mortars, and a couple of 18-pounder long guns. How to use them?

Just then, Kendall recalled, there appeared "a little fat, pursy, pot-bellied Englishman, the owner of a neighboring brewery, who was profuse in kind offices. The suburb of San Cosme, taken by assault, had been given up by Worth to sack, and his men were at it.[11] Perhaps the Englishman thought his own premises inside the Garita would be entered," but more was at stake:

. . . while we all drank his beer, the ordnance officer drank his information.

"You have lived some time in the city of Mexico, my little man?" quoth Worth.

"Seventeen years, off and on," responded the Englishman.

"You know the city then?"

"Like a book."

"And which is the best part of it? Where do all the rich people live?"

"Right over that tall tree you see there."

"Right over that tallest tree there?"

"Exactly."

He did not imagine, poor fellow, that immediately behind him and unbeknown to him the ordnance officers were "taking sight" with his pointing fingers; and training their pieces: the object of Worth was to "pitch in" round shot and shell, into the best part of the city. Of course it took some little time to lay the platforms for the mortars, and meanwhile the little fat man was used.

"And the Archbishop," queried Worth, "where does he reside?"

"Right over that tallest house there," continued the fat brewer, pointing to the dwelling where the Prussian Minister then resided, while the ordnance officers were behind him taking sight and aim. . . .

"And the National Palace, the Grand Plaza, the Cathedral, the

[11] Semmes, *op. cit.*, 355–56, denies that there was any sacking.

Plateros?" continued Worth, as noted points in the beautiful city came to his mind.

"Beyond the Alameda, and right under that star," answered the Englishman, pointing, Huger and Stone behind him "lining" as old bee hunters term it. Hagner would also have been on the lookout, only that he was hard of hearing. An excellent officer was Hagner.

Meanwhile the platforms for the two 10-inch mortars were laid, and every thing was ready to "open" when all of a sudden it got through the little fat man's skull that he had been "pumped."

"But you are going to bombard the city," said he. . . .

Bang! Whang! went the 18-pounders.

"And my wife and children are living up there!"

Slam! Boom! went the two mortars.

"God bless my soul! You'll tear the whole city to pieces! And my poor wife, she's timid, and—"

Bang! Whang! went the 18-pounders again: it took longer to work the mortars, but as fast as they could be wiped out and cleaned they were kept in active play.

It may not seem altogether so right for a man to sit down and split his sides laughing after a long day's work of carnage and strife: but who could help it, as that blue coated pursy little Englishman, who had unconsciously given Worth a thorough reconnaissance of the entire city of Mexico . . . commenced jumping and skipping about with the regularity of a first class acrobat. I am laughing now as I tell the story —I can't help it.

A short time after Worth started shelling the city, Kendall continued, "a deputation from the Ayuntamiento came hurriedly down to San Cosme with intelligence that Santa Anna had evacuated the city . . . and that it was at our mercy. Here ended the war between the United States and Mexico. . . ."[12]

Two days later, Kendall met the little fat Englishman on the street and asked if any of his family had been hurt in the bombardment. "Scared, that's all," he replied.

On the morning of September 14 Kendall rode with Worth and his staff into the grand plaza, and waited while some of Quit-

12 Kendall, letter to the *Picayune,* dated Boerne, August 2, 1867.

man's officers raised the flag on the National Palace. "Worth might have done it the night before," Kendall wrote later, for Santa Anna, after releasing all of the thieves and murderers from the city's prisons, had fled with his army. "There was a fuss at the time as to who placed the first American flag on the National Palace; it was a foolish fuss: the gallant officers of each division were all trying to unfurl the banner in the heart of Mexico and adventitious circumstances aided one of them."[13]

Worth had advanced to within three squares of the Plaza at six o'clock that morning, but was ordered by Scott to wait there until Quitman took possession of the Palace. The coldness between Scott and Worth, which had begun at Puebla and was increased by Scott's criticism after the battles of Churubusco and Molino del Rey, was soon to break into an open quarrel that was a sad commentary on the brilliant campaign just ended.

As they watched the flag raising ceremonies, Kendall wrote later, "I told Gener'l Worth distinctly . . . that I had done with glorious war's alarms, and all the pomp, and pride, and circumstance thereupon attendant: . . . that I was going home to New Orleans, that if ever an enemy threatened the city I would turn out with a musket and help drive them off, that I would never again put myself in the way of whistling bullets in foreign countries."[14]

But he was a long way from realizing this dream.

They watched General Scott ride into the plaza, bearing himself like a proud conqueror. Kendall reported that he was mounted on a horse some eighteen hands high, rigged out in full regimentals, and with military hat and yellow feathers top-knotting all, he loomed like a steeple above his fellows. Worth, Twiggs, Persifor F. Smith, and his principal officers had been camping out the night before, and were shabby enough, while Beauregard was begrimed with mud from the ditches in which he had worked all night.

A half hour later, as Worth and his staff were riding to-

[13] *Ibid.*, August 28, 1867.   [14] *Loc. cit.*

ward the Alameda, they were all fired upon from the roof and windows of the convent of San Francisco, probably by criminals whom Santa Anna had released from prison.[15] Fighting continued for two days, until General Quitman was appointed civil and military governor of the city. During these days, Kendall continued to collect news for the *Picayune,* and at the first opportunity dispatched another courier with the story of the capture of the city, the numbers of killed and wounded, the fighting in the streets, and attempts to negotiate a treaty of peace.

News of the end of the campaign reached the *Picayune* by boat from Vera Cruz, and it printed rumors on October 5, followed with Kendall's letters from Tacubaya and Mexico in its issue of October 14. So many of his stories had come through that the paper printed them on October 15, 16, and 17, including in the latter issue two maps which had been drawn for Kendall by an army engineer showing Scott's operations on September 13, and Worth's operations at Molino del Rey.

The couriers continued to elude the guerrillas until November 6, and with each bundle of letters Kendall usually included copies of Mexican and Anglo-Saxon newspapers. For, as was the case at Matamoros, Monterrey, Vera Cruz, Jalapa, and Puebla, the printers ever present with the army began to publish newspapers soon after the occupation of Mexico City.

Peoples and Barnard, who had abandoned their *American Star No. 2* at Puebla and marched out with the troops, now brought out another version of this paper at the capital on September 20 which they called *American Star, Mexico.*[16]

Peoples counted on a certain amount of revenue from the army, from the printing of forms needed for the various departments. After the armistice of August 24, Scott wanted the articles of agreement printed, and Peoples volunteered to enter Mexico City ahead of the troops. There he printed the articles,

15 Semmes, *op. cit.,* 353, says that Colonel Garland was wounded in this attack.
16 Complete files of this paper, September 20, 1847, to May 30, 1848, are in the Library of Congress.

smuggled them through the streets, and delivered them to Scott at Tacubaya.

All during his stay in Mexico, Peoples had been correspondent for the *Delta,* signing his correspondence "Chaparral," but after the establishment of the New Orleans *Crescent,* March 5, 1848, by his old employers on the *Delta,* Alexander H. Hayes and Sam McClure, he became the correspondent of this new paper. During his last months as a publisher in Mexico City he became involved in bitter competition with *The North American, Mexico,* which was started September 29, 1847, by William C. Tobey, Kendall's friend whose correspondence in the Philadelphia *North American* was published over the signature of "John of York."[17]

Besides the *Star* and the *North American,* two other American papers were started in the Mexican capital, the *Rover,* and *Yankee Doodle,* a humorous weekly edited by H. R. Courtney from the press of the *North American.*

While Kendall watched the rivalry of these papers in Mexico City, he also noted the increased activity of the *Delta's* correspondents in the capital. Freaner, copying Kendall's spectacular method of sending dispatches by special courier, began to hire riders to get his own and Peoples' letters through to the *Delta's* agent at Vera Cruz.

The *Delta,* a strong Democratic organ under the leadership of Judge Alexander Walker, now had a wide following among the Democratic editors of the United States, many of whom believed that Kendall's Whig leanings had influenced his stories.

---

[17] The *North American* was forced to suspend publication, probably because of its critical editorial in the issue of February 10 headed, "Vexatious Delay of a Bearer of Despatches." It reappeared March 2, as a partnership venture of "Tobey, Callahan and Co.,"—the same Charley Callahan of the *Picayune,* who had been associated with Peoples and Barnard. Tobey stayed on in Mexico City to wait for the commission as second lieutenant which he had been promised. This was awarded on March 3, and soon afterward he went back to Philadelphia with the Pennsylvania troops. In July he resigned from the United States Army and again joined the staff of the Philadelphia *North American.* Issues of the *North American, Mexico,* for November 30, 1847; January 19, 24, February 10, 11, and a one-sheet extra of March 6, 1848, are in the Library of Congress.

The *Delta's* great boast at this time was that Freaner's story with the list of killed and wounded in the battles before Mexico City was widely copied by other newspapers throughout the United States. Freaner's list of casualties included mention that Kendall was slightly wounded, and in a later letter he added a joking explanation that both he and Kendall were casualties. A bullet, he said, struck Kendall in his horse's ear, while he himself was wounded in his horse's saddle. Both of the victims, he reported, were doing remarkably well.

20

Kendall's
peace treaty scoop

THE FIGHTING WAS OVER, but there were many things for Kendall to do before he could turn his job over to subordinates and leave for home. While Trist struggled with the elusive Mexican government in an effort to negotiate a peace treaty, while Freaner was building up the *Delta's* courier service, while Scott was wrangling with his officers, Kendall was busy planning the book he was going to write on the principal battles of the war.

He watched with concern, and a measure of distaste, the quarrels which developed after Mexico City had been captured. While peace negotiations dragged slowly forward, and while detailed reports of the campaigns were being compiled for the War Department, Scott became convinced that there was a conspiracy afoot to strip him of the glory of winning the war.

Duncan's "Tampico Letter" and the *Delta's* "Leonidas" dispatch came to light[1] and Scott issued a blazing order which hinted

[1] For "Tampico Letter," see above, XVIII, p. 204n; for origin of "Leonidas" Letter" see XVIII, 210. Also *Delta*, September 9, 1847, April 7, 1848; *Picayune*, September 16, 18, 21, 24, 1847; New Orleans *Crescent*, May 10, 1848, and Thirtieth Congress, first session, *Senate Executive Documents, Doc.* 65, p. 14. Scott's General Order No. 349 read in part, "It requires not a little charity to believe that the principal heroes of the scandalous letters referred to, did not write them, or specially procure them to be written, and the intelligent can be at no loss in conjecturing the authors—chief, partizans, and pet familiars. To the honor of the service, the disease—pruriency of fame, *not* earned—cannot have seized upon half a dozen officers (present), all of whom, it is believed, belong to the same two coteries. . . ."

that numerous officers were involved in a petty scramble for publicity. Angry correspondence ensued. Generals Worth and Pillow and Colonel Duncan were placed under arrest, the President ordered an inquiry and, pending this, relieved Scott of his command.

The dispute was echoed in the newspapers, and became a bitter political issue on the eve of the presidential election. Kendall found himself caught in the crossfire of the newspaper barrage, and his own dramatic stories of the campaigns were declared to have been slanted in such a way as to ignore the deeds of officers who were members of the Democratic party.[2]

A year was to elapse before the disagreeable affair reached an anticlimax in the hearing of charges against Pillow. While this wrangling gained headway, Kendall kept up his letters to the *Picayune,* telling of news from Mexico, of rheumatism among the troops, of the Spanish theater, of an earthquake that shook the city. But he spent a great deal of time with Carl Nebel, the French artist whose recent book, *A Picturesque and Archaeological Voyage in Mexico,* had made him widely known. Within a month after the capture of Mexico City he and Kendall had entered into an agreement to join in the publication of a work for which Nebel was to make the drawings and Kendall to write the text.[3]

Through Kendall's last letters from the capital there ran a continuous note of homesickness. "They may say what they will about the climate of Mexico—its clear skies, delightful temperature, etc., etc.," he wrote, "—but give me the region of the lower

[2] See Boston *Post,* October 4, 1847, for complaint of political slant of Kendall's correspondence. Also Washington *Union,* October 22, 1847, which charged that Kendall had not only "almost entirely passed over the services of Gen. Pillow, who has never received from the *Picayune* the justice to which his merits entitle him," but also insisted that Kendall made "indiscreet, illiberal and unjust reflections upon the administration. . . ."

[3] Shortly afterwards, Colonel James Duncan wrote Kendall, "I see Navel [Nebel] on the street he says he is getting on well with his pictures—now that I am in limbo I cannot go to see them, or I should give you some account of them." Duncan to Kendall, November 22, 1847, in Kendall papers.

Mississippi after all has been said and sung."[4] He found his first opportunity to leave late in October when Scott sent his first military train out of the city since its occupation, under the escort of Colonel William S. Harney of the Second Dragoons.

The *American Star, Mexico,* in its issue of Thursday, October 28, 1847, announced his departure in a lengthy paragraph, stating that his letters had been copied into almost every journal in the Union. Callahan stayed on in Mexico City as correspondent, and when Kendall reached Vera Cruz D. Scully began to send in letters to the paper, later moving his headquarters to Mexico City. The courier service which Kendall had set up continued to operate under their supervision.

Before he left, General Worth wrote him:

My dear Kendall. If it does you no good the commendation of an old soldier can do you no harm—be this as it may I cannot part with you without an expression of my high and grateful appreciation of the value of your services on my staff in several of the principle [*sic*] conflicts with the enemy in this Campaign—Churubusco, El Molino del Rey & in the final attack upon & capture of the City.[5]

Friends who remained in the capital had many errands for him to run on his way home. General Persifor Smith asked him to pick up his belongings and take them to New Orleans. Smith's letter added:

The flag the Regt of Mo Riflemen carried they had made in Puebla it cost $210 I should like the ladies of N. Orleans to present the flag to the Regt. if they will subscribe the money & place it in the hands of the paymaster there to the credit of the Regt. & then present the colors to me by letter it will answer the same as if they had had it made. Send me some late Phil[a] letters from Vera Cruz or New Orleans.[6]

Before he reached home, Colonel Duncan had written:

I wish you would make some inquiry about my pony that belonged

[4] *Picayune,* October 21, 1847.
[5] Kendall papers, Worth to Kendall, Mexico City, October 29, 1847.
[6] *Ibid.,* Smith to Kendall, November 1, 1847.

to poor Ridgley[7]—May brought him to N. Orleans and there left him, and be d----d to him—why he didnt send him to Baltimore I can't imagine—I wish whoever had him in possession you would ask to write to Andrew Ridgley, Esq Baltimore and say that the horse is subject to his order. I must owe somebody for his keep—let the bill be sent to me and I will pay it.

I wrote to Col. Peyton on the subject while we were at Puebla—but the letter fell into the hands of the enemy.[8]

When Kendall reached Vera Cruz, Dr. J. J. B. Wright, major surgeon in the army, wrote asking for publicity for the medical corps. All of the corps of the army had received full justice at Scott's hands, the doctor complained, except the medical corps. Scott, he believed, had never been kindly disposed to his medical staff, hence his studied neglect of all mention of it in his dispatches.

"You, my dear sir," he stated, "have been present and have had a fair opportunity, during this whole war, to judge of the manner in which the Medical Staff has done its duty. If at some leisure, and convenient moment, you would give to the Country, through the 'Pic.' an intimation of the little credit that is due us, poor Devils, as a distinct corps of the Army, you would confer an essential favor on it, and impose personal obligations on us individually."[9]

General Worth added a last request:

... if Charles is with you, do me the favor to flog him—the rascall hired my wagon to a damned rascally french Tailor to transport his goods—my stores were thrown into one of the wagons &, as *made* and *provided*, stolen en route.[10]

At Vera Cruz Kendall bought another pony for his little nephew, George Kendall Rix, and shipped it, along with his favor-

[7] Randolph Ridgley, Brevet Captain A.A.G., promoted for gallantry at Buena Vista and Resaca de la Palma. Accidentally killed October 27, 1846.

[8] Kendall papers, Duncan to Kendall, November 22, 1847.

[9] *Ibid.*, Wright to Kendall, Vera Cruz, November 20, 1847.

[10] *Ibid.*, Worth to Kendall, Mexico, January 12, 1848.

ite Spriggs, to his sister Kate in Mobile. To her, also, he sent most of the mementos he had picked up on the campaign with General Scott. Most of these were lost when Kate's home was burned. For Kate there were gifts that included Mexican songs—she felt "very foolish trying to sing or rather pronounce them,"—and when the horses arrived she wrote, "they are looked upon as wonders coming from Mexico."

Among the editorials that welcomed him when Kendall reached home on November 25 was one in the New Orleans *National* which stated:

> To the enterprise and ability of this gentleman (Mr. Kendall) the people in every section of the Union, and the Government itself, have, for a long time, been indebted for the earliest and most reliable intelligence, communicated through the *Picayune*, from the seat of hostilities in Mexico.[11]

At such elaborate praise, however, the *Delta* protested. It quoted excerpts from a number of newspaper items praising "Mustang's" work, and insisted that he was every bit as good a correspondent as Kendall. It also pointed out the difficulties the *Delta's* reporters had faced in getting news through to Vera Cruz.[12]

After Kendall's wounded dispatch rider had galloped into Vera Cruz with his stories of Contreras and Churubusco and the armistice, the guerrillas had gained possession of the road and shut off communications for more than two weeks. Both Kendall and Freaner dispatched courier after courier with duplicate messages. The first of "Mustang's" stories of the fall of the city was intercepted and he saw it shortly afterwards in a copy of the *Nacional*, published at Atlixco. He sent another copy that eventually got through.[13]

News of the terms of the armistice, with the official corre-

11 Reprinted in the *Delta*, November 26, 1847.
12 *Loc. cit.* See also issues of November 13 and 28, 1847.
13 *Ibid.*, October 23, 1847.

spondence, came to light through a copy of a pamphlet published by the Mexican government, which reached Vera Cruz and was forwarded from that city.[14] In this interval one of "Mustang's" express riders was captured, "hung by his neck to a tree, with the words 'Cerreo de los Yankees,' pinned to his clothing."[15]

When some anxiety was felt as to the fate of Scott's official reports of the battles of Contreras and Churubusco, the *Delta* boasted that these dispatches came through with "Mustang's" letters, "enveloped and directed to the editors of the *Delta*. They were immediately mailed to the war department. . . ."[16]

Franklin Pierce, disgusted with the quarrels among the various officers, had finally gained permission to leave Mexico. He wrote Kendall that he hoped to be in New Orleans by New Year's Day, adding, "my object in writing is to say that you must be ready to go *north* with me & make the snow fly in February over the *Mont Vernon* hills and along that region. . . . Yr friend Frank Pierce."[17]

But before Kendall could leave New Orleans to visit the boyhood home where he and young Pierce had spent so many happy hours, there was the matter of arranging for the remaining big story that was to come out of Mexico. This concerned the long and tedious negotiations Trist was carrying on with the Mexicans, and the peace treaty that eventually was to be signed. The entire *Picayune* staff in Mexico was watching developments, and every precaution had been taken to get the news to New Orleans without delay.

On February 2 Trist completed negotiations with the Mexican peace commissioners, a matter which had been pending since December 9, and went out to Guadalupe, on the anniversary of the Purification of the Holy Virgin. There, on the altar of the holy cathedral, the Treaty of Guadalupe Hidalgo was solemnly

---

[14] Rives, *Op. cit.*, II, 518.
[15] *Delta*, November 9, 1847.
[16] *Ibid.*, November 10, 1847.
[17] Kendall papers, Pierce to Kendall, November 27, 1847.

signed. Trist had been recalled by President Polk during the previous October, but had chosen to stay and negotiate the treaty.[18] Now that the treaty was signed, it was urgent to get it to Washington as quickly as possible. For this task he chose Freaner, who had been marking time in Mexico, waiting for the big story.[19]

At last Freaner's waiting was at an end. Early on the morning of February 3 he galloped out of Mexico City followed by a company of mounted rifles. Instead of a story for the *Delta* he carried, concealed in his clothing, Trist's treaty for Secretary Buchanan and Scott's dispatches for Secretary Marcy.

He had not traveled far before he found that his escort, because of numbers, could not keep up with him. He rode on ahead, caught up with a troop of Illinois cavalry, and traveled with it. Again, numbers delayed his escort and he struck out alone. In the foothills east of the capital he met a detachment of rangers under Lieutenant Fortunatus Lilly, who turned back and rode with him through the bandit-infested roads to Puebla. From there he hastened on, sometimes alone, sometimes accompanied by cavalry, and reached Vera Cruz in three days. The *Picayune* courier, with the story of the treaty, followed close on "Mustang's" heels.

At Vera Cruz the United States steamer *Iris* was put at Freaner's disposal and he sailed directly for Mobile. The steamer *New Orleans* was ready to leave with the *Picayune's* dispatches, but through the interference of the army commander of the port she was detained for two days to prevent the private news stories from getting ahead of the official convoy. Captain Edward Auld

18 Milo Milton Quaife (ed.), *The Diary of James K. Polk* (Chicago, 1910). III, 344.

19 During this tiresome interval at the capital, Freaner spent a vague and little-remembered week making a thorough investigation of a shipment of "very suspicious looking barrels, demijohns, etc.," which had been brought in the supply train from Vera Cruz. After attentive and unceasing efforts, which left him prostrate each night with symptoms of bricks in his hat, he was able to report to the *Delta* that the shipment contained "nothing more nor less than the very best Monongahela and Bourbon, at least 20 or 25 days old, and branded 'Rectified.' " *Delta,* January 14, 1848.

of the *New Orleans* rose to this challenge, however, and drove his ship through "on an extraordinary run," passing the *Iris* before she reached the Balize and docking at New Orleans Saturday afternoon, February 12, about the time Freaner landed at Mobile.[20]

Without rest Freaner pushed on toward Washington, while the *Picayune* was getting out its edition of February 13. Excited crowds swarmed along Camp Street as they had when Kendall's great story of the Battle of Monterrey came in, and it was two o'clock before the first express rider galloped away with his saddlebags stuffed with copies of the *Picayune* for the northern press.

By this time Freaner was forty-eight hours ahead and was traveling at top speed along the stage line. After the *Picayune's* rider left Mobile he began to gain rapidly, and when he reached Montgomery "Mustang" was only one day ahead.

The dashing expressman caught him at Charleston, and from there they finished the race neck-and-neck, so that the *Picayune* boasted, ". . . the news reached Washington by our columns simultaneously with Mr. F. . . . Full details were laid before the public from the *Picayune* by the Baltimore papers of the morning of the 21st."[21]

"Mustang's" appearance in Washington created a sensation among newspapers of the country. In his seventeen-day dash from Mexico he had little opportunity to pay attention to his appearance. He wore a blue jacket and pants, one leg of which was strapless, while the lack of suspenders displayed a fold of checkered linen over his waistband. In a broad-brimmed tarpaulin hat, his face covered with bristling whiskers, he looked like one of the bandits along the Jalapa road.

He took a cab at the wharf, though the hackmen were rather

[20] Accounts of this boat race were published in the *Delta,* March 5, 1848; *Picayune,* February 13, March 1, 1848, and October 24, 1885.

[21] *Picayune,* March 1, 1848. The Charleston *Courier,* February 18, 1848, reported that Freaner passed through the city "yesterday," and in the same issue it carried the news of the treaty from the *Picayune* of February 13 which "arrived yesterday afternoon."

shy of him, and rode directly to the home of Secretary Marcy, without waiting to change the clothing he had worn on the two-thousand-mile journey. "Knocking at the door of the house," the *Delta* related, "our friend was received by a pug-nosed servant, who, judging from appearances, came to no favorable conclusion as to the character of the visitor, and peremptorily informed him that the Governor couldn't be seen.

" 'I must see him,' was the reply of 'Mustang,' and to the utter astonishment and great indignation of the servant, he entered by the door and quietly seated himself in the hall. The servant retired, and presently a lady appeared, and in a very positive manner informed the unseemly intruder that the Governor could not be seen, as he was taking his afternoon nap.

" 'Very well, madam, I will keep him company, and, as I have not slept a wink for six days, I will take a little siesta in this chair.' "

When Marcy appeared, frowning and yawning and asked who he was, "Mustang" replied, " 'Sir, I am directed by General Scott to deliver this despatch immediately upon my arrival,' at the same time drawing a sealed well-worn document from some remote corner of his clothes, to the very great embarrassment of the lady,"—he handed it to the Secretary and left.

A short time afterwards, a messenger from the War Office arrived at Tuttle's hotel, sent his card up to Freaner and asked to see him immediately. Freaner sent word that he was taking his siesta and couldn't be interrupted.[22]

While the President apologetically broke the sabbath to discuss the treaty with his cabinet, the *Picayune's* express riders were dashing on up the seaboard with its great story.

The Baltimore *Sun* in its issue of Monday morning, February 21, carried the account of the treaty, saying "We have received

[22] *Delta,* March 10, 1848, related this incident in relation to Marcy. Its issue of March 16 repeated the incident, carried in the Boston *Atlas,* but this paper stated that it occurred in connection with his delivery of the treaty to Secretary Buchanan. Polk in his diary, February 19, 1848, states that Freaner arrived "after night," and that "About 9 o'clock Mr. Buchanan called with the treaty."

by 'overland express' for the Baltimore *Sun* a copy of the New Orleans *Picayune* of the 13th, one day in advance of the mail, containing the following—" The Baltimore *Argus* published the same story that evening.

The Washington *Daily Union* of February 21 carried the story with the introduction, "We lay before our readers the following very interesting intelligence which we received in the New Orleans *Picayune*. We are sure our readers will excuse us from giving any explanation or speculations this evening upon these matters. . . ." Its editors, Thomas Ritchie and John P. Heiss, although they published Polk's official organ, apparently had not been given any news of the treaty by their patron.[23]

The next day's issue of the *National Intelligencer* carried the *Picayune's* story.

The *Union's* New York correspondence, dated February 21, began with this paragraph: " 'yere's the extra Sun—got the treaty with Mexico-h!' shout the newsboys through the streets, and at once the whole town *arrectis auribus astat*. The papers have got from the *Picayune* an outline of the terms of a treaty said to have been accepted by General Scott from the Mexican Congress."

By 1848 telegraph lines had been extended southward to Petersburg, Virginia, and enterprising New York newspapers had stationed reporters there to intercept the *Picayune* express riders and telegraph brief summaries of the more important stories. Thus it was that the *Sun* and the *Herald* had extras on the streets of New York when the Washington *Union* was setting the type from the *Picayune*. The *Evening Post,* therefore, copied the treaty story, on the afternoon of the twenty-first, from the *Herald's* telegraphic bulletin, and the *Herald* on the next day ran the complete story from the *Picayune,* which in the meantime had arrived by the pony express. In Philadelphia the *Public Ledger* and the *North American* and *United States Gazette* got copies

[23] Although this paper had lambasted Kendall for his partisanship, it regularly received copies of the *Picayune* by pony express. See its issues of February 21, 22, 23, 25, 28, 1848, in Library of Congress, for items credited to the *Picayune*.

of the *Picayune* in time to pick up the full account in their issues of February 22. Copies had reached Boston in time for publication in the *Atlas* and the *Courier* on February 23.

Freaner had made a remarkable trip from Mexico City to Washington, but his official assignment sealed his lips on the big story he carried, so that he could not give it to the *Delta*. But the machinery Kendall had set up functioned smoothly, and the dramatic race across the gulf enabled the *Picayune* to break the news in papers from New Orleans to New England.

21

Paris—
revolution and romance

THREE WEEKS on board a Cunard liner from New York to Liverpool gave Kendall the first respite from frenzied activity which he had known in years. His efforts in New Orleans to keep up with developments in Mexico and make preparations for the handling of the story on the treaty had been frantic.

Already the *Picayune's* boom for Taylor was gaining momentum, and Kendall was drafted to go to Washington on behalf of the Taylorites, to try to mend the Whig breach. When news of his business leaked out the Mobile *Register* commented, "If he does not keep his mission more of a secret, we will recall him."

At every step on his trip northward from Washington he was greeted with acclaim growing out of the popularity of his war stories in the *Picayune,* and he received a flood of invitations to join honorary societies and to attend public balls and dinners in honor of returning military heroes. The Whigs of Philadelphia invited him to a public dinner on February 22, urging him to add the influence of his name "to a movement which may result in the SALVATION OF THE CONSTITUTION, and the rescue of the Nation and the Union from the perils which surround them." But these events took little time from his preparations for his first trip to Europe. While he packed, he looked forward only to a short business trip and a well earned vacation. He did not dream that in a few weeks he would again hear bullets whistling around his ears and would cover a dramatic revolution for the *Picayune.*

As Kendall paced the decks of the Cunard liner, *Britannia,* on her three weeks' voyage from New York to Liverpool, other ships sped westward with the news that Louis Philippe had abdicated before the fury of a Paris mob late in February, 1848. This was the signal for widespread uprisings, and within a few months nearly half of the rulers on the continent either had been forced to grant political concessions to their restive peoples or had been forced from their thrones.

It was for this turbulent Europe that Kendall had sailed on March 11, to enjoy a vacation and to publish a book. The vacation was postponed while he wrote long letters to the *Picayune* about the political turmoil, and it was three years before his book, the *War between the United States and Mexico, Illustrated,* was ready for the public. When he finally returned in 1856, after frequent hurried trips across the Atlantic, he brought with him his young wife and growing family, whose existence had been known only to his closest friends.

He had little warning of these dramatic events as he rode up to London from Liverpool on April 9, 1848. There he learned that unrest, simmering since the fall of Louis Napoleon, had swept across the Channel to reach its climax next day with a monster Chartist demonstration.

Metternich and his allies had restored monarchy to Europe after the close of the Napoleonic Wars in 1815, but they faced a rising tide of nationalism that was to echo through half a century. France was appeased, temporarily, with the show of representative government under the charter which Louis XVIII granted on his restoration to the throne. The ultraroyalists continued to gain power, however, under their leader, the Count of Artois, who became King Charles X in 1824. Disputes over the titles to land confiscated by the state and transferred to farmers during the Revolution reached a climax with the uprising of the legislature in 1830. Charles abdicated and Louis Philippe, of the Orleans line, became King of the French under a limited monarchy with popular sovereignty.

This uprising was the signal for revolts in Germany, Belgium, and Italy. In England, with the death of King George IV and the election of parliament for William IV, the Whigs gained fifteen seats through a campaign of reform. They gained concessions, but in 1838 the Chartists renewed the agitation which reached its climax about the time Kendall landed.

Louis Philippe started out conservatively in France, with a cabinet composed of the bourgeoisie, but leaned more and more toward absolute monarchy after political flurries in 1835 and 1840. The King's corrupt minister, Guizot, insisted on ever increasing royal power, while the people demanded a loosening of electoral restrictions. By 1848 only two hundred thousand persons had the right to vote in France, and the government of businessmen was distinctly antilabor. Factory conditions were terrible, with wages ranging from fifteen to seventeen cents a day, but when the workers sought to organize, the Napoleonic code preventing strikes was invoked.

Repressive measures prevented the populace from circulating political leaflets, cartoons or pamphlets, and from holding meetings; but they did not prevent banquets. A banquet was scheduled in Paris for February 22, 1848, and when Guizot ordered it stopped the delegates who had assembled from all over France milled about the streets and joined the mob in a patriotic demonstration. When royal troops tried to break it up, the National Guard intervened and, with the mob, forced Guizot to resign.

This might have ended the turmoil, but the mob attempted to charivari Guizot and the royal guard fired into the crowd, killing thirty-five persons. The infuriated mob bombarded the palace, and Louis Philippe abdicated in favor of his grandson. Before the succession could be confirmed, however, the mob broke into the legislative hall and demanded a republic. Strife and bloodshed recurred through the ensuing months, until Louis Napoleon was elected president in December.

As had been the case in 1830, the French revolt started another political earthquake in Europe. It spread into the Near

East where the weakened Ottoman empire was facing difficulties with Russia which were to lead to the outbreak of the Crimean War in 1854.

When Kendall reached London he learned of a monster demonstration planned by the reformers, under the leadership of the blatant Feargus O'Conner. A huge petition, bearing six million signatures, had been prepared. A half-million workers were to assemble at Kennington Common and march on Parliament with this fabulous document.

The alarmed government forbade the procession, called out armed forces, commissioned a hundred and seventy-five thousand special constables, and placed public buildings in a state of defense.

Here was a news story made to order for Kendall. The book and the vacation could wait. He elbowed his way through the crowd to watch while O'Conner and his ally, Ernest Charles Jones, were taken into custody. Then he himself was arrested and spent two anxious hours in Bedlam prison explaining that he was not a dangerous and suspicious character.[1]

When he had talked his way out of prison and sent his story to the *Picayune*, Kendall crossed to France, still intent on the business of color engravings for his *Illustrated History*. In 1848, Paris had the only workmen who could produce these plates. But on his first morning in Paris, the *rappel* sounded before six o'clock, and he rushed out to the boulevards. The sidewalks were jammed with men, women, and children, crowding in the rain towards the Champs Elysées where a ceremony of presenting the flags to the battalions was to take place. Thousands of white handkerchiefs waved from the windows, all the grisettes of Paris were out in their neat white caps, trying to preserve their stockings from the mud, "and where do you see such stockings, so white and close fitting, as in this same Paris?" Kendall wrote.

Kendall lacked knowledge of France, knew little of its lan-

[1] Kendall later related this incident in a letter to the *Picayune* from Boerne, August 28, 1867.

guage and less of its politics. For years his interests had centered in the great American Southwest, which remained his first love throughout his life. Yet, while work on the book lagged, he ranged through the boulevards and made frequent trips to other news centers, sending back letters to the *Picayune* which were marked with all of his earlier curiosity, freshness, and sharpness of detail. His concern was to give New Orleans something different; a clear and vivid picture of what the common people in France were doing and saying and thinking. And he never forgot that New Orleans was French, and interested in the same things that interested the French people.

By this time the telegraph lines had been extended southward into Georgia,[2] and brief summaries of international news reached New Orleans many days ahead of Kendall's dispatches. Yet the *Picayune* filled its front page and sometimes its second with his letters, and its circulation soared as newsboys cried in the French Quarter, "All about the French Revolution!"

Indeed, much of the United States had keen interest in the revolution which, in the minds of Americans, was to bring republican institutions to France. When the first news arrived in Philadelphia, there was a public meeting in the park to express sympathy with the revolutionary movement. Stands were built, and speeches in various languages told of the movement in progress in nearly every European kingdom, looking toward freedom "from the bondage of monarchy."[3]

But while Kendall watched the troops parade and the bands play and the crowds throng to ceremonies on the boulevards and in the theaters, he grew skeptical of the thin veneer of democracy. He soon concluded that the leaders of the French democratic movement were demagogues, and their supporters the rabble who

[2] See Point Coupée *Echo*, April 8, 1848, which quoted the *Picayune* of April 1 as saying that a special express, "seventy-two hours ahead of the mail," had brought a copy of the Georgia *Constitutionalist*, "containing a telegraphic despatch from the North, announcing the arrival of the British mail steamer Caledonia, at Boston."

[3] The Philadelphia *North American and United States Gazette*, April 3, 1848.

wished only an escape from anything that resembled work. Commerce and trade and the small tradesmen were being crushed by the unsettled conditions which attend a revolution. At the first warning of a political demonstration, merchants closed their stores and barricaded their windows, and there was a growing fear that the city would be given over to pillage.

Liberals in Italy and in Poland were clamoring for assistance, and in Vienna the prime minister's forced resignation and flight to England had been the signal for a rising against the Hapsburgs which spread over Europe. Kendall reported to *Picayune* readers the story told on the streets of Paris to the effect that the crown prince of Prussia had escaped to England only after his tormenters had rubbed his nose in the gutter and forced him to beg for his life.

For a while the French crowds were appeased by fetes and parades, but while Kendall heard the ominous rumblings over the continent and watched the storm clouds gather, he predicted that when the treasury was empty carnage would follow. By June the impoverished government could not feed all of its hungry people who had been promised "a new existence, an exemption from all care, an abundance of everything." When some of the workers' spokesmen deemed the proffers of the Assembly unacceptable, they made plans for open resistance, demanding a return to monarchial government.

During the night of June 23 the insurgents threw up barricades in the street; they upset omnibuses and coaches, and by noon the *rappel* was being sounded furiously all over Paris.

Kendall was in the Palais Royal, getting shaved, when the alarm sounded. Hastily he tied his cravat and rushed into the street, where he saw the jewelers and money-changers taking their decoy wares from the windows, and watched groups of frightened women and children running for a place of safety. The insurgents in the streets, all excited, all talking, were working furiously at their barricades, and leading them on was an actress, decked out in a red scarf and Phrygian cap.

244

A volley of bullets fired by the National Guard whistled past and crashed into the barricades, the crests of which were instantly alive with insurgents, who returned the fire. Kendall squeezed into a doorway where there was a little protection from the flying bullets, and watched while the National Guard stormed the barricade in the street before him. The insurgents retreated, leaving their killed and wounded on the cobblestones. He remained through the evening, as close to the fighting as the guards would permit, and early the next morning he reported that cannon had been brought up to dislodge the insurgents from their position across the Seine.

During the twenty-fourth and twenty-fifth the battle raged, and because so many New Orleans readers knew Paris as their own, Kendall wrote in great detail of the chief rallying places of the insurgents and of the destruction in these quarters. On Sunday, June 25, he climbed the hill of Montmartre to watch the fighting, and when the insurgents were routed at sundown he followed their retreat. He was not as near the center of fighting as he had been with General Worth at Monterrey, at Cerro Gordo and in the Valley of Mexico, but he was much closer to the spattering bullets then he had expected to be when he started on his vacation.

When the revolt was crushed, the National Assembly staged another fete—a huge funeral procession for those who died in the revolution which exiled Louis Philippe and established the provisional government. It was the most imposing spectacle Kendall had ever seen. An immense hearse, drawn by sixteen horses "richly caparisoned in black," was followed by two hundred priests, members of the National Assembly, judges, a large number of civil functionaries, and richly uniformed cavalry and infantry.

In the Champs Elysées the aerial ships and flying horses attracted crowds, and sword swallowers and montebanks plied their trade. Places of amusement and the theaters reopened, while in the National Assembly Victor Hugo urged free theatricals as a means of preventing tumultuous assemblages on the street. With this idea Kendall rather contemptuously agreed. The French, he confided to *Picayune* readers, were much too fond of amusement and not sufficiently concerned with work.

For a time Paris was quiet, but the monarchist cause had gained headway. The National Assembly was terrified when a regiment entered Troyes shouting, "Vive Louis Napoleon!" Since the name of Napoleon became a rallying cry for the disaffected, the National Assembly decided to admit Louis Napoleon to a seat, and Kendall watched the mounting landslide which was to sweep the future emperor into the presidency of the Republic in December.

When affairs in Paris quieted down, Kendall turned his attention to Russia and Spain, where vigorous steps were being taken to stem the tide of liberal ideas sweeping in from France. Business in connection with his *Illustrated History* took him to Brussels, Amsterdam, and Hamburg, and he witnessed a great demonstration in Berlin in favor of liberty and equality. He decided that there, as in France, the idle and dissolute or mischief-making demagogues were causing the trouble, which was paralyzing trade and industry.

He reported that the Pope was forced to leave Rome and flee to Naples, that destruction and civil war were engulfing Spain, and that there was little peace and prosperity in Hungary. The liberals were crushed in Austria, but shortly afterwards the emperor abdicated in favor of Francis Joseph I, whom Kendall described as a lad of much spirit, and "so far as a boy but little more than eighteen years of age can have principles, is liberal enough."

Summarizing the events of 1848, Kendall concluded that the masses "lacked three great essentials to success; an education which would teach them the uses of liberty, the patience which would guide them as to when and where to strike for its attainment, and the determination which stops not this side of the grave in carrying out its object."[4]

[4] Kendall letter to *Picayune*, Paris, January 1, 1849.

This was not a popular opinion in the United States. Later in 1849 President Taylor removed Mr. Robert Walsh from the consulate at Paris for expressing similar sentiments in his correspondence, which was published in the *Journal of Commerce* and in the *National Intelligencer*. Democratic newspapers assailed Kendall's stand as being that of "a yankee Whig, of the *Picayune*, blue-bellied breed," but he insisted that France was not yet ready for democracy.[5]

Newspapers from home brought items of far greater interest to Kendall than criticism of his correspondence. New Orleans, wallowing in the depression following the Mexican War and hard hit by another cholera epidemic, took heart when the California gold rush got under way. With boom times, work speeded up on the customs house near the foot of Canal Street, where Henry Clay had laid the cornerstone; Madame Pontalba was building fabulous apartments flanking the Place d'Armes, and a new municipal hall was being built fronting Lafayette Square. Kendall wrote to the *Picayune*, "I wish to know if there is any truth in the marvelous stories . . . all about those gold mines in California? One feels strongly prompted, on reading about them, to shoulder a shovel and start at once."

Had he been home, Kendall undoubtedly would have gone along with many of his old newspaper friends who followed the call of adventure to the Pacific coast. Captain Tobin, former *Delta* correspondent, went by way of New York with General Persifor F. Smith, who was appointed governor of California. The *Picayune* employed Durivage, whom Kendall had trained as a Mexican War correspondent, and his old rival, Freaner, to cover the gold-rush story in California. With each mail a special California edition of the *Picayune* was dispatched to the coast.

Kendall was delighted with another home tie when Colonel Richard M. Hoe, famous American designer and builder of printing presses, was called to Paris to install a press for *La Patrie*.

[5] *Picayune*, January 29, March 24, October 29, 1849; *Delta*, October 17, October 27, 1849.

During 1849 there were frequent and lengthy gaps in Kendall's correspondence for the *Picayune*. Many times there had been false rumors in various newspapers in the United States, saying that he was married. But not a word of the courtship he now had been pressing for a year reached his confreres at home.

At this time he was just turned forty, handsome, well known and traveled, with plenty of money to spend and the will to spend it.[6] Soon after he arrived in Paris the American consul had introduced him to Adeline de Valcourt, a tall blonde girl of eighteen whose mother was of the French nobility and whose father had ruined himself in the cause of Napoleon. When the family found itself without income, and not wishing to dispose of its possessions, Adeline decided to become a governess. She was beautiful, had more than ordinary musical ability, was utterly courageous, with a delightful sense of humor, and she inspired Kendall's complete devotion. He always insisted that he loved her at first sight, and the letters he wrote to her deserve to rank with the world's great love letters.

One obstacle alone stood in the way of their marriage. Adeline de Valcourt was a Catholic, although as she sometimes exclaimed in later years, "but not be-gotted!" Kendall had no religious prejudice. Later, in Texas, he built for her a little Catholic church which one may see today, rising from a steep hillside in Boerne.

But in Mobile, Alabama, lived the matriarch who thought George Wilkins Kendall was the only man in the world. Abigail Kendall, widowed since 1843, was a fanatic Presbyterian who would bitterly oppose such a marriage for her son. Correspondence with the *Picayune* and work on his *Illustrated History* suffered while Kendall persuaded Mme. de Valcourt to take her daughter to Antwerp for their marriage. He was determined that while his mother lived, no whisper of such an event should reach her.

[6] Besides his royalties from his book, *Narrative of the Texan Santa Fe Expedition,* which was a best seller, the final accounting of the *Picayune* showed that he was drawing $4,000 a year from the paper at this time.

When Mme. de Valcourt yielded, Kendall combined a trip to see the English Derby with a visit to his London tailor. The engagement ring he bought for Adeline was a wide pointed oval, set with diamonds and emeralds, held by a narrow gold band. Her wedding ring was of plain gold, and he bought her wide bracelets of heavy gold. For himself, he bought a fine gold watch, and had it engraved with a buffalo, reproduced from one of the illustrations in the *Narrative of the Texan Santa Fe Expedition.*

One of his gifts to her, which she wore always, had romantic associations with his adventures in Mexico. Her blue eyes wide with wonder, this young French girl listened as the tall, handsome American told of having rescued a Mexican child from bandits. When he took the youngster home, its mother took from her neck the heavy gold chain and hung it around his own. Now he gave it to his bride.

So they were married in Antwerp, with a Presbyterian ceremony as well as the Catholic service, Kendall's friend, J. H. Dillon from London, serving as best man. After they spent two months touring the capitals of Europe, Kendall established his wife and her mother in an apartment in Paris, and later in a little house in the quiet suburb of Chaville. Across the Atlantic, only Kendall's banker, Westray, in New York, and Holbrook knew of the marriage. Holbrook doubted the wisdom of secrecy, and protested to Kendall that it might in the future lead to trouble for his wife.[7]

But Kendall was obdurate. What would be a source of unreasoning grief to his mother, he was determined, should not be known while she lived.

[7] Letter from A. M. Holbrook to Mrs. Kendall, dated New Orleans, December 17, 1872, in Kendall papers. After Kendall's death, the secret marriage did cause trouble for Mrs. Kendall in the settlement of the estate. See letter from F. Westray to Mrs. Dane, New York, October 17, 1873; and from S. F. Wilson to Mrs. Kendall, New Orleans, August 11, 1868, also in Kendall papers.

22

Reporter
on the boulevards

DURING THE YEAR after Kendall's marriage his life, so far as the public knew, moved along in the same groove, but he was at home in as domestic surroundings as a man ever created for himself. With his wife and his mother-in-law, whom he affectionately called "mother," he lived quietly in an apartment in Paris. There were frequent visits from his wife's two brothers, Adolphe and Alexandre, and her two sisters, Henriette and Louise.

Adolphe, two years older than Mrs. Kendall, became an officer of rank in the French Army, and later lived with the Kendalls in Texas. Alexandre, who was twenty-five when Kendall married, was a lieutenant in the French Navy; and both brothers became members of the Legion of Honor.

Besides actual members of the family there were a changing number of servants, carefully chosen to please Kendall, who was particular to have a good cook with a pleasant voice and a neat appearance. After they moved to a house in Chaville there was a backyard garden which Kendall cultivated himself, raising corn and vegetables for the table.

As time passed a few close friends came to know of the secret marriage, but Abigail Wilkins Kendall and Kate Rix knew nothing of the French Catholic family into which their George had married.

Paris was quiet and France enjoyed peace after the inauguration of Louis Napoleon as president of the Republic. By 1850 workmen were "fully employed," tourists crowded the cities, and without audible protest the thrifty middle class watched their dearly bought liberties undermined by an aggressive government. Kendall kept a stream of editorial correspondence flowing toward the *Picayune* office, but no longer were there revolutions and riots and bloodshed to cover.

Keeping the flavor of the spicy stories which had built up the infant *Picayune* in 1837–38, he wrote of queer cases in the courts of Paris, of a great rat hunt in the sewers of the city, of a journeyman painter who wagered he could eat a lighted candle and died from the effects, and of the great ladies who carried their pet cats and dogs, in elaborate cradles made up with fine embroidered linen, into the large airy building which was a hospital for sick pets.

Then misfortune struck the *Picayune*. A great fire swept Camp Street, and along with twenty others the *Picayune* building was destroyed. Kendall heard of it on March 4, three weeks after it happened, but he could not leave Paris at once. His brief vacation had now stretched out to two years; but the *Illustrated History* was not quite finished, and he and Adeline were awaiting the birth of their first child.

A flood of books on the Mexican War already had appeared, but Kendall was not one to put copy or illustration between covers until he was certain neither could be improved further. He had received a copy of Ripley's book on the war,[1] and had laughed heartily over it with General Ethan Allen Hitchcock when they met in Paris.

At last the baby arrived, on May 29, 1850, and was named Georgina de Valcourt Kendall. Less than two months later Ken-

[1] Roswell Sabine Ripley, *The War with Mexico* (2 vols., New York, 1849); Hitchcock told Kendall it had been written at General Pillow's house in Tennessee, and they agreed that it was "little more than a defense of General Pillow and an attack on everybody else." See Ethan Allen Hitchcock, *Fifty Years in Camp and Field* (New York and London, 1909), 356, March 30, 1850.

dall was in New York signing an agreement with D. Appleton and Company to publish *The War Between the United States and Mexico, Illustrated*. The price of the book, in various bindings, ranged from thirty-six to forty-eight dollars a copy.[2]

In New Orleans Kendall arranged for book agents to carry the work up and down the river and into remote parts of the state. He looked over the new *Picayune* building rapidly going up, and congratulated his partners that not an issue of the paper had been missed because of the fire. They discussed the secession crisis looming as Congress debated compromise measures, and agreed that the paper's policy should be to oppose the madness of South Carolina and avoid or postpone secession.[3]

Kendall noted that the *Picayune* had won another civic campaign when contracts for new paving on Levee and Chartres streets stipulated square granite blocks instead of the round cobblestones against which the paper had complained for so long. He saw the new wharves under construction in the Second Municipality, and the new bridge across Canal Carondelet at Marias Street, and visited the St. Charles Theatre to see the new drop curtain that was the talk of the town.[4] He went to Mobile for a brief and dreaded visit with his mother and sister, who were grieving over the death of Kate's eldest son, his own namesake.

Then he hurried on to Texas where the project of his dearest

[2] Appleton bound, advertised and distributed the book for a commission of five dollars per volume. Kendall and Nebel shared all costs including printing, lithographing, and hand-coloring the plates at three shillings each. The text, on pages 18 by 24 inches, was printed in the *Picayune* shop, and the New Orleans *Crescent*, April 2, 1850, referred to it as "the finest typography ever executed in New Orleans."

[3] *Picayune*, May 20, 1850; *Crescent*, July 30, 1850. The Columbia *South Carolinian* had declared that not a paper in New Orleans, with the exception of the *Delta*, was "true to the South." The *Picayune* insisted that whenever secession came it would be "with the intent and with the certainty of all the consequences of civil war, and no man needs delude himself with any hope of the contrary." Kendall had seen too much civil war in Paris to welcome the prospect.

[4] The curtain was a triumph of theater decoration of the period. The design was a Florentine landscape as described by Boccaccio, with a lake bordered by villas and a background of mountains, while the bottom of the frame contained a picture of the Mississippi River, with a female figure representing Louisiana.

dreams was taking shape. In the midst of secession talk and the distant rumblings of civil war, louder than they were to be again until the storm finally broke, people were turning to the security of the land. Immigrants were pouring in a steady stream into northern Louisiana and over into Texas, while others came to New Orleans to take ship for points along the Gulf coast.[5]

It was not secession talk which shaped Kendall's project, for his dream of a home in the beautiful hills of Texas had been growing since his trip to the Republic on the Santa Fe Expedition adventure in 1841. Tucked away among his papers was an old parchment deed signed by Anson Jones, the last president of the Republic, granting to Kendall four thousand acres of land far out beyond the frontier. And he had another hastily penned deed to a tract on the Brazos River, signed by J. Pinckney Henderson and witnessed by Mirabeau B. Lamar when the happy-go-lucky Texans were camped below the Rio Grande before General Taylor's advance on Monterrey.

But neither of these was the idyllic spot he sought as the home for his beautiful young wife and their tiny daughter. Theirs should be an estate built on a vast and prosperous sheep ranch. Kendall had interested three other partners in the venture; Holbrook, his old Mexican War friend Captain Forbes Britton, and W. A. Weed, a Vermonter whom he had met in Mexico at the time of the Santa Fe Expedition. They had purchased a flock of Mexican ewes and added to it a few pureblood Merinos that Kendall had secured in Vermont, and were pasturing their sheep on a tract of land on the Nueces River while they looked for a more favorable ranch site. Kendall made a brief trip into Texas, then returned to Paris, leaving Weed to look for new lands.

Weed made little headway, and Kendall soon was on his way back across the Atlantic, this time accompanied by Mrs. Kendall.

[5] The New Orleans *Crescent,* December 19, 1850, quoted the Caddo (Louisiana) *Gazette,* stating that in six weeks 343 families passed through that town on their way west, bringing 1556 Negroes, 1365 horses and mules, and 375 oxen. Alabama, Mississippi, Tennessee, Arkansas, Georgia, Kentucky, Louisiana, Virginia, North Carolina, and Missouri were represented in successively decreasing numbers.

253

He assured Mme. de Valcourt that, although he was not ready to announce his marriage in the States, every precaution would be taken to forestall any comment. Leaving always ahead of her, he would then, as an acquaintance, meet and escort her to the places chosen for her reception, where all arrangements had been made. Mme. de Valcourt felt that it would be a great opportunity for her daughter to see the country which would be their future home.

His wife followed him across to New York, then to the Ohio River, and by easy stages down the Mississippi where, as Mlle. de Valcourt, she met many of Kendall's friends. She arrived in New Orleans in time to share the excitement of the visit of Jenny Lind, whom P. T. Barnum was taking on a tour of the country. They saw her driven in state with Mr. Barnum to her apartment in Mme. Pontalba's building, and attended her concert, when front seats sold for twenty to twenty-five dollars, after the first had been auctioned off to D'Arcy, the hatter, for two hundred and twenty-five dollars.

After Mrs. Kendall returned to France, Kendall listened once more to the call of adventure when an expedition started from St. Louis to attend the Indian council at Fort Laramie. It was to the *Picayune's* interest that he go, for such negotiations were important news, and newspapers carried in detail the treaties made with the different tribes.

At St. Louis he met the ten "amateurs" who were joining Colonel D. D. Mitchell, Indian agent in charge of the expedition. Among them were Colonel A. B. Chambers, editor of the St. Louis *Republican;* Kendall's English friend, Dillon, who had been best man at his wedding, and H. C. King of Georgia, who was to settle beside him in Texas in 1860 and become Kendall's closest friend for the rest of his life.

They spent two days swapping yarns with old friends, buying horses, groceries, ammunition and all kinds of camp equipment, running bullets, and cleaning their guns and revolvers. They all got their hair cut short so that any scalping party might be at a disadvantage, and piled two wagons with boxes labeled "Old Bourbon," "Sazarac '95," "Potted Lobsters," and "French Preserved Meats." Then they started out for Fort Kearny to meet Colonel Mitchell, an escort of dragoons, and his fifty wagons loaded with provisions and presents for the Indians.

At Fort Laramie they expected to find the different bands of the Sioux nation, the Arapaho and Cheyenne tribes, and delegations from the Crow and Snake, Comanche, Cayuga (Kiowa), and Utah tribes. On the first night out, rain drenched Kendall and his companions and made the roads almost impassable. The overloaded wagons stuck in the mud, "not in one creek, but in every one," and as the mules could not drag them out the men were forced to put shoulders to the wheels and help them. Covered with mud and worn with fatigue, on the third day they began to lighten the wagons, throwing overboard five hundred pounds of wet and damaged sugar, coffee, and meat.

From Pottawatomie Post, consisting of a dozen log houses, Kendall sent a letter to the *Picayune* and another to his wife, complaining of the bad luck that had permitted them to cover only half of the scheduled two hundred miles. The rains continued and they reached Fort Kearny ten days behind time, to find that Colonel Mitchell had left a week before. While they rested and repaired their gear, Indians stole some of their mules, and they decided to give up the trip to Fort Laramie and go instead to a smaller council in the Pawnee country. This was the last of Kendall's ventures into the wilds in search of news for the *Picayune*.

He was back in Paris in January, 1852, reporting that there had been another revolution and commenting that "the little previously left of the Republic of '48 has been completely swept away." In the previous December Louis Napoleon had issued a manifesto proclaiming a temporary dictatorship, dissolving the hated Assembly, and calling for a plebiscite on the proposal to let him revise the constitution. This constitution was promulgated in January, and late in the following year he became emperor in name, as he had been in fact for more than a year.

While Kendall wrote of politics and the Mardi Gras, of the Prince-President's fetes and the antics of Parisians along the boulevards, or complained of Americans idolizing Kossuth, there appeared a growing note of nostalgia in his letters. More and more often he contrasted the crowded streets, the dark, damp, disagreeable living quarters in Paris and London with the rocks and rills of Texas.

In the spring, as a diversion, Kendall and his wife spent two months in England and Scotland visiting historic landmarks and taking in the Derby, but they spent more of their time looking over farms and flocks and watching sheep dogs work out. By now Kendall definitely was looking for sheep dogs and a shepherd for his ranch in Texas. He was not successful in his search on this trip, however.

In September he was in London again, en route to America, leaving Mrs. Kendall at home awaiting the arrival of their second child. Urgent letters from Weed, in Texas, and from his publishers, made the hurried trip imperative. Mrs. Kendall was gloomy at the prospect of their separation, but he promised to be back by December.

His first stop in London was at the shop of his tailor,[6] then he went on to Scotland. There, on the banks of the Tweed, he found a resourceful young shepherd, Joe Tait, who was willing to go to Texas to take care of Kendall's flocks. He bought two fine Leicester sheep and four Scotch collies. The Leicesters did not prove a profitable investment, but Tait and the fine sheep dogs contributed greatly to Kendall's success.

He sent Tait on to the ranch on the Nueces River, where their flocks were grazing, while he stopped briefly in New Orleans, then hastened on to Corpus Christi to join Weed.

The cabin of the little mail sloop had hardly room for two persons, yet a half-dozen crowded into it for the rough passage

[6] A receipted bill in the Kendall papers shows that for twelve pounds he purchased "two pairs of fine checked doeskin pants, one pair of grey doeskin and one pair of checked tartan pants, two commodore vests, one angola traveling vest with mahogany buttons, and one fine angola traveling coat."

between Corpus Christi and Indianola. In this cramped, uncomfortable place, filled with "myriads of musquitoes," Kendall and his partner were forced to share their quarters with a woman, her twelve year old daughter, and two Negro servant girls. Through the monotonous day and night the little boat sailed close to the shore, and it was two o'clock on the following afternoon before the passengers sighted Indianola. The wind blew a gale, and Kendall, who usually had great contempt for seasickness, was violently ill.

Even in this situation, his sense of humor made it possible to joke, in his letter to his wife, about one of the Negro girls who had never been to sea before, and who "said she should die; she knew she must die." Every thing he saw, and a great deal of what he thought and felt, proved material for Kendall's busy pen as he wrote voluminous letters to his lonesome young wife in Chaville. At every stop, in crowded steamer cabins, by the campfire, under the dim light in remote post offices, he paused to dash off a letter to her. They were revealing letters, showing at once his devotion, his anxiety for her welfare, his high good humor, his burning ambition and his quick fits of depression.

Both Kendall and Weed needed a sense of humor on this journey, for Kendall was driven by the determination to find exactly the land he wanted for the permanent location of his ranch. Weed had left his wife and two children in Vermont and did not expect to see them for a year to come.

The two had already made one horseback trip from Corpus Christi into the interior of Texas. But the water was not good in this region, and although he found plenty of land at a good price, Kendall refused to buy. He wrote his wife, "I will have clear and bright water, where we can bathe, and where we can also have shade trees and every other comfort."

So they pushed on, first by mail sloop from Corpus Christi to Decroins Point, then by a small sailboat to Indianola, and from there on horseback to Fort La Vaca, Victoria, Labadie, and Goliad. They slept on the ground, which was not a new experience for Kendall; but he was now a man of forty-three who suffered from frequent colds, and the damp, chilly November nights left him numb. Continued hardships brought on an attack of bone fever and rheumatism, but he refused to be delayed.

At Goliad, Weed found a letter from his wife, and Kendall stopped in a small store "with forty people around," to send a note to Adeline. No suitable location yet offered, so they pushed on over the terrible road to San Antonio, Kendall riding his little black mare, Addy. It was nearly nine o'clock in the evening when they crossed the bridge into the city, "tolerably well tired down" after a land hunting trip of nearly a week along the banks of the Cibolo. Kendall went at once to the post office. The letter he expected was not, however, to bring word of the baby's arrival, but he was eager for any news from his wife and small daughter. The office was closed, but the postmaster lived nearby, and Kendall argued so persistently that the postmaster came down to the office and gave him his mail.

Under the flicker of a street lamp he stood on the corner and read his letter from his wife, then hurried to his room to answer. "I look at every child I see," he wrote, "but find no one who can in any way compare with our dear little girl."

In the morning he took stock of his appearance. His clothes were soiled and shabby, his hat out of shape from frequent rains, his face and hands burned black from exposure. On the boulevards of Paris, he decided, he would "pass for the roughest specimen of red republican or Socialist," but since he was not now "on a wife hunting expedition," he would not change clothing until he got back to New Orleans.

He drove in a carriage into the region around San Antonio and came back to write his wife that his search for land was near an end. He was enchanted with the rolling hills and the clear streams. And he hastened to assure her that she would like the city itself. "Here in San Antonio the society is excellent," he wrote, "and I can assure you that it is quite aristocratic. Many of the army officers reside here, with their families, a railroad is soon to be built to the coast, and by the time we are ready to live here it will be the finest situation in the world."[7] At this time he was planning that only a few weeks of each year would be spent on the farm, with the family residence in San Antonio. He made three more unsuccessful trips into the surrounding hills, one to the southwest with a guide, then a drive over to Seguin, and a ride from there through an uninhabited stretch to New Braunfels.

His enthusiasm returned when he reached this little German settlement and found the progress it had made in the seven difficult years since its establishment. The town had its beginning on March 21, 1845, when Prince Carl zu Solms-Braunfels, commissioner general for the Adelsverein, the society of German noblemen of Mainz, Germany, camped with a group of immigrants on the east bank of Comal Creek. The Verein, organized in 1842, intended to establish in Texas that feudal society which Napoleon's conquests had shattered in Europe.

But annexation of Texas to the United States, for which Kendall had worked so enthusiastically, ruined their plans for a feudal society, and Prince Solms returned to Germany. Baron Otfried, Hans von Meusebach, who was later Kendall's neighbor and close friend, took over as commissioner general and made frantic efforts to take care of the four thousand immigrants who were on their way to Texas. In spite of a staggering debt and slim credit, he bought additional land to the northwest where the town of Fredericksburg later was established. The immigrants arrived during the Mexican War, when the United States had bought up all available horses and mules, and the new settlers were obliged to march to New Braunfels, suffering incredible hardships. After two years the company became insolvent and the immigrants—more than seven thousand of them—had to shift for themselves. But individual enterprise triumphed, and when Kendall visited New Braunfels in 1852 he was able to describe it to his wife as "the great German settlement," where "regular nobility" lived in log houses and raised fine, hearty children.

[7] Kendall papers, Kendall to Mrs. Kendall, November 8, 1852.

Here his long search for land ended; on November 23 he wrote Mrs. Kendall that he had found a place that would suit them exactly. It was "a pleasant and verdant valley, surrounded on all sides by rough, rocky and rugged mountains," seven miles northwest of New Braunfels.

The tract he had selected was "about six times as large as all Paris," and "admirably adapted for raising both sheep and horses." It had rich grass, the beautiful stream roared like a young Niagara, and von Meusebach would be their neighbor within an hour's ride.

On the land Kendall saw bears, antelope, deer, wild turkeys, and some proud, beautiful mustangs. "I know that you would like the spot for its many romantic beauties," he wrote his wife, not realizing that his idea of romantic beauty might not be the same as that of a young woman whose only contact with the wilds of nature had been in the well ordered parks of Paris and in the countryside along the Seine.

Flushed with victory and pride in finding this ideal homesite, Kendall gave Weed power of attorney to go to San Antonio and buy the land, while he started back to New Orleans where he hoped to receive news from his family. But a speedy trip was something he longed for in vain. At the San Marcos River high water had carried off the ferryboat and the stage could not cross. It was nine o'clock at night, but at Kendall's frantic urging the passengers set to work building a raft, and by eight the next morning were all safely over. They made their impatient way to Gonzales, where another stage was supposed to be waiting for them, since it ran only every other day. Kendall's quick anger flared when he found that the stage and mailbag had been gone an hour. The tavern keeper, anxious to get their custom for two days, had sent it off to Indianola, empty.

Kendall was infuriated. After "high words with the scoundrel," he went out in search of other transportation. He was able to hire a wagon and team, on condition that the passengers walk a part of the way. The roads were heavy and muddy, but he

Adeline de Valcourt Kendall   George Wilkins Kendall

(about the time of their marriage)

covered the hundred miles in time to catch the steamer *Fashion* for New Orleans. The letter waiting for him brought word that his wife had been safely delivered of a boy.

When Kendall had written his wife from London on September 1, he promised her that the land hunt would be over in six weeks and within two months he would be on his way home again. But two months had stretched into three and he was still weeks away from Paris.

He stopped for a brief visit with his mother and Kate in Mobile, then headed north by the mail route which had caused the *Picayune* editors so much grief over delayed news in the past. He took the steamer on Saturday evening for Montgomery, changed at midnight Monday for the train for West Point on the Chattahoochi River, had an hour for breakfast before taking the stage, over horrible roads and swollen streams, and reached Augusta by daylight on Wednesday. There was no time even for a cup of coffee before catching the Charleston cars, and at Charleston he caught the mail steamer for Wilmington without a moment to spare. There he boarded a river steamer for Washington.

Congress was in session, and at another time he would have liked to stay over for the inauguration of Franklin Pierce as president. But he hurried on to New York where he bought doors, windows, and flooring for his ranch house, at a saving over prices in New Braunfels. He hoped to be in Paris by New Year's Day, but broken machinery delayed the *Franklin* and she could not sail. This was an annoyance, since he now would have to go by way of Liverpool. He had purchased canvasbacks, hams, and other American delicacies as a gift for his wife, and it would require considerable trouble and expense to take them through England. He took them along anyway, but they spoiled in an unusually warm, rainy spell between New York and Boston, and he had to throw them overboard.

It was mid-January before he was at home in Chaville with his wife and daughter and his new son, William.

23

Last vacation
in Europe

KENDALL'S JOY over reunion with his family was soon disturbed by news that disaster had struck his Texas venture. When he had left his flocks on the Nueces, to search for a better ranch site, they were thriving; but while he was en route for Paris a severe blizzard swept over his range. Many of the sheep, caught without adequate shelter, froze in the unprecedented snow and sleet.

It was a serious blow to his dreams for immediate success of the undertaking, but during the next few months, while he was combing the boulevards of Paris for news, he also was making definite plans for restocking his range.

He wrote the *Picayune* that Louis Napoleon had arranged another brilliant diversion for the French people; this time it was his marriage to Marie Eugénie de Montijo de Guzmán. Kendall considered this marriage the boldest act, to date, in the Emporor's career, the result, he said, of two causes: "a great love for the lady . . . and . . . to spite the Princess Vasa who preferred the suit of some petty one-horse potentate, with two acres and a half of tillable land which he calls a dukedom, somewhere in Germany."

He covered the royal ball at the palace of the Luxembourg, and concluded "It is a part of the system of Louis Napoleon to keep the French continually surfeited with amusement or excitement of some kind, and as long as the money lasts they may be kept tranquil. . . ."

But Kendall was marking time until the annual spring sheep auction at Rambouillet. While he was in Spain, Napoleon Buonaparte had selected all of the best Merino sheep in that country and sent them to Rambouillet to be bred with the greatest care. One hundred of the sheep were to be sold at the national farms in April, and Kendall took his wife and Georgina along to the sale. Bidding ran high, from two hundred and fifty to six hundred francs, but he bought several of the fine animals for shipment to Texas.

Just as he had been interested in talking with the cab drivers, the chambermaids, the people in the streets to get their reactions during the Revolution, Kendall now was greatly interested in the French farmers who attended the auction. He had breakfast with eleven of them, "jolly, ruddy, substantial men," courteous and some of them "fair drinkers," for after breakfast he counted twenty-two empty bottles on the table.

He told *Picayune* readers of the breakfast menu, for he had arisen at six o'clock and traveled half a hundred miles and was pleased with the light wine, the cold, well seasoned pork pie, veal cutlets, mutton chops and stewed kidneys, the fat, delicious shad, a roast, a regular course of vegetables, pies, cakes and pastries, fruits and coffee, with "delicious French cream (they call the latter brandy in some parts of the States)." The charge was three francs, not quite sixty cents.

His sheep hardly had been loaded for shipment when he heard further disturbing news from Texas. Weed had been unsuccessful in San Antonio in locating the owner of the land Kendall had selected for his ranch near New Braunfels. The owner was reported to have returned to his home in Ireland. So Kendall hastened to Dublin, covering the great exposition of art and industry for the *Picayune* and spending many weary hours looking for the man who owned the Texas land. He left an agent to continue the search and returned to Paris.

There he bought type for the *Picayune,* and pear trees, vines, and other plants for the ranch. James Gordon Bennett, publisher of the New York *Herald,* dropped in for a visit and the two friends spent a half-hour discussing the idea of making printing paper out of Texas prairie grass.

In Paris bad news from Texas again caught up with him. An epidemic of liver rot broke out among his sheep and carried away more than half of those that had survived the blizzards.[1] Kendall wrote Weed to transfer the remaining sheep to the New Braunfels region, and made plans to hasten to Texas himself in an effort to avert complete disaster.

He was on his way by the last of August, all the while writing voluminous letters for the paper. He was particularly eager to make this trip as quickly as possible, for his third child was expected, and more than ever Kendall dreaded this separation. But in Boston he received a letter from Holbrook warning him that yellow fever was raging in New Orleans, and urging him not to come south before it was over.

A diversion offered, of the kind Kendall welcomed most—a hunting trip with a group of congenial friends. There were his old friend, Porter of the *Spirit of the Times;* Vincent Wallace, musician and composer; M. Placide, comedian and manager of the New Orleans Varieties Theater, and Colonel Charles of the New York militia. They went to Booneville, New York, and rode twenty-five miles into the wild country where Kendall delighted his friends with his camp cooking.

When he returned from his vacation he found a long-delayed letter telling him that the plague had struck within his family circle. His sister, Kate, wrote that their mother had died at the age of eighty. This news moved him deeply, but with it came the realization that now his mother would be spared the shock and grief that would have accompanied news of the marriage which had brought so much happiness to him.

[1] Kendall summarized these misfortunes in "Sheep Raising in Texas," *Texas Almanac* for 1861, pp. 166–170.

On his way back he went over into Vermont to see Mrs. Weed, to take her the recent news he had of her husband who had been in Texas for two years. In order to travel on Sunday he had to hire a team and carriage, since "in Vermont they are too religious to allow the locomotives to work on such a day. They have no objection, however, to hire out their horses for money, and we engaged a fine team."

He went by Washington to ask President Pierce to give one of Holbrook's brothers a government job of some sort. The man was poor, with nothing to do, and a wife and eight children dependent upon him. "Think of that," Kendall wrote his wife. "Eight! It makes me nervous whenever the fact comes to my mind." The President promised a job for Holbrook's brother, and Kendall put in a word in his own behalf. He wrote Mrs. Kendall that he had been assured that the coming Congress would take a copy of his *Illustrated History* for each member. "If so, it will put some eight thousand dollars in my pocket at once—a comfortable sum, and which I would like much to have."[2]

His trip to Cincinnati was delayed by difficult and annoying rail connections, but he arrived in time to buy horses to ship to Texas. As usual, too, he had time for a brief visit with his newspaper friends. The next day's issue of the Cincinnati *Daily Columbian* carried this item:

HE'S IN! George Wilkins Kendall of the New Orleans *Picayune* is at the Burnet. George is *enroute* for home—if he has any such place on the hemisphere—New Orleans. Kendall is a man whose history can only be appreciated hereafter. He is here to-day, gone to-morrow; we read of him in Paris, and understand he hails from New Orleans. He

---

[2] Kendall, letter to Mrs. Kendall, dated Burnet House, Cincinnati, November 3, 1853. There is no record in either the *Congressional Globe* or the *Statutes at Large* of Kendall's *Illustrated History* being purchased by Congress. The appropriation deficiency bill, which was passed during the last days of Millard Fillmore's term as president, included an amendment stating: "Hereafter, no books shall be distributed to members of Congress except such as are ordered to be printed as public documents by the Congress of which they are members." *The Statutes at Large and Treaties of the United States of America,* (Boston, 1855), X, 188.

travels more, sees as much, in one year, as some of us learn in a life time. "Got up" in the hills of Vermont, starts out to see what is gone on in the South—all of a sudden he makes a fortune, and goes round to see the world. All we could ask for the general good of mankind is, that George would marry off—and perpetuate his ilk.[3]

"George" must have smiled to himself to observe how well he was keeping separate his public and his private life.

He had hoped for a speedy passage down the river from Cincinnati, but a careless pilot ran the boat aground on a sand bar. For three days he paced the decks, played whist, and finally, for consolation, turned to the Bible and read several chapters of Job. This was one of the evidences, increasing as the years passed, of the impatience which stamped his character. Always he had chafed at obstacles, but his energy and his resourcefulness carried him past barriers which turned back less determined men. These characteristics made him a versatile reporter, a successful publisher, a great correspondent, and a pioneer who contributed immeasurably to the development of his adopted state.

Later he was to suffer the bitter disappointments of adverse weather, of a choking wartime blockade, of devastating Indian forays, and of epidemics in his flocks—obstacles beyond his strength and patience to endure. Happily for him now, these dark years of the future were curtained. As usual his arrival in Texas served as a tonic for his fretting spirit.

After a brief stop in New Orleans he caught the first boat for Indianola. His slow progress over the muddy roads up from the coast was offset by a chance meeting with a settler. When the man learned his name, he asked if he were the same man who wrote "that Santa Fe Expedition book." Acknowledging the authorship, Kendall learned that his descriptions of the state had induced the man to come to Texas, where he had made a substantial start

[3] Issue of November 4, 1853. A marked tear sheet of this paper is included in the Kendall papers, along with many others mentioning his name. It is probable that he sent such clippings to his wife when he was on his trips, and that she preserved them carefully with his letters.

toward prosperity. Later his writings were to prove such a magnet for immigrants that inquiries became a burden, but now the incident was a source of pride.

His gloom over the delays which lengthened to six weeks his trip from New York to New Braunfels lifted when he reached the ranch. The enterprising agent in Dublin had completed the deal for the land, Weed had constructed a small but livable house, and their sheep were thriving. One flock numbered more than two thousand, and another seven hundred, almost entirely of lambs. Early next morning Kendall was out catching fish and shooting quail for breakfast. Rapture shone through every word of the frequent letters he sent to his wife. He longed for his family, but even without them he was at home, in the one place in all the world where his roots went deep and he found complete satisfaction in his surroundings.

Adeline's letters telling him of the birth of their third child, Caroline, reached him on December 9. From what she wrote he was fearful that the baby might not live, and he was terribly concerned over this and his wife's health as well. But he could not leave the ranch at once; Weed had gone north to bring back his family, and in his absence there was much to do. Kendall was building more shelters and pens for the sheep, and ploughing land for the corn planting. That year they had raised two thousand bushels, and hoped for more in 1854.

So in spite of forebodings about his wife and baby, he worked with his men, driving them on with his own energy. He wrote his wife that he was living a wild, strange life, wearing the coarsest clothing, with nothing to drink except coffee, and nothing to eat except bacon, beef, sweet potatoes, and corn bread. This fare was varied with fish and game when he could take time out from his labor. He had only a pipe to smoke. Probably this statement, from a man who had formerly ordered the finest Havana cigars, two thousand at a time, was enough to warn her of the change that was taking place in this restless, ever moving dynamo who was her husband.

He was careful, however, to add that they would not always live in this way.

One of his workmen on the ranch was Dutch, one French, one Scotch, and one English; and there were the Mexican shepherds. Each day Kendall had to speak three languages besides his own. So he cautioned his wife that it was important that their children learn languages, that they must have a German nursemaid, and not forget their English. German he considered a rude, uncouth language, almost too difficult for him to master, but most important for Adeline and the children to learn.

Probably at this time he gave up his dream of living most of the time in San Antonio, with only a few weeks each year on the ranch, for the letters now revealed a foretaste of weary years to come. The ewes began to drop their lambs, and Kendall was annoyed and astonished, for Weed had assured him that none were due before March. Unseasonably warm weather following Christmas warned of a norther and made Kendall drive himself and his men to build additional shelters.

The expected blizzard struck on January 7, and night and day they nursed the lambs by a great wood fire, saving many but not all.

Then a prairie fire raged close to the ranch and Kendall rode many miles trying to hire a man to plough fireguards, but in every direction the settlers were busy. While one man went out to round up his five yoke of oxen, Kendall and another helper worked furiously to save fence rails threatened by the fire.

Company came immediately after this strenuous effort. Fortunately he had a ham, a loaf of wheat bread, and fresh meat to offer the three over-night guests. He gave up his cot and slept in blankets on the floor.

Weed had secured a Negro woman as a cook, and at this time Kendall purchased another household slave. She was Nelly, a mulatto girl, who cost him seven hundred dollars.[4]

By late January Kendall estimated his holdings in Texas to be worth twenty thousand dollars. The ranch was running smoothly, and he left for France, impatient to see his new daughter. Isolated on the ranch, he had scarcely known what was going on in the world, but when he arrived in New Orleans early in 1854, he learned that war had broken out between Russia and Turkey while he was on his way to Texas. Already there were indications that England and France would be drawn into the conflict.

The inevitable struggle for supremacy in the Near East finally came to a head in the dispute between France and Russia over supervision of the holy shrines in Palestine. When Russia's demand for a protectorate over all Christians in Turkey was rejected, the Czar's troops moved into the Turkish principalities along the lower Danube, where fighting continued late in 1853.

While he waited in New Orleans for a West India mail steamer to take him to Europe, telegraphic dispatches revealed that England had seized all Cunard liners to transport troops to Turkey.

[4] Nelly proved an annoying responsibility until after the Civil War, and her case was an excellent example of the burden which a few slaves placed on the small slaveowner who operated without the services of an overseer. She was poorly clad when Kendall bought her, and had caught a violent cold in the bitter weather. Kendall wrote his wife about Nelly's illness, ". . . last night when I came in from work, I found her groaning and taking on in great pain, and saying that she must die. She complained bitterly of pains in her hips, back, and what we call the stomach. And what to do for her I did not know. The old cook, who has had a great deal of experience, said she had caught a violent cold, and was putting cataplasms and hot water in bottles all over her. . . . I thought we should lose her. On inquiring, I find that she has neither chemise nor petticoat—nothing at all of the kind—the people of whom I purchased her never having furnished anything of the sort. All this I knew nothing at all about—she never hinted to me that she was cold, poor thing! or that she wanted clothes, although I always thought that her frock set very slim upon her. Tomorrow morning I am going to New Braunfels to purchase both flannel and thick cotton stuff for chemises. . . . The man of whom I purchased her must have been simply a brute, or else he would have given her warmer clothes to wear." Kendall papers, Kendall to Mrs. Kendall, January 26, 1854.

Mrs. Kendall, who was shocked on her trip from the coast to New Braunfels to learn that on his infrequent visits the minister often performed the marriage ceremony for a pioneer couple and at the same time christened the children already born to the union, was embarrassed by Nelly's promiscuous mating instincts. When Nelly produced a child each year, Mrs. Kendall remonstrated with her about her conduct, but Nelly invariably gave the reply, unanswerable from her viewpoint, "Why Mis' Kendall, I'se making Mr. Kendall rich."

269

Kendall determined "to go directly to the line of operations on the Danube, to witness and describe the active progress of the war."[5]

However, he made no mention of these plans in his letters to his wife. He wrote her that he had attended performances of Sontag, Ole Bull, and Julien's band in New Orleans, and had been invited to attend a fancy dress and masquerade ball at the St. Charles Hotel. He was beginning to tell his friends about his marriage, and was pleased at their astonishment.

He went by Mobile to tell Kate of his little family in Chaville, but was annoyed to find her house so full of company that he had no chance to visit with her. He told her husband, William Rix, about his marriage as they were driving down to the wharf.

Mrs. Kendall met him in Liverpool and accompanied him to London where he gathered war news for the *Picayune* before they went on to Chaville. There he got acquainted with the tiny Caroline and cultivated his backyard garden. His vacation ended, however, when news came that France and England formally had declared war on Russia. Still considering the possibility of going to the war front, Kendall returned to Paris to write the *Picayune* of the sentiment for war, less strong in France than in England, of the uneasiness as to the course Austria would follow, and of the dullness of business in the city.

He soon realized that for many reasons his proposed trip to the lower Danube was inadvisable. All horses and other means of transportation had been snatched up by the fighting forces. All available interpreters had been forced into service with the armies, and at the same time every line of communication was threatened by wandering "swarms of Bashi-Buzouks, ever ready to knock any helpless party on the head with as little compunction as so many lawless Comanches." When the Russians moved toward the lower Danube, he wrote the *Picayune*, "the occupation of newspaper writers was gone."

While he was making this decision, another correspondent

5 Kendall letter to the *Picayune*, Paris, June 12, 1854.

started for the Bosporous and the Crimea where in the next two years he was to gain fame which prompted the English to claim for him the title Kendall had earned eight years before—that of "the first modern war correspondent." He was William Howard Russell of the London *Times,* whose vivid stories of a mismanaged campaign and suffering troops caused the overthrow of the Aberdeen ministry and sent Florence Nightingale and her little band of nurses sailing eastward on their famous errand of mercy.[6]

The decision to leave the reporting of the Crimean War to others must have raised a serious conflict in Kendall's mind. When he was in New Orleans making plans to go to the front, the fighting along the Danube might have echoed with the call of adventure, with the possibility of profit to the *Picayune,* as the Santa Fe Expedition, the Indian councils, and the Mexican War had brought profit through his reporting. However, his dispatches from France when the war was gaining momentum indicated that he was convinced *Picayune* readers were not vitally interested in details of the conflict in the Crimea, a war in which Louis Napoleon hoped to win over clerical opponents at home, and through which England saw a chance to strengthen her interests in the eastern Mediterranean.

He must have known that the paper's gain through his increased reputation as a war correspondent would be offset by the great cost and hardship of such an enterprise, which would be more difficult for an American than for an Englishman. In spite of his fondness for adventure, Kendall was a canny businessman who considered the financial aspect of his undertakings, and it is difficult to see how direct coverage of a campaign along the shores of the Black Sea could have been anything but a heavy drain on the *Picayune.* Furthermore, the paper, because of a general business stagnation in the South, was not now in a position to undertake a great financial gamble.

[6] John Black Atkins, *The Life of Sir William Howard Russell, C.V.O., LL.D., the First Special Correspondent* (London, 1911).

There was also a personal angle which Kendall undoubtedly turned over in his mind. He was now forty-five years old, and if he went to the Crimea it would mean the postponement of his plans for taking his family to the ranch in Texas very soon. Having made up his mind not to go to the scene of war, Kendall sent his wife to Abbeville for a brief vacation, putting her on the train with the promise that he would look after the household in her absence. At the end of three days he was so completely worn down with domestic chores that he urged Mrs. Kendall to return so they could go together on a long vacation trip through Switzerland.

They changed their plans and routed their trip through Brussels, Frankfurt, Stuttgart, Munich, Heidelberg, Baden, Strasbourg, and Nancy. Cholera was raging along the route, and because of this they enjoyed superlative service in the almost deserted hotels. The once gay tourist centers were gloomy places, but he wanted his wife to see everything she could on this farewell tour. Next year they would be leaving for America.

Perhaps without admitting it, he realized that some day he himself would feel a nostalgia for the capitals of Europe, for the opera and the boulevards, the good hotels and the choice wines he prized so highly. Whether or not he knew it then, the time was to come when, from the remoteness of a ranch west of New Braunfels, he would write to *Picayune* readers with wistful reminiscence of this last vacation in Europe.

24

A family
moves to Texas

BEFORE he could take his family to Texas, it was
necessary for Kendall to make one last trip to
complete preparations at the ranch. In addition
to the melon, pear, and apple seeds he had taken on his previous
trips, he now secured olive trees and grapevines from the south
of France.

By this time warning had come of a grief which Kendall at
first refused to believe. It was becoming apparent that Caroline,
now a year old, was deaf. Worry over this growing fear increased
his gloom during his tedious journey.

In England he was delayed by his gunsmith, and by his failure
to find an India rubber cape with a hood to keep the rain off while
riding horseback. Finally he got aboard ship with nine parcels.
These included his trunk and carpetbag, a gun for a friend in
Louisiana and a fishing rod for himself, a basket containing
brandy, whiskey, and his favorite wine, Vieux Ceps; a box of
Bordeaux, a Scotch blanket for his head shepherd, a package
which the consul in London wanted him to deliver in San Antonio,
and finally, his umbrella.

He had booked passage on the *Strato,* which his friends had
recommended as the newest, best and fastest ship running. But
the British government had sent the *Strato* to Sevastopol as a
troop ship, and Kendall was forced to take the *Parana,* an old

slow steamer, wet and dirty, which had been undergoing repairs at Southampton. She was jerked out of dock with the repairs half finished, and her indifferent accommodations for fifty passengers were shared by nearly three hundred. Worse still, she was going around by Haiti.

The weather was rough, and water stood two feet deep in some of the staterooms. Although Kendall lifted his trunk to a settee, its contents became damp and mildewed. There were at least a dozen French milliners and fancy dressmakers on board, and when at last the sun came out, "it was a sight to see them bring out their *moire antiques* and *dernieres modes de Paris*, generally all mouldy and stained, to dry in the sun."

Kendall's cabin mate was a dapper little Frenchman, very reticent about his calling, who was going to Mexico. When he discovered that Kendall's shirts were mildewed he offered a generous supply, and Kendall was amazed to discover that they fitted perfectly although the Frenchman was slight of stature. Every morning he would find a beautiful linen or lawn shirt laid out for his use, and other passengers marveled and commented on their perfection and the extent of his supply.

Enjoying the furtive envying glances which his glossy shirt fronts attracted, Kendall during the tropical weather accepted the luxury of two a day, even while he wondered how the Frenchman happened to own so many shirts, and why he was showing such unparalleled generosity. Some time later he learned that the little Frenchman kept a fancy goods and hairdressing establishment in Mexico, and always had the finest assortment of perfumes, gloves, and shirts in the capital. Since soiled or worn clothing paid no duties, Kendall had been helping his cabin mate smuggle his shirts through the Vera Cruz customs house.[1]

Kendall arrived in New Orleans at two o'clock on the morning of January 5, 1855, six weeks after he had left Europe, and immediately hastened to the *Picayune* office with news he had

[1] Kendall related this incident in a letter to the *Picayune* from Boerne, June 16, 1867.

written for the paper. Four printers were there, and he set them to work at once.

As he read his way through a stack of accumulated mail next day, he learned that a disastrous business depression had settled over New Orleans during the winter. Once-rich merchants were failing at an alarming rate. The Mississippi tributaries had been too low for navigation and produce had just begun to come in. He urged his wife to be prudent in her expenditures, since "it is now too late to hope to make much money this year, and if we can obtain enough to live upon we shall be fortunate. . . . The times will be still harder in the old world unless the war is soon brought to a close. I wish that the stupid Russian Emperor had to bear all the evil he has caused on his own shoulders."[2]

Kendall's trip to Texas again was filled with annoyances. Seeking to avoid the slow stage trip inland, he shipped a mare aboard the steamer, but a norther blew the water so completely out of Matagorda Bay that the ship could not get to the wharf. He landed in a small boat, walked to Indianola and not until the next day was he able to get his hungry mare ashore. But once on the road to New Braunfels his spirits soared, and he wrote his wife enthusiastically from the ranch. There, he insisted, the weather was more pleasant in February than it was in France at any season of the year, with fruit trees in full flower and every little grove alive with singing birds.

The larger ranch house was going up, but even now his dreams outran the New Braunfels establishment. Forty miles to the west lay the larger tract of land he had purchased from the Republic of Texas in 1845, and one of his flocks now was pastured there. Only the frequent and deadly forays of Indians had kept back the tide of settlement in that direction, but when the Indian menace was removed, his broad acres there would be the site of his great ranching establishment.

With this dream in mind, he hitched a team to a Jersey wagon and started across the hills to this future homesite. Some half-

[2] Kendall papers, Kendall to Mrs. Kendall, New Orleans, January 11, 1855.

dozen German families lived in the first four miles; then for eight miles there was not a house. Another German settlement, then a wilderness of prairie and post oak woods for nearly thirty miles.

Kendall lost his way, and as he camped at night by a beautiful spring wolves howled in the distance, but he had a good rifle beside him and was not afraid. Next day he found the place at Post Oak Spring where Weed had said he would see their sheds and camp, only to find that everything had been swept away by a prairie fire. Some thirty sheep were walking on their knees, their feet badly burned, trying to feed upon the burned-off grass.

It was not until nightfall, when a small German boy came in driving one of his flocks, that he learned that about half of his sheep had survived the fire. Among them was his fine Merino ram, "Old Poll," which had also weathered the bitter storms of 1852 and the disease that had ravaged his flocks during the following season.

The sight of his remaining flock revived his spirits and he walked over the hills, planning the home he would build there some day. The Palace of St. Cloud might surpass it in size and beauty, he wrote his wife, "but the park of St. Cloud, for natural beauty, does not come up to our Post Oak place, and so you will yourself say when you come to see it."

He did not write her that one reason for not building there immediately was fear of Indians, whose depredations were greater in this region than around the little town of Boerne, six miles to the west. But to the *Picayune,* he wrote of the alarm among his shepherds at Post Oak, of how they spent the night in an armed watch, and of how his best shepherd left because of fear of Indians.

When he returned to New Braunfels letters from France informed him that his wife, in response to his admonition about expenses, had given up the house in Chaville and moved to a larger one in Passy, where she could let out rooms to English tourists. The suggestion that they take roomers was one Kendall promptly vetoed in his reply.

The Kendall Family

Georgina de Valcourt   *Caroline Louise*
George Wilkins   *Adeline de Valcourt*
Henry Fletcher   *William Henry*

By now Kendall had accepted the fact that Caroline would never be able to hear and would never have a normal life. Turning over in his mind the best way of providing for her, he decided to invest in real estate in San Antonio. His friends told him that the lots he selected would be worth a handsome sum one day or another, and so it proved, for the famous Menger Hotel was built directly across the street, and "Liline's lots" became a substantial part of the family inheritance in later years.

In San Antonio he visited his old Santa Fe Expedition friend, Antonio Navarro, who hugged him "in true Spanish fashion" when they met; but he refused the many invitations to social functions which his other friends showered upon him, and spent his evenings bathing in the San Antonio River.

Mrs. Kendall, completely ignorant of the details which were occupying so much of her husband's time, was finding his absence much more trying than former separations. She had the entire responsibility of moving from Chaville to Passy, her fourth child was expected in June, and she was being bled in an attempt to relieve constant and exhausting headaches.

When Kendall once more had the ranch running to his satisfaction he started again for France. His impatience mounted at the annoying delays in travel, at missed connections in New York, at the rough passage across the Atlantic; and on June 16 he reached Havre, ill with chills and fever, his head ringing from the quinine he had taken. He stumbled through the customs and made two visits to the prefecture of police about his passport before he took the train for Passy, where Henry Fletcher Kendall was born on June 18, 1855.

Within a short time he had slipped back into his former routine of foreign correspondent, writing to the *Picayune* about Colonel Samuel Colt's arms factory in Belgium,[3] of the Siege of Sevastopol, and of Queen Victoria's visit to Paris. He made a trip to

[3] Both nations were using Colonel Colt's arms, and there was some criticism because his guns were finding their way to Russia. But the Colonel, undisturbed, dipped snuff from a brilliantly decorated snuff box, a gift from the Sultan of Turkey, and proudly wore on his finger a diamond presented by the Russian Emperor.

London to meet Judge Falconer, and there they collaborated on an additional chapter for Kendall's new and seventh edition of the *Narrative of the Texan Santa Fe Expedition*.[4]

Letters to the *Picayune* continued while Kendall tackled with a light heart one of the jobs he liked least of any he had to do—that of moving. But this time the difficulties and annoyances could be disregarded, for at last he was taking his family home to his beloved Texas.

The sturdy little Henry Fletcher was too young to endure the hardships of the journey; he was left with his grandmother and a wet nurse. And Caroline, that beautiful afflicted child whose future was her parents' especial and constant concern, was left in the home of the famous Dr. Houdin, one of the few men anywhere who had been successful in teaching deaf-mutes to articulate.

While she tried to keep her husband undisturbed by the annoyances of the move, Mrs. Kendall supervised the packing of her red velvet sofa and armchairs, the red velvet carpet with its design of darker red leaves, the red damask curtains, and the real lace glass curtains which were to appear as such incongruous luxuries in the stone-floored farm house above New Braunfels. There were also the fine mahogany bedroom pieces, and the little blue-damask-covered sofa-bed, whose chains let the ends down to extend its length, and the great dining table and the spacious china cupboard. With her own hands she wrapped each Sevres china fruit plate, each fragile coffee cup.

Without tears, she said goodbye to the tiny baby and the little girl who would never hear her voice, and turned her face toward her husband's country, "that beautiful Texas."

---

[4] Falconer's manuscript, relating incidents which occurred while he and Kendall were separated on the western plains, is included in the Kendall papers.

25

Gentleman rancher

K ENDALL LEFT HIS FAMILY in Mobile after the long trip from Havre, while he hastened on to locate a house for them in New Orleans. After searching intermittently for two weeks in the worst cold spell in the memory of the city's "oldest inhabitants," he found lodgings in the house of Mrs. Rice, on Julia Street, near St. Patrick's Church. He rented the second and third stories of the house—a parlor, dining room, bathroom, and three bedrooms.

It was April before he could leave the *Picayune,* so severe was the epidemic of winter illness among the staff members brought on by the bitter weather. In the meantime, he added another item to the fine pieces of furniture brought from France. It was a new Chickering piano, which visitors later noted as one of the luxuries of the far-famed Texas ranch.

The first leg of the trip from New Orleans was uneventful, but rain fell incessantly when the family started inland. Kendall's two fine bays plodded through the mud, pulling the high-wheeled Jersey wagon in which he rode with Mrs. Kendall and her sister, Henriette, Clara Melchert, the German governess, and the two small children, Georgina and William.

Four mules pulled a wagon loaded with trunks, and after them came twelve yoke of oxen with the huge wagon of household furniture. In spite of distressingly slow travel, Kendall was filled with excitement at bringing his family home to the ranch. There would be no more separations, no more dashing about to catch dirty trains and slow boats, no more gloomy forebodings as to what might be happening during his absence. For four years he had worried in Texas about his family in France, and in Paris he had longed to know what was going on at the ranch. Now all that was ended.

To him it was a matter of course that they should stop at ranch houses for the nights while on the road, and that they should find poor food and scanty accommodations. Henriette, convent bred and very timid, was not so complacent when at the first German farmhouse where they stopped she was expected to share a bed with Clara, Georgina, and Billy. And when the six-teen-year-old son of the family made his way into the bedroom, evidently intending to share their quarters, she gave way to a series of frightened screams.

The boy's mother came running, lighted lamp in her hand, and was surprised at Henriette's terror. "What would you?" she asked with annoyance. "It is his bed—he has no other place to sleep!"

Next day they went on in the cold April rain, the four-year-old Billy became ill with colic, and the young French wife's bewilderment grew into distress and something like fear. On the third day the rain whipped into a storm and a bolt of lightning, striking a large tree near the road, killed a horse seeking shelter beneath it. Huddled in the front seat beside her husband, she finally asked, "George, where are the beautiful plains of Texas you have told me so much about?" Surprised at her question, Kendall waved his hand expansively at the drenched landscape, and said proudly, "My dear, here they are!"

When the exhausted family reached the ranch house they found Mrs. Weed in bed with a new baby, in the large, sunny bedroom Kendall had intended for his wife. The rest of the house was cramped, disarranged, and crowded with furniture until Mrs. Weed became well enough to travel and she and her family left the ranch.

The plan of the ranch house was simple—four rooms and a gallery on the ground floor, three rooms formed by burlap partitions in the attic, and the kitchen a single room under a separate roof. From the downstairs bedroom a closed stairway led to the stone cellar, one of the few in that part of the country; and a closed stairway led from the dining room to the attic.

Gradually Mrs. Kendall reduced her household to order. She spread sheepskin rugs on the floors, and furnished the attic for Clara and the children. It took weeks of work before things were in sufficient order to hang the lace curtains and lay the red carpet in the living room. Then they set up the new piano, draping it with Kendall's handsome red and brown blanket, souvenir of his campaign below the Rio Grande, and even before life in the household settled down into a routine, neighbors dropped in for "music and dancing in the evening." There were numerous guests; almost every week Count Rittberg or Baron Roggenback and his wife, or others, came to dinner.

As readily as he had changed to a new mode of life on his brief, earlier trips to the ranch, Kendall put aside his role as correspondent and continental traveler and became a frontier rancher in earnest. His money now paid for shoeing the horses, repairs on the ambulance, for leather for the mill band at the new mill he was building at Post Oak, "badly made, as the saddler was ruddy with lager beer." It went for seeds and farm and household supplies from New Braunfels and New Orleans and San Antonio, for salaries to Clara and to an almost incredible number of laborers whose needs he must care for in a truly feudal manner.

With this change came the pleasures of planting—peaches, olives, cherries, figs, and cedar trees—the fun of all sorts of experiments with varieties of seeds, the labor of cultivation, and an exasperating, heartbreaking struggle with the weather, a struggle which was to end only with his death.

He continued his letters to the *Picayune,* picking up news items around the countryside. He was in San Antonio to witness the arrival of the caravan of camels, with their Arab attendants, which the federal government introduced in the quixotic hope of domesticating them for western Texas, and of making them useful in the desert beyond the frontier. Their appearance caused a general stampede of all the horses in sight.

Before the horses that had broken their bridles had been caught, the stage arrived with news that the Democrats at Cincinnati had nominated Buchanan and Breckenridge for the coming presidential race, and there was a rush toward the saloons for celebration.

San Antonio hardly had settled back to normal when there was new cause for excitement. A wagonload of ice arrived from Indianola, and there was another scramble to the barrooms by all the thirsty souls in the city. Kendall quoted for *Picayune* readers the following prices: "Brandy and plain water, ten cents; brandy and iced water, fifteen cents."

Repeatedly he reported his delightful visits to his frontier sheep ranch at Post Oak Spring, where he went twice a month on an inspection trip and hunting expedition, and to grind meal for himself and his neighbors. To a friend he wrote, "I counted forty-seven deer playing near my wagon the other day—two of them bucks nearly as large as mules! I'll have those bucks yet, sure."

But always, on these trips to the west, he was alert for any sign of Indians. "Two things are certain," he wrote the *Picayune,* "The government is bound to take care of the Indians within the limits of Texas, and as well to protect the life and property of every one of her citizens." All was well when he made his last trip to Post Oak, but he added, "Today I am not certain that my shepherds have not been killed and scalped, and my flocks scattered. Within the last month or two the Indians have been on every side of me: my great good fortune has so far been that the rascals do not seem to have contracted a taste for mutton."[1]

Kendall roared with laughter at the sight presented by his shepherds at Post Oak. Instead of "crooks on their shoulders and perhaps lutes under their arms," as poets were wont to describe

[1] Kendall letter to *Picayune,* New Braunfels, December 23, 1856.

the gentle folk who tended the flocks, each was ready to stand off a full-fledged Comanche raid. Standard equipment for guarding a flock of eight hundred sheep included a doublebarreled gun, a Bowie knife and a Colt's six-shooter, and each shepherd wore a ferocious beard and moustache.

Mrs. Kendall must have felt more than a tinge of longing for Paris when Holbrook wrote of the gay social season in New Orleans and the gorgeously dressed ladies at the Gaiety Theatre on Mardi Gras night. Except for infrequent trips to San Antonio and New Braunfels with her husband on business, her life was centered at the ranch home which already was widely known as a frontier show place. Even as Kendall worked through the long days laying rail fences, or building new sheep pens, and even when all hands turned to for the strenuous twelve-day ordeal of shearing the flocks, the house was "boiling over" with company. These daily details Kendall recorded each night in his diary.[2]

When drouth descended on the land and dried up the springs and waterholes, the family rode daily to Waco Spring to get water for household use and to bathe. Kendall had to send his flocks from New Braunfels to Post Oak for water and pasture. By July the situation was desperate, and the whole family drove over to Post Oak Spring, put up tents and slept on the ground.

At this time Kendall made one of the few diary entries which ever indicated that he was aware to the slightest degree of Mrs. Kendall's distaste for the life she was living in "this beautiful Texas." She and Henriette were having their first experience with outdoor living, and everything went wrong with them. Kendall wrote that they were "not very well satisfied with camp life," and

[2] With the beginning of 1857, he started a daily record of his activities which continued until his last illness. Using a little leather-bound black book, probably similar to that in which he stored up his reservoir of jokes he later converted into feature stories and cryptic editorial paragraphs for the infant *Picayune* twenty years earlier, Kendall now wrote daily of the weather, of his expenditure for incidentals, or of the norther that froze his turnips and blighted the young corn. In his diary of 1857 he used a pencil and the entries were brief. Thereafter he used pen and ink, and the pages were packed with comments in his scrawling, almost microscopic, writing.

283

when he returned from a fishing trip at nine o'clock in the evening with no fish, he found them "in anything but a good humor."

They had sent for Joe Tait, the head shepherd, to act as a guard, and Kendall in his diary called the situation "a funny affair all round." But the next day he caught a fine mess of trout, neighbors came over bringing cucumbers and other vegetables, and life went fairly smoothly during the two weeks they remained in camp.

Rains came eventually, but without moderation. Floods swept away the rail fences and damaged the cogwheels at the mill. November brought a cloud of grasshoppers which stripped the fields. Although Kendall's letters to the *Picayune* continued to extoll the virtues of the country, his diary recorded that around New Braunfels there was fear of famine.

Fall came, and with it sowing time. There were five different kinds of seeds from the United States Patent Office. And there was the annual introduction of Nelly's "young stranger," as Kendall always referred to the infant, and four dollars to pay the midwife for her care.

By trial and error, Kendall was still learning the secrets of successful sheep ranching. Ahead lay the most profitable years of his Texas venture—perhaps the most contented years of his life. These were years when he established himself as the foremost sheep raiser in the South, when his praises of Texas brought immigrants streaming into the state from all parts of the nation, when friend and stranger alike turned to him for advice about lambing and shearing and dipping sheep, about planting and the price of lands.

During these lush years there crept into his *Picayune* letters occasional echoes of the political strife which was growing over the nation. For the most part, however, he wrote of the glories of Texas, its wonderful opportunities, its healthful climate, and the riches awaiting all who came with energy and a will to work. The call of adventure that rang through his stories of McCulloch's rangers before Monterrey and of Scott's troops charging toward the halls of the Montezumas still echoed in his writings. But now he told of adventure on a new frontier in a land which his pen had helped acquire, whose borders he had helped defend and extend, whose economic future he now worked to secure.

In addition to his regular contributions to the *Picayune,* widely copied by other newspapers, and his replies to individual queries, which often found their way into print, his annual articles for the Texas *Almanac* were an important feature of that magazine. By the spring of 1858 he realized that he had been conducting a one-man colonization campaign for his beloved Texas. He was receiving inquiries by the hundreds.

On January 1 of that year he had written to his old friend, Jim Oake of the Boston *Post,* who for many years had served as correspondent for the *Picayune* under the pen name of "Acorn," and Oake published the letter in the *Post.*[3] Immediately a new deluge of letters poured into the post office at New Braunfels, all clamoring for information. By April 5, Kendall confided to his diary, "Jim Oake's publication of the Boston letter put me to a heap of trouble."

When Holbrook visited Boston in August, he reported to the *Post* that Kendall already had spent more than one hundred dollars in postage during the past four months in answering correspondence growing out of the "Acorn" letter alone. These letters asked about the "climate of Texas, the soil, the best location for raising sheep and other stock, the price of land, what kind of public schools there were on the frontier, and how many churches and of what denomination."[4]

The *Post* poked good-natured fun at Kendall, but added further to his avalanche of letters by picking up a paragraph from one of his more recent articles. "The *Picayune* of the 27th ult.," the *Post* stated, "has a letter from Kendall, in which he thus talks about 'balm' in the Texas swamps:—

"We shall have an abundance and to spare this fall. The wheat crop

[3] Kendall papers, clipping dated Boston, February 1, 1858.
[4] Undated clipping in Kendall papers, identified as Boston *Post,* August, 1858.

is already of course gathered, and the yield has been immense. The corn crop—much even of the second planting, which was put in the ground after the grass-hoppers had left—is as good as made, and the yield will be great. Cotton looks well in every quarter, and from the sugar-growing sections we have no other than the most flattering accounts. Of peaches and melons we have enough for all creation, our stock of all kinds—cattle, horses and sheep—is fairly rolling fat: wild grapes, plums and cherries may be gathered in profusion unknown in other countries: of sweet potatoes, tomatoes, cabbages and other vegetables we are raising all that we can eat, and our entire population is more than hopeful—it is joyous. Gov. Runnels can afford to give us two thanksgivings this year: we can't get enough in one day. There's balm in Texas."[5]

The tide of inquiries rose again. Frequent diary entries note that he "spent most of afternoon writing letters," or "continued to write letters most of the day." His patience ended when a dissatisfied settler in Wisconsin wrote early in October, 1858, asking for many details about Cooke, Fannin, and Colin counties, roughly five hundred miles from Kendall's home.

Kendall at this time had two ranches, four large flocks of sheep, a grist mill, and a stock of horses and cattle to look after; and a newspaper to write for. So he sat down and poured all of his enthusiasm for Texas into a thirty-six-hundred word letter and sent it off to the *Picayune,* to be printed into circulars. At the outset he urged that copies he sent be reprinted in local newspapers, for, he asserted, "I shall esteem it as an especial favor if all my old fellow members of the editorial craft will give me a place in their columns, as by so doing they will save me a world of trouble."[6]

He repeated what he had written for years in the *Picayune* about the climate, the soil, the cheap lands, the bubbling springs, and the abundant opportunities of the San Antonio region. As to

[5] This article appeared in the *Picayune,* July 27, 1858, indicating that the Boston *Post* item was published in the following month.

[6] A copy of this circular letter, dated "New Braunfels, Comal County, Texas, October 13, 1858," is in the Kendall papers.

health, he pointed out that the only physician serving the settlers within twenty miles around Boerne ran a grist mill for a
livelihood.

When his bundle of these circulars came from New Orleans,
the task of letter writing, at least for the present, was simpler.
He either mailed a copy to each distant inquirer, or sent one along
with a hasty note. He boasted in the circular that his profit in his
sheep raising venture had been seventy per cent each year during
1857 and 1858. He told tall tales about the opportunities in Texas,
but he was living a success story of his own.

Mistakes he had made in his early ventures and losses he
had sustained would have discouraged a less hardy beginner. Of
the twenty-four thoroughbred American and French Merinos
shipped to his Nueces ranch in 1852, only two survived the blizzards and disease and fire. But in 1858 hundreds of their progeny
dotted his ranches, proud descendants of these lords of the flocks.

Under the watchful eye of Joe Tait, Kendall's Scotch shepherd, the sheep had multiplied amazingly, and careful breeding
of acclimated Mexican ewes to the best Merino rams from Vermont and New York and France had brought a sharp increase in
the wool clip. In 1856 he sheared 2,800 pounds of wool; this had
jumped to 5,100 pounds the next year, and to 9,000 pounds in
1858. In two years his flocks had more than doubled.[7]

Frequent diary entries read, "McKinney bought buck lambs
for $50. . . . Rec'd for 2 merinoes $125.00. . . . Rec'd for bucks
$125. . . . Rec'd of Y. B. instant sight draft to pay for Buck
$250.00."

From constant inquiries and from his own experience, Kendall devised a system of sheep husbandry suited to the hill country above San Antonio. Ewes were at least two years and fully
grown before they were bred. The breeding season was limited to
six weeks, so that all the lambs would drop between March 25
and May 1, and be weaned by August 16. In the fall he divided
the lamb flock, providing fodder and shelter for the weaker lambs

[7] G. W. Kendall, "Sheep Raising in Texas," *Texas Almanac*, 1859, pp. 126–27.

through the coldest days of winter. Each day shepherds drove the stronger flocks to ranges several miles away, while the weaker ones grazed close at home.

By crossing thoroughbred, heavy-wooled Merinos with Mexican ewes already acclimated, Kendall by 1858 had a grade of sheep which could endure the bitterest storms without shelter and subsist on the open range in the depths of winter as well as through the hot summer months. Constant vigilance, however, was necessary in following this pattern, and securing and keeping competent shepherds was one of Kendall's incessant worries. Negroes, he concluded, did not make good shepherds, for they needed too much sleep. Mexicans were not easily persuaded to come to the remote ranch. On one occasion he spent two hot summer days in San Antonio before he found two Mexicans who promised to come. He advanced them money for the trip to Post Oak and gave them an order for shirts at a local store. That was the last he saw of them.

Despite his labor troubles however, Kendall in 1858 was able to operate two widely separated establishments and to live the life of a gentleman rancher and genial host to innumerable guests. This was due to the faithful service of Tait, who looked after the rapidly multiplying flocks at Post Oak. Kendall was dreaming, these days, of the perfect ranch home he intended to build there, once the Indian menace was removed. His holdings, extending into the low, rolling, oak-covered hills surrounding the valley, now had grown to six thousand acres.

But while he worked and planned, friends and strangers crowded his modest ranch home above New Braunfels. Neighbors, friends from New Orleans, visitors from New England, settlers who had read his descriptions of Texas and were moving to the state, dropped in to see him. Of all the visitors who made their way to the rancho above New Braunfels, Kendall perhaps was most delighted to see his tall, slender partner, Lumsden, and Westray, his New York agent and long-time friend, who came for a two weeks' stay in January, 1860. They bought ammunition "enough to slay all the birds on the place," and soon had the porch festooned with ducks, geese, doves, rabbits, partridges, robins, and chaparral cocks.

When they tired of bird pies and small game there was a dinner of mutton cutlets, pumpkin pies, and Vieux Ceps. Kendall took them hunting at Post Oak, but deer were scarce after the epidemic of black tongue which had killed so many of the animals in the mountains during the previous summer. Back at New Braunfels, the guests amused themselves with bird hunting again while Kendall superintended his farm tasks and answered innumerable letters. Neighbors dropped in after dinner, and when his guests had retired for the night he closed his diary with such comments as, "Parlor crowded, but had a very pleasant evening," or "Another pleasant evening: sociable game of whist."

This visit was the last time Kendall saw his much loved partner. In September, 1860, Lumsden took his family north for a vacation, and they were among the three hundred passengers drowned when the *Lady Elgin,* an excursion steamer on Lake Michigan, collided with another boat and sank in a storm.[8]

After Lumsden and Westray left, the house was not quiet for long. Kendall's diary recorded the names of many others who dropped in. Among them were Mr. Lawrenson and two friends from Maryland, and Colonel Kinney and former Governor Porter. "Mr. Terry called with a letter from Kate Rix's husband," and "Mr. Gibson called with a letter from Henry J. Raymond," of the New York *Times.* Among his visitors was G. W. Morris, an old Santa Fe prisoner, and for the second time, Kendall "helped him along on his road," as he recorded in his diary. On a tragic winter night, eighteen years earlier, Kendall had fished a hidden coin from his clothing to bribe a Mexican guard who was ready to knock the exhausted Morris in the head, cut off his ears, and throw his body in the ditch beside the bleak trail across the Jornado.

The visit of George D. Prentice, publisher of the Louisville

8 *Picayune,* September 14, 16, 25, 26; October 3, 1860.

Journal, was an important occasion. Very soon Prentice, with whom Kendall had sparred verbally for so many years, was to be the best loved and worst hated editor in Kentucky because of his part in keeping that state out of the Confederacy. Soon his was to be one of those unhappy families of which one son fought for the South and another for the North.

While Kendall was so vigorously telling readers and visitors about the glories of this sun-bathed paradise, his own fame spread to the far corners of the state as one of its most romantic and successful figures. This brought about a result he hardly had expected. Before he knew it, his friends were booming his name for election as governor of Texas. On May 19, 1859, after a trip to San Antonio, he made the terse diary entry, "Saw Mr. Richardson of Galveston *News,* and talked for first time about the governorship: decidedly opposed to nomination."

But Richardson and Kendall's friends who were dissatisfied with the administration of Governor Runnels refused to consider his "decided" opposition. The Galveston *News* and the San Antonio *Herald,* with the enthusiastic support of Kendall's German neighbors around New Braunfels and Boerne, launched the campaign. Kendall, the *News* insisted, had raised a monument to himself, through introduction of fine-fleeced sheep to Texas, which would outlive all politicians.[9] Within a month he had received such a flood of letters offering support that he was forced to resort to a published denial of his candidacy. "I have no taste for the calling of a politician," he wrote, "have never been in the business, and am too old to learn a new trade."[10]

Need for a larger house became urgent in December, 1858, when Mme. de Valcourt arrived from France with Fletcher, who had been her charge since he was five months old. The Kendalls took both their children to meet their brother and grandmother in New Orleans, and this trip was the occasion of their first ride on

[9] See Galveston *News* and San Antonio *Herald,* May 19, 1859. W. Richardson was publisher of the *News* and also of the *Texas Almanac.*
[10] *Herald,* June 18, 1859.

the first railway in Texas. After four days on the stage they crossed the Brazos River on the way from Richmond to Harrisburg. Kendall's diary contains only the brief comment, "did not much like the bridge." Years afterwards his daughter, Georgina, remembered the excitement of this crossing. The bridge was a rickety pontoon affair, and to avoid stalling on it, the engineer opened the throttle of his snorting little engine, plunged down the bank and onto the bridge at a great rate and up the opposite bank before stalling. The crossing was considered so perilous that passengers walked across the bridge ahead of the train, and waited, in some doubt, as the train followed.[11]

When Kendall arrived in New Orleans, Holbrook handed him a hundred dollars "on account of Sorin oil company," an oil investment dividend nine months before the world's first commercial oil well was discovered.[12]

After a visit with Kate in Mobile, the family plunged into a round of theaters and visits to friends in New Orleans. Kendall enjoyed chatting with Brantz Mayer, former secretary of the United States legation in Mexico, and L. S. Hargous, former United States consul in Vera Cruz, both of whom had worked hard to secure his release from prison after the Santa Fe Expedition.

Within ten days he was bound once more for Texas, proud of the two fine mares and the new wagon he had purchased in New Orleans. He was pleased at being spared the stage ride up from Galveston to New Braunfels, but Mme. de Valcourt could scarcely have enjoyed the six days of driving in a wagon over heavy roads as her first introduction to Texas.

This was Kendall's first absence from his frontier home in nearly three years, and was to be his last visit to New Orleans

[11] This line was then known as the Buffalo Bayou, Brazos and Colorado railroad. See "Texas' First Railroad," *Southern Pacific Bulletin,* February, 1938, pp. 1–4.

[12] Kendall diary, December 16, 1858. Colonel Edwin L. Drake brought in the first commercial producer near Titusville, Pennsylvania, on August 27, 1859. See C. B. Glasscock, *Then Came Oil* (New York, 1938).

until after the Civil War. In New Orleans he had bought a barrel of apples, packed in oats for safe shipment. As an experiment, he sowed the oats in his garden on February 28, and despite the drouth he reaped a small crop on June 16. According to family tradition, this was the beginning of oat culture on the frontier, and thereafter the oats from the apple barrels were saved for late winter planting.

Routine on the ranch went smoothly again and the family was happy to be almost reunited. Only Liline remained away from the fireside. She was to stay with Dr. Houdin until her education was completed. Billy was seven, able to accompany his father on short hunting trips, and the sturdy little Fletcher thrived in his new surroundings. Mme. de Valcourt soon became acquainted with Cumming Evans, a neighboring rancher who was Henriette's suitor, and who admired the way in which Mrs. Kendall rode alone so fearlessly about the countryside and handled the business correspondence of the ranch.[13] Kendall found his mail had stacked high during his absence, with inquiries from prospective settlers, and demand for sheep for stocking new ranches had sent prices soaring. Buyers hustled off to Arkansas and Missouri to secure sheep which could be driven overland, and shipments came by gulf steamers.[14]

At this time Kendall suffered a loss which was to deprive him of much of the time he had devoted to writing, gardening, hunting, and fishing, and the entertainment of his numerous guests. Joe Tait, his ever reliable head shepherd, left to set up a ranch of his own over on the Fuente Frio. He had stood long vigils during the spring storms at lambing time, supervised the shearing,

[13] Kendall papers, Holbrook's letter dated New Orleans, April 11, 1861, in which he called her "a pattern woman" for her pioneer neighbors.

[14] Kendall diary, New Orleans, December 18, 1858; "Was up at daylight this morning and down on board the 'Survanne': Saw Colin Campbell and his sheep, all for Texas." When Sam Houston retired from the United States Senate and returned to Texas early in 1859 he sent out a collection of blooded rams from Louisiana and planned to enter the "shepherdizing business," but he laid aside this plan to defeat Runnels in the bitterly contested election for governor. See James, *The Raven*, 392.

The Post Oak Spring Ranch Home

From a painting, 1862

divided the flocks and nursed the sick ewes. He was to be succeeded by a series of head shepherds, none of them as competent or energetic as he. Eventually Kendall had to take over the job himself, and the time was to come, during the gloomy days of the war, when Fletcher and Billy had to go out on the range with the flocks.

Tait's departure hastened Kendall's plans for moving to Post Oak. Instead of building the big ranch home of which he had dreamed, he rebuilt and enlarged the shepherd's house near the pens on the slope west of the spring, and added servants' houses, an outdoor kitchen, a carriage house, and barns.

Before the family started preparations for moving, Kendall was called to Richmond, Texas, to collect an old land debt. He made the trip in a blizzard, and on his return went to bed with a severe cold. More disconcerting than the cold, however, was the sentiment for secession which he had found to be sweeping across the plains of Texas. Occasionally, on his visits to San Antonio, and in his chats with friends in New Orleans, he had heard talk of disunion, but had not considered it serious. Few of his German neighbors at New Braunfels and Boerne had slaves, and slavery was not an economic issue in that region. Nor was it an important issue with Kendall, for actually his slaves were more of a burden than a help.

But in January, 1861, at every stage stop on his trip down toward the coast, he found nothing but angry, threatening talk against the Union. Now he realized that this talk meant war for Texas. Up at the capital a group of officials had started the circulation of a petition for a secession convention and Governor Houston hastily called a session of the legislature. While Kendall was overhauling his cellar preparatory to moving, "Maverick, Hyde, Walder and other representatives" came by on their way to Austin. A week later he noted in his diary that he had seen "Mr. Anderson, Dr. Howard, Mr. Corolan and Herbert," also en route to the capital.

After much commotion, the family moved to Post Oak early

in February. Their new home was comfortable—a compact stone structure with bedrooms, a parlor, and a dining room on the main floor, and an attic for Clara who still stayed on as governess and tutor. But on every hand there was evidence that they were on a newer, more dangerous frontier. The shepherds still went out armed like border ruffians. The region was sparsely settled, and the tide of visitors, both friend and stranger, almost subsided.

Late one evening Mrs. Kendall was sitting by the fireside awaiting her husband's return from a trip to New Braunfels. The children, Mme. de Valcourt and Henriette were in bed, and the place was still except for the crackling of the logs in the fireplace and the ticking of the empire clock on the mantle. Suddenly there was a slithering sound and the clock stopped. She looked, and there, coiling itself around the alabaster pillars of the clock, was a rattlesnake.

She might have shot the snake with the loaded rifle which stood nearby, but she could not bring herself to destroy the valuable clock so carefully brought from France. Finally, terrified but determined, she took up the fire tongs and snapped them on the snake's head. Holding the tongs with all her might, she carefully drew the snake from the clock, and, as it lashed about with rattles whirring, thrust it deep into the fire and held it there until its writhings ceased.

With this episode her transition from a timid young Frenchwoman to a resourceful American pioneer wife must have been complete. There were to be times when she knew fear, and when she was disconcerted by the raw life so far from her sheltered girlhood existence, but nobody ever denied her courage.

Kendall's sheep were still flourishing, despite the hard winter, but a careless neighbor was having difficulty. On January 15, 1861, he wrote in his diary, "Saw Mr. Green; his sheep scattered, and many with the scab. A most annoying matter." Later this scourge was to sweep through the whole region.

Although his days were filled with the details of ranch work and concern for his sheep, it is evident from his diary that Kendall's thoughts were more and more on the rapid course of events at Austin. Despite the efforts of a minority group of Unionists, an ordinance of secession had been submitted to the people. The ills of the country, and the tragic days which lay ahead, he felt, could be blamed on the blundering politicians. He took up his pen on January 20 to pour out his resentment.

"Save and except Seward," he wrote, "there is not a man in Washington who would have rated a third-rater twenty years ago, and Seward himself is as rotten as an apple I kicked out of the way in my grand-father's orchard in New Hampshire, thirty-six years ago last October.

"If any man worked hard for the annexation of Texas to the United States, it was your humble servant: . . . *I am sorry for it —I wish that. . . ."*

He laid the letter aside unfinished, but his disgust for politicians remained throughout his life.

He wrote a letter to the *Picayune* on February 23, telling of the death of Captain Britton, his friend during the Mexican campaigns and his longtime partner in the ranching venture. Then with a heavy heart he rode over to Boerne to mail the letter and to cast his vote in the secession election.

The majority of the German residents of Boerne opposed secession and there was great excitement in the little town. Before he went to bed Kendall wrote in his diary, ". . . much excitement about election: majority against Secession." But he knew that the rest of the state would support the Confederacy and the war to come.

26

Troubles accumulate

K ENDALL'S IMMEDIATE CONCERN, after the secession of Texas, was the safety of the frontier. Federal outposts had proved at least a threat to marauding Indians, but withdrawal of these troops meant that either the Confederacy or Texas frontiersmen must patrol the fringe of settlements or there would be frequent and disastrous raids. Eventually, when the state failed to heed his frequent pleas, Kendall had to organize his neighbors into a ranger patrol.

Now, with the war under way, he felt the need of speeding up the spring wool clip; but heavy rains and labor shortage stretched the task out to two months. Finally, when he had loaded eighteen thousand pounds of wool on Mexican carts and sent it off to New Orleans, he was not sure that it would reach its destination. Already the Yankee gunboats had clamped a tight blockade along the Atlantic seaboard, and Kendall was cut off from his usual market in Atlanta. To his great relief the wool got through to New Orleans, but this was his last shipment to that city during the war.

After the wool was shipped, the Kendall household invited the neighbors in for the wedding of Henriette to Cumming Evans. Kendall also found time to add to the growing pile of manuscript of his "History of the Mexican War," which he had been working on since the publication of his brief *Illustrated History,* nine years earlier. But it was difficult to find much time for writing. Wolves killed some of his finest rams, the lambs got into his sweet potato patch and stripped the vines, and wild cattle repeatedly broke into the cornfield.

By November his shepherds began to complain about receiving their wages in paper money, and Kendall had "a great row" with them. He searched for new shepherds in San Antonio, and finally hired two Germans in New Braunfels. When he returned to the ranch he found that all of his old shepherds had left.

The new hands were becoming accustomed to their work when Kendall took Billy into the hills to inspect one of the new sheep camps on January 17, 1862. He had not been gone long when Mrs. Schlosser, the wife of one of his shepherds, came running, terrified, across the valley to the Kendall ranch house, her three-year-old child in her arms, to say that four Indians had chased the head shepherd into the shepherd's house.

Mrs. Kendall immediately gathered the household into one room, with all the arms and ammunition on the place. When the head shepherd came running up she sent him and a mounted helper to look for the three flocks out with Schlosser, Fechler, and Baptiste. When dusk fell she put on her husband's hat and overcoat, took a rifle, and paced the front gallery keeping guard. From the back windows of the house Clara, Mrs. Schlosser, and the children watched until darkness settled over the Post Oak hills.

Kendall came home after nightfall to this scene of excitement and confusion, and went at once to look for the missing shepherds. Two of the flocks came straggling in without dog or shepherd, but the third flock could not be found. While his wife continued to pace the gallery in the darkness, Kendall sent word to the neighbors to come to Post Oak in the morning, and until after midnight he continued to hunt the sheep through fog and darkness. No sound save the screeching of owls answered his shouts, and he returned to spend the rest of a gloomy night watching.

Neighbors who came at daylight to join the search for the missing shepherds brought word that the Indians had killed a Mr. Rheinhart who was cutting wood for Mr. King within sight of the town of Boerne. Soon the sound of barking led them to the naked body of the young German boy, John Fechler, pierced with seventeen arrows and resting against a tree. The dog, Fanny, was licking away the blood from his wounds, trying vainly to revive him. They left her with the body and followed the trail of the Indians down to a rough crossing of a rocky ravine. There, partially in the water, lay the body of the Mexican shepherd, Baptiste, with four arrows in his back. His dog, Pink, stood guarding him.

They buried the victims in the evening, and on Sunday a large crowd looked all day without success for the missing Schlosser. His sheep came in alone that day, but it was nearly three weeks later that his body was found, mutilated and full of arrows.

Monday all farm operations stopped and the farm hands, much against their will, were armed and sent out with the sheep. Kendall secured additional arms, ran bullets, and conducted target practice on the ranch.[1] Mr. King loaned him a Negro boy to work in the fields, but it was late January before he was able to secure three Mexican shepherds who were willing to go out with the flocks. By early February Kendall was convinced that his appeals for border protection were unavailing, and he organized his neighbors. Diary entries recorded frequent scouting trips in an effort to intercept raiding parties.

Despite the press of work, the ranch staff took time out to vote for the choice of county seat. Blanco County had been divided in January, 1862, by the legislature, and "Kendall County" created with Boerne as the county seat.[2]

The labor problem was somewhat relieved in March when

[1] For Kendall's protests against the Indian menace, see his letters to the *Picayune*, May 5, 1861, to Governor F. R. Lubbock, February 8, 1862, and to Colonel S. M. Baird, January 18, 1865.

[2] Historical markers in the county read, "Kendall County, created January 10, 1862, organized February 18, 1862. Named in honor of George Wilkins Kendall, 1809–1867, Poet, Journalist, Author and Farmer; one of the founders of the New Orleans Picayune; Member of the Santa Fe Expedition; Most successful sheep raiser in the Southwest."

Holbrook sent the slaves, John and Harrison, from the *Picayune* office to the Post Oak ranch. He acted just in time to save his slaves; soon the mail was being captured by the Yankee blockaders in the gulf, and a month later the city was in the hands of the federal troops.[3]

By April the *Picayune* had stopped coming, and Kendall was unable to learn until months later the difficulties Holbrook was having to keep the paper going. It was closed for a day because General Benjamin F. Butler disliked one of its articles, and resumed only after explanation and apology.[4] In June Kendall received word from Holbrook through a friend who had slipped across the river and made his way to Texas. Holbrook sent fifteen hundred dollars and "a sad description of the times there. . . . the doings of the notorious General Butler."

Alexander H. Hayes, Kendall's old newspaper friend, came from New Orleans to Post Oak on October 14, bringing another letter from Holbrook. Business in the city, he said, was terrible, and the *Picayune* was making only about two-thirds of its expenses, but he would try to continue in some way. He was sending regularly the two hundred dollars each month to Louise de Valcourt in Paris for Liline's education, but was not sure how long he could continue to do so.

He smuggled another letter through to Kendall in November, with the report that business was *"dam gone busted!"* and that he was thinking of turning the *Picayune* office into a grocery store, since that was the only business in town in which there was profit.[5] This was Kendall's last news from Holbrook until after the war.

In July, 1862, Kendall sent off three hundred grade rams to

[3] On April 11, 1861, Holbrook had written, "We expect an army of Black Republicans to come up the Mississippi any day, & at this moment we have no protection for the city, and it will take a month to provide protection for us. The mouth of the Miss. River I think will be blockaded in the course of four or five days."

[4] *Picayune*, August 2, 1862. General Banks suppressed the paper in 1864, from May 23 to July 9, because it had published a bogus proclamation taken from the New York *World* saying that the President had issued a surprise call for 400,000 more troops and had appointed a national day of fasting and prayer for victory.

[5] Kendall papers, Holbrook to Kendall, New Orleans, November 14, 1862.

Mexico, but before he could get a permit to start the flock toward the border he had to go to San Antonio and take the oath of allegiance to the Confederate government.

Drouth ruined the prospect for fresh vegetables, labor troubles added to his depression, and he was especially discouraged when it was necessary to send nine-year-old Billy and seven-year-old Fletcher out on the range with the flocks. Kendall grieved because they were missing the advantages he had planned to give them.

Georgina started to school at the convent in San Antonio in September, and he missed her greatly. Visitors called, Henriette and Mr. Evans came to chat, the piano tuner came and spent the night, and the midwife arrived for her annual care of Nelly, whose baby died that year.

A rare bottle of the carefully hoarded Vieux Ceps brought Kendall's nostalgic comment, "When will the old times come back?" and he closed his diary for 1862 with the hope that there might be truth in the news of another victory for Lee in Virginia.

With markets disrupted and cash scarce, Kendall tried during the winter of 1862–63 to put the ranch on a subsistence basis. He hunted wild hogs and cured hams and smoked bacon, dug and bedded the sweet potatoes carefully, shot a wild steer that kept breaking into his crib, put down a barrel of corned beef, and brought in venison as often as possible. His early garden included parsley, eschalots, corn, carrots, peas, cress, artichokes, white mustard, spinach, tomatoes, and endive. He cleared another patch and planted squash, melons, okra, and more tomatoes, all the while feeling sorry that he had to work with a worn-out plow and tired oxen.

He struggled through shearing and finally sent nearly nineteen thousand pounds of wool to his agent in San Antonio to be freighted to Eagle Pass and marketed in Mexico. Later he made frequent shipments overland to Shreveport, getting groceries and other supplies in the returning wagons. He was hard pressed to get the silver and gold which his shepherds demanded, and as often as possible he paid them in merchandise which he had been able to buy with paper money or to take in trade for rams and wethers, for hides, tallow, sweet potatoes, or sheepskins. Sale of these products brought in an income of $1,219.50 in 1863, while the cost of running the ranch that year was $4,949.55. And in December the wool, which provided the main money income, was still in storage.

Salt was inferior in quality and increasingly hard to get. He spent nearly four hundred dollars without getting a sufficient supply for his flocks, and resorted to mixing the salt with wood ashes to make it go farther. But several of his fattest lambs died of a liver affliction which he eventually blamed on the ashes.

He complained repeatedly in his diary of high prices. Cabbage, which a year previously had sold for a dollar a head, was now three. Domestics and calicoes were five dollars a yard, coffee fourteen dollars a pound, and "a fair article of whiskey one hundred and twenty five dollars a gallon." Soon the barkeepers were charging three dollars for a drink; barbers got two dollars for a shave and three for a haircut, and an ordinary pair of work shoes cost thirty-five dollars.

Kendall's war assessment was nearly two thousand dollars, yet, difficult as the financial situation was, Mrs. Kendall subscribed one hundred dollars for the benefit of the Texas hospital in Virginia, and Kendall donated twenty bushels of wheat to the frontier rangers. He had the neighborhood threshing machine, but it was by now so old and rickety that it made slow work, and threshed only sixteen bushels in a long day of hard, dusty labor.

December went out with snow and sleet and cutting cold, and thirty-five lambs died during the blizzard. Then drouth followed, and by March Kendall wrote in his diary, "A crop dries up and makes no moan, but the starving lambs die uttering the most plaintive cries!" Bad colds, influenza, and whooping cough attacked the whole family. Kendall declared himself the worst of any of them, and in his extreme depression he felt it ridiculous that his wife should be afflicted with the whooping cough.

Through the spring he drove himself to plant and water, while the creek got lower and lower and wild cattle flocked into the valley by the hundreds, tearing down fences and destroying crops.[6] April came, and shearing time, but the extra help Kendall had counted on was away for a scout, for there had been another Indian raid up near Fredericksburg. Nelly had twins, which Kendall considered "too much of a good thing for war times."

But shearing was finished at last, at an enormous cost of Kendall's own energy, with the help of what transient labor came his way. Through July and August he cultivated tobacco, now his most profitable crop. Then Kendall discovered something which caused even war to seem quite unimportant. The dreaded scab had appeared among his sheep. He fought the disease through October without success, and early in November decided that all of them must be dipped regardless of the cost.

What the cost was, the cash accounts in his 1864 diary did not show. By this time Kendall was so deeply in debt, so pressed for time, so discouraged and so depressed, that he no longer kept the careful reports of previous years. For the first time he put expenditures and receipts in the same column, and he was cutting expenditures to what seems an impossibly low point, or neglecting to record them. When he made a trip to San Antonio, he camped by the road at night to avoid bills for a hotel and meals.

But he recorded that he spent one hundred and fifty dollars for sulphur and eleven dollars and fifty cents for extra labor for

6 Through the remainder of his life Kendall was confronted with the menace of increasing herds of range cattle, which multiplied rapidly when the markets were cut off by the federal blockade in the gulf. Repeated entries in his diaries expressed determination to fence them out, but this was something he never got done. These increasing herds formed the basis of the great cattle drives through the Indian Territory to Kansas railheads beginning in 1866 and lasting until the early 1880's. Edward Everett Dale, in *The Range Cattle Industry* (Norman, 1930), 26–28, states that before the war the cattle drives from Texas had lessened, as they were not profitable, and that the number of animals in Texas increased rapidly during the last two or three years before the war. He points out that after the capture of New Orleans and Vicksburg "the provision storehouse of Texas was virtually closed to the South except for the use of the limited number of troops in the Trans-Mississippi Department."

dipping, in addition to weeks of his own labor and that of his eight hands. Countless cords of wood had to be cut and rock hauled to burn for lye and lime. Through December his preparations continued. Christmas of 1861 was to Kendall nothing but a most unwelcome interruption of work. Most of the Negroes had colds from exposure, but he kept them at work as much as possible. He sent one of them to Boerne to borrow kettles and barrels for the dipping, another to haul ashes for the hopper, while he himself set out to hunt lost horses. Nine long, cold hours on Christmas Day he spent riding in fruitless search, and returned to Post Oak after dark, fearing the Indians had stolen them.

It was January 5 before he was ready to start dipping. In his inexperience and eagerness to do the job thoroughly, he made the lye too strong in the mixture, and by night the men's hands were bleeding. He changed the mixture, but two of his men finally had to quit, and he sent another to find extra help, while the work continued despite a norther which blew in with a cold rain. It was January 21 before the five thousand sheep were dipped, and dozens of them died because of being dipped in bitter weather. Even when he had finished, Kendall was not sure that his makeshift, wartime recipe for dip would stem the disease.

The strain and exposure had drained Kendall's health and vitality. He was unable to work much during February because of a bad attack of rheumatism; but nearly one hundred lambs died in a storm, and crippled though he was, he had to work all of one bitter day, cleaning the pen and carrying out dead sheep. Almost immediately there was another terrible storm, and, when a lamb flock became lost in the whirling drifts of snow, he wrote, "persecution by the elements can go no further." Remnants of the flock came straggling in during the next five days, before Kendall found the frozen body of the shepherd, Josey, down by Mustang Hill. They buried the shepherd, and Billy and Fletcher were once more out with the sheep. Bad weather lasted through lambing time, and the scab continued its ravages.

Through the winter and early spring reports of declining Confederate fortunes had drifted in, but it was not until May 1 that confirmation came of the rumors that Lee had surrendered on April 9. "Starvation and desertion have whipped this great general—not the federals," Kendall wrote sadly. With the report there came also news of Lincoln's assassination, and Kendall predicted gloomily, "Times of lawlessness and insecurity are upon us."

Late in May Kendall heard that General Kirby Smith had surrendered and that Houston had been sacked. When he went to San Antonio to get a doctor for Billy, who showed symptoms of the dreaded scarlet fever, the town was in tumult with soldiers helping themselves to merchandise in the stores.

Hearing of the Confederacy's defeat, one at a time the Negroes slipped away from the ranch. Nelly departed with her five progeny, to the great relief of the Kendall family. Harrison and Uncle Billy and his wife left but could find no place to stay, and returned within a short time for food and shelter. The Negro, John, stayed until July, then left, but he too came back crying to be kept on the ranch. He stayed until his death several years later.

When shearing was over, Kendall realized dipping must begin again immediately. He was determined to be better prepared for this undertaking than on his first attempt, when he and his men dipped the sheep by hand in barrels and kettles. So he sent for Wolf, the stonemason, to quarry rock and build a dipping vat and platform. After numerous delays the vat was completed, but when the work started he found that it leaked. Wolf had to serve a term on the jury before he could come to make repairs.

Finally the vat was made leak-proof and Kendall was jubilant as the work of dipping proceeded so swiftly. The sheep were driven up a chute, into the vat, then on to a platform where the excess of the solution drained off the animals and back into the vat. He dipped one flock after another, and was so delighted with the results that he sent word to his neighbors to drive their flocks over for dipping.

Labor remained scarce, for Indians were still stealing horses and killing settlers in the neighborhood, and Kendall had difficulty persuading Mexicans to work on the ranch. In addition there were frequent reports of renegade "bushwhackers" operating in the region. So Kendall slept in the field with the ewe flock at night, and sent Billy out again with the lamb flock. Billy proved expensive help. To his great grief, he lost Kendall's favorite five-shooter on his first trip out, and though Georgina came to help him search through the tall grass, they could not find it.

But there was at least plenty to eat on the ranch in the summer of 1865. By continual watering, the Kendalls had melons, okra, tomatoes, cucumbers, and beans. These had cost the added price of constant watching to drive away the cattle.

Life on the ranch was settling back to normal, and the *Picayune* was coming regularly again. For the first time in years, wool was worth saving, since it could be marketed with certainty. During the war years Kendall had not bothered to shear the wethers before one was killed each day for meat; now it was again worth doing. Wool brought twenty-four cents a pound, and in November Kendall sent off more than three thousand pounds, which brought him $917.76, less some ten dollars for the hauling.

Kendall now was hurrying to get things in shape for a trip to New Orleans, the first in seven years. He ploughed and sowed, tramped in the rye with the old ewe flock, and dipped his scabbiest sheep a second time. Preparations for his journey were slowed down to entertain a visitor, whose arrival on December 9 was to change the course of Mrs. Kendall's later life.

He was Benjamin F. Dane, who came from Boston with a Mr. Lincoln, stopped in New Orleans, and, with a letter of introduction from Holbrook, came to Post Oak looking for a place to settle in the "mountains" of Texas. Six years after Kendall's death he was to marry Mrs. Kendall, and take over the care and management of Post Oak Spring ranch.

As final preparations for the trip were made, Kendall took Georgina to make farewell calls. She was now fifteen, and her

305

schooling, delayed by the war, was to be completed in the school of her choice in New Orleans.

The isolation of the ranch had not caused the real education of the Kendall children to be neglected. Georgina spoke French and German and a little Spanish, and after Clara left, her father took over the supervision of her spelling lessons. Every night while she stood wearily holding the sperm oil lamp as he shaved before the mirror of the great armoire, he improved the time by drilling her in spelling the longest and hardest words he could think of at the moment.

The trip down to the coast was little different from earlier ones, but Kendall's temper and endurance had been drawn thin by his years of disappointing, heartbreaking toil, and he complained bitterly that the mattresses in the roadside inns were "stuffed with corncobs and the pillows filled with pecan shells."

The crowded steamer out of Galveston had poor accomodations, and many old Confederate soldiers on board had no place to sleep. Kendall gave his berth to one of them to use during the day, while he, as in former times, gossiped with the men on deck. Soon after breakfast on the second day they reached the Balize, glad to see the Mississippi again after an absence of seven years. They passed Fort Jackson and the wrecks of old gunboats sunk during the war, and through squalls of rain could see the orange groves yellow with fruit. It was after midnight when Kendall came ashore, leaving Mrs. Kendall and Georgina to spend the night on board. His first object was to find an oyster bar, where he ate a dozen raw oysters before he went to the *Picayune* office, and later to the St. Charles Hotel.

He hired a coach next day to bring his family to the hotel, and went about town delivering letters and messages entrusted to him by Texas friends, then back to the *Picayune* office.

After the long absence from civilization and the years of drudgery and privation, Kendall felt a very human determination to have "the best of everything for a short time." He had no real idea of his financial situation, for there had been no settlement of

Picayune affairs since before the war. Nor was there time for a settlement now, for Bullitt was at his plantation in Kentucky, Holbrook was ill, and Kendall was too busy enjoying his vacation.

So, ignorant of the enormous deficit he had piled up in his account with the paper, Kendall set about enjoying his stay in New Orleans to the full. Almost every evening he took Mrs. Kendall and Georgina to the theater. During their three weeks they heard "La Traviata" and "Il Trovatore" and "Faust," saw the Keans in "Much Ado About Nothing," and "School for Scandal," and Mrs. Howard in "Fun Land." Places of amusement were doing a thriving business that reminded Kendall of the rushing times of 1837, when he and the *Picayune* were young together.

During the days he purchased sal soda and great hogsheads of tobacco for sheep dip, and two forty-gallon kettles for mixing the solution; groceries and ammunition, crockery and glassware —items denied for four years by the blockade.

New Orleans had improved greatly in appearance in seven years, and Canal Street was as gay as Broadway or the boulevards of Paris. But among the old friends whom Kendall met at every turn there was little gaiety. Most of them had been ruined by the war, and told long stories of trials, troubles, and disasters. On New Year's Day there were few who kept the holiday as of old, and there was no disposition to celebrate the anniversary of Jackson's great victory over the British on January 8.

Back in Texas a letter in English was waiting from Liline, and Kendall's mind leaped ahead to a return to Paris and the sight of the child who was always in his thoughts. The next six months were directed toward that end. Mrs. Kendall, who now was attending to a large part of her husband's business correspondence, was much concerned about the mounting debt to Dr. Houdin, Liline's teacher. Holbrook wrote her that he had sent two drafts totaling 1700 francs, that he would make more payments as fast as possible, and advised that they leave Liline in France at least another year.

A fatal quarrel between the shepherds developed unexpectedly in February and delayed Kendall's departure. Kendall, up at daylight, found Anselmo drunk and ordered him down to the dipping place. Andrew, another shepherd, came up to the house and complained that Anselmo was insolent, but Kendall sent him back to work. While he was sitting at breakfast, Kendall heard a shot, and hurrying down to the vat he found that Andrew had shot and killed Anselmo, who had run amuck and attacked him with a drawn knife.

The coroner decided Andrew had shot in self-defense, but Kendall told Andrew he could not stay at the ranch because of the feeling aroused among the other Mexicans. Despite his dismissal, all the shepherds left five days later, and Billy, with the guests, Dane, Lincoln, and a Mr. Langston who had been visiting at the ranch for several months, took care of the sheep until Kendall could go to San Antonio for more shepherds early in March.

By the middle of June the new wool clip of seventeen thousand pounds was shipped, and the Kendalls started for France. The boys stayed in New Braunfels at the home of Mrs. Gustav Benner,[7] Dane and Lincoln stayed at the ranch to take care of the sheep on shares of the next wool crop, and the fields were leased to a Dr. West for cropping.

Kendall stopped in San Antonio to talk with General Heintzleman about the perennial Indian problem on the frontier, and Heintzleman referred him to General Philip Sheridan in New Orleans. In Indianola he heard of the tragic Negro riots of July in New Orleans, but he did not foresee the omnious political repercussions which were to follow, nor their effect on the entire reconstruction program in Louisiana.[8] He was more excited

[7] Mr. Benner, postmaster of New Braunfels until his death in 1857, had come with Prince Solms and had charge of the commissary department of the colony. After his death, Mrs. Benner became the first postmistress of the United States, but was displaced for having served under the Confederacy. L. E. Daniell, *op. cit.*, 748–51.

[8] A rump session of the constitutional convention, prompted by the radicals who hoped to oust Democratic officers and gain control through disfranchising the Southerners, had been called to meet in New Orleans July 30, 1866. When the meeting was attempted, a riot broke out between Negroes and white police, and

The Four Old Men of the Picayune, *1866*

G. W. Kendall   S. F. Wilson

A. M. Holbrook   A. C. Bullitt

about the successful laying of the Atlantic cable. "News in two days from London and Paris! Think of that!" he exclaimed.

After joining Georgina in New Orleans, they visited for a day with the Bullitts in Louisville, stopped by Niagara Falls, and then went on to Cortland, New York, to see Henry S. Randall, president of the National Wool Growers' Association. After a brief visit in New York with Dillon and Westray they sailed, and early in September saw their daughter again after an absence of nearly eleven years.

Paris no longer held the lure for Kendall which it had in his younger days. After visiting with his old friend Lausseure, and with General P. G. T. Beauregard, who was stopping in the city, Kendall within two weeks was writing that the weather was miserable and that he would be glad to get out of Paris.

Mrs. Kendall stayed with Liline in New York while Kendall took Georgina to call on his relatives in New Hampshire and Vermont, then on to Boston where he had breakfast with Franklin Pierce. Back in New York there were parties to attend and calls to make on Greeley, Colonel Hoe, George H. Giddings, who had an important contract for constructing a double-wire telegraph from New Orleans to San Francisco, and Frank Chickering, with whom they had music in the evening.

Mrs. Kendall did not share her husband's fondness for Greeley. After her first meeting with him she queried, "George, who is that very *dirty* man?" and he replied, "That, my dear, was Horace Greeley."

After breakfasting with Greeley, Kendall took his family on to Washington for a brief stop and calls at the White House, at

---

four whites and thirty-four Negroes were killed and one hundred and forty-five persons were wounded. This bloody riot, with earlier agitation over the "black codes," provided the arguments which enabled the radical Congress to enact its legislation for the military reconstruction of the ten seceding states, which marked the beginning of eleven years of reconstruction government in Louisiana. See New Orleans *Crescent,* July 31, 1866; for a review of newspaper opinion of the period, see the *Picayune,* March 5, 1871.

the French embassy, and on General Dick Taylor, and by November 10, 1866, they were in New Orleans again.

Kendall had been hurrying from place to place ever since he left Texas. Now, for the last time, he settled down briefly and took over the editorship of the *Picayune*. In the ensuing three months while he again controlled the paper he was able to set the policy which was to carry it through the turbulent days of reconstruction that lay ahead.

27

At rest
in the hills

HOLBROOK HAD BEEN ILL for more than a year and the *Picayune*, between his infrequent visits to the plant, had been run by younger staff members. Before he could straighten out the turmoil he found in the office, Kendall had much to learn about the developments which had converted Louisiana into virtually an armed camp since the convention riots of the previous July.

This bloody outbreak, which had made so slight an impression on Kendall when news of it reached him in Texas, had resulted in the appointment of a Congressional investigating committee which now was on its way to New Orleans to determine the future policy of the United States government toward the state. Responsibility lay heavily on editorial shoulders.

The white citizens of Louisiana felt a strong need for some workable policy which would fix the Negro's place in society and establish some sort of labor system replacing that swept away by emancipation. The state had always feared the free Negro, and now her people sought some system by which former slaves could be fed, cared for and forced to work in return.

Kendall often wrote in his diary that his freed Negroes would miss "their bread and mutton," and in different words *Picayune* editorials now told of the hardships emancipation had brought to the colored population, uprooted and often starving. Some on the *Picayune* staff, vitally interested in politics, tried actively to use that means of making the North understand the problems of the South. But Kendall, long disinterested in politics, had no illusions about the *Picayune's* power to stem the tide of hatred which the radicals in Congress held for the southern states. Before this bitterness had subsided, the former Confederates had been disfranchised and the state government turned over to the Radical Republican party, which included "loyal" whites and newly enfranchised Negroes. Not until 1876 was the state to see the withdrawal of the Federal troops which supported the hated "black and tan" government.

The hope of the South, Kendall asserted when he rolled up his sleeves and took charge of the *Picayune* in December, 1866, lay in its agricultural and industrial progress. This progress he determined to foster through the columns of the *Picayune* as he had fought to develop it by encouraging immigration to Texas, by his articles in the *Texas Almanac,* and by his establishment and development of Post Oak.

While other New Orleans editors[1] railed at the unreasoning fury of the radicals in Congress and at the hopeless political situation in Louisiana, Kendall echoed again and again his belief that industry—hard work—was "the only thing which can restore the country."[2]

Within a short time the *Picayune* circulation increased in Mississippi, in Alabama, in the outlying districts of Louisiana, and particularly in Texas. Development of Texas now was the keystone of Kendall's strengthening of the *Picayune,* for since its establishment, the *Picayune* had outstripped its competitors

[1] One of these was A. B. Bacon, a New Yorker who had joined the *Picayune* staff in 1862, after a career as a lawyer, politician, journalist and a member of the legislature in Mississippi and Texas. He had unwisely referred to General Butler in uncomplimentary terms, was arrested and sent to Fort Jackson for the duration of the war. Now he was back on the staff, fighting actively for the Democratic party.

[2] Kendall's "back to the farm" movement stands out as the most striking feature of New Orleans journalism of late 1866 and early 1867 when, with this exception, newspaper comment in the city was devoted almost wholly to local and national politics.

in Texas news, in circulation and in advertisements directed particularly to settlers in the Lone Star state.[3]

In the years ahead, when the carpetbag government tightened its strangle hold on Louisiana, and when contemporary newspapers fell by the wayside, Holbrook and his staff kept the paper alive by following the policy which Kendall had firmly established.[4] In the decade before the Civil War, New Orleans journalism was unsurpassed by any in America, but when the reconstruction period ended the *Picayune* found itself the city's only survivor of all the great English-language newspapers of the prewar days.[5]

But while Kendall was struggling to establish this policy, he found the work a difficult strain on his health. When General Beauregard urged him to go up to Compton to meet the Congressional committee, he was suffering from an attack of "bilious dysentary," and the morphine which the doctor gave him only increased the difficulty of work, so he stayed in New Orleans. He felt that he would give anything "for a whiff of the air of Post Oak hill and a drink of Post Oak creek water," and to get away from the incessant din of firecrackers which boys on the streets shot by way of Christmas celebration.

[3] See *Picayune* statement, August 15, 1872, of "most important business complications from the direction of Texas, where most valuable patronage is received."

[4] In 1872 the *Picayune* became the first newspaper in New Orleans to employ an "agricultural editor," when D. Dennett of the Franklin (Louisiana) *Planters Banner* was added to the staff with this title.

[5] The *Delta* was confiscated by General Butler and converted into a Union paper, then discontinued. The *True Delta* expired at the beginning of the reconstruction period and its plant was used to publish the carpetbag organ, *The Republican*. The *Crescent* was confiscated, revived by its publisher, Colonel J. O. Nixon, but failed in 1868; the *Commercial Bulletin* also was revived but died in 1872. Papers which flourished briefly in New Orleans during reconstruction days included the *Daily Southern Star, The Herald, The Bulletin, The Commercial,* the *Daily News, The Advertiser, The Tribune, The Sunday Delta, The Republican* and the *Weekly Delta*. *The Times,* which was established in 1863, had an up-and-down existence until it was purchased and consolidated with the *Democrat* in 1881, and the *Times-Democrat* was merged with the *Picayune* in 1914 to become the present *Times-Picayune*. The *Bee,* a French and English newspaper of the prewar days, became wholly French in 1873.

No matter what the pressure of business, there was no neglect of friendly duties. He went to visit with Duncan Kenner, noted turfman who had once named a horse for him, and, with Mrs. Kendall, called on General E. G. Lee and Mrs. Lee, who were talking of going to Texas. When Dillon came in from Havana, Kendall took him to the St. Charles restaurant for steamed oysters, and arranged a very special stag dinner for him at the St. Louis Hotel.

A. H. Hayes died suddenly, and Kendall had the sad duty of writing the obituary of this old friend whose long life had been so intimately connected with New Orleans journalism. After the funeral, he went with other friends to the loft of Sam McClure's saloon where the old man's trunks were stored, and with pangs of nostalgia helped dispose of them. He noted in his diary that Hayes had "saved newspaper clippings and everything else he had ever owned."

In his spare time Kendall took Georgina and Mrs. Kendall to the theater and the opera, and as he shopped for the ranch,[6] for books and clothes for Billy and Fletcher, he worried about Liline who was ill with an acclimating fever.

But there was less and less spare time. Holbrook's ill health continued, and often Kendall arrived at the office early in the morning and worked until toward midnight. The weather was bitter in January, 1867; he felt the cold in his "very marrow," and his nerves rebelled at the screams of children in the streets, playing in the snow they had never seen before.

Utterly wretched, taking medicine constantly, regretting the time lost because of the steady stream of callers, but always stopping to chat as long as they were inclined, and making up his work later, Kendall watched the *Picayune* grow sturdy and strong again as he pumped his own life blood into it. His struggle con-

[6] Mrs. Kendall bought a Florence sewing machine and took lessons in its use, while Kendall selected a handsome new ambulance for the ranch. He bought her an elaborate cast-iron bathtub with a built-in charcoal burner for heating the water. After his death, this bathtub was listed in the inventory of his estate as a "washing machine," and valued at forty dollars.

tinued until late in February when Holbrook returned to work. Bullitt came down from his plantation, and the partners reached a settlement for the first time in seven years. Bad as the news was to Kendall, he was "heartily glad" to know just how he stood financially.

Over the period from May 1, 1839, to May 31, 1867, when the balance was finally determined, his total cash earnings from the paper had amounted to almost one hundred thousand dollars. But he had drawn out more than that, and had to assume one third of Lumsden's interest in the paper at the time of his death. In the seven years prior to the settlement, Kendall's earnings on his share amounted to only fifteen thousand dollars, and now he found that he owed the partnership more than twenty-eight thousand dollars.[7]

Holbrook came back to the office again, but Kendall was nevertheless unable to slow down the pace which steadily was ruining his health. He suffered constantly from colds and lumbago, and now his eyes were giving him difficulty in the close work under the gas lights. The stream of requests for "situations by poor fellows who were once rich" depressed him, and "exciting political news from Washington, where madness rules the hour" created a fear that the South had not yet seen the worst of her troubles. Eagerly his thoughts turned again to Post Oak, which much needed his attention and where his history of the Mexican War remained unfinished.

An annoying personal difficulty arose before he could leave the city. In an effort to solve the insoluble labor problem, he arranged with his brother-in-law, Alexandre, for the Le Sage family to emigrate from France, and paid their passage to New Orleans together with that of a French girl named Artemise de Valois, employed for Mr. Evans and Henriette.

The Le Sage family arrived and according to contract started

[7] Kendall papers, statement of the cash earnings of the *Picayune* from May, 1839, to May, 1867. Bullitt's plantation had drained the paper to a far greater degree than Post Oak had done, so that after assuming his share of Lumsden's interest, his indebtedness to the *Picayune* was nearly fifty thousand dollars.

on to Indianola, but Artemise de Valois refused to leave the city. Kendall had her arrested, but still she refused to go to Texas. He had her arrested a second time, but could find no way of holding her to her five-year contract, and furiously concluded that the labor laws were sadly defective. There was no way to force her to repay her passage money, and nothing to do but to go without her.

Kendall left his family in San Antonio and went home to find that the bachelor management of Lincoln and Dane during his absence of eight months had worked havoc on the ranch. The house was very dirty, the muslin sagged from the ceilings where the roof leaked, everything was worn, broken down and dilapidated, and the sheep and lambs were "in deplorable plight."

March rain was cold, there was no green grass on the prairies, scores of dead lambs lay about and the old ewes were almost starving. The house was in such disorder that Kendall went to Boerne to write his letter for the *Picayune,* which under the new contract he was to do weekly, and he dreaded the arrival of his wife, and Liline who would see the place for the first time.

The only bright spot was that the Le Sages had arrived and started to work like Trojans. Most willingly Kendall paid the sixty dollars for their passage up from the coast. Le Sage worked steadily in the garden, his wife took over the kitchen, and their little boy, Francois, showed promise of becoming a good shepherd.

Returning to a house which Kendall admitted was scarcely habitable, Mrs. Kendall became ill from overwork before she got her household under control. Mme. de Valcourt came back from Twin Sisters, where she had been living with Henriette, riding in state in an oxcart for lack of better transportation at the moment she wanted to come. July came, and Kendall went to San Antonio to meet Georgina and bring her, with Billy and Fletcher, home from school. For the first time in twelve years, he wrote with satisfaction, all the children were together. Post Oak settled down to its accustomed routine of work and visitors.

Kendall went hunting with his new breech-loading shotgun, a gift from Dillon which pleased him greatly, and he went fishing with Billy and Fletcher and little Francois.

But his health was no better than it had been in New Orleans. He had several teeth pulled, spoke often of being too tired to sleep, and complained frequently of a pain in his side which he could not account for, an ailment which increased after he was thrown from his horse. Formerly he had never been fatigued by riding, but now a trip to Boerne on horseback made him very sore.

No longer did his letters to the *Picayune* flow easily, full of cheerful tales of ranch activities, developments in Texas, or invective against a government which failed to protect the pioneers against the Indians. Now they were largely reminiscent of his great days, filled with incidents which had occurred in Mexico or in Paris. The pen which had started the *Picayune* with laughing, satiric sketches of New Orleans life, had made vivid the ill-fated Santa Fe Expedition, had relayed to the whole American press the events of the Mexican War, and had preserved for posterity a carefully written history of that struggle,[8] was running dry.

He had brought to exiled Frenchmen in Louisiana column after column telling of the revolutionary movements which shook Europe. For twenty-five years he had written of the wonders of

[8] This history, which in his opinion was to be the great work of his life, was never to lie between boards as he had planned. His briefer illustrated history of the Mexican War had been widely popular in the early 1850's, but many efforts of his family to get the longer history published resulted in tragic failure. Immediately after his death publishers rejected the manuscript because interest was centered in the more recent Civil War. Efforts were resumed but came to an abrupt halt with the death of his older son, William. Georgina, now Mrs. Fellowes, took up the project again, but dropped it when her husband died. Fletcher, a graduate of the United States Military Academy, wrote the last chapter and tried to get the work published, but in the midst of his negotiations, he died. Mrs. Fellowes lost her only son after she had renewed correspondence with publishers. Death had cast a spell over the manuscript, and it was suggested that the stack of yellowed sheets be destroyed. Mrs. Fellowes, however, could not forget the oft-repeated instructions of her father when she was left alone in the house on his short trips to Boerne: "If the house burns, and you are not able to save anything else, be sure to carry out the white box of papers on top of the armoire in my room." Finally, she gave the manuscript to the University of Texas.

Texas, and his pen had done more than any other to bring settlers there. He had written countless galleys of copy explaining to farmers and sheep raisers of the Southwest how to meet and conquer their problems, and countless more telling of the success or failure of his experimental planting of crops in the new country.

Now his pen had reached the bottom of the page. When he wrote his weekly letter to the *Picayune,* it dealt almost exclusively with the past, as if there were no present and would be no future. Only his articles to the *Texas Almanac,* telling of the problems of sheep raising and his solution for them, showed any of his former fire and ease of composition.

An old injury which he had almost forgotten—the crushed ankle that he sustained in a fall in the darkness at the outset of the Santa Fe Expedition, and which kept him in a Jersey wagon during the first weeks of his trip across the plains—returned to torture him. His foot swelled so he could hardly bear a shoe, and kept him from moving about much through late August and early September, but he took the boys to San Antonio to school, and tried without success to find a cart for the farm work, which he declared was much worse needed than the new ambulance.

Then he spent the rest of the day going from place to place in San Antonio, in spite of his bad foot, trying without success to borrow money to promote a factory for the manufacture of woolens in New Braunfels. Discouraged, he wrote in his diary, "Was doomed to utter disappointment during the day as were doubtless many others; Money tight, business dull, and no confidence in the future, the accursed political demagogues the cause of it all."[9]

Discouraged with failure, home he went through rain and mud, to find three callers, and the workmen idle because he had not been there to supervise. Desperately he put them to work relaying the pasture fence, while he doctored rams for worms and

[9] September 5, 1867. Times were hard for borrowers in 1867, and money had a mercurial quality. In December, Mrs. Kendall received a draft for $146.48 currency, and sold it for $108.39, silver. Yet then as now, industry survived by means of credit.

despaired at finding so much scab among them. Then he made a trip to New Braunfels in a wagon, over heavy roads, borrowed the needed funds, and visited the woolen factory which was waiting only for a new engine to set it whirling. He found a rickety wagon to use on the ranch, and went back to struggle with his letter to the *Picayune*.

Through a hot September he plowed with the oxen and gathered corn against a scourge of grasshoppers that ate everything in sight. They stripped the sweet potatoes, but Kendall seemed almost indifferent. Things had become so desperate on the ranch that he seemed numbed, and had not even the energy to rail at things gone wrong, as formerly.

The situation among the sheep was bad and was to become worse. A year later Mrs. Kendall wrote to Mr. Randall in New York:

> The sheep business is not very flourishing in Texas. Almost every one who has sheep is anxious to sell them, but there are no buyers. Some very good grade sheep were sold at 50 cents a head two weeks ago. It is almost impossible to keep the scab out of the flocks, because stray scabby sheep get in, and introduce the disease as fast as it can be cured. Every one in this part of the country has had bad luck with their lambs. . . . We had 1500, and have only 500 left. . . .

Of those times, Mrs. Kendall never liked to speak in later life. She was only thirty-seven when she was left alone on the ranch, with four children to care for and establish in life. These things she did.

Much happened to her later. She sent Billy to live with Kendall's sister Kate, in Royalton, Vermont, where he died, unmarried, at twenty-five. She saw Fletcher a major in the army, a graduate of West Point, and followed with pride his military career and the lives of his children, Adeline de Valcourt Kendall and Major William Henry Kendall. In 1913, she read of his funeral in the National Cemetery near Vancouver, Washington.

She sent Liline to school at Jacksonville, Illinois, to learn to

read and write English, and she outlived the beautiful girl with
the sad gray eyes, to whom Kendall had been so devoted. Her
mother, Mme. de Valcourt, was drowned while crossing the
Guadalupe River on the way back from visiting Henriette in
1873, and that same year Georgina married Eugene J. Fellowes
and went to live in Chicago, and Mrs. Kendall herself became
Mrs. Dane. She lived to be ninety-four years old, and if anyone
ever intimated that she did not understand Americans, she would
retort, "I ought to! I married two of them!"

But that was later. Now, on October 9, 1867, Kendall sat at
his desk by the window of the low, white ranch house, and wrote,
"Dark, damp, and showery this morning, with occasional sharp-
ish showers. No great amount of rain fell, but sufficient to do a
deal of good. Commenced laying—"

Kendall laid down his pen, to write nothing more. The history
of the Mexican War remained unfinished until his son, Fletcher,
wrote the final chapter. The box on the armoire with "father's
manuscript" gathered dust, while his wife recorded the progress
of his illness, which lasted seven days. On Monday, October 21,
she picked up the tiny black volume of Kendall's diary for 1867,
and wrote:

My dear husband died at $\frac{1}{4}$ to nine o'clock p.m. on the 21st of
October, 1867, of congestion of both lungs. Dr. Morse tried every
remedy he knew, but he could not save him. I sent to San Antonio for
another Doctor, but he came at half past ten, it was too late!

Bibliography

Kendall Papers

EARLY LIFE: Shortly after the death of George Wilkins Kendall in 1867, his widow and daughters began to collect information about his early life. Letters to Mrs. Kendall and her daughter, Georgina Kendall Fellowes, from relatives in New England, covering nearly a half-century, form an important part of the Kendall papers. In this period the family collected copies of wills, deeds, and scores of letters from relatives, establishing the genealogical line and relating incidents in Kendall's youth. Important among these is a letter from William Rix, Kendall's brother-in-law, written in the spring of 1868 to Mrs. Kendall, giving details of her late husband's life up to the time of the establishment of the New Orleans *Picayune* in 1837. A letter from Kendall's parents, dated Philipsburg, Quebec, April 26, 1818, to his aunt in New Hampshire, sheds light on his early schooling.

SANTA FE EXPEDITION: Fortunately, Kendall signed his initials to a great many of his letters and dispatches to the *Picayune*, so that his activities after the establishment of the newspaper can be followed in its files. In his later years he grew reminiscent and related many incidents of his boyhood, of his early wanderings, and of his first years on the *Picayune*. Family letters, most of them from Kendall's sister, Kate, cover the period from 1842 to 1848. The papers include a contract between Kendall and Harper and Brothers for the publication of his two-volume work on the Santa Fe expedition in 1844, a mass of Kendall's notes for revision of later editions of the work, and a manuscript written by Judge Thomas Falconer covering a portion of the journey across the plains in 1842 when the two friends were separated.

Invitations to join learned societies, after his dramatic return from the Santa Fe expedition, found their way into the family archives. Two deeds mark Kendall's land-hunting expeditions after his early visits to Texas. One, signed by Anson Jones, president of the Texas Republic, records the transfer to Kendall from the Republic of Texas of 4,106¾ acres of land at Post Oak Spring on July 31, 1845. The other, which was witnessed by Mirabeau B. Lamar, transferred 3,400 acres of land on the Brazos River from J. Pinckney Henderson to Kendall on August 28, 1846. "A statement of co-partnership affairs of Lumsden, Kendall, Holbrook & Bullitt in Daily & Weekly Picayune from 18th Nov. 1844 to 31st Dec. 1845" gives invaluable information on the early operations of their publishing venture.

MEXICAN WAR PERIOD: Letters to Kendall from General Franklin Pierce, General W. J. Worth, General Persifor F. Smith, Colonel James Duncan, and Alexander Bullitt supplement the great mass of newspaper material by and about Kendall during the Mexican War. The Kendall papers include a typescript of his unpublished history of this war, together with hundreds of newspaper clippings and tear sheets which he assembled in the preparation of this work, some of them identified as the work of Yankee printers who followed General Winfield Scott's troops into Mexico. Unique among these items is a scrapbook history of the war, by an unknown compiler. Contracts, statements, receipts for work done by engravers and artists shed light on the work involved in the large illustrated history of the war which Kendall published in 1851 with Carl Nebel, the French artist. Hotel and steamboat menus, invitations to dinners, balls, and political rallies for war heroes, and bills from tailors and haberdashers are indications of the hectic days Kendall spent in America and in Europe immediately after the war.

RANCH LIFE: One hundred and eighteen letters from Kendall to Mrs. Kendall in Paris cover the period from August 15, 1851, to January 16, 1856, dealing with business, his land-hunting expeditions, his travels, friends he met, developments on the ranch, and current events. There are two letters from Mrs. Kendall to Kendall, written from Chaville, 1854. Eighteen letters from A. M. Holbrook to Kendall and Mrs. Kendall cover the period from 1857 to 1873, dealing with purchases for the ranch, conditions of the *Picayune*, social events in

New Orleans, comments on Mrs. Kendall's activities on the ranch, news from friends and other partners, the Civil War as it affected the *Picayune*, business settlement after Kendall's death, arrangements for his tombstone, and advice about the children's schooling. History of the *Picayune* is revealed in this business settlement, and in the inventory of property and effects of Kendall filed in the Second District Court, New Orleans, March 2, 1868, including equipment and holdings of the newspaper and Kendall's ranch property. The papers include one letter to Kendall's widow from Pearl Rivers, who later became the owner of the *Picayune*.

Kendall's diaries, with daily entries from January 1, 1857, to October 15, 1867, form the most valuable commentary on his pioneering venture in Texas.

Further details of his ranch life are shown in his record of marks and brands, his tax receipts from 1854 to 1866, statements from his bankers and business agents, letters from friends who visited the ranch, eight letters in French, written in 1854, concerning his purchase, shipment, and insurance of sheep from the Rambouillet flocks in France; and copies of Kendall's letters to Governor F. R. Lubbock, Colonel S. M. Baird, and Governor J. W. Throckmorton, dealing with Indian depredations on the frontier.

Family scrapbooks include clippings of newspaper comments on Kendall's published works, his war experiences, his ranch life, and reminiscences of fellow printers after his death.

Official Documents

Congressional Globe, Thirty-second Congress, second session, XXVI. Washington, 1853.

Executive Documents:

Twenty-seventh Congress, second session, *Docs.* 49, 266, 271.

House Journal, fifth Texas congress, first session.

Papers of Mirabeau Buonaparte Lamar, from the University of Texas papers. Edited by C. A. Gulick, Jr., Austin, 1921. Numbers 913, 1049, 1162, 1773.

Report of Postmaster General, November 30, 1839. Twenty-fifth Congress, second session.

Senate Documents:

    Twenty-seventh Congress, second session, *Doc.* 278.

    Thirty-first Congress, first session, *Doc.* 32.

Senate Executive Documents:

    Thirtieth Congress, first session, *Docs.* 1, 56, 65.

    Thirty-second Congress, second session, *Doc.* 14.

Statutes at Large and Treaties of the United States of America, X. Boston, 1855.

Statutes at Large of the United States of America, V. Boston, 1854.

Texas Diplomatic Correspondence, II.

Newspapers

American Flag. Matamoros, Mexico, July 4, 1846, to July 29, 1848.

American Star No. 2. Puebla, Mexico, July 1, 8, 1847.

Atlas. Boston, Massachusetts, February, 1848.

Bee. New Orleans, Louisiana, 1837–67.

Commercial Bulletin. New Orleans, Louisiana, February 17, 1837, through 1860.

Courier. Boston, Massachusetts, May 26, 1826, to February, 1848.

Courier. Charleston, South Carolina, February, 1848.

Courier. Natchez, Mississippi, 1848.

Crescent. New Orleans, Louisiana, 1848–62, 1865–68.

Daily Advertiser. Boston, Massachusetts, May 19, 1848.

Daily Enquirer. Cincinnati, Ohio, January and February, 1848.

Daily News. Galveston, Texas, August 15, 1939.

Daily Union. Washington, D.C., February, 1848.

Delta. New Orleans, Louisiana, 1845–62.

Evening Post. New York, February, 1848.

Examiner. Richmond, Virginia, May 10, 1864.

Flag of Freedom. Puebla, Mexico, October 27, 1847.

Gazette and Comet. Baton Rouge, Louisiana, October 6, 1861.

Herald. New York, January, 1847, through March, 1848.

National Intelligencer. Washington, D.C., March, 1846, to March, 1848.

National Journal. Washington, D.C., January through June, 1826.

Niles' National Register. Washington, D.C., November 6, 1830, through 1842.

North American. Mexico, November 30, 1847; January 19, 24, 1848; February 10, 11, 1848.

North American. Philadelphia, Pennsylvania, June 1, 1846, through February, 1848.

Observer. New York, November, 1841, through January, 1842.

Picayune. New Orleans, Louisiana, 1837–77.

Picket Guard. Saltillo, Mexico, May 3, 21, 1847.

Public Ledger. Philadelphia, Pennsylvania, January and February, 1848.

Republic of Rio Grande and Friend of the People. Matamoros, Mexico, June 6, 16, 30, 1846.

Republican and Argus. Baltimore, Maryland, January, 1847, through November, 1848.

Sun. Baltimore, Maryland, February, 1848.

Times. New Orleans, Louisiana, 1862–76.

Tribune. New York, February, 1848.

Tropic and American Republican. New Orleans, Louisiana, 1844–46.

Weekly Advocate. Baton Rouge, Louisiana, October 6, 1861.

Weekly Picayune. New Orleans, Louisiana, 1838–67.

Pamphlets and Bulletins

Anonymous. *Jack Hayes, the Intrepid Ranger.* Bandera, Texas, n.d.

Barker, Jacob. *Suspension du Nacional Advocate.* New Orleans, 1863.

Fanning, Clara Elizabeth (ed.). *The Book Review Digest,* New York, 1913.

Fellowes, Georgina de Valcourt Kendall. *A Short Biographical Sketch of the Kendall Family.* San Antonio, Texas, 1939.

Miller, Edmund Thornton. *A Financial History of Texas.* Bulletin of the University of Texas, Austin, Texas, 1916.

The Picayune's *Guide to New Orleans.* New Orleans, 1903.

Seeligson, Mrs. Lelia. *A History of Indianola.* Cuero, Texas, n.d.

Periodicals

Adams, Ephraim Douglas (ed.). "Correspondence in British Archives concerning Texas," *Southwestern Historical Quarterly,* XVII, 1913, 1914.

Barker, E. C. "The Texan Revolutionary Army," Texas Historical Association *Quarterly*, IX, 1906.

———. "The Texan Declaration of Causes for Taking Up Arms against Mexico," Texas State Historical Association *Quarterly*, XV, 1912.

———. "The U. S. and Mexico, 1835–1837," *Mississippi Valley Historical Review*, I, 1914.

Biesele, R. L. "Prince Solm's Trip to Texas, 1844–1845," *Southwestern Historical Quarterly*, XL, 1936.

Bolton, Herbert Eugene. "Some Materials for Southwestern History in the Archivo General de Mexico," Texas State Historical Association *Quarterly*, VII, 1904.

Burton, E. Bennett. "Texas Raiders in New Mexico in 1843," *Old Santa Fe*, II, 1915.

Christian, A. K. "Tariff History of the Republic of Texas," *Southwestern Historical Quarterly*, XX, 1917.

Cox, Isaac Joslin. "The Southwest Boundary of Texas," Texas State Historical Association *Quarterly*, VI, 1903.

Edwards, Herbert Rook. "Diplomatic Relations between France and Texas," *Southwestern Historical Quarterly*, XX, 1917.

Garrison, G. P. (ed.). "Diplomatic Correspondence of the Republic of Texas," *American Historical Association Report*, II, 1907.

Hart, W. O. "The New Orleans *Times* and the New Orleans *Democrat*," *Louisiana Historical Quarterly*, VIII, 1925.

Kendall, Amos (ed.). *Kendall's Expositor for 1841: containing an epitome of the Proceedings of Congress at the Memorable Extra Session: also, Dissertations upon Currency, Exchanges, The Tariff, and Other Topics With A Summary of Current News*. I. Washington, 1841.

Kendall, John S. "Journalism in New Orleans between 1880 and 1890," *Louisiana Historical Quarterly*, VIII, 1925.

Lestage, H. Oscar, Jr. "The White League in Louisiana and Its Participation in the Reconstruction Riots," *Louisiana Historical Quarterly*, XVIII, 1935.

Marshall, Thomas M. "Commercial Aspects of the Texas-Santa Fe Expedition," *Southwestern Historical Quarterly*, XX, 1917.

———. "Diplomatic Relations of Texas and the United States, 1839–1853," Texas State Historical Association *Quarterly*, XV, 1912.

————. "The Southwestern Boundary of Texas," Texas State Historical Association *Quarterly,* XIV, 1911.

O'Meara, J. "Early Editors of California," *The Overland Monthly,* XIV, 1889.

Overdyke, W. Darrell. "History of the American Party in Louisiana," *Louisiana Historical Quarterly,* XV, 1932.

Phillips, U. B. "The Central Theme of Southern History," *American Historical Review,* XXXIV, 1928.

Ramsdall, Charles W. "The Changing Interpretation of the Civil War," *Journal of Southern History,* III, 1937.

Russ, William A. "Disfranchisement in Louisiana, 1862–1870," *Louisiana Historical Quarterly,* XVIII, 1935.

Spell, Lota M. "The Anglo-Saxon Press in Mexico, 1846–1865," *American Historical Review,* XXXVIII, 1932.

Spillman, W. J. "Adjustment of the Texas Boundary in 1850," Texas State Historical Association *Quarterly,* VII, 1904.

Terrell, A. W. "The City of Austin from 1839 to 1865," Texas State Historical Association *Quarterly,* XIV, 1911.

Winkler, E. W. "The Cherokee Indians in Texas," Texas State Historical Association *Quarterly,* VII, 1904.

————. "The Seat of Government in Texas," Texas State Historical Association *Quarterly,* X, 1907.

Books

Acheson, Sam. *35,000 Days in Texas*. New York, 1938.

Adams, Ephraim Douglas. *British Interests and Activities in Texas*. Baltimore, 1910.

Allen, Edward Monington. *Authors' Handbook*. Scranton, Pennsylvania, 1938.

Allen, Hervey. *Anthony Adverse*. New York, 1936.

Anderson, Robert. *An Artillery Officer in the Mexican War*. New York and London, 1911.

Atkins, John Black. *The Life of Sir William Howard Russell, C.V.O., LL.D., the first Special Correspondent*. London, 1911.

Auchampaugh, Philip Gerald. *Robert Tyler, Southern Rights Champion*. Duluth, Minnesota, 1934.

Bancroft, H. H. *History of Texas and the North American States*. San Francisco, 1890.

Beale, Howard K. *The Critical Year: a study of Andrew Johnson and Reconstruction*. New York, 1930.

Bieber, Ralph B. *Southern Trails to California in 1849*. Glendale, California, 1937.

Binkley, William C. *The Expansionist Movement in Texas*. Berkeley, California, 1925.

Bleyer, Willard Grosvenor. *Main Currents in the History of American Journalism*. Boston, 1927.

Bolton, Herbert Eugene. *Athanese de Mezieres and the Louisiana–Texas Frontier, 1768–1780*. Cleveland, 1914.

———. *Guide to Materials for the History of the United States in the Principal Archives of Mexico*. Washington, D.C., 1913.

Bonnell, George W. *Topographical Description of Texas*. Austin, 1840.

Bowers, Claud G. *The Tragic Era*. Cambridge, 1929.

Bradley, Glenn D. *The Story of the Pony Express*. Chicago, 1923.

Brown, John Henry. *Indian Wars and Pioneers of Texas*. Austin, 189–.

Buckingham, James Silk. *The Slave States of America*. London, 1842.

Bullard, F. Lauriston. *Famous War Correspondents*. Boston, 1914.

Burgess, John W. *Reconstruction and the Constitution, 1866–1876*. New York, 1902.

Carter, Howell. *A Cavalryman's Reminiscences of the Civil War*. New Orleans, n.d.

Casteneda, Carlos E. (ed.). *The Mexican Side of the Texan Revolution*. Dallas, 1928.

Chapman, Arthur. *The Pony Express*. New York, 1932.

Christian, A. K. *Mirabeau Buonaparte Lamar*. Austin, 1922.

Claiborne, J. F. H. (ed.). *Life and Correspondence of John A. Quitman*. New York, 1860.

Clapp, Theodore. *Autobiographical Sketches and Recollections during Thirty-five Years' Residence in New Orleans*. Boston, 1857.

Connelley, William E. *War with Mexico, 1846–1847. Doniphan's Expedition and the Conquest of New Mexico and California*. Topeka, Kansas, 1907.

Cook, James M. *Fifty Years on the Old Frontier*. New Haven, 1923.

Cox, James. *Historical and Biographical Sketches of Texas and Texas Cattlemen*. St. Louis, 1895.

Crane, W. C. *Life and Selected Literary Remains of Sam Houston*. Dallas, 1884.

Daniell, L. E. *Texas, the Country and its Men*. n.p., n.d.

de Peyster, W. *Personal and Military History of Philip Kearny*. New York, 1896.

Didimus, H. *New Orleans as I Found It*. New York, 1845.

Dodd, William E. *The Cotton Kingdom*. New Haven, 1912.

Dumond, Dwight. *Southern Editorials on Secession*. New York, 1931.

Dunning, William A. *Reconstruction, Political and Economic*. New York, 1907.

Durbin, John Price. *Observations in Europe, Principally in France and Great Britain*. New York, 1844.

Duval, John C. *Early Times in Texas*. Dallas, 1936.

Edwards, Frank S. *A Campaign in New Mexico with Col. Doniphan*. Philadelphia, 1847.

Elliott, Charles W. *Winfield Scott*. New York, 1937.

Emory, Lieutenant Colonel William Hensley. *Notes on a Military Reconnoissance*. Washington, D.C., 1848.

Falconer, Thomas. F. W. Hodge (ed.). *Letters and Notes on the Texan-Santa Fe Expedition*. New York, 1930.

Ficklin, John R. *Reconstruction in Louisiana*. Baltimore, 1910.

Fleming, W. L. *Documentary History of Reconstruction*. Cleveland, 1906–1907.

————. *Sequel of Appomattox*. New Haven, 1919.

Folson, Charles J. *Mexico in 1842: a description of the country, its natural and political features; with a sketch of its history, brought down to the present year*. New York, 1842.

Foot, Henry S. *Texas and the Texans*. Austin, 1935.

Fortier, Alex. *History of Louisiana*. Chicago, 1900.

Freeman, Douglas. *Life of Robert E. Lee*. New York, 1934.

Furber, George C. *Twelve Months Volunteer; or Journal of a Private in the Campaign of Mexico*. Cincinnati, 1857.

Gayarre, Charles. *History of Louisiana*. New Orleans, 1885.

Gibson, George Rutledge, and Bieber, Ralph P. (eds.). *Journal of a Soldier*. Glendale, California, 1935.

Giddings, Luther. *Sketches of the Campaign in Northern Mexico*. New York, 1853.

Glasscock, C. B. *Then Came Oil*. New York, 1938.

Greeley, Horace. *Recollections of a Busy Life*. New York, 1868.

Green, Thomas J. *Journal of the Texan Expedition against Mier*. New York, 1845.

Gregg, Josiah. *Commerce of the Prairies*. Dallas, 1933. (Reprint edition.)

Hall, A. Oakey. *The Manhattaner in New Orleans, or Phases of "Crescent City" Life*. New Orleans, 1851.

Harper, Henry. *The House of Harper: a century of publishing in Franklin Square*. New York and London, 1912.

Henneman, John Bell (ed.). *History of the Literary and Intellectual Life of the South*. Richmond, Virginia, 1909. "Southern Editors," by George Frederick Mellen; "The Southern Press," by Norman Walker.

Hitchcock, Major General Ethan Allen. *Fifty Years in Camp and Field*. New York and London, 1909.

Hudson, Frederic. *Journalism in the United States from 1690 to 1872*. New York, 1873.

James, Marquis. *The Raven*. New York, 1929.

Jay, William. *A Review of the Causes and Consequences of the Mexican War*. Boston and Philadelphia, 1849.

Jewell, Edwin L. *Jewell's Crescent City Illustrated*. New Orleans, 1873.

Kendall George Wilkins. *Narrative of the Texan Santa Fe Expedition*. New York, 1844.

———, and Carl Nebel. *War between the United States and Mexico, Illustrated*. New Orleans and New York, 1851.

Lee, Sidney. *Dictionary of National Biography, XXXVI. London*, 1893.

McDermott, John Francis (ed.), Albert J. Salvan (trans.). *Tixier's Travels on the Osage Prairies*. Norman, Oklahoma, 1940.

Macdonald, Helen Grace. *Canadian Public Opinion on the American Civil War*. New York and London, 1926.

McMaster, John Bach. *The Encyclopedia Americana*. New York, 1937.

———. *History of the People of the United States*. New York, 1914.

McMurtrie, Douglas C. *A History of California Newspapers*. New York, 1927.

Magoffin, Susan Shelby. *Down the Santa Fe Trail and into Mexico, 1846–1847*. New Haven, 1926.

Marryat, Captain Frederick. *Narrative of the Travels and Adventures of Monsieur Violet*. Boston, n.d.

Marshall, T. M. *A History of the Western Boundary of the Louisiana Purchase, 1819–1841*. Berkeley, California, 1914.

Martineau, Harriet. *Retrospect of Western Travel*. London, 1838.

Masters, Edgar Lee. *Whitman*. New York, 1937.

Mayes, Edward. *Lucius Q. C. Lamar*. Nashville, Tennessee, 1896.

Mott, Frank Luther. *American Journalism*. New York, 1941.

Myers, William Starr (ed.). *The Mexican War Diary of General George B. McClellan*. Princeton, 1917.

Nixon, Pat Ireland. *A Century of Medicine in Bexar County, Texas*. San Antonio, 1936.

Norman, Benjamin Moore. *Norman's New Orleans and Environs*. New Orleans and New York, 1845.

Oswandel, J. J. *Notes on the Mexican War*. Philadelphia, 1885.

Owsley, Frank Lawrence. *King Cotton Diplomacy*. Chicago, 1931.

Parton, James. *General Butler in New Orleans*. Boston, 1892.

Pike, Zebulon. *Account of an Expedition to the Source of the Mississippi and through the Western Parts of Louisiana*. Philadelphia and Baltimore, 1810.

Powell, William H. *List of Officers of the Army of the United States from 1779 to 1900*. New York, 1900.

Quaife, Milo Milton (ed.). *The Diary of James K. Polk*. Chicago, 1910.

Ramsdall, C. W. *Reconstruction in Texas*. New York, 1910.

Reid, Samuel C., Jr. *The Scouting Expeditions of McCulloch's Texas Rangers*. Philadelphia, n.d.

Richardson, R. N. *The Comanche Barrier to South Plains Settlement*. Glendale, California, 1933.

Rightor, Joseph. *Standard History of New Orleans*. Chicago, 1908.

Rives, George Lockhart. *The United States and Mexico*. New York, 1913.

Robertson, James A. *Louisiana Under the Rule of Spain, France and the United States*. Cleveland, 1911.

Robinson, William Morrison, Jr. *The Confederate Privateers*. Cambridge, 1928.

Root, Frank A. and Connelley, William Elsey. *The Overland Stage to California*. Topeka, Kansas, 1901.

Sabin, Joseph. *Dictionary of Books Relating to America*. New York, 1868–1936.

Salmon, Lucy. *The Newspaper and the Historian*. New York, 1923.

Scott, Lieutenant General Winfield. *Memoirs of Lieut.-Gen. Scott*. New York, 1864.

Secomb, D. F. *History of the Town of Amherst, Hillsborough County, New Hampshire,*. Concord, N. H., 1883.

Semmes, Raphael. *The Campaign of General Scott in the Valley of Mexico*. Cincinnati, 1852.

———. *Service Afloat and Ashore during the Mexican War*. Cincinnati, 1851.

Smith, Arthur D. Howden. *John Jacob Astor, Landlord of New York*. Philadelphia and London, 1929.

Smith, Charles J. *History of the Town of Mont Vernon, New Hampshire*. Boston, 1907.

Smith, Justin H. *The War with Mexico*. New York, 1919.

Stephenson, Nathaniel W. *The Day of the Confederacy*. New Haven, 1920.

———. *Texas and the Mexican War, a Chronicle of the Winning of the Southwest*. New Haven, 1921.

Stevens, Major Isaac I. *Campaigns of the Rio Grande and of Mexico*. New York, 1851.

Taylor, Benjamin F. *Short Ravelings from a Long Yarn, or, Camp and March Sketches of the Santa Fe Trail*. From the notes of Richard L. Wilson. Chicago, 1847. Reprint edition, Santa Ana, California, 1936.

Thompson, Waddy. *Recollections of Mexico*. New York, 1846.

Thrall, H. S. *Pictorial History of Texas*. St. Louis, Missouri, 1879.

Tiling, Moritz. *German Element in Texas from 1820–1850*. Houston, Texas, 1913.

Upham, Charles Wentworth. *Lectures on Witchcraft, Comprising a History of the Delusion in Salem, in 1692*. Boston, 1832.

Wagner, Henry S. *The Plains and the Rockies*. San Francisco, 1937.

Warmoth, H. C. *War, Politics and Reconstruction; Stormy Days in Louisiana*. New York, 1930.

Watterson, Henry. *Marse Henry, an Autobiography*. New York, 1919.

Webb, J. J. (Ralph P. Bieber, ed.). *Adventures in the Santa Fe Trade*. Glendale, California, 1931.

White, Laura A. *Robert Barnwell Rhett, Father of Secession*. New York, 1931.

Williams, Amelia. *Following General Sam Houston from 1793–1863*. Austin, 1935.

Wise, John S. *The End of an Era*. Boston and New York, 1899.

Yoakum, Henderson K. *History of Texas from its First Settlement in 1685 to its Annexation to the United States in 1846*. New York, 1856.

Young, G. M. *Victorian England, Portrait of an Age*. London, 1936.

Index

Abell, Arunah S.: 22

Aberdeen, George Hamilton Gordon, Lord: becomes British foreign minister, 110; meets American Abolitionists, 126; opposes Texas annexation, 127, 130, 132; New Orleans press opposes diplomacy of, 128; abandons intervention plans, 131

Abolition: 14, 126, 127, 129, 146n.

Acklen, Captain C. B.: 172, 175

Adams, John Quincy: 46, 125

Adelsverein: 259

Alamo, the: 55

Albany (N.Y.): Kendall in, 3, 11

Albuquerque (N. Mex.): 45, 87

Allen, Hervey: 89n.

Allis, S. D.: *Picayune* war correspondent: 182

Amherst (Mass.): early home of G. W. Kendall, 4, 6, 7

Ampudia, General Pedro de: 153, 182; captures Mier prisoners, 118; threatens General Taylor at Rio Grande; at battle of Monterrey, 170–78

Amsterdam (Holland): 246

Anderson, Robert: 218n.

Antwerp (Belgium): Kendall married in, 249

Appleton, D. and Co.: publishers of Kendall's *The War Between the United States and Mexico, Illustrated,* 252

Armijo, Governor Manuel: 70n., 79n.; natives arming under, 78; captures Texan Santa Fe expedition, 81–83;

sends prisoners to Mexico, 85; reports capture of Texans to Santa Anna, 117; clashes with Texans under Charles A. Warfield, 119

Arista, General Mariano: 197; places spies in Texas, 78n.; assumes command at Matamoros, 149; threatens Taylor's communications, 152; delivers ultimatum to Taylor, 153; meets Taylor at Palo Alto, 156

Ashland: Kendall visits, 38

Astor House: 106

Audubon, John James: 41

Augusta (Ga.): on express route, 261

Austin, Stephen F.: 46

Austin (Tex.): 63, 70, 77, 90, 148; Lumsden visits, 37; established by Lamar, 43–44; Kendall in, 51–52, 54; Texan Santa Fe expedition starts from, 57–58; Texas convention meets in, 139

Austria: 246

Baker, Alexander, with Texan Santa Fe expedition: scouts ahead of expedition, 70; captured in New Mexico, 78; killed by New Mexicans, 82

Balize, the: 34, 235, 306

Ballowe, Captain: 173, 175

Baltimore: 24, 123, 235

Bangs, Samuel: 162

Bankhead, Charles, British minister to Mexico: 133; reports Santa Anna's war moves, 131

Banks' Arcade: 20, 97, 99

KENDALL OF THE *Picayune*

THIS BOOK HAS BEEN SET

IN LINOTYPE OLD STYLE NUMBER SEVEN

IN THE ELEVEN POINT SIZE WITH

LONG DESCENDERS

AND HAS BEEN PRINTED ON

WOVE ANTIQUE

PAPER

UNIVERSITY OF OKLAHOMA PRESS

NORMAN